GodSpace

WE ACT
Middle School Division
Christmas 2007

May the Joy of Christ be with you
Now and throughout the New Year.

To order additional copies of
God Space,
call
1-800-765-6955.

Visit us at
www.reviewandherald.com
for information on other Review and Herald® products.

GodSpace

From all about me
to all about Thee

Tompaul Wheeler

REVIEW AND HERALD® PUBLISHING ASSOCIATION
Since 1861 | www.reviewandherald.com

Published by Review and Herald® Publishing Association, Hagerstown, MD 21741-1119

This book was
Edited by Penny Estes Wheeler
Copyedited by James Cavil
Designed by Trent Truman
Cover art by Photodisc
Typeset: 10/12 Universe 55

PRINTED IN U.S.A.

11 10 09 08 07   5 4 3 2 1

Library of Congress Cataloging-in-Publication Data

Wheeler, Tompaul, 1976-   .
  God space : from all about me to all about Thee / Tompaul Wheeler.
     p. cm.
  1. Teenagers—Religious life. 2. Devotional calendars. 3. Spirituality—Adventists.
4. Christian life—Adventist authors. I. Title.
  BV4447.W49 2007
  248.8'3—dc22
                              2007025019

ISBN 978-0-8280-2027-5

Visit the author at www.tompaulwheeler.com

DEDICATED

to

Judye Estes

To know her is to love her

ACKNOWLEDGMENTS

At the end of many of the readings in this book you will see mysterious initials: RB, HC, JD, JE, LH, SP, etc. What do they all mean? Well, each set of letters is the code for real, live people! Let me introduce them to you:

Ryan Bell lives with his wife and their two daughters in Hollywood, California. He is the pastor of the Hollywood Seventh-day Adventist Church and writes a blog at www.ryanjbell.net.

Heather Crews serves as pastor for church life at the Keene, Texas, Seventh-day Adventist Church.

Jessica Dorval is a senior nursing major at Union College and a Lincoln, Nebrask, native. In her spare time she enjoys reading, writing, photography, traveling, and experimenting in the kitchen. She hopes to one day become a nurse practitioner and volunteer running clinics in developing countries.

Judye Estes is a brilliant chef and wordsmith. She lives in Hagerstown, Maryland.

Lisa Hermann is a neurology resident at Vanderbilt University Medical Center in Nashville, Tennessee. She enjoys traveling, cooking, and reading mystery novels by the pool. She's married to Tompaul Wheeler.

Sonia Perez is a youth pastor in Beltsville, Maryland. She loves God.

Jill Pole is a pseudonym.

Ben Protasio is a Web designer, graphic artist, and photographer—and the only Guamanian Filipino Jewish Adventist Oregonian I know. He lives with his wife, Kimberly, and their two daughters, Mahal and Daniela.

Christy Rasmussen lives in Maryland and works for the Adventist Development and Relief Agency. She enjoys reading biographies, writing e-mail, experimental cooking, and long conversational walks with friends. She looks forward to a career as a clinical psychologist.

Bret Schlisner is a pastor for public campus ministries in San Luis Obispo, California. He likes to preach on uncomfortable subjects, read the Bible, talk about Jesus, write and lead praise music, and surf.

Kristine Stuart is a pastor's wife, mom, writer, and artist. She and her husband, Dave, live in Jamestown, North Dakota, with their three children.

Gerald Wheeler is a book editor. He's the author of more than a dozen books, including *God of the Whirlwind, Saints and Sinners*, and *The Two-taled Dinosaur*. He loves model trains.

Penny Estes Wheeler is the author of such books as *The Appearing, The Beginning*, and *With Long Life*. She enjoys scrapbooking and travel.

Katy Wolfer is a designer and videographer in Berrien Springs, Michigan.

I couldn't have pulled this book out of a hat without y'all. You have my eternal thanks!

—Tompaul Wheeler

Dear Reader,

Have you ever felt that sometimes God can seem like so much outer space? That life should be more than a long fight for last place?

What if we were to give God more than just shelf space? Maybe we could go from self-centeredness to discipleship.

But how to do this?

That's what this book is all about. You'll discover a mix of topics:

Innovations. The arts. Music. Media—even a few gems of poetry.

Adventism. Adventist history, doctrine, and personalities are on display here.

All about the Bible. Biblical, spiritual, archaeological, and sociological insights.

Science. The universe, from neurons to nebulae. Real perspective on evolution, creation, medicine—and everything else God has made.

Spirit. Devotional stories with a twist of lemon and a dash of cinnamon.

Life. Relationships. Every-day life.

Missions—at home and abroad. Short-term missions, cross-cultural issues, and witnessing on the "home front."

And there may even be the occasional quiz, space to write your own thoughts, prayers, goals—and a recipe or two!

But most of all, I pray that you will determine to put God in first place—and, along the way, discover God's incredible mission for your life!

—*Tompaul Wheeler*

INSIDE OUT

Listen, I tell you a mystery.
1 CORINTHIANS 15:51

Welcome to a brand-new year.

We may not have ever met, but I'm willing to guess two things about you: You're not as close to God as you'd like, and there are a few things about yourself you wouldn't mind changing. That is, if you're anything like me.

Whether you're reading this on January 1 or October 14, this book is your ticket to a new year and a new you—not from the outside in, but from the inside out. You won't find any get-fit-, get-rich-, or get-smart-quick schemes, but you will find plenty of insight, knowledge, and perspective to plug into your life.

You'll read about people who kept their cool, made wise choices, and gave their all for God's kingdom. People who changed their world by standing for what they believed in, relying on the Holy Spirit and the incredible power of love. We'll go behind the scenes of the Bible to see how it came together, what's really going on between its pages, and how its first readers would have understood it—and clarify a few things that probably never made sense to you. We'll explore science from neurons to nebulae, and what it tells us about God (and what God tells us about science).

We'll look at the nitty-gritty of everyday life, from family and life choices to romantic relationships. We'll explore the challenges, history, and possibilities of missions—across the street and around the world. We'll even investigate Seventh-day Adventism—its personalities, its controversies, and its potential.

We'll dig deep into spirituality, wrestling with issues of God's character and plans for our lives. We'll see how God works in the world today, shaping, leading, and still allowing people to make their own choices. We'll find some answers—and a whole lot more questions to chew on.

When Job's three friends tried to comfort him with pat answers and empty platitudes, God told them they needed to repent of their smugness. God told Job that he'd have to live with ambiguity. So even though there won't always be easy answers to difficult questions, we'll see that with God, sometimes we just need to embrace the mystery.

Adventism

RED-EYE RELIGION

*The mind of sinful man is death,
but the mind controlled by the Spirit is life and peace.*
ROMANS 8:6

I read a letter to the editor last week that bugged me.

An earnest Christian wrote to the *Adventist Review* about how low our church standards have fallen. Why, it used to be, said he, that you could tell a church member just by looking at 'em, but now most just look like anybody else. Indeed, today's church members wear pretty much the same things other people do.

I wondered if that letter writer did much traveling. Some people collect Hummel figurines, Barbie dolls, or comic books. I collect airports. (And Pez dispensers, but never mind that.) Last time I added it up, I'd landed or taken off from more than 60 airports. Last week I added Memphis; this month I'll add Atlanta. And as tiring as traveling can get, with red-eye flights, bad meals, late luggage, and unexplained delays, it's still one of the best ways I've found to practice one of my favorite sports: people-watching.

People seem to let their guard down when traveling (and I'm not just talking about that guy hollering into his mobile phone). The real person comes out. It's not always pretty. Sitting in Baltimore a while back after learning that my flight would arrive too late to catch my connection to Peru, I involuntarily eavesdropped as another man came unhinged. He didn't dress any different than anyone else, but everything about his attitude and demeanor declared that the Holy Spirit did not live in him.

Coming back from the same trip, I boarded a plane with a group of fellow mission-trippers, most of whom I hadn't met. Yet despite the fact that they wore the same shorts, sandals, and tops as any other tourists, picking them out was easy. You could see their relationship with God right in the peace and smiles on their faces.

Yes, your relationship with Christ should impact the choices you make, from clothes shopping to channel surfing, but not because you're afraid that God will judge you or that someone will gossip about you. Your choices change because *God changes your priorities*. When you consider the price Jesus paid to save you, the suffering of the world around you, and that whatever you do for another person you're really doing for Jesus, you won't look at the world the same again.

HOW THE BIBLE WAS WRITTEN

The Teacher searched to find just the right words,
and what he wrote was upright and true.
ECCLESIASTES 12:10

When Christians think about how the Bible writers wrote, many imagine something like my note taking in college biology classes. Professor Hare began each class by declaring, "Pencils poised." My classmates and I hurriedly took notes as he lectured.

While occasionally the writers of the Bible recorded the very words they heard in visions and dreams, they also used many different additional methods to compose the Bible. Frequently they could write from personal experience, as when the apostle Paul describes his missionary journeys. Often, though, they would begin writing only after careful research. Luke tells us that he wrote his Gospel after having "carefully investigated everything" (Luke 1:3). He didn't receive his Gospel already put in words through a vision directly from God, but he talked to eyewitness and others. Perhaps he used writings that others had compiled. (Ellen White tells us that as a child, Timothy studied a collection of "teachings and lessons of Christ" that already existed before anyone had written a complete Gospel.) Finally, when Luke had gathered his material, the Holy Spirit helped him to choose the messages he should present, and carefully guided him in the writing.

The authors of Kings and Chronicles consulted historical records, such as the annals of the kings of Israel and Judah. Or they got information from prophetic writings that did not get included in the Bible, such as the writings about or by the prophets Nathan, Ahijah, and Iddo (2 Chronicles 9:29). The Holy Spirit inspired the biblical author what the spiritual significance of some event was, but the human author would check historical documents for the event's details.

Sometimes the Bible's writers included things they had gathered from non-Israelite sources. For example, the book of Proverbs contains many sayings that had appeared earlier among the wisdom literatures of Egypt and Assyria, and some of the psalms and parts of the book of Lamentations echo the wording of non-Israelite hymns and poetry. But always the Holy Spirit guided the Bible writers, so that we can trust that they faithfully presented God's messages.

GW

science

EVOLUTION / PART 1

*Cursed is the ground because of you; through painful toil you will eat of it
all the days of your life. It will produce thorns and thistles for you.*
GENESIS 3:17, 18

Ever since Darwin built on previous ideas of life's origins and presented his theory of evolution in *The Origin of Species*, a battle has raged.

Christians have sputtered to respond, hugging their Bibles ever tighter. They've tried to reclaim science to prove that God did it all, with mixed results at best. In their quest to defend God they've often claimed far more than the Bible ever did (such as that species have never changed at all). Meanwhile scientists have learned more and more about how life works—though what it all adds up to is anybody's guess. They've found more dots, but connecting them is as challenging as ever.

For the Bible believer wading into the debate, several challenges await. One is to not reduce God's work to a mere mathematical formula. Another is to allow the Bible to tell its story with its own agenda, not our modern one. A third is to remain humble and remember that God has given us sufficient information and evidence to believe, despite some major questions posed by evolution.

Let's take a brief look at some of the issues and principles that shape the creation/evolution debate, and what we can and can't say for certain.

1. According to the Bible, the world has experienced at least two major operating changes since God finished creating it. When Adam and Eve sinned, God changed how nature and our bodies operate. Our bodies grow old and die. Thistles and thorns appeared—and, we may infer, so did claws, viruses, parasites, and poisons, all of which simply didn't exist before we allowed sin in. The world doesn't operate by the same rules it did when God created it. Sin has warped life. 2. The second operating change was at the Flood, when God rearranged the planet in ways we'll never definitively know. All that science can study about life's origins is distorted by this reality, leaving our information incomplete.

It also means that what we call miracles—the spontaneous remissions, the voice of God suddenly revealed—occur when the world, just for a moment, works the way it was always supposed to, before the shadows fell. *Continued.*

EVOLUTION / PART 2

God's voice thunders in marvelous ways;
he does great things beyond our understanding.
JOB 37:5

2. Species do change (a fact zealous creationists were initially slow to acknowledge), but they never change anywhere near as much as evolution requires. The various species of, for example, cats—lions, tigers, leopards, the fluffy *Felis domesticus* currently hiding in my closet—may have all descended from the same ark-riding ancestor, but countless experiments have failed to show any evidence that it is possible for animals to evolve new organs or body structures.

3. Major arguments for evolution often boil down to circular reasoning and presuppositions. For example, organs considered vestigial (leftover parts from earlier species) have been considered evidence for evolution. Yet almost all the human body parts once considered vestigial have been found to be quite useful after all. Darwin thought that flightless birds were terrific evidence of evolution, yet, as biophysicist Cornelius Hunter notes: "If a penguin's wing is highly efficient for swimming, then why should we think it is vestigial, aside from simply presupposing it was formed by evolution? The idea that vestigial structures can in fact be perfectly useful makes the argument subjective" (*Darwin's God: Evolution and the Problem of Evil*, p. 33).

Darwin and successive evolutionists have argued against the idea of a divine Creator by suggesting that patterns in nature are illogical. The late biologist Stephen Jay Gould wrote, "Odd arrangements and funny solutions are the proof of evolution—paths that a sensible God would never tread but that a natural process, constrained by history, follows perforce" (*The Panda's Thumb*, pp. 20, 21). But this tells more about the scientist than it does about God or life, and ignores the reality of a world warped by sin.

4. The fossil record provides challenges to both evolution and creationism. Scientists have found that fossil records consistently match the developmental sequence that evolution proposes, yet huge gaps leave out the intermediate species that would be necessary for such massive change. Stephen Gould and paleontologist Niles Eldredge proposed "punctuated equilibrium" to explain this, suggesting that at certain points evolution just works really, really fast—if you blink, you'll miss it. *Continued.*

EVOLUTION / PART 3

*He who forms the mountains, creates the wind, and reveals his thoughts to man,
he who turns dawn to darkness, and treads the high places of the earth—
the Lord God Almighty is his name.*

AMOS 4:13

It's easy to get caught up in the various issues of evolution and creation—microevolution versus macroevolution, contradictions in the fossil record, the Cambrian explosion, dinosaurs, and Neanderthals. Both conventional creationism and evolution leave a multitude of unanswered questions.

As King David wrote: "I praise you because I am fearfully and wonderfully made; your works are wonderful, I know that full well" (Psalm 139:14). Genesis tells us we're made in God's image, appreciating beauty, wisdom, and wonder. Though sin has corrupted everything in us and around us, warping and distorting all that should point to its Creator, God still calls to us and promises to restore us.

Biologist Ariel Roth wrote, "It is estimated that there are around 100,000,000,000,000 connections between nerve cells in the human brain. That we can think straight (we hope most of us do!) is a witness to a marvelous ordered complex of interdependent parts that challenges suggestions of an origin by random evolutionary changes. How could such complicated organs develop by an unplanned process?" (*In Six Days: Why 50 Scientists Choose to Believe in Creation*, p. 89).

Ultimately a Christian has to consider evidence both material and immaterial, natural and supernatural. The mystery and history of their own relationship with God. The examples of people they know who live life energized by their walk with God.

For me the greatest evidence for a loving, creating God is the incredible change I've witnessed, change that evolution can't match. It's the friends and family members who began to transform, slowly but surely, from self-centered cynicism to hopeful allegiance. It's the power of the Holy Spirit turning bitterness and brokenness into sweetness and togetherness.

Before the Flood people saw amazing evidence for the Creator-God, including an angel guarding the gates of Eden, but still chose to ignore Him. Belief and conviction is never simply external. It must happen in the heart.

BIRTHDAY BLUES

Unless the Lord builds the house, its builders labor in vain.
PSALM 127:1

I spent my thirteenth birthday painting my bedroom in our new house. Then my parents decided they hated the color. Too green, they said. Needed more blue, they said.

My whole day spent in backbreaking, muscle-aching toil? A waste. So I let my parents repaint it. No use doing something unappreciated. I swore off hard physical labor.

When I turned 14, I was eligible to work for pay, though I stayed home on my birthday. I wanted to put off this physical labor business as long as possible, and I figured that my birthday was as good an excuse as any.

But the very next day, there I was as part of the academy grounds crew. Mowing lawns. Weeding flower beds. Our boss drove around comfortably in his big roofed tractor while we pushed mowers in the scorching sun. He stood around giving directions while we carried logs from place to place. I learned a lot about hard work from him. (Specifically, how to avoid it.) And my heart hardened toward manual labor.

Through what must have been divine intervention, I was released after a mere two weeks to the happy world of office work. On my fifteenth birthday I didn't mind working. Photocopying, typing, sending faxes—no problem.

But God wasn't done with me yet. He impressed me to go to the Dominican Republic for the Ultimate Workout mission trip. I still harbored ugly memories of outdoor work, but God kept calling. I wondered how He was so sure I was the right guy for this. Eight hours a day in the hot sun doing hard labor! I'd tried this before, right?

But God is persuasive, so I fund-raised and sacrificed on frills so I could spend two weeks in construction in the D.R. I wondered, *What will be different this time?*

At the beginning of the trip I was reluctant to try new things, but I soon got in the spirit. And on my sixteenth birthday, in Santo Domingo, I determinedly scooped up dirt with a shovel. I bent down, again and again, picking up rocks. I pushed a wheelbarrow full of concrete blocks and dumped it into a ditch. I poured wet mortar into holes.

I had to admit it was actually fun. But why the difference? Maybe it was that instead of doing something with myself in mind, I was doing something totally for someone else.

CARICATURE DEVELOPMENT

So God created man in his own image, in the image of God he created him.
GENESIS 1:27

Everybody loves a substitute teacher.

OK, so that's a lie. My sanity during my third-grade teacher's maternity leave was preserved only by the listening ear of visiting Week of Prayer speaker (and noted author) Sally Streib. And when Mrs. Zane taught my eighth-grade art class, well, I was still a few years shy of calling her a friend.

Mrs. Zane asked us to draw portraits of our fellow students. My friend Christine seemed an excellent subject. Long dark blond hair, an oval face, round glasses, a prominent nose. Picasso couldn't have been more pleased with a subject than I was.

Christine sat down beside me and straightened her posture while I started to sketch. I exaggerated her features, turning her face into a zany jumble of curves and angles, exactly as I'd intended. I'd followed the renowned style of art known as a caricature. When I finished my depiction, Christine loved it, and I only wished I had a camera handy to capture her grin.

Mrs. Zane, on the other hand, was horrified. "This picture is hideous!" she exclaimed. "Why did you draw such an ugly picture of a nice girl?"

"It's a caricature," I tried to explain. "Like political cartoonists or people at a state fair draw. It exaggerates someone's features for comedic effect. Like a skinny tall man in a big black hat—voilà, Honest Abe."

Mrs. Zane snorted, unconvinced. And if I'd ever prided myself on straight A's, it would have ended that day.

Mrs. Zane saw only ugliness in my caricature, but the ugly truth is that they're everywhere. Some of the worst caricatures are words—demeaning, degrading, dehumanizing words. In the business world men used to refer to women around the office as "skirts." Today's bigots toss around labels that mock people for their traits or alleged actions. Slant-eyes. Wetbacks. Ragheads.

When we tag people with taunting labels that sum up with a put-down, we lose out. We lose the contribution their perspective could bring us. And we lose a bit of our own humanity as we deny theirs.

AMERICA WAKES UP

I will be exalted among the nations.
PSALM 46:10

How does a brand-new, ever-expanding country entertain itself? Would you believe . . . religion?

Before the Revolutionary War, Americans had a take-it-or-leave-it attitude toward Christianity. People had moved over from Europe (where governments had spent the past few centuries arguing over which version of Christianity to enforce), and most were quite happy to get church off their backs. Thus most of America's founders were deists, who thought that God probably created everything somehow sometime a while back, but had better things to do these days than babysit a planet.

The zany extremes of the anti-religion French Revolution in the 1790s took a bit of the sparkle off deism, and America's official religious neutrality inspired Americans to give religion another spin. Soon the Second Great Awakening had Americans seeking spirituality, and curious people willing to try something new.

The new nation inspired scores of new denominations, as people started churches for every inclination. Methodist and Baptist churches mushroomed as people flocked to a fun new innovation called camp meeting—revival meetings held in the great outdoors, with plenty of room for everybody and lots of singing, shouting, and general hoopla. Preachers reminded listeners just what wretched sinners they were, but assured them that Jesus offered a new life. And to show that their religion was more than just talk, Christians started working to end slavery and other evils the founding deists had neglected to ban. Even America's growing slave population embraced Christianity, finding that what their hypocritical masters paid lip service to just might free their minds and bodies.

By the time he was murdered by a mob at age 38 in 1844, New Englander Joseph Smith had reported angelic visions, claimed to have discovered and translated long-lost revelations from golden plates hidden in the New York hills, founded the Church of Jesus Christ of Latter-day Saints, led a growing group of followers to the Midwest, attempted to found a "new Zion," and run for president of the United States.

And then there was William Miller.

Bible

AND GOD SAID

In the beginning God created the heavens and the earth.
Now the earth was formless and empty, darkness was over the surface of the deep,
and the Spirit of God was hovering over the waters.
GENESIS 1:1, 2

If any part of the Bible is controversial, it's the beginning verses. Is it literal? metaphorical? both?

Genesis 1 tells how God took a dark, desolate, and deserted mass of nothingness in space, whipped it into shape, and made it home to all manner of life, including the crowning part, humans He designed after Himself. So what's really happening?

The Bible's creation story isn't unscientific—it's *nonscientific.* Genesis doesn't try to give an in-depth examination of everything that happened. It addresses the questions and issues that the ancient Israelites faced, rather than the exact issues and questions we might ask. It talks in theological terms, not twenty-first-century scientific ones. It has implications for modern science, but it speaks in theological language. We need to find the theological message before we see how it applies to our scientific questions.

The incredible things God does in Genesis 1 set the pattern for what He does later. For example, God divides the waters when He creates the world, brings them back together again at the Flood, and divides them again when the Israelites cross the Red Sea. God tells His children to be fruitful and tells them what to eat in the Garden of Eden, and gives a similar message to Noah and his family after the Flood. The rest of the Bible refers to these acts again and again, all the way through to Revelation.

Genesis assures us that an eternal God is in control. Other people groups believed that people and the world were created more or less by accident as various gods squabbled with each other. Their gods had not always existed, but just popped up as a result of natural forces (a bit like the theory of evolution). Their gods were not eternal, but would someday disappear again as the universe returned to chaos. People worshipped and feared various forces of nature as gods, such as the sun and the moon, but Genesis tells us that every natural force is under the one God's control.

God loves creating something new and beautiful out of chaos. It's His specialty—and He can't wait to do it in your life.

RIPOFF RELIGION

What has been done will be done again; there is nothing new under the sun.
ECCLESIASTES 1:9

I first encountered the phenomenon at a youth event when I was 13. T-shirts featured suicide pillar-pusher Samson knocking a pagan temple down with the words "Lord's Gym" in a logo that looked suspiciously like that of the fitness joint Gold's Gym. Suddenly a horde of cheap knockoffs exploded in the Christian marketplace, imitating movie posters, soda ads, and even cartoon characters. Most of today's witness wares are a little more self-assured and include more original offerings, such as caps proclaiming "I [Heart] Christian Boys" and beach sandals that print "Jesus Loves You" in the sand with every step. Yes, there's always a market for cheesy witnessing. When I drive past certain church signs, for example, I'm always ready for another bad pun or pithy epiphany:

To prevent sinburn, use sonscreen
This church is prayer-conditioned!
Worry: a dark room where negatives develop

OK, so I actually kind of like that last one. It doesn't rely on Christianese jargon, and sounds almost like something Solomon would have written if he'd been in a metaphorical mood and knew his way around a predigital camera. It says, "Life may bring struggles, but you can make it. Don't focus on your troubles; let this church help you." Except, you know, not in so many words.

Still, Jesus told His disciples that it takes more than words to enter His kingdom. Jesus said, "Not everyone who says to me, 'Lord, Lord,' will enter the kingdom of heaven, but only he who does the will of my Father who is in heaven. Many will say to me on that day, 'Lord, Lord, did we not prophesy in your name, and in your name drive out demons and perform many miracles?' Then I will tell them plainly, 'I never knew you. Away from me, you evildoers!'" (Matthew 7:21-23).

Describing people who trumpeted their Christianity but whose religion was only skin-deep, Jesus quoted Isaiah: "These people honor me with their lips, but their hearts are far from me" (Matthew 15:8). God wants more than just our lips—or bumpers or torsos. He wants nothing less than our hearts.

And whatever you do, don't be a ripoff. Be an original—just as God made you.

KARAOKE SUPERSTARS

I have hidden your word in my heart.
PSALM 119:11

Karaoke is not my cup of tea.

Hanging out at a friend's house the other night, Lisa and I learned the first rule of karaoke: It's a lot more fun if you're actually good at singing.

Lisa makes no claims to singing skills. I'm generally good at technically staying in tune, so the song is at least recognizable, but suffice it to say that neither of us has ever been invited to do special music. When we found ourselves in a group who loved singing along music tracks while the computer scored them and judges popped up afterward to critique their efforts, I decided the only thing to do was forestall the inevitable.

Unfortunately I fumbled the perfect opportunity right at the beginning: a Johnny Cash song. Of course there's only one Man in Black, but the way I see it, Cash basically talked his way through a lot of his songs—the world's official first rapper. There was also the added benefit that I could anticipate most of the words. Instead I made the mistake of choosing to mime singing a seventies ballad in Lisa's ear, one I knew exactly seven words to—the song's chorus-sung title. Forced to play along, I bombed out. When the sardonic judges appeared at the end of my pathetic performance, they shook their cartoonish heads, asking, "Why did you even bother to show up today?"

The amazing thing, though, was the number of songs that I suddenly remembered the lyrics to, including ones I hadn't heard in years. There's a funny thing about music—it greases the skids of memorization like nothing else. When I was 6 years old, a Sabbath school teacher taught me the books of the Bible in order. Unfortunately, while I can still sing a lilting "Genesis, Exodus, Leviticus, Numbers, Deuteronomeeeee . . ." I still get stymied in the minor prophets. Even after all these years I still can't remember just what comes after Micah. And of course I know "Matthew, Mark, Luke, and John" is followed by Acts and Romans, but the Epistles get kinda hazy too. If my life somehow depended on it, I think I'd sing real fast and then pronounce a triumphant "Revelation!" at the end.

I had a seminary classmate who, though blind in both eyes, had memorized much of the Old Testament—in Hebrew. He made me reconsider just what qualifies as a disability.

RELAX

Come to me, all you who are weary and burdened, and I will give you rest.
Take my yoke upon you and learn from me, for I am gentle and humble in heart,
and you will find rest for your souls. For my yoke is easy and my burden is light.
MATTHEW 11:28-30

"The water will support you if you let it. And I won't let you sink."
My cousin Heather, ace swimmer and lifeguard, waited patiently while
I, the world's worst swimmer, tried not to think about sinking. We
stood in the campus pool at a quiet time of the day, having the pool to
ourselves save for a group of senior citizens doing water aerobics in
one corner.

I tried not to eye Heather too skeptically. Sure, I trusted this girl,
who I could not remember not knowing, but 18 years of experience
(and frustrated swim teachers) had also taught me how water worked.
Drop a rock, a spoon, or me in the water, and sinking was certain.

I held my breath, then remembered I was supposed to be relaxed. I
leaned back and let my feet and knees rise to the water's surface.
"There you go," Heather said, her hand on my shoulder. "Now let go
and float. Perfect!"

Heather lifted her hand. I closed my eyes and let go of the world.
The water held me, cushioned me, soothed me. For the first time in
my life I floated.

After a life of wealth, women, and power, King Solomon figured
out that life is what happens when you're trying too hard. At the end
of Ecclesiastes, his classic meditation on the meaning of life, he
summed up everything life had taught him:

"Be happy, young man, while you are young, and let your heart
give you joy in the days of your youth. Follow the ways of your heart
and whatever your eyes see, but know that for all these things God
will bring you to judgment. So then, banish anxiety from your heart
and cast off the troubles of your body, for youth and vigor are meaningless" (Ecclesiastes 11:9, 10).

Stop. Relax. Kick off your shoes and feel the grass beneath your
feet. Dip your ears beneath the bathwater and listen to your heartbeat.
Tune in to the Holy Spirit. Let go of the world. And no matter what
threatens to drown you, trust God to hold you up.

Mission

YOUR TIME, YOUR TOUCH

When Jesus landed and saw a large crowd,
he had compassion on them and healed their sick.
MATTHEW 14:14

Visiting Nicaragua's Mosquito Coast with the frontier nursing class from Union College, I felt as if I'd stepped back in time a thousand years or two.

Children carried their younger siblings about in the sizzling sun. Farm animals were as ubiquitous and ultimately unobtrusive as squirrels in American suburbs. The village's young men played baseball in the afternoon, and in the evening the young women took their turn on the field. The houses are wood built on stilts (before the civil war they were still bamboo). Malnourishment and traditional values means kids mature slowly, but adulthood comes far too soon. I couldn't tell you how many pregnant 15-year-olds came to the clinic already nursing a 1-year-old.

The men work the fields, the women care for the children, and the children have plenty of room to roam. They giggled and bolted from my cameras, then peeked around the corner to make sure the game was still on. We listened to their hearts, scrubbed away their scabies, and prayed we'd made a dent. The littlest patients etched our minds the most—the 3-week-old with a staph infection, her teenage mother quiet but hopeful, her father long gone. The alert but merely 11-pound toddler we took to Puerta Cabezas for proper treatment. Baby Kevin made eye contact and tracked movements, but he could neither speak nor crawl. We waved his grandparents goodbye as they stepped into a cab for the city hospital and his chance for a healthy life.

The people Jesus ministered to in ancient Judea lived incredibly similar lifestyles. Minimal education. Boys hitting the fields as soon as they could swing a knife. Girls married as soon as they could bear a baby. Lives hampered by maladies that modern societies have practically forgotten.

Mark 6:34 says, "When Jesus landed and saw a large crowd, he had compassion on them, because they were like sheep without a shepherd." The needs of the people around you may not be as obvious as those I've just described, but their spiritual needs are just as stark. They crave connection. They're hurting for lack of trust, of love, of God. They need your ear, your time, your touch.

THE MAN WHO PREVENTED NUCLEAR WAR

Better a patient man than a warrior.
PROVERBS 16:32

You've probably never heard of Stanislav Petrov. But if it weren't for him you probably wouldn't be alive to read this, and I wouldn't be around to write it.

September 1983 was a dark time in the so-called cold war between the United States and the Soviet Union. On September 1, 1983, the Soviet Union shot down Korean Air Lines Flight 007 after it strayed into Soviet airspace, believing the plane's presence was a deliberate provocation. All 269 passengers died, including U.S. congressman Lawrence McDonald. The world protested the attack on a passenger plane, and U.S. president Ronald Reagan condemned it as a crime against humanity.

As part of the deterrent system of Mutually Assured Destruction (MAD) both the U.S. and Russia kept thousands of nuclear missiles aimed at each other. Soviet premier Andropov obsessed about a potential surprise nuclear attack. And then it happened. At 12:40 a.m. September 26, 1983, alarms went off in a bunker near Moscow where Petrov watched a computer for signs of a nuclear attack. The red start button blinked. A satellite in outer space signaled that America had launched an attack. It was Petrov's responsibility to notify his superiors so they could launch an immediate response.

Petrov froze in shock for about 15 seconds. The system declared that the U.S. had launched five Minuteman missiles in all. Should he notify his superiors so they could fire back? Or was it simply a computer error? Alarms pierced his ears, screens and lights flashed, and he shouted into a telephone in one hand, an intercom in the other, while another officer ordered him to stay calm and do his job.

"I had a funny feeling in my gut," Petrov recalled when the world finally learned his story 15 years later. "I didn't want to make a mistake. I made a decision, and that was it." Suspecting that five missiles were too few to be real, he declared, "False alarm."

In the documentary *The Red Button and the Man Who Saved the World*, Petrov said he simply did his job. "I was the right person at the right time, that's all. For 10 years my late wife knew nothing about it. 'So what did you do?' she asked me. I did nothing."

Nothing had fully prepared Petrov for such a scenario, but when it came, he was able to look past paranoia and make the right choice.

Adventism

WILLIAM MILLER

And he said unto me, Unto two thousand and three hundred days;
then shall the sanctuary be cleansed.
DANIEL 8:14, KJV

In the early 1800s western New York was one happening place to be.

Over in Palmyra, Joseph Smith announced that an angel had told him that every Christian religion was wrong. In Hydesville, sisters Kate and Margaret Fox introduced modern spiritualism when they claimed to hear a dead person rapping on the walls of their house.

The Shakers, whose stylistic furniture lives on (although their no-sex policy ensured their family tree wouldn't), operated several communal farms in the area. On the other side of the plate, when they weren't making silverware the Oneida community practiced group marriage and believed they were already sinless.

Low Hampton's own William Miller had no such newsmaking ambitions. After seeing some action in the War of 1812, he preferred a quiet, farming life. He'd grown up Baptist and become a "God's gone fishing" deist, but his brushes with death and the loss of family members left him wondering about the afterlife. And considering how his much smaller army had somehow managed to defeat the Brits left him wondering if maybe God sometimes pulled a few strings after all.

Miller tried easing himself back into Christianity, keeping a pew warm on Sundays while still talking like a good deist in public, but he soon found himself falling in love with Jesus. Wanting to be sure of his beliefs, he started studying the Bible verse by verse by verse. After two years of hard-core study (1816 to 1818) he slowly came to a shocking conclusion: Bible prophecy predicted the world had only about 25 years left.

Miller wasn't sure what to do about this new conviction. In his day most people believed Jesus would return at the end, not the start, of Revelation's thousand years, once the world had begun to get better and better. He spent another 14 years centuple-checking his argument, and he just couldn't shake it. He knew that if it weren't true, talking about it would deceive people. But if it were . . . He couldn't in good conscience keep quiet. In 1832 he told God, All right, I'll preach about it—but only if I'm invited. When a half hour later that invitation came, he kinda sorta wished he'd stayed a deist.

THE FIRST COMMANDMENTS

A new command I give you: Love one another.
JOHN 13:34

Honor your father and your mother. Don't steal, covet, or commit adultery. Remember the Sabbath. Words to live by, but they were chiseled for fallen, sinful people. Adam and Eve didn't need to keep a tablet of stone propped up by the tree of life so they'd remember not to tell a lie or covet someone else's spouse.

After Jesus' sacrifice we no longer sacrifice lambs, worry about becoming ceremonially unclean, or stone adulterers. But what if we could go back to the beginning? What commandments did God give sinless Adam and Eve?

"Be fruitful and increase in number. . . . Rule over the fish of the sea and the birds of the air and over every living creature that moves on the ground" (Genesis 1:28). God put us on this planet to work it. Maybe we've got that "be fruitful and multiply" part down pretty well, but we haven't done the greatest job taking care of our more slippery or fuzzy friends. From the giant sloth (the size of a small car when it meandered about South America) and mighty mastodon to the lowly dodo bird, we've hunted animals to extinction. We've polluted air, ground, and ocean in the name of progress and survival.

God then announced that everybody would enjoy a hearty vegetarian diet—even all the animals (verses 29, 30). And finally, His latest creation completed and looking pretty fine, He took a break: "By the seventh day God had finished the work he had been doing; so on the seventh day he rested from all his work. And God blessed the seventh day and made it holy, because on it he rested from all the work of creating that he had done" (Genesis 2:2, 3).

So there you have it. God commanded us to work and take care of His creation and rest weekly in honor of the Creator. That's what would shape our lives if we'd never sinned. Work would build character, and the Sabbath would keep us spiritually rooted.

People who trumpet the Ten Commandments usually like 'em for one big reason: They tell us what not to do, and that makes it easy to lord over other people (so much for having no other god before the Lord, when that lord is yourself). Jesus summed up the law in three words that should have gone without saying: Love one another.

LIVE IT UP

If anyone would come after me,
he must deny himself and take up his cross and follow me.
For whoever wants to save his life will lose it, but whoever loses his life for me will find it.
MATTHEW 16:24, 25

Life is a race. Life is a journey. Life is not a spectator sport. Life is what you make it. Life is not a dress rehearsal. Or as Shakespeare wrote in *As You Like It*: "All the world's a stage, and all the men and women merely players." Which sounds profound and poetic and all, but I seem to have lost my script.

In reality, you wake up one day, and without having ever asked for it, you're alive on this broken planet. Soon you're supposed to know how to do things on your own, but everything feels preprogrammed. Maybe you know somebody who knows somebody who can make things happen for you. Maybe you end up poor and alone. In the end, it seems like life's a gamble and whatever happens to you was probably gonna happen anyway.

Is that it? Is life just making money and staying healthy? Is there more to it than just enjoying what you can while it lasts? More than just trying to impress people who don't care, learning things that don't matter, and achieving things that won't last? Maybe we've got it all backwards—or maybe we shouldn't try to fit into a backward world at all.

"For whoever wants to save his life will lose it, but whoever loses his life for me will find it. What good will it be for a man if he gains the whole world, yet forfeits his soul?" (Matthew 16:25, 26).

Self-preservation works in the short term, but in the end you've lost yourself. Jesus offers an amazing invitation to a life centered on more than self-preservation. It's risky—but rewarding. It's dangerous—but fulfilling. It will stretch you, mold you, and break you—and remake you, a "new creation."

It's not about power or about who gets the credit. It's about letting God use you in ways you never expected. It's about laying everything on the line for what you truly believe in. It's about rejecting the world's standards of grandeur and standing up for something bigger than yourself.

And it's in those moments that you're truly alive.

WEIGHT TRAINING

The testing of your faith develops perseverance.
JAMES 1:3

The last semester of college, things were looking great. The previous semester had been a whirlwind of cramming and catching up, but now the best events of the year were still ahead.

And then I discovered one little hole in my transcript: I needed another PE credit.

As snappy as their uniforms looked, I knew I wouldn't be joining the baseball team anytime soon—not unless I liked riding the bench. And basketball? The less said, the better. Cross-country? With my asthma-damaged lungs, I'm lucky to make it across campus in a hurry. Which left one area I'd never really tried before: Weight lifting.

The previous college I'd attended charged a fee to use its weight and exercise facilities, and I'd been too poor to pony up the cash. But now I attended a university with a weight room free and open to every student, and suddenly "Yeah, that'd be a good idea" became "Now or never—at least if I want to graduate." Walking two to five miles each day back and forth from my apartment to campus, I already felt pretty healthy, so I figured I might as well take it to the next level while I had the chance.

The supervising teacher showed me around the weight room, and we covered what I'd do on my own schedule to meet the standards for credit. I committed to working out three times a week for the semester, lifting weights of increasing poundage and exercising various arm, leg, and abdominal muscles.

The first day started slowly but smoothly. It was on my walk home that things really hit me. I felt sore nearly everywhere, from my calves to my clavicles. My body simply ached as never before. Yet somehow the soreness was a good soreness. I sensed it wouldn't last. And sure enough, the next time I worked out I didn't feel so pained afterward, and soon I stopped feeling sore at all.

When you work to strengthen your muscles, you traumatize muscle fibers. When the body repairs the damage, it builds your muscles bigger and stronger than before.

I think faith works the same way. It can hurt to stretch your faith, to risk everything to trust and follow God. But sometimes faith is a muscle that must be torn before it can grow.

LONE SHEEP AMONG WOLVES

Yet I reserve seven thousand in Israel—all whose knees
have not bowed down to Baal and all whose mouths have not kissed him.
1 KINGS 19:18

When *Mission: Impossible* debuted as a weekly TV series in 1966, it featured an elite group of agents who worked together week after week to rescue hostages, foil nefarious Communist plots, crack codes, and keep vital secrets from falling into enemy hands. Every week they managed to pull it off thanks to high-tech gadgets, audacious disguises, nerves of steel, and dedicated teamwork.

When *Mission: Impossible* rebooted in 1996 as a movie, the premise completely changed. The team was no longer to be trusted. Now it was one man against the system, making his way on his own. And who needs friends or colleagues when they can hang on to a helicopter while explosions rock the Chunnel train tunnel?

At first glance the Bible seems chock-full of lone sheep among the wolves. After clocking and burying an Egyptian slavemaster, Moses runs off by himself into the wilderness. Elijah hides out with only ravens for company. But then it falls apart. Moses is stuck with sheep for 40 years while the Israelites slaves keep working and dying. Elijah celebrates an incredible display of God's power by running for His life. When God asks him what he's doing out in the desert, he whines, "I've been so zealous for You, God, and now Jezebel's trying to kill me!" God tells him to get up and get moving, 'cause there's plenty to do—and 7,000 other faithful people who can back him up.

In the Garden of Gethsemane, Jesus begged His friends to stick by His side while He wrestled with His looming mission and impending death. "I'm grieving My heart out," He told Peter, James, and John. "Stay awake with Me awhile."

Today's society celebrates individualism, but that's not how God created us. We need to reach out and stick together. Research demonstrates this in some surprising ways. When scientists at Carnegie Mellon University exposed people to live cold viruses, those with strong social networks were four times less likely to get sick than the socially isolated were. As people get older, studies show that joining a club or association can cut their risk of dying in the next year by 50 percent. Love and community isn't just a warm and fuzzy luxury for people with too much time on their hands. It's a matter of life and death.

UN-BELIZE-ABLE

The King will reply, "I tell you the truth,
whatever you did for one of the least of these brothers of mine, you did for me."
MATTHEW 25:40

A pale mist of blood and bone dust wafts up as I hold a flashlight in an open-air sanctuary. I am at a small academy in Burrell Boom, Belize, Central America. I can see the sweat pooled in my gloves, not so much from the heat but from the persistent changing of them. That one day I lose count at 48 pairs of gloves. In the meantime Sean, the dentist I assist, is in the process of saving a pair of buckteeth on a 12-year-old girl.

A team of eight American dentists and dental assistants set up shop in the chapel of this tiny school. Now it's a dental clinic. Pews were set back and dental chairs were brought in, though calling them dental chairs was a joke. They were, in fact, four old, rickety, and threadbare folding chairs that could recline. They were fitted with a pair of crudely welded aluminum "skis"—locking restraints to keep the chairs from folding in on the patient. Sanitization relies entirely on tap water and a few packets of unpronounceable disinfectants that make chlorine look like Kool-Aid. Sean instructs me on how and where he wants things. Two days ago I was an oaf on the plane insisting on another bag of pretzels; today I am a dental assistant in the middle of a jungle.

The girl lay frozen as the drilling began, and I pointed a pen-sized flashlight at her mouth. She had two very faint gray spots on both of her front teeth. Sean began to drill. In seconds the two buckteeth exposed their core. Inside, they were fully rotted. It was gritty and grimy, with the same consistency as wet charcoal. These were her permanent teeth, and she had probably been in pain for weeks. Sean drilled out the decay, leaving a clean circular pit in each tooth. I fumbled, trying to find the just right color of filling to load into the filling applicator. Clumsily, in sticky gloves, I managed to get the filling cartridge loaded, and handed it to a very patient Sean.

Now he's finished. Sean tells the girl not to eat until the numbness goes away. She smiles and leaps out of the mutant recliner. A boy hops right in. His teeth are worse.

Oh, by the way, welcome to the mission field. There is blood, spit, and puss. There are no easy answers, and it's hardest when you are supposed to be the fixer. And guess what? Jesus just might be calling you here.

BP

JANUARY 22

MISS INDEPENDENT

Do not conform any longer to the pattern of this world,
but be transformed by the renewing of your mind.
ROMANS 12:2

Independence and conformity are full of contradictions.

For as long as I can remember, people have told me how independent I am. I had a strong will and wanted things my own way. Sometimes independence was a good thing, like learning to cook for myself. Other times it seemed more negative: "The world does not revolve around you!" In school I learned that the American culture is quite individualistic, but many Asian cultures are collectivistic. In other words, Americans look out for number one (me) and collectivistic cultures look out for the good of the group (us). When I learned that my attitude was typically American, it seemed to validate me. I was normal. It was OK to be independent, because this characteristic of Americans sparked the age of innovation and invention.

But I struggled. Christianity is all about putting others before yourself—right? *Turn the other cheek. Walk the extra mile. We're part of the body of Christ.* Suddenly, being independent seemed wrong again.

Then I learned how Christians are supposed to be separate from the world; in the world, but not of it. Jesus said, "If you belonged to the world, it would love you as its own. As it is, you do not belong to the world, but I have chosen you out of the world. That is why the world hates you" (John 15:19). Did this mean that I could take pride in being unique? Did that mean going to church on Saturday and all the things that made me different than the other kids in my neighborhood were something to be proud of?

Paul wrote, "You are still worldly. For since there is jealousy and quarreling among you, are you not worldly? Are you not acting like mere men?" (1 Corinthians 3:3). So is brotherly love what *truly* makes Christians different from the world? Reading that, I was back full circle. The other was greater than the self. Independence seemed rubbish next to interdependence.

But maybe it's like healthy fats. Maybe there is a healthy independence. Don't just ingest the church's doctrines—study the Bible for yourself. Stand up for what you believe. Be true to your convictions. And don't be afraid to stand out.

KW

THE MIDNIGHT CRY

But you, Daniel, keep the words secret and the book sealed until the time of the end.
DANIEL 12:4, NRSV

That day will bring about the destruction of the heavens by fire,
and the elements will melt in the heat.
2 PETER 3:12

Though the American William Miller is the most famous person to have preached about Jesus' soon return in the early 1800s, people around the world discovered Daniel and Revelation's end-time predictions. Mostly ignored for centuries, now people dug into these two prophetic books and began pulling out interpretations. From 1821 to 1845 missionary Joseph Wolff, the converted son of a German rabbi, traveled throughout the Middle East, Africa, and India proclaiming Jesus' soon return.

In *Secrets of Daniel: Wisdom and Dreams of a Jewish Prince in Exile*, Jacques Doukhan writes, "Jews and Muslims had caught the same religious fever. On the Jewish side in the Hasidic movements of eastern Europe many expected the *Mashiah* to come in . . . 1843/1844. The Baha'i Muslims reached the same conclusion. . . . Whatever reasons may explain this historical phenomenon, it is interesting that it happened in tune with the prophecy. It was a symptom of intense longing and waiting" (p. 189).

Back in America, though he did no advertising, church after church in town after town invited Miller to preach. To every audience he explained how the prophecies of Daniel 8 pointed to 2300 years after 457 B.C. as the date when the sanctuary would be cleansed. If the sanctuary was Planet Earth and the cleansing was the fire of Jesus' return, that meant the Second Coming would be around the year 1843.

For Miller's message to really catch fire, though, would require some mass media marketing. Enter Joshua V. Himes, one of history's first and greatest public relations managers. The Boston pastor took his cue from Matthew 25:6: "At midnight the cry rang out: 'Here's the bridegroom! Come out to meet him!'" Himes printed millions of copies of his newspapers *Signs of the Times* and *Midnight Cry*, and found the largest tent in the United States for Miller to preach under. More than a half million people around the country came to hear Miller. And thanks to the newspapers, Miller's message reached around the world.

Bible

GOD AND EVE / PART 1

The Lord God commanded . . . , "You are free to eat from any tree in the garden;
but you must not eat from the tree of the knowledge of good and evil,
for when you eat of it you will surely die.
GENESIS 2:16, 17

They were the perfect couple in a perfect world. They had everything going for them. Absolutely everything. Fresh from the hands of God, Planet Earth held all that their hearts could desire. Excitement. Beauty. Sheer, rollicking fun. And enough challenge to keep things interesting. It was all theirs—except for the one tree.

I try to imagine their world. Flowers tumbling across hillsides. Trees reaching toward the clouds. The river that flowed through the middle of the garden. Tame beasts nuzzling their hands while a rainbow of birds wheeled and dove in the distance. And Adam and Eve. Have any two people ever been more in love? On what journeys did their strong legs take them? What did they talk about at night as they lay on their backs in pillows of grass, the stars hanging like clusters of fruit just out of their reach? And above and beyond, encompassing and right there with them, was God.

How He must have loved those exhilarating first days. Can't you just see Him grabbing Adam and Eve by the hand in His joy to show them yet another surprise! And every day would be more joyful, every year richer, than the one before. Only they must beware of the tree with the curious name: the tree of the knowledge of good and evil.

Good, they knew, though they hardly knew they knew. Everything, you see, was good. But evil? They had no knowledge of that. Yet God specifically said, "Don't eat from this tree. If you do, you will die." A command and a warning. Did they stop to think about it? So much more filled their lives.

I'd like to know the number of their carefree days. How many Sabbaths did God spend with them hiking in high green mountains, explaining mysteries we don't yet know? Had certain animals become favorites, tagging along as they worked? Had they held new-hatched chicks and wondered at the balls of fluff? And how was it that one day Eve paused long enough by the forbidden tree to hear the enemy's confidential whisper, "Did God really say, 'You must not eat from any tree in the garden'?" (Genesis 3:1).

And why didn't she run for her life? *Continued.*

PW

GOD AND EVE / PART 2

And I will put enmity between you and the woman, between your offspring and hers;
he will crush your head, and you will strike his heel.
GENESIS 3:15

Hiding in the forbidden tree, just within reach, the serpent spoke to Eve. "Did God really say, 'You must not eat from any tree in the garden'?" he asked.

"O, no," Eve replied. "We can eat from all the trees but one." Her eyes must have opened wide. "It's this one! This tree. God said that if we eat from it, or even touch its fruit, we will die."

Eve had misquoted. God hadn't said they'd die if they touched the fruit, but Satan didn't disagree. He almost had her, for she'd stopped to listen. "Ah, you will not die," he said. "God knows that when you eat the fruit your eyes will be opened, and you will be like God, knowing good and evil." He spoke the truth, the terrible, tragic truth, for lies are always strengthened by adding truth.

See Eve looking through the sun-gold leaves as the serpent picks a fruit and holds it out to her. See her hesitate a moment, weighing the awful words. Feel Heaven's anguish as They watch and wait. See her take the fruit, breathing in its sweet scent. *No, Eve. Drop it. It's not too late. Run, Eve . . .*

She put it to her mouth and took a bite. The juice ran down her chin. She waited. Shafts of sunlight still fell across her face, but everything had changed. She had made a choice. She trusted the serpent instead of God, and there was no turning back. The fruit was sweet in her mouth, but in the sweetness was the bitterness of all to come. For Eve, and Adam, too, did become like God—knowing evil as well as good. Knowing deception, anger, hatred, illness. And like Digory in C. S. Lewis's novel *The Magician's Nephew*, Eve discovered that once rung, the bell cannot be unrung. There was no going back.

The violent death of her son Abel was only the first of millions upon millions. Slaughter in battle. Epidemics. Disease. Systematic starvation, ethnic cleansing. Alexander the Great, Attila the Hun, Ghengis Kahn, Stalin. Rape as a tool of war.

They had to leave the Garden, of course. But God told them all was not lost. Though death was now a fact of life, God Himself would come to earth to live and die. And through His death, they could live again in joy. Forever.

PW

THE DEVIL'S DUE

You believe that there is one God. Good!
Even the demons believe that—and shudder.

JAMES 2:19

Countless pages have been written questioning how God can watch a suffering world without doing more to stop it. But I have another question: How can demons derive such endless pleasure from our suffering?

For starters, sin is acidic, destroying all it touches. The only reason beings dedicated to pure evil have managed to survive for thousands of years is because God has allowed it to be so.

Maybe it's all a matter of perspective. Maybe they see earth as one big video game. Or maybe it's the music in their ears. Maybe they're listening to a different soundtrack that turns our planet into one big dark comedy, like a remixed movie trailer that turns a horror thriller into a breezy, carefree chick flick. With scratched headphones blaring a hip, postmodern, preapocalyptic soundtrack in their ears, our anguish is hilarious, our confusion uproarious.

Or maybe they just love themselves too much.

In *People of the Lie* psychologist M. Scott Peck described his rare encounters with people he could only classify as evil: wholly self-centered and narcissistic. They see themselves as forever blameless, always put-upon, all their problems someone else's fault. They view others only as objects to manipulate for their own needs. They have no sense of empathy, the ability to identify with others' feelings.

For demons with the universe's oldest persecution complex, there's nothing to exist for but to thwart the One they feel has done 'em wrong. And since Jesus walked the earth for a mere three decades and now can't be touched by their efforts, the only way they can get back at God is through His children. It's a pathetic existence, but it's kept them entertained for quite a while. Like kids who hide and toss marbles into the paths of unsuspecting shoppers, demons live to deceive, to distract, to knock us off our feet.

When Jesus showed up to heal two men possessed by demons, the evil ones trembled in His presence. "Are You here to punish us early?" they quaked. Demons know that their time is short. And while Jesus' return is bad news for them, it's great news for us.

THE QUEST

"You still lack one thing.
Sell everything you have and give to the poor, and you will have treasure in heaven.
Then come, follow me." When he heard this, he became very sad,
because he was a man of great wealth.
LUKE 18:22, 23

Quests. That was the topic de jour in my English class. I attended an experimental magnet high school that synced the English and history classes. As we studied the Middle Ages we also read *Beowulf* and *Sir Gawain and the Green Knight*. (Sure, it sounds whimsical, but have you ever read Old or Middle English?)

We were also forced to do silly, time-consuming projects that didn't teach me much but were worth a big chunk of our grade. This time each student had to come up with and pursue a quest, something that we must search for and find. I collected vintage lunch boxes, so I searched for the perfect lunch box and thermos.

But the quest that caught my eye was my classmate Elle's. Elle epitomized fashion, wearing something new every day. She tried new styles and looked to New York and Milan for inspiration. Her quest—to find the most amazing vintage dress? To come up with the perfect outfit? No. Her quest was to go with less. She wanted to see how many of her amazing clothes she could do without. Elle donated four huge garbage bags stuffed to the brim with her treasures to the local thrift shop. She wasn't trying to be unfashionable or dumpy. She just realized that she had "too much" when others had none.

"That isn't a quest," our teacher scoffed. Suddenly 24 indignant 15-year-olds yelled at him. Dragons couldn't have been fiercer. We'd grown up with Elle, we understood her sacrifice, and we saw her growth. She understood the true meaning of a quest. It wasn't to find the ultimate something-or-other, but to grow.

The rich young ruler was willing to do anything to fulfill his quest for the kingdom of heaven, anything but leave his security. Anything but risk the pain of growth.

What is your quest?

What keeps you from growing?

LH

Mission

JESUS LOVES PORN STARS

For all have sinned; all fall short of God's glorious standard.
ROMANS 3:23, NLT

In 2006 a pair of independent California pastors, Mike Foster and Craig Gross, directors of the anti-porn ministry www.xxxchurch.com, paid to print a Bible with "Jesus loves porn stars" emblazoned on the cover. They planned to give the uniquely titled Bibles to workers in the adult film industry. The first publisher they approached returned their money and refused the job, saying that as much as they appreciated the pastors' intent, such titling was misleading and inappropriate.

Foster and Gross conceived it as a way to break barriers with a group of people who would not otherwise consider looking at a Bible. Was it really such a bad idea? Granted, the title could be misinterpreted, but so was Jesus. He faced head-on too many issues people would rather ignore; reached out to too many people society disregarded.

We usually picture Jesus in nice nature settings. There are endless posters of Him hanging out with sheep, lions, and children in fields of bluebonnets and daisies. It's such a comfortable view of Him.

We like to think that our God deals with kids and large fuzzy mammals, not despicable people. Oh, wait. I forgot to mention that we are all despicable. Some of us have just been fooled into thinking that there are levels of sin. Sin is sin. Being "a little sinful" is like being "a little dead." Only Jesus' grace can set us apart—and that offer is open to anyone and everyone.

So the truth is, yes, Jesus does love porn stars. He loves you, too, and with the same powerful love that has transcended the ages. Porn stars, addicts, ballet dancers, murderers, and even (gasp!) churchgoers have an equal shot at heaven. Jesus sees us for what we were supposed to be, not how we are now. If Jesus measured you merely on your present condition, you wouldn't even see the glint of the pearly gate, just the loveless abyss of eternal death.

The difference is that you have today to accept the grace of a God who doesn't grade on a curve. There's no A-through-F level of goodness with grace. You want it? You got it. Now go. Find someone who can benefit from this truth, no matter his or her background or occupation.

BP

UNDERGROUND

I, the Lord, have called you in righteousness. . . . I will . . . make you to be a covenant for the people . . . , to free captives from prison and to release . . . those who sit in darkness.
ISAIAH 42:6, 7

Johan Weidner grew up watching his father go to jail—again and again.

It was the early 1920s. Staying out of jail would have been easy enough for his father, a Seventh-day Adventist minister, but it was a matter of principle. The Swiss government repeatedly fined him for refusing to pay the fine for not sending Johan and his sister, Gabrielle, to school on Saturday. Pastor Weidner could have paid up, but he believed that governments should never force people to violate their conscience, so his acknowledging his act as a crime by paying a fine was out of the question.

Johan studied in France and Switzerland before starting his own business. Gabrielle studied in London, becoming fluent in several languages, before moving to Paris to work for the Adventist Church. Then the Nazis invaded France, and their father's fearless example shaped everything they did next.

Johan and Gabrielle joined with other members of the French Resistance to organize the Dutch-Paris underground network to save the lives of people wanted by the Nazis. A network of volunteers helped Jews, downed Allied airmen, and others escape to safety. With a wide assortment of fake identity cards and passports, and a limitless supply of pluck, Johan moved fearlessly through Nazi-occupied Europe. The German gestapo arrested and tortured Johan in 1943, but he told them nothing. But after another member of the Resistance revealed everything, on February 26, 1944, the gestapo arrested Gabrielle, tortured her, and sent her to the Ravensbruck concentration camp for slave labor. In February 1945 the Soviet army liberated her camp, but, her health broken, she died within days.

The gestapo arrested Johan again and shipped him to Germany, but he jumped the train and escaped to Switzerland. After the war government after government honored him for saving the lives of more than 1,000 Jews and more than 100 Allied airmen. Before his death in 1993 he lit a candle at the opening of the Holocaust museum in Washington, D.C.

For Johan and Gabrielle, doing right was far from easy. But it was all their consciences allowed, thanks to a father who valued doing the right thing more than his own comfort and security.

Adventism

ELLEN

For we are God's workmanship, created in Christ Jesus to do good works.
EPHESIANS 2:10

Growing up in frigid Portland, Maine, Ellen Harmon couldn't stand her school reading textbook. The 1830s schoolbook featured a little girl named Ellen as its main character—a (flawless) Victorian angel of a child. With her prim blouse, puffy sleeves, and ruffled skirt, the imaginary paragon of perfection fit the title of one of the lessons: "A Good Girl."

As if that wasn't enough prissy propaganda for a classroom, the religious textbook hammered home the Christian virtues. As Ellen later described it, it presented "religious biographies of children who had possessed numberless virtues and lived faultless lives." Ellen despaired to compare herself to such models. "If that is true," she kept telling herself, "I can never be a Christian. I can never hope to be like those children."

One afternoon when she was 9 years old Ellen and her sister Elizabeth were walking home from school with a friend when an older girl ran toward them, enraged. The three started running away, but when Ellen turned to see how far behind them the angry girl was, a rock smashed into the center of her face.

She awoke in a store, blood gushing from her nose, her dress drenched crimson, blood staining the floor. A stranger offered to take her home in his carriage, but she didn't want to dirty his vehicle, so she declined. Elizabeth and her friend carried her home. She lay in a coma the next three weeks. Only her mother had faith she'd live.

When she first saw her reflection, "every feature of my face," as she later described, "seemed changed. . . . The bone of my nose proved to be broken. The idea of carrying my misfortune through life was insupportable. I could see no pleasure in my life. I did not wish to live, and I dared not die, for I was not prepared."

As she recovered, her warped face haunted her in the reaction of old friends who'd no longer play or confide with her. She turned to God for comfort, and felt love.

But there's something usually forgotten about Ellen White: Elizabeth was her twin. And even though they weren't identical, every time Ellen looked into Elizabeth's pretty, perfect face, it must have been like looking in some tragic, magic mirror.

YOUR FAVORITE PASTA

Greet all your leaders and all God's people.
Those from Italy send you their greetings.
HEBREWS 13:24

Tired of digging in at potluck with nothing to show of your own good cooking? Want to wow your friends and convert your enemies? Your time has arrived, thanks to some fantastic recipes from my favorite chef, Lisa Hermann.

What you'll need:
    6 cups water
    1 tsp. salt
    16 oz. chunky pasta (bowtie, spiral, rigatoni, or penne)
    1/3 cup virgin olive oil
    2 cloves garlic (minced or chopped)
    1 can sliced black olives
    Sun-dried tomatoes or halved cherry tomatoes
    1/2 tsp. ground red pepper
    1/2 tsp. rosemary
    1/2 tsp. basil
    1/2 tsp. oregano
    Sun-dried tomatoes or halved cherry tomatoes
    Feta cheese

Preparing the pasta:
    Bring to a boil 6 cups of water and salt. Set a timer to the shortest length of recommended cooking time per instructions on box. Add pasta to boiling water, quickly returning water to a boil. At this point start the timer, and place a colander in the sink. Boil until pasta is firm but cooked through (usually takes the lesser time of cooking directions). Now dump the pot of pasta into the colander. Let water drain, and place pasta back in pot. Set aside.

Preparing the sauce:
    On medium heat in large skillet or wok, heat olive oil until almost steaming, then sauté garlic until it turns golden (between 1 and 2 minutes). Hint: brown means burned. Add olives, tomatoes, and spices. Cook for about 2 minutes, then pour into pot of pasta. Add the feta cheese and place on low heat, stirring until feta is slightly melted. Ready to serve!

                                                                            LH

Science

SPIT AND NEUROSCIENCE

Jesus asked, "Do you see anything?"
He looked up and said, "I see people; they look like trees walking around."
MARK 8:24

The blind man we meet in Mark 8 quite possibly lost his sight well after birth. The man's distorted view is very similar to a case in neurologist Oliver Sacks' book *An Anthropologist on Mars*. Sacks documents the case of a man named Virgil, who regained his sight later in life. While an operation repaired his eyes physically, his brain had a difficult time making sense of what he was seeing. Virgil saw his cats as globs of black and white, and struggled with depth perception.

Virgil and this man that Christ healed could not process what they saw. The blind man in Mark 8 was more fortunate than Virgil, for he had the Great Physician with him. After Jesus healed the man's eyes, He asked him what he could see. The man said that he saw people, but they looked like trees. Jesus wasn't just doing a vision check; He was dealing with the science of the brain. After placing His hands on the man's face, he could see clearly. Jesus had the knowledge to realize that vision sometimes requires two healings: a healing of the eyes and a healing of the brain's ability to see.

Then there was the man born blind (see John 9:1-7). There is a good possibility that the man had no eyes at all, just sockets. That may explain why people could hardly recognize him later in the chapter— his face was filled with a pair of sparkling new eyes. As the passage goes, Jesus took dirt, spit in it, and put it into the man's eyes, then told him to wash his eyes in a nearby pool. He does, and suddenly he's looking at a new world.

While some may think that the mud was some sort of salve, or provided some curative property, let's look back to what we're made of. We are made of mud, the Play-Doh of the Lord. So Jesus just scoops up a handful of dirt and molds a pair of eyeballs. Let's see your optometrist pull that off.

That brings it all back to the spit. It seems gross in our age of technicolor mouthwashes, but people believed that the spit of the firstborn in the family had curative properties. But the healing power of the spit applied only to the immediate family. Knowing this, Jesus acted as the big brother to the two men. Jesus signified that He was the eldest son in the family of man, and the firstborn of God.

BP

THE WORD MADE FLESH— OR STONE? PART 1

The Word became flesh and made his dwelling among us.
JOHN 1:14

The Bible's message is revolutionary. When was the last time you noticed?

We've gotten so accustomed to a felt-set, junior-camp-skit view of Scripture that its radical, turn-the-world-inside-out imagery and outlook has lost all its bite. To us, Samaritans have always been saints, beggars were ever choosers, the last have always been first, children have always been heavenly . . . and none of it means a thing.

Such thoughts as stated above shocked their original hearers, but to us it's just elevator music. Scripture constantly decries the workaday, lion-eat-lamb world we're so accustomed to, proclaiming a radical new arrangement, yet we lie in foggy sleep, tethered securely to the way it's always been.

The Bible's visions of the new earth aren't just pretty pictures peeled from a Prozac ad. They're a refutation of the entire power structure this world is built on. Overturned are predator and prey, master and slave, favored and rejected, replaced by a new world of interdependence and grace. When that future spills into our here and now, people get flabbergasted.

Just then his disciples returned and were surprised to find him talking with a woman. But no one asked, "What do you want?" or "Why are you talking with her?" (John 4:27).

Good call, disciples.

In Jesus' kingdom world God confides in the ignored, prodigals are pampered, and prostitutes beat preachers to heaven's door. But Christianity has become about self-congratulation. We can excuse anything when it's done for the supposed good. We've created a culture in our own image, baptized it, and can't tell the difference anymore.

The religious leaders were fine with Jesus as long as His message was just words on a page with no application to real life. Words on a page were hunky-dory with them, because they could always be manipulated, obfuscated, or origamied to support a power structure that kept them at the top and everyone else below. But the Word made flesh—that they could not tolerate. Words on a page were easily ignored. The Word made flesh, the word in action, transformed everything. *Continued.*

spirit

THE WORD MADE FLESH— OR STONE? PART 2

I will give you a new heart and put a new spirit in you;
I will remove from you your heart of stone and give you a heart of flesh.
EZEKIEL 36:26

What happens when you try to use God to make yourself look good? You miss God even when He's standing right in front of you.

One of the most startling things about the book of John is how much of it is one long conversation between Jesus and religious leaders who just didn't get Him. John 5 tells of one such encounter. One Sabbath in Jerusalem Jesus picked a man out of the crowd and healed him. Religious leaders spied the man carrying his mat and accused him of breaking the Sabbath. The man said, "The man who healed me said to carry it away."

The leaders boiled inside. They should have known that Jesus was behind this! They tracked Him down and started giving him a hard time: Jesus was ruining everything their religion was about! Jesus told them that they could study the Bible all they wanted, but without His loving attitude, it was pointless. "You search the scriptures because you think that in them you have eternal life; and it is they that testify on my behalf. Yet you refuse to come to me to have life" (John 5:39, 40, NRSV).

Jesus' opponents treated the Bible as a spinning wheel of texts: Put your hand in, pull out some texts, find a few you like, and toss back the ones that don't fit your agenda. Their checkerboard of verses patted them on the back, congratulated them for their zealous religiosity, coddled their arrogance, backed up their prejudices. As Jon Paulien wrote: "Jesus violated man-made rules about Sabbathkeeping to heal a man. The Pharisees were more concerned with petty rules than with the health and welfare of a human being" (*The Abundant Life Bible Amplifier: John*, p. 128).

A year before a friend of mine rejoined the Adventist Church, while he still rejected most of Adventism, we discussed Adventist doctrine. He'd grown up in the church and spent years studying church history, so he knew the doctrines better than I did. However, he lacked the core relational aspect that brings them to life.

God's Word made flesh calls us to lives of action, to break bonds of suffering, suspicion, and superstition. The word made stone leads to self-interested fundamentalism. The Word made flesh reaches out with love and grace.

THE GOOD NEWS CAN GET YOU KILLED

"They got up [and] drove him out of the town, . . . [to] throw him down the cliff.
LUKE 4:29

What can turn an adoring crowd into a murderous mob?

Back in civilization after His wilderness temptation, Jesus traveled the Galilean countryside teaching and healing. By the time he reached His hometown the buzz was everywhere. The Nazareth synagogue overflowed with people eager to see what Jesus would say and do. He took the scroll and began to read from Isaiah: " 'The Spirit of the Lord is on me, because he has anointed me to preach good news to the poor.'"

The people applauded: "Isn't this the carpenter's son? He's certainly grown up. Just listen to the confident way He expounds the Scriptures!"

Then Jesus dropped the bomb. "You want to see me do what you heard I did in Capernaum. But the truth is, no prophet is accepted in his hometown. There were many widows in Israel in Elijah's time, yet Elijah was not sent to any of them, but to a widow in Zarephath in Sidon." (Hint: Sidon is not Israel.) "And there were many lepers in Israel in Elisha's time, but none of them were healed—only Naaman the Syrian." (Clue: Syria and Israel are worlds apart.) And in the next minute Jesus is being run out the synagogue by a murderous crowd intent on His demise. What just happened here?

Here's Jesus' point: *God's healing and liberating work extends beyond Israel's borders.* That may not sound that scandalous on the surface, but it's like suggesting that God's grace extends to Muslims, Buddhists, Hindus and atheists—not as popular a view as it should be. Jesus pointed out that Israel's own stories suggest that at certain times in history, in the times of two of Israel's celebrated prophets, God *preferred* the Gentiles.

Imagine your preacher saying, "There were many Christians in America, but none were blessed by God like a young Muslim in downtown Los Angeles." I daresay that would raise a few eyebrows. The speaker might even find himself or herself run out of church by an angry crowd. Yet central to Israel's story and faith, and thus central to the Christian story, is the truth that God is the God of all nations.

Today millions of people claim exclusive access to the truth, or even to God Himself. But God is no more willing to be limited to one group today than he was in the days of Elijah, Elisha, or Jesus.

RB

Innovation

DISCIPLES: STICKING IT TO THE MAN SINCE A.D. 30

For do I now persuade men, or God? or do I seek to please men?
for if I yet pleased men, I should not be the servant of Christ.
GALATIANS 1:10, KJV

Furniture salesman. It was gonna be a dead-end job for me, but it sure beat a few more weeks tearing up the want ads. Initially my new boss agreed to give me Saturdays off. But with each new week he tried to schedule me on Sabbath.

Whether it was schedule conflicts or "forgetfulness" on the boss's part, by the third week I got smart to what was happening. I finally asked why he always rescheduled me even though we had specifically agreed about Saturdays. He finally said that if I wanted to keep this job, I had better get off of this fanatical church stuff.

"This is a business," he snapped. "We haven't got time for that." He admitted that he'd hoped I would finally yield to the scheduling and disregard our initial agreement.

"Well," I replied, "it looks like you will just have to deal with it."

That's right. I just told this guy, my sole source of income for my wife and baby daughter, that he would have to "deal with it." It had taken me weeks just to get this podunk work. Losing it meant losing my car, defaulting on school loans, and missing out on things like food.

My boss and I stood quietly for a moment. I counted the wrinkles between his eyebrows. He glared at me for a stint, made a guttural *humph*, and walked off.

I had every Sabbath off from that point on. The Holy Spirit had stepped in on my behalf and took the yoke when I needed Him to.

You can't please everybody. No one can serve two masters. Would you jump off a cliff if everybody else did? Yada yada yada. You've heard those clichés since you were knee-high to a felt board. But here's what all those clichés mean: you have chosen to serve a God who is not always a welcome citizen here on this planet.

You don't have time to waste trying to please everyone. You are too valuable to God for doing greater things. Yes, really. That's why He calls you to follow His lead. With each move you make for Him, you'll see people trying to seek *your* approval. And when that happens, direct them to your Manager.

BP

UNWORTHY

For it is by grace you have been saved, through faith . . . the gift of God.
Ephesians 2:8

Ellen Harmon's devastating injuries left her too weak to get much out of school. The teacher assigned the girl who'd smashed Ellen's face to be her assistant, but the strain of studying left her in a sweat, and her teacher recommended that she take more time to recuperate. Ellen never spent another full term in school.

Sunday school was another story. Ellen still resented that God had let her be so injured, but didn't dare let anyone know how she felt. Now on top of feeling beaten down, she felt guilty for feeling beaten down. The Christians around her seemed "so much nobler and purer" than she felt.

Then a major newsmaker showed up in town: William Miller. People swarmed in to hear him. Ellen remembered hearing about him four years earlier, and now she and her friends came to listen as he slowly and methodically explained how Bible prophecy pointed to their time. Ellen felt conviction, but still worried about her worthiness. She'd stay up all night, begging God to save her, but not quite believing He could. Then one night she dreamed that she met Jesus and He welcomed her with love and encouragement.

Ellen's mother suggested she share her feelings with a preacher in Portland, Elder Levi Stockman. He put his hand on her head and, teary-eyed, said, "Ellen, you are only a child. Yours is a most singular experience for one of your tender age. Jesus must be preparing you for some special work." He talked with her a little more, then said, "Go free, Ellen. Return to your home trusting in Jesus, for He will not withhold His love from any true seeker."

Ellen's heart soared. As she later described in her autobiography *Life Sketches*, "During the few minutes in which I received instruction from Elder Stockman, I had obtained more knowledge on the subject of God's love and pitying tenderness than from all the sermons and exhortations to which I had ever listened." At a prayer meeting that night she felt her depression at last lifted, replaced by joy in Jesus.

When William Miller returned a second time, in 1842, when Ellen was 14, the public responded even more enthusiastically, but local churches denounced the "fanatics." Ellen's family found itself expelled from their own church.

Bible

THE RAINS CAME DOWN AND THE FLOODS CAME UP

The Lord was grieved that he had made man on the earth,
and his heart was filled with pain. So the Lord said,
"I will wipe mankind, whom I have created, from the face of the earth—
men and animals, and creatures that move along the ground,
and birds of the air—for I am grieved that I have made them."

GENESIS 6:6, 7

Though their folk stories varied widely, countless ancient cultures took the reality of a devastating worldwide flood for granted.

An ancient Chinese legend tells of Nu Wa, who mended the world after a great flood. Sumerians of ancient Mesopotamia believed that when the gods decided to destroy the world, Ziusudra rescued the world's animals and birds in a big ship. The Hareskin people of what is today Alaska believed that Kunyan ("wise man") knew a flood would come, so he built a raft for himself and his family. People mocked him and said they'd just climb trees, but when the flood came, only Kunyan and his family survived, along with many animals and birds they rescued as they floated.

The Tarascan of northern Mexico believed that God asked a man to build a large house to store animals and food. When it rained for six straight months, the house floated safely on top of the waters, saving the animals and all who had helped build it. As the waters began to recede, the man sent out a raven and a dove to check on things. The Yaqui people of Mexico believed that it rained for 14 days, destroying all life. Only the noble Yaitowi and his family survived at the top of a hilltop, along with some animals in groups of seven.

The Bible's picture of the antedeluvian (pre-Flood) world is of a place richly blessed by natural resources and beauty, yet the inhabitants squander it all on themselves. They forget the Creator, who made it all possible, trusting in and worshipping themselves and whatever their imaginations conjure. God had entrusted His principles to the descendents of Adam and Eve's son Seth, but their association with Cain's self-serving children corrupted them as well. Only a few lived to honor the God who made their luxurious lives possible.

The Creator decided to uncreate, to reverse His actions in creating the world just long enough to scrub the slate clean. Human nature, of course, is not so easily cleansed.

DO-IT-YOURSELF VEGETARIAN CHILE

Daniel then said to the guard whom the chief official had appointed over Daniel,
Hananiah, Mishael and Azariah, "Please test your servants for ten days:
Give us nothing but vegetables to eat and water to drink.
Then compare our appearance with that of the young men who eat the royal food,
and treat your servants in accordance with what you see."
DANIEL 1:11-13

I always hear about chili cookoffs, chili fests, and award-winning chili. It all sounds so difficult and foreign.

On the other hand, this is my mom's chili. She used to whip this up industrial-size. We would freeze the leftovers and eat chili for months on end. I remember taking the leftovers to high school, where my friends would crowd around begging to eat it. Once when my class discussed party eats, my friend Abby piped up, "Or Lisa's mom could just make chili."

My mom's vegetarian chili became legendary in my public high school. No one knew it was so simple. Here is the basic recipe, and you can add some pepper to it to make it as spicy as you like. I like it as is with some Fritos corn chips on the bottom and sharp cheddar on the top.

Ingredients:
    2 cans (15 oz.) kidney beans
    2 cans (15 oz.) black beans
    1 cup salsa
    1 small (about 6-8 oz.) can diced tomatoes
    1 small (2 oz.) can chopped chili peppers
    1 tsp. chopped garlic
    1 bag of Morning Star ground burger or 1 cup dehydrated TVP
    3 cups of water

Directions:
    Combine all ingredients into a large pot. Simmer over medium heat for 1 hour.

LH

spirit

SPIRITUAL JOURNEYS

The path of the righteous is like the first gleam of dawn,
shining ever brighter till the full light of day.
PROVERBS 4:18

When I was 16, a church youth leader asked my group to draw a graph of my spiritual journey. Apparently it was "supposed" to look more like a zigzag than a nice straight line tilting upward. Frankly, though, I didn't get it. I grew up in a home with smart, decent, non-petty parents who let me grow at my own pace. I figured I got to know Jesus a little better every day, and, well, I hadn't blasphemed lately.

The years since then, on the other hand, have zigged and zagged with the best of them. The path God's nudged me to take has, more often than not, not been the one I've chosen. The closer I get to God, the more inscrutable He becomes. He seems to lead me one direction, but it dead-ends. He prepares a table before me, but I'm unable to eat from it. I strain to hold on and somehow sneak a peek around the corner.

I think of a quote from C. S. Lewis' *The World's Last Night and Other Essays*:

"I dare not leave out the hard saying which I once heard from an experienced Christian: 'I have seen many striking answers to prayer and more than one that I thought miraculous. But they usually come at the beginning: before conversion, or soon after it. As the Christian life proceeds, they tend to be rarer. The refusals, too, are not only more frequent; they become more unmistakable, more emphatic.'

"Does God then forsake just those who serve Him best? Well, He who served Him best of all said, near His tortured death, 'Why hast thou forsaken me?' When God becomes man, that Man, of all others, is least comforted by God, at His greatest need. There is a mystery here which, even if I had the power, I might not have the courage to explore. Meanwhile, little people like you and me, if our prayers are sometimes granted, beyond all hope and probability, had better not draw hasty conclusions to our own advantage. If we were stronger, we might be less tenderly treated. If we were braver, we might be sent, with far less help, to defend far more desperate posts in the great battle" (pp. 10, 11).

Despite what televangelists might suggest, the Christian life is not all punch and pudding. Sometimes you have to roll with the punches. But grace is never far from sight.

FRIENDS AND NEIGHBORS

If one falls down, his friend can help him up.
ECCLESIASTES 4:10

They say no man is an island, but if I suddenly had to choose one to be, I'm thinking Australia. Sure, it's technically a continent, but I think kangaroos are worth the argument.

Sometimes I think my spiritual life boils down to me, myself, and the Holy Spirit, but that's not reality. A lot of friends and family have shaped and unshelled me through the years, and I owe them all a bucket of gratitude.

What people have affected your spiritual journey?

_____
_____
_____

What events have affected your spiritual journey?

_____
_____
_____

Where do you think your spiritual journey is headed?

_____
_____
_____

What dangers do you think may lurk in your spiritual journey?

_____
_____
_____

When have you felt closest to God? farthest away?

_____
_____
_____

Where do you see yourself spiritually in the future?

_____
_____
_____

HIS SPECIAL PLACE / PART 1

When I called, you answered me; you made me bold and stouthearted.
PSALM 138:3

"Doctor! Doctor!" the men shouted. Shaking himself awake, Eric looked down from the bamboo window to see three wild-looking men. Their bodies were greased, each grasped a sword and an oil lamp, and one held a piece of paper up to him. It was a note saying that a drugged man had chopped up a woman and her son. "Bring all your needles and sutures," he read. Could he do it? For just an instant Eric let himself think back . . .

He saw himself kneeling by his mother, repeating the words of her prayer. "And when I grow up," *and when I grow up,* "may I be a missionary," *may I be a missionary,* "at the four corners of the earth," *at the four corners of the earth.* "And remember," she often said, "God has a special place where you can serve Him better than anyone else."

After graduating from college, Eric had taken a two-year nurses' course. Then he and his wife, Agnes, accepted the church's call to do medical work among the Karen spirit worshippers of Burma (now Myanmar). From large tropical ulcers, to toothaches and stomach aches, to a man gored by an elephant, Eric had cared for them all. But nothing prepared him for this midnight hike and the sight he saw when he opened the door of a small house.

"It's terrible! I don't know if they're still alive," the headman said, pushing him inside. By the light of his lantern he saw two bloody bodies. Just then the boy gave a yell. At least he was alive. Eric stepped over to the woman, and blood oozed around his feet. She was most likely dead, and he thought he was going to faint.

"No, you don't," he said aloud. "Get hold of yourself!" It worked, and soon he knelt in the boy's blood, doing his best to comfort him. He had a bad gash in his neck, but it had missed the large veins. Quickly Eric sutured and bandaged it and other wounds. Carrying the boy to the door, he gave him to the headman, then asked for help. The man who came fainted into his arms. At last a little old grandma stepped up. "I'll come and help," she said. "I'm so old and skinny that the evil spirits won't hurt me."

They knelt beside the woman. Her forehead was split open. Through the slash in her cheek they saw her teeth and tongue. Her left arm had been hacked off below the elbow, and a feeble drip of blood came from that arm. *Continued.*

HIS SPECIAL PLACE / PART 2

Trust in the Lord with all your heart . . . and He shall direct your paths.
PROVERBS 3:5, 6, NKJV

Seeing the drip of blood coming from the woman's severed arm, Eric put on a tourniquet and stopped its bleeding. He and his elderly helper bound up her split forehead. Carefully Eric sutured and bound her almost severed cheek the best he could, then sutured and bound the flesh of her other arm. Then he asked for hot milk.

A few minutes later he carefully placed a teaspoon of milk to her lips, and the almost-dead woman took it and swallowed. Eric gave her another, and another. After taking a half cup she opened her eyes and looked at Eric, who knelt above her. "I'm not going to die," she said slowly.

At that Eric told the headman that the woman was alive but must get to the government hospital 60 miles away. He hesitated. "Do you think she can live that long?"

"It's a miracle she's still alive," Eric told him. He explained that she needed much more care. The headman made a decision. He got the largest canoe in the village and six strong men to paddle it. Eric wrote a letter to the doctor, then watched them disappear into the darkness. Some weeks later a woman came into the jungle clinic. Her face was a crazy patchwork of scars. Eric looked at her, puzzled. "Don't you remember me?" she asked. It was his midnight patient, who sobbed out her thanks. "If you hadn't come, I would have died. But you weren't afraid of the night. You weren't afraid of the fiend who chopped me up. And now both my son and I live."

"Of course she lived," said the other patients looking on. "Isn't he our own Dr. Rabbit, and wasn't the rabbit the most clever animal and the best doctor in the jungle?"

And Eric knew that this little jungle clinic was exactly where God wanted him to be. For his last name was "Hare," and his patients had quickly named him Dr. Rabbit. As the years passed, those spirit worshippers learned to worship the true God. More clinics were established, and schools. The nationals became nurses and ministers and administrators. And during World War II, when all foreigners had to leave, they kept the church alive. Despite hardship, starvation, and even torture, not one Sabbath passed without the believers meeting together. They did not let go of God.

Adventism

THE GREAT DISAPPOINTMENT

Then I took the little book out of the angel's hand and ate it,
and it was as sweet as honey in my mouth. But when I had eaten it,
my stomach became bitter. And he said to me,
"You must prophesy again about many peoples, nations, tongues, and kings."
REVELATION 10:10, 11, NKJV

As William Miller preached Jesus' very soon return, his new colleagues dug yet deeper into their Bibles to figure out what it was all about. In 1840 Josiah Litch pointed out from the Bible that God's end-time judgment of sinners would happen before the Second Coming. In 1843 Charles Fitch preached a sermon based on Revelation 18, urging "Millerites" to "come out of Babylon"—to leave, he said, their home churches that didn't accept Jesus' impending return. More and more of Miller's followers left or were kicked out of their churches by their annoyed congregations. Though they pained to lose friendships and spiritual ties, they knew it would hardly matter in a few months' time, when they were hanging out in heaven.

When 1843 came and went without Jesus showing up, Millerites were disappointed but not depressed. Eventually they figured out something they'd overlooked in their calculations: there was never a year 0 (because A.D. 1 immediately followed 1 B.C.). Aha—that meant the prophecy pointed to 1844 instead.

In March 1844 the eminent Hebrew scholar Dr. George Bush, from New York University, published an open letter to Miller. The date might be right, he said, but it wouldn't be the Second Coming. "Your error, as I apprehend, lies in another direction than your *chronology.* You have entirely mistaken *the nature of the events* which are to occur when those periods have expired."

Then in August 1844 Pastor S. S. Snow upped the stakes. Having studied the Jewish ceremonial calendar, he declared that the prophecy would be fulfilled on the Day of Atonement, the tenth day of the seventh month of the Jewish year—October 22, 1844.

When Millerites heard him at a Millerite camp meeting in New Hampshire, they felt ecstatic. This was it! Jesus was just around the corner, and there was a world to warn. They no longer had to worry about money or health or success, only for the salvation of souls. But when October 23 rolled around, many wept until they could weep no more.

THERE AND BACK AGAIN

So the Lord scattered them from there over all the earth,
and they stopped building the city.

GENESIS 11:8

After the Flood tore the planet apart, leaving a handful of survivors scrambling to adapt to a new world, God renewed His covenant with His people. He first sent wind to separate the water from dry land, just as He had at His original creation.

God had told Adam and Eve to "be fruitful and increase in number; fill the earth and subdue it" (Genesis 1:28). He now told Noah and his descendants to do the same, except that now the world's animals would fear them. As God had told Adam and Eve to eat fruits and vegetables, so He now told Noah, "Everything that lives and moves will be food for you. Just as I gave you the green plants, I now give you everything" (Genesis 9:3).

Though Noah's descendants fruitfully multiplied, they ignored the part of God's command that urged them to spread out and fill the earth. "We've got to stick together, or we'll end up scattered," they said, so they moved east to Shinar (perhaps what we know today as Sumer, in modern-day Iraq) and decided to see what they could accomplish without God's help. They decided they could "make a name" for themselves. Previously things and people had always received their name from someone else—creation from God, animals from Adam, children from parents—but the presumptuous people of Shinar were, as the old joke goes, self-made people who worshipped their makers.

The people named their city Babel, which meant "gate of the gods" (and gave us the name Babylon), but because a similar-sounding Hebrew word means "confusion," that's how we remember them. When they attempted to build a tower that would touch the sky (and perhaps protect them from another flood), God decided it was time to step in and break up the party. Before then, everyone had spoken the same language, so God gave different people different languages, and people hooked up and headed out with the people they could understand.

Yet God didn't want things to stay that way. Beginning with Abraham (through the descendants of whom all nations would be blessed), God has worked to bring them back together. In the New Jerusalem, God's own great city, all peoples, tongues, and nations will at last gather together.

Science

WHY TEENS CRAVE THRILLS

One day Jonathan son of Saul said to the young man bearing his armor,
"Come, let's go over to the Philistine outpost on the other side."
But he did not tell his father.
1 SAMUEL 14:1

They're hungry. They're sleep-deprived. They're easily addicted—
and incredibly talented. And most of them haven't even graduated
from high school.

People used to think that teens were just like adults, only pimplier.
You can make babies, you can drive a plow. Make us proud, kid! In
today's world, though, you're more likely to hear teens judged and
criticized. Politicians promise to "get tough" on juvenile crime. TV
reporters ramble about the latest disturbing trends of teen behavior.
And authorities wish youth would act like adults—but don't let them.

Their brains suddenly start rewiring, as an explosion of new neuro-
transmitters causes them to crave the new, the fresh, the outlandish.
Meanwhile increased amounts of dopamine in the brain spurs reward
anticipation, and suddenly teens whose bodies would have rejected
artificial stimulants now relish them. Studies of rats show that before
puberty they shun drugs like cocaine, but suddenly desire them in
adolescence. "Older rats and people aren't attracted to cocaine. . . .
If you look at stimulant abuse according to age, there's very little risk
until you hit puberty. . . . But between 11 and 14, the risk jumps four
times." Such research explains why almost no smokers start the
habit after 21.

Yet, writes former *Psychology Today* editor Robert Epstein, "The
truth is that [teens] are as competent or virtually as competent as
adults across a wide range of adult abilities. And long-standing studies
of intelligence, perceptual abilities and memory functions show that
teens are in many instances far superior to adults. . . . Almost without
exception, the reckless and irresponsible behavior [of teens] is the
teen's way of declaring his or her adulthood, or, through pregnancy or
the commission of serious crime, of instantly becoming an adult under
the law. . . . [Yet] when we treat teens like adults, they almost immediately rise to the challenge."

It just may be up to the church to lead the way.

WILL THIS BE ON THE TEST?

*The hand of the Lord was upon me, and he brought me out by the Spirit of the Lord
and set me in the middle of a valley; it was full of bones.*

EZEKIEL 37:1

Anatomy and physiology class was the scholastic highlight of my senior year of high school. I'd taken a similar class the year before, but this one meant college credit—and the teaching of the incomparable Mr. Lee.

Mr. Lee never raised his voice or even told many jokes, but my classmates and I still thought he was awesome. He made anatomy and physiology fascinating and fun (even if he did have something bizarre stored in a jar in his office). We learned that every hole and bump on our skull has its own name, like the internal occipital protuberance (where the four main parts of the top of your skull fuse together) and foramen magnum (the slot the spinal cord sticks through). I also learned that when it comes to dissection, nothing beats a savvy lab partner with a steady hand. (Thanks, Sean.)

When Mr. Lee assigned the skeleton test, we knew not to sweat it. Studying together in the library, we memorized the bones from cranium to phalanges. Humerus? Check. Femur? Check. Thoracic vertebrae? Check. We just had to remember what was connected to what. The hip bone's connected to the leg bone (aka the femur). The leg bone's connected to the knee bone (aka the patella). Simple. Easy as a jigsaw puzzle.

We strode into the classroom oozing confidence, ready for a few rounds of Name That Bone. But our faces fell. Something was amiss. Bones were scattered around the room at various locations, stripped not only of their muscles and skin, but of their context. This wasn't the connect-the-dots we'd expected and prepared for—this was a crime scene! When the test was over, we all knew we'd bombed. (Well, except Sean.)

When our scores came back, we discovered that Mr. Lee had ignored the top score (thanks, Sean) and counted the second-best score as 100 percent. Thanks to that adjustment I actually passed that test, and ended up with a B in the class. Today Sean's a nurse . . . and I— well, I married a neurologist.

However much we may bone up for God's judgment day, we don't know the half of it. The only way we'll pass that test is through God's grace, with Jesus' perfect score substituted for our miserable attempts to score on our own.

WALK SOFTLY AND CARRY A BIG JESUS

In quietness and confidence shall be your strength.
ISAIAH 30:15, NKJV

If you've ever seen a Jackie Chan movie, you'll realize that each film was just a scaffold on which to hang fight scenes. In each movie he was always in control, calm and composed. Even when he's blind-folded and balancing on a grocery cart, fighting an entire bloodthirsty gang, he could find time to blurt out a philosophical maxim.

Dignified reserve. Take any hero, male or female, and they've got it. They don't freak out when the enemy approaches. There's no doubting, no lack of composure; just a steady hand and a watchful eye. It's part of why people so love those costumed crime fighters. They are the eye in an otherwise turbulent storm. Superman rarely doubted his own strength, and even when he did, he persevered. It's as if Supe went forth with nothing more than his obligation to do what was right.

Then there's you. Your fight with the enemy is not punctuated with wisecracks. No 20-foot-tall robots or crowd of ninjas crouch on your doorstep. Instead your opposition is a motley team of insipid fear, hollow doubt, and baseless guilt. You can't physically knock out or rip these bad boys apart. And your enemy knows that. How do you fight what you feel?

So you beat yourself up instead, which works well for Satan. He wants you to freak out and feel unable to defend yourself. And here's where the sick truth sinks in: you can't defend yourself alone. And all that cool-reserve stuff hits the fan blades of reality.

Yet you've got an awesome strength by your side. Your trials probably aren't so glamorous, but they're not supposed to be. In the seemingly endless melodrama of your life, remember that this chaos is not your domain. You come from a Creator who left His burial sheets folded in the tomb when He rose. He is not chaos. Satan's the one who plays that up. In quietness you recognize that it is God who leads you, and your confidence builds knowing that you are His to be led.

Your strength lies in who you rest on—but you saw that coming, right? So as the formidable forces loom over you and the storm starts to rage into a personal typhoon, quit trying to be self-confident. Be Christ-confident instead.

BP

THE ONE-PAGE GUIDE
TO WITNESSING

But God demonstrates his own love for us in this:
While we still yet sinners, Christ died for us.
ROMANS 5:8

"So where do you go to church?" If asked, what would you say? If you say, "I'm a Seventh-day Adventist," what then? Token references to nice hospitals, vegemeat, and having a "unique" belief of going to church on Saturdays?

Then there's all the theological baggage and historical trivia. What are these stories of beasts coming out of the oceans and a woman being fooled by a snake? (Great, there's a snake act involved too.) There's talk of spirits, new wine, blood, and virgins with lamp collections. And that's just the cookie-cutter stuff.

While you reel back from the interrogation, your face has an uncanny resemblance to a deer in front of a pickup at 2:00 a.m. You may want to rationalize or lessen what you just encountered. You may even try to defend all or part of what's thrown at you, only to find that trying to make excuses for misunderstandings only confuses things more. So instead, take a breath, and let oxygen and the Holy Spirit take it from there.

Let loose crazylike and start with the truth. Start with a Man who was born of human DNA and God. Tell about His career as a carpenter, how He was trained to cut and set wood, then was cut and set on wood. He lived 2,000 years ago, and immediately a following began. They followed Him because they'd heard stories of what He did before being seized by the Romans and, on popular demand, executed. His closest followers recorded His ability to heal those who were blind or mutilated. He fed thousands with a prayer and a fish basket! He could resurrect the dead. And not just the recently dead—in one instance the guy had been dead four days.

But the Man who awakened the dead was killed for not being what people expected of Him. They could not handle the truth. The truth was that He was the Son of God. Three days later He came back to life. Now He's in heaven awaiting the day when He'll return to destroy our dying world and create a new one. He loves you and wants you to be part of that new world. If you run into someone bent on confrontation, toss in the reminder that a Seventh-day Adventist is a follower of Jesus Christ. If that ruffles their feathers and they unload with bits of bad info and rumors, send a prayer upward for direction. The Holy Spirit has your back.

BP

Innovation

LOVE/HATE RELATIONSHIPS— WITH YOURSELF

*All who fear the Lord will hate evil. That is why I hate pride,
arrogance, corruption, and perverted speech.*
PROVERBS 8:13, NLT

"I don't get it. I hate that I'm just too stupid," one of my students exclaimed.

"This world will do more than enough in trying to tell you how stupid you are," I snapped back. "Don't fulfill the lie."

"Hate" is a word that has lost its meaning in our abuse of it. Seriously, outside of sin, what or whom do you really hate? Waking up early? Those shirt tags that itch? Spam e-mail? Do you really hate those things, or do they just annoy you? The reason you should "hate" any-thing—let alone yourself—should be because it is not of God.

"Perverted speech" in Proverbs 8:13 sounds like a cussing session. But you start perversion the moment you start to dog yourself down. Did you catch that? If God never called you stupid, why do you do it? And if God didn't, who did? That's right, Satan—the accuser. And Satan will use any tool to break down your God-given abilities and gifts.

Some people actually hate themselves and don't even know it. And while you may not think that you've ever beaten yourself down, think back to kindergarten. When a teacher asks the class who can draw, all the hands in the room shoot up. Fast-forward to high school. The teacher asks the same question, and you might see three people raise their hands. Did you raise yours? And whether you did or did not, did you notice the huge loss of drawing capability?

A high school friend of mine could draw any comic book character he saw. More than imitation, he created new scenarios for the heroes, and even new characters. He free-sketched faces and body forms. In art class he worked in acrylic, pointillism, and even clay, all with aston-ishing results. But even as the class encouraged and praised his abil-ity, he would brush off the compliments. He hated how "bad" he was. He focused on the negative talk—perverted speech—he gave himself and allowed it to poison his whole person. Teachers encouraged his abilities and even suggested art schools. He seemed to balk it all. The last I heard of him, he was working as a stock clerk at a grocery store.

God did not create dim bulbs. He created souls lit with passion and capabilities. If you're currently hiding yours under a bushel, light it up and let it blaze.

FALLOUT

The visions of the evenings and mornings that has been given you is true,
but seal up the vision, for it concerns the distant future.
DANIEL 8:26

The day Ellen Harmon and family waited for Jesus to return, October 22, 1844, the famous General Tom Thumb, two feet one inch tall, appeared in their hometown, available for citizens' viewing for a mere 12½ cents. The legendary P. T. Barnum had trained the 7-year-old to sing, dance, and imitate famous people, and in a world without television, radio, or movies, the sideshow was the hottest ticket going.

But while the famous dwarf came and went, Jesus never showed up at all. The Millerites crashed from cloud nine to rock bottom. As Ellen later reflected: "Mortality still clung to us, the effects of the curse were all around us. It was hard to take up the vexing cares of life that we thought had been laid down forever. It was a bitter disappointment that fell upon the little flock whose faith had been so strong and whose hope had been so high. But we were surprised that we felt so free in the Lord, and were so strongly sustained by His strength and grace."

The Millerites struggled to figure out the suddenly upside-down world they had so recently expected to exit. The prophecies had seemed so clear. Did they just need to wait a little longer? Had they been deceived? What was really going on?

Some said Jesus had come—just, you know, spiritually speaking. As historian George Knight describes, some of them got a little wacky. "Some claimed to be sinless, while others refused to work, since they were in the millennial Sabbath. Still others, following the biblical injunction that they should become as little children, discarded forks and knives and crawled around on their hands and knees" (*A Brief History of Seventh-day Adventists*, p. 29).

For others, though, the sense that something *had* happened on October 22, 1844 stuck with them. Daniel 8:14 predicted that a "sanctuary" would be "cleansed." Where? How? Methodist farmer Hiram Edson was the first to suggest an answer. After praying with friends on October 23, he was walking across a field when suddenly an insight flashed into his mind: the sanctuary in heaven. It was as Josiah Litch had said: before Jesus carried out His judgment at the end, He first had to perform a trial. Fair was fair.

Bible

FATHER ABRAHAM AND MOTHER SARAH

By faith Abraham, when called to go to a place he would later receive as his inheritance, obeyed and went, even though he did not know where he was going.
HEBREWS 11:8

Abraham. Man of God. Righteous and bold. Faithful and true. Willing to do whatever God said, even if it meant sacrificing his own son. A veritable paragon of virtue. It's such a dramatic and romantic picture. Too bad it's not as true as we'd like.

We imagine Abraham sitting in church when God calls his number, then he and Sarah pack their bags and move to Canaan. Then Sarah gets anxious because didn't God promise a baby in the bargain, so she nags Abraham to procreate with her servant, and that turns out just about as well as might be expected. When God drops by in person to announce that senior citizen Sarah can finally start knitting baby clothes, she snorts in the background. But within a year Isaac is born, and they all live happily ever after, an interrupted child sacrifice only strengthening the family bonds. Hallelujah.

Somehow we've painted Abraham as Mr. Faithful and Sarah as Ms. Skeptical, and lost the well-rounded, real people who actually walk the pages of the Bible. The reality is Abraham didn't even grow up in a Yahweh-worshipping home (Joshua 24:2 tells us that Abraham's father worshipped false gods). When God showed up to change his life (and the history of the world), He was a stranger, and He didn't spell out religion as we know it all at once. He just said, "Follow My lead, and trust Me to do what I promise."

Set off and leave everything you know behind . . . easy as kissing your half sister, right? No. When they left their family in Haran, they gave up their ancestral rights to land and inheritance. If they were to survive, Yahweh had better be telling the truth.

The truth is, ol' Abram ("exalted father"), redubbed by God, Abraham ("father of many nations"), had as hard a time holding on to faith as any of us do. Abraham had his questions, his doubts, his mistakes he just couldn't shake without embarrassing himself a few times. Fortunately God put even more faith in Abraham than Abe put in Him. He knew that even though Abraham was jumpy and skittish, he could be bold and true. He knew that even though Sarah was suspicious and impetuous, she would laugh with joy instead of scorn if she just held on.

BRAIN + BODY = YOU

And the Lord God formed man of the dust of the ground,
and breathed into his nostrils the breath of life; and man became a living soul.
GENESIS 2:7, KJV

Mind melds. Shape shifting. Body swaps. Science fiction loves to explore what it means to be human through zany scenarios during which the usual rules are twisted out of shape—but at that extreme there's very little science left in the fiction.

Numerous religions believe that people's "spirits" can survive apart from the body. Hindus believe that our spirits leap from body to body when we die, reincarnating until we finally get things sorted out. People fear ghosts in hotels and battlefields. Even most Christians believe that when we die, our souls go to heaven or hell. Yet the Bible and science both agree: our minds and bodies are inseparable. Kill your brain or kill your body, and "you" aren't there anymore.

I've admittedly not watched a lot of TV that included so-called mediums pretending to talk with dead people, but I've never heard any of them say, "Yeah, I've got your grandpa on the line, but he doesn't remember you—you know, Alzheimer's and all that." Nope; somehow, despite really fuzzy communication skills ("I'm sensing something to do with yellow and the number 7"), these alleged spirits land in the spirit realm with their brains restored.

The word "soul" in the Bible has confused a lot of people, but the Bible is clear—you don't *have* a soul; you *are* a soul. The Hebrew word for soul, *nephesh*, simply means a person, and is even used to describe animals (Leviticus 24:18) and fish (Isaiah 19:10).

Our memories, our emotions, and our consciousness all have a physical basis. Our memories are stored in our brain's web of neurons. Brain chemicals regulate our emotions, which are affected by all manner of stimuli, from food to light to touch to drugs. Distortions in our brain chemistry and makeup cause mental illness. Our bodies are incredibly complex creations. When our consciousness is impaired, we're no longer there.

Adventism's emphasis on the mind-body connection has made it one of the most health-conscious religions in the world. As Ellen White wrote: "The brain nerves which communicate with the entire system are the only medium through which Heaven can communicate to man and affect his inmost life" (*Testimonies for the Church,* vol. 2, p. 347).

spirit

DAYS OF NOAH

And because lawlessness will abound, the love of many will grow cold. . . .
But as the days of Noah were, so also will the coming of the Son of Man be.
For . . . they were eating and drinking, marrying and giving in marriage,
until the day that Noah entered the ark, . . .
so also will the coming of the Son of Man be.
MATTHEW 24:12, 39, NKJV

People love to talk about how much better things used to be—and how bad things have become. Crime. Violence. Disrespect. Money. Marriage. Morality. It all used to be so much better, right? Today's divorce rates/crime statistics/war/sexuality/youth/corruption/drugs are worse than ever—right? And isn't it all a sign of the end of the world?

Is society really worse than ever? Think about it. In the 1850s divorce was rare, but the American life expectancy was several decades shorter than it is today. If things didn't work out with one spouse, chances were one of you would have another go at it before too long. A hundred years later overt racial and gender prejudice still shaped American laws and lives. Are things better today than 50 or 150 years ago? In a lot of ways, yes.

Today opportunity has expanded around the world, and people live longer, richer, healthier, more peaceful lives than ever. Today crimes like child and domestic abuse, sexual assault, and racial prejudice are no longer hidden in the dark, as they were for most of history. For millions of people the "good life" is here, and despite tragic things that are easier than ever to ignore on the news, life is safer (if not simpler) than ever. It's not quite the picture that people have always painted of a world in its last gasps.

But it's the picture that Jesus painted—a world in which people are so satisfied with their self-sufficiency that they hardly think of eternal issues. He compared the end of the world with Noah's day, when people went along "eating and drinking, marrying and giving in marriage" as if everything were fine and nothing were going to change. It reminds us that even when life seems hunky-dory and dandy, the sun is shining and flowers are in bloom, there's more to life than the pursuit of temporary happiness. We've got an eternity to live for—today.

SPIRITUAL GROWTH / PART 1

*"My dear children, for whom I am again in the pains of childbirth
until Christ is formed in you, how I wish I could be with you now and change my tone,
because I am perplexed about you!"*
GALATIANS 4:19, 20

One of the finest Christians I know is someone I've rarely seen eye
to eye with.

I'll call him Mr. Jones. He's dedicated and driven, and loves working for God and serving people. But though I've seen him soften and
become more humble over the years, he's got a rigid side to his personality. Mr. Jones sees Christianity as primarily a list of dos and
don'ts that keep people from sinning. Sometimes people have complained that he's too quick to judge them for their looks or other weaknesses he perceives.

The funny thing about Mr. Jones, though, is that he used to be a
pretty public sinner. He got drunk. He cussed people out. He was
everything he might condemn today, yet now that he's a Christian he's
gone to an opposite, legalistic attitude.

A friend I'll call Brad called me the other night and asked, "Do you
think the church brainwashes people?"

"Well," I said, "what scientists might call brainwashing—and it's all
very debatable—is generally a very intense thing in a very controlled
and secluded situation, so it's rather difficult to do on a broad scale.
Why do you ask?"

"Well," he replied, "when we're kids we're taught simplistic songs
such as 'Jesus Loves Me.' With songs like that, and the constant teaching of relying on Jesus as your savior and leader, etc., isn't it brainwashing?"

"It's teaching a worldview on an age-appropriate level, to be sure.
But most people find it pretty easy to go their own way when they
grow up."

"Maybe," Brad said. "I dunno—it seems very . . . calculated to me."

"Well, if you believe in something strongly you tend to want to
pass it on to your kids, whether it's religion or the value of money and
hard work. Which is not to say that people can't be manipulative. One
of my friend's moms used to sit by her bed at night and pressure her
by saying that the rest of the family was going to heaven and that she
hoped that her daughter would be there too. I think that's fundamentalist thinking that can warp people." *Continued.*

SPIRITUAL GROWTH / PART 2

When I was a child, I talked like a child, I thought like a child, I reasoned like a child.
When I became a man, I put childish ways behind me.
1 CORINTHIANS 13:11

"Seriously," Brad said, "my old girlfriend just flipped! She went nuts. She used to be this smoking-hot, up-for-anything person, but now she won't wear anything but skirts down to the floor and has been telling me all these crazy conspiracy theories. I know that this can come from any religion, but seriously!"

"Ah," I said. "I've known a few people like that. It's a very black-and-white, no nuance worldview. But the healthiest religion is centered on relationships, not rules."

The truth is that going from one extreme to another is human nature. And it's actually pretty healthy—to a point. Someone who's had no spiritual roots, just doing whatever feels good at the time, living for the moment, may need to take a breather and enjoy some structure for a while.

Psychologists suggest four stages of spiritual growth that everyone potentially experiences, though people may remain in one stage for many years or a lifetime. We're wired to go through these stages, and as long as we don't stagnate, it's a healthy process.

Very young children are in the first stage, self-centered and chaotic. They think the world revolves around their immediate desires for pleasure and gratification. Some people never leave this stage. Most of us revisit it more often than we'd care to admit.

The second stage might be called blind faith. A person has learned to play by the rules, how to live in a community. Think of a 7-year-old. You can tell them something outrageous, and unless they know they've been fooled a few times, they're gonna believe you. It's a black-and-white world in which people follow authority and rarely question their beliefs. For many, it's a very comfortable place.

The third stage is skepticism and curiosity. Preteens and teenagers usually experience this stage as they wrestle with making their religious beliefs their own, and not just hand-me-downs from their parents.

In the fourth stage, people become more comfortable with ambiguity. Similar to Job at the end of his Old Testament book, they recognize that they don't have all the answers, but they trust a God who does. They are willing to put their lives in His hands.

QUALITY COUNTS

*"See, I have called by name Bezalel son of Uri son of Hur, of the tribe of Judah:
and I have filled him with divine spirit, with ability, intelligence, and knowledge
in every kind of craft, to devise artistic designs, to work in gold, silver, and bronze."*
EXODUS 31:2-4, NRSV

Hanging out one Saturday night, Lisa, our friend Jesse, and I decided to head to the video store to find a movie to watch. As we perused the shelves searching for a mutually agreeable motion picture, I spotted one that just looked lame. Its cheesy cover art and bad graphics screamed "Don't waste your time. I'm just here to keep has-been actors employed!"

I pointed to the video box and leaned toward Lisa. "That looks like a Christian movie—wait, it *is* a Christian movie!"

Lisa and I laughed heartily yet ruefully, pondering why so many movies made by Christians look like they belong, quality-wise, next to titles like *Zombie Mutants 4: The Vengeance.* Meanwhile Jesse, who is Jewish and thus blissfully unaware of much of what his religion's most successful spin-off has been up to lately, looked at us as if we were insane.

So what about "Christian art"? Sometimes it's hard to pin down what "Christian" means, or whether it should ever be used as an adjective at all. Maybe "Christian movie" or "Christian music" makes about as much sense as "Christian car." The problem comes when Christians think a few "Jesus loves you"s make up for their intellectual and artistic laziness. Worse still, Christian art and literature too often paint a dishonestly rosy picture of a Christian's life. Instead of the Bible's gritty honesty we find a cheery world populated by bland do-gooders who neither sin nor sweat and who, once they accept Jesus, never struggle or suffer again. The pictures may look pretty, but they don't tell the truth—and can't connect with an audience trapped in the real world.

The Bible is an artistic masterpiece. From its classic stories to its mind-bending poetry, unflinching warts-and-all biographies, and piercing wisdom, it's defined and inspired art for centuries. And while a spiritual elitism runs counter to everything the gospel stands for, I believe that one of the best ways to witness for the Creator is to be truly creative.

FEBRUARY 27

Adventism

THE ROAD TO HEAVEN

Even on my servants, both men and women, I will pour out my Spirit in those days.
JOEL 2:29

The dejected Millerites continued meeting in Ellen Harmon's hometown, often at her parents' home. They continued to wrestle with the question *Where was God in all this?*

And then an answer came from where they least expected it.

Hanging out at a friend's house in December 1844, Ellen, now 17, was still recovering from tuberculosis. Her lungs had bled and she could hardly breathe lying down, but she'd accepted her friend's invitation to get out of her own house for a bit. As she and four other young women knelt together in morning worship, she suddenly found herself in vision.

She saw the group who'd believed in Jesus' soon return climbing a mountain path, a bright light shining behind them, guiding their way. An angel told her that the light was the "midnight cry" message Miller had preached. The path was dangerous, but they'd be safe as long as they kept their eyes on Jesus.

"We should have gotten there by now," someone said. Then Jesus waved in the distance, light shining from Him, and they pushed on, crying "Hallelujah!" Yet others said, "This has all been a mistake—God is not in this," and they stumbled off the path into the darkness below. The faithful pressed on, not even stopping when attacked by opponents. Then Ellen saw what they'd waited for: the Second Coming and the New Jerusalem in heaven, with its tree of life and resurrected loved ones.

Ellen's friends watched, astounded, as she witnessed her vision, her eyes gazing into the distance, unresponsive to their attempts to speak with her. When she came out of her vision she was thrilled by what she'd seen, dejected to see dismal earth again after glimpsing heaven, and appalled by the responsibility to share this message from God with other people. She begged God to give the job to someone else, someone stronger, someone more sanguine. A week later she had another vision, of the ordeals and challenges ahead for her. When in a third vision she told an angel she was afraid she'd get full of herself, the angel said that if she ever felt as if there were something special about her, her fragile health would keep her humble.

HAGAR AND ISHMAEL / PART 1

Now Sarai, Abram's wife, had borne him no children.
But she had an Egyptian maidservant named Hagar; so she said to Abram,
"The Lord has kept me from having children. Go, sleep with my maidservant;
perhaps I can build a family through her."
GENESIS 16:1, 2

It's a plot worthy of a telenovella. She did everything she was asked as a servant, and then, when she wasn't needed anymore, her spiteful boss fired her, leaving her destitute in the desert.

It all started when Abraham's wife couldn't stand the shame of childlessness any longer, and suggested to ol' Abe that since God was taking His sweet time making her pregnant, Abe might as well have a kid through her servant Hagar. Since anything her servant owned was legally hers as well, Sarah figured that a surrogate-born son beat no son at all.

Naturally that went just about as well as you might expect. Sarah resented Hagar's pregnancy just as much as she'd probably come to resent the very act of lovemaking with her so-called patriarch of a hus-band. Stung by Sarah's sudden cruelty, Hagar—just as so many of God's children in the Bible—fled to the wilderness.

God found her at a spring. And as God was known to do in the Bible when He found His children hiding in shame, He asked a gentle question: "Where have you come from and where are you going?"

"I am running away from my mistress Sarai," the pregnant slave breathed.

"Return to your mistress," God urged, "and submit to her." And then He did the unexpected. God gave Hagar the same blessing He'd previously given Abraham: "I will so greatly multiply your offspring that they cannot be counted for multitude."

And then Hagar herself did the unexpected. She became the only person in the Old Testament to give God a name of her own. "You are *El-roi*," she said, pondering, "Have I really seen God and remained alive after seeing Him?" (Genesis 16:8-13, NRSV).

Like us, Hagar was born into slavery. Like us, Hagar tried to do what she was told would make everybody happy, and got only grief for it. And like we should all be, Hagar was overwhelmed by the love of an accepting God. *Continued.*

Bible

HAGAR AND ISHMAEL / PART 2

*God heard the boy crying, and the angel of God called to Hagar from heaven
and said to her, "What is the matter, Hagar? Do not be afraid;
God has heard the boy crying as he lies there."*
GENESIS 21:17

So Hagar headed home—back to the father of her child, back to the
most hostile work environment you could imagine. She gave birth to
her son, Ishmael: "God hears."

Years came and went. God reestablished His covenant with
Abraham, and this time He told Him he would be the father of a multitude of nations. Sodom turned to soot. Ishmael grew up into an energetic teen.

And then Sarah herself gave birth. The uneasy truce between slave
and master was over.

Feeling that Ishmael had slighted her son, Sarah demanded
Abraham send Hagar and Ishmael packing. Abraham's heart ripped.
Ishmael was his son. How could he send him away? But God told
Abraham that for His promise to be fulfilled, Hagar and Ishmael
needed to go, and yet, "I will make a nation of him also, because he is
your offspring" (Genesis 21:13, NRSV). Even the unwanted son would
be blessed.

Hagar and son soon found themselves in the wilderness yet again.
She feared that this time both she and her son would die of exposure,
and she couldn't bear to look on his suffering. Yet God told her they
had not been forgotten. Pointing her to a well full of water, God said,
"Come, lift up the boy and hold him fast with your hand, for I will
make a great nation of him" (verse 18, NRSV).

In *The Book of Beginnings* Gerald Wheeler writes, "Scholars have
noticed many interesting parallels between the story of Hagar and that
of Moses. . . . For example, both flee oppression into the desert and
come to a well. . . . Both encounter God. . . . Moses learns the name of
God . . . , while Hagar goes beyond Moses to name the deity. . . . The
Lord tells both of them to return to the oppression they had escaped
from. Eventually they were expelled from their bondage back into the
desert. . . . In the desert God delivered them from death, particularly
from thirst. . . . And both became heads of a great people consisting of
12 tribes. . . . God cared just as much for Ishmael and his descendants
as He did for Isaac and his future offspring. After all, the Lord had
promised Abram that he would be 'the ancestor of a multitude of
nations' (Genesis 17:5, NRSV)" (p. 107).

PROVIDENCE

For he will command his angels concerning you to guard you in all your ways;
they will lift you up in their hands, so that you will not strike your foot against a stone.
PSALM 91:11, 12

I once drove over a mailbox. In a car. I was 4 years old.

Packing up after visiting some friends in Kentucky, my father had decided to pack me first. These were the days before child car seats and mandatory "kids ride in the back" rules. It was also a time that all that certain cars needed to start rolling was to push their gearshift into neutral. Sitting there by my lonesome, I started looking around. And pushing things. Including that gearshift. The car sat atop a small hill, but not for long.

My sister Bronwen first noticed my forward motion. Jumping up and down shouting, she finally got my parents' attention. My mom sprinted toward the car, which had flattened a standing mailbox and now headed toward a brick wall.

My mom found herself on the passenger's side of the vehicle. If somehow she could yank open that door, climb in, and put that gear back in place, disaster could be averted. Unfortunately, that front passenger door jammed nearly 100 percent of the time. It always took a few hard yanks—but not this time. This time she peeled the door open like a can opener. Leaping inside, she grabbed me, jammed her left foot on the brake, grabbed the wheel, and stopped. that. car.

But that perpetually jammed door—angels? adrenaline? a very lucky coincidence? Afterward it jammed as dependably as before.

When I was 6, I slipped from the top of a metal jungle gym during recess. "You went straight down, like an arrow," observers said. My head bounced off the ground. The next I knew, I was lying on a cot in the elementary school sickroom. And despite what my sisters might tell you, the doctors found no damage.

Miracles. Sometimes they're hard to pick out. If there's one thing I can say for certain about miracles, it's simply this: *They're unfair.* Unfair to the millions who suffer every day, who pray and pray and die anyway. Unfair to those left behind when nothing stops the car or the cancer. But if there's one more certain thing, it's this: Miracles are one way God's love shines through the cracks in this broken world, and remind us that soon we won't need angels to protect us.

THE TRUE VALUE OF YOU

Jesus . . . for the joy before him endured the cross, scorning its shame.
HEBREWS 12:2

I wouldn't be surprised if some of my old college professors thought of me as cocky or a know-it-all. I've always thought of myself as a confident hard worker, with an intense side, who knew her goals. I knew medical school would be a new playing field, academically, socially and spiritually, and suddenly I wondered about my responsibility for witnessing. I prayed for humility, a spiritual discipline I knew I lacked.

I felt overwhelmed and unprepared for the intensity of med school. I was used to the intimate classes of a small college, but now I was just another seat in the auditorium. I sat among graduates of the most prestigious learning institutions and older students who had already spent years researching and publishing. My grades were no longer the best, and I "knew" more wrong answers than right. Soon my outspokenness turned into silence. My self-confidence vanished. I felt timid in small groups, doubtful of my abilities. I had been humbled. But had I truly been given the gift of humility?

Over dinner a friend told me her pain. She had heard that an old boyfriend had gotten married—to a girl he'd sworn he was over. She felt worthless and silly. All of the time they had spent together, was he thinking of *her*? Was she always second best? I felt speechless. Here was my good friend whom I admired. She had helped me so often through difficult times. She was brilliant, yet she couldn't even see her own merit. Finally I gathered the only words I could find: "This doesn't mean that you are worth less or that she is worth more. Your value is independent of this news."

We try to prove our worth by showing how we're better than other people. We derive value based on our ranking with our peers. When we become distant from our Creator, from whom we've derived our worth, we have to search for value elsewhere.

Humility isn't cutting yourself down. When Jesus washed His disciples' feet, He didn't lower Himself, because even in human form He was still God. Instead, He increased *our* value. When He washed his disciples' feet He lavished love onto them. Jesus was confident in His position. He was not afraid of servitude devaluing Him. Humility is being so confident in your value that you do not need praise to determine your worth. It liberates you to serve, to treat others as though they are worth the world.

LH

KINDERGARTEN CONDESCENSION

"Let no one despise your youth, but set the believers an example
in speech and conduct, in love, in faith, in purity."
1 TIMOTHY 4:12, NRSV

One day in kindergarten my teacher announced we'd all get to contribute recipes to a cookbook. That sounded pretty fun—if anyone loves eating, it's a 5-year-old—and I pondered what my contribution would be. Deciding that I knew how to make instant pudding, I happily waited my turn to be interviewed.

When, at last, the inquisitive adult, pen and paper in hand, came to my desk, I was ready. Carefully I explained the simple steps: pour the chocolate pudding mix into a glass jar, add milk, screw on the lid, and shake, shake, shake till it was good and thick. Voilà: a tasty treat for you to eat.

I thought I was finished, but the adult, looking oddly frustrated, started asking such questions as "Where do you buy the pudding mix?" I thought that was a random question but tried to be helpful just in case there were actually people who didn't know where groceries were sold.

However, when the cookbook was assembled and choice selections were read aloud to an appreciative parental audience, I realized I'd been had. The crowd guffawed at the various recipes calling for plenty of gumdrops and jelly beans. Then someone read my recipe, and I barely recognized it. That woman had taken my nonchalant answers to her pesky questions and weaved them into my nice, straightforward recipe to make me look silly. I was peeved. I thought, *Dude, if you wanted me to give you something funny, why didn't you ask?*

Too bad the condescension doesn't end when you start first grade.

Popular media worships young people with countless magazines chronicling the every move of the young and the beautiful ("Hey, they go shopping too!"). But too often the church ignores youth and young adults. They're excited to get you baptized when you're 12, they entertain you a few times in your teens, and then they seem to forget you exist until you're 35—or just wonder whatever happened to you.

In taking its youth for granted, the church is harming itself almost as much as its young people. Next week we'll look at what you can do to make a difference.

MISSING BEAUTY

*He had no beauty or majesty to attract us to him,
nothing in his appearance that we should desire him.*

ISAIAH 53:2

On an ordinary Friday morning a thirtysomething guy dressed in jeans and a T-shirt stood in a busy subway station, removed his instrument from its case, and began to play some of the most beautiful music ever written. Violinist Joshua Bell, recognized as one of the best classical musicians in America, was taking part in an experiment arranged by the Washington *Post* to see if people would acknowledge the sublime amid the cacophony of the daily grind.

Nobody knew quite what to expect, but what *did* happen was far removed from anyone's best guess. Of the nearly 1,100 people whose morning commute took them past Mr. Bell, only seven stopped to listen for any length of time; a meager $32 accumulated in his open case during the 45-minute concert. For someone accustomed to recognition and acclaim, the indifference was surprising. "I started to appreciate any acknowledgment, even a slight glance up. . . . When you play for ticket holders," Bell explains, "you are already validated. I have no sense that I need to be accepted. I'm already accepted. Here, there was this thought: *What if they don't like me? What if they resent my presence?"*

For most, it seemed a question of priority: the rush to an early meeting, the irritation of having a cell phone call drowned out by the insistent strings, the iPod piping some other tune directly to the ear. Though one man didn't notice anything special about the music, he said he would have dropped a few dollars—if he hadn't just spent all his cash on lottery tickets. Among those who did take notice were former music students who appreciated the skill on display, and children captivated by the sparkling notes even as their parents rushed them away.

On an ordinary Friday morning 2,000 years ago, a thirtysomething guy dressed in a purple robe and a crown of thorns quietly claimed to be the Son of God and was summarily dismissed by the crowds.

"As one from whom others hide their faces he was despised, and we held him of no account"(Isaiah 53:3, NRSV).

CR

ADVENTISM GETS ITS GAME ON

*Now the Bereans were of more noble character than the Thessalonians,
for they received the message with great eagerness
and examined the Scriptures every day to see if what Paul said was true.*
ACTS 17:11

The Christians who'd believed that Jesus would return in 1844 splintered into various groups. Some decided that nothing had happened. Some kept setting dates for Jesus' return. And a few started digging deeper into the Bible to see what Daniel's 2300-day prophecy had been about after all, and what other truths they might have missed.

Several had recently started observing Saturday as the Sabbath. They took another look at what the Bible says about death and decided it was just a dreamless sleep. People aren't born immortal, they decided, not destined to forever fly or fry, but would escape the eternal nonexistence of death only if they believed in Jesus.

The new "Adventists," though hardly 100 now existed, soon earned a nickname: "the Sabbath and shut-door people." As the small group hammered out what they believed, they didn't give much thought to mission. (After all, what is a mission without a message?) *Perhaps*, they thought, *the door of salvation, the same as the door of Noah's ark a week before the rain fell, is now shut tight.* But as their work began to attract people who hadn't even been interested in the 1844 hoopla, they began to realize that God was calling them to something much bigger than just rounding up former Millerites.

In 1846 Ellen Harmon became Ellen White when she married an ambitious, can-do young preacher named James. Their marriage shocked some who believed that, since Jesus was coming soon, marriage was surely a worldly waste of time. Meanwhile, that year Ellen received a vision telling her that the end would not be for a while yet, as the "time of Jacob's trouble" would come first. Some who had rejected the Holy Spirit's work in recent years had "shut out" the Holy Spirit, committing the "unpardonable sin," Ellen believed, but many more would still be open to their message.

By 1848 the group had nailed down the essentials, and that year Ellen White saw a vision that changed everything—and told them they needed to get busy. She'd seen, she said, their publishing work surrounding the world "like streams of light." Now that they knew what they believed, it was time to start spreading the word.

Bible

SODOM AND GOMORRAH

Now this was the sin of your sister Sodom: She and her daughters were arrogant,
overfed and unconcerned; they did not help the poor and needy.
EZEKIEL 16:49

What words do "Sodom and Gomorrah" bring to your brain? Utterly sinful? Sensory overload? Sex maniacs? For most people, the names conjure images of decadence and depravity. Partying, fornicating, you name it. But for the prophet Ezekiel, writing under God's inspiration 1,000 years later, Sodom's sin could best be summed up as selfishness.

Arrogant. Overfed. Unconcerned. While people suffered around them, the citizens of Sodom just rolled over and grabbed another bag of chips.

I've heard a lot more politicians or Christian activists speak out about sexual immorality than plain old greed. After all, greed is the very foundation of our world today. If some poor sap falls through the cracks, tough luck.

There's no denying that Sodom and Gomorrah's sexual viciousness added to the sins that brought God's wrath. Yet I've got a hunch that that wasn't what sealed their fate. In the Gospels Jesus forms instant bonds with numerous people with shameful sexual histories, yet the arrogant, the overfed, and the unconcerned won't give Him the time of the day. While Jesus told the woman caught in adultery, "I don't condemn you," He blasted the arrogant, overfed, and unconcerned for their hypocrisy.

When Abraham rescued his nephew Lot and Lot's neighbors from four pillaging kings who'd robbed them and taken them hostage, two people met up with them. The godly Melchizedek offered Abraham bread and wine and a blessing, yet the king of Sodom, ignoring ancient tradition and customary courtesy, offered Abraham nothing but demands: "Give me people; take property yourself."

When God's angelic investigators took one last look at Sodom, making a personal appearance to see how the people would treat them, Lot showed them due hospitality. In a time without hotels or Taco Bells, a healthy society revolved around hospitality. But the rest of the people thought only of themselves. As far as they were concerned, visitors were there just to be used and abused. And though God had promised Abraham he'd spare Sodom if only 10 of them were righteous, that night their number was up.

"AN ART OF SOUND IN TIME"

Then I heard what sounded like a great multitude,
like the roar of rushing waters and like loud peals of thunder,
shouting: "Hallelujah! For our Lord God Almighty reigns."
REVELATION 19:6

"An art of sound in time." That's how my dictionary defines music, and I like the sound of that. The thing is, music may be the universal language, but it sure has a lot of different dialects.

My dad enjoys classical. I bug out when a song doesn't seem to be going anywhere after the first minute. My grandfather enjoyed country music. "It tells a story," he told me when I asked why, but I think too much of modern country is self-parody. I like a song with soaring melodies and guitars, that pulls like gravity and swings like the tide. I like lyrics that remind me that I'm more than skin and bones.

Music has incredible spiritual power. It's probably a good thing, though, that the Bible doesn't include notes for any of its songs, or we would be tempted to think that they're the only way to play them. Of course, that hasn't kept generation after generation of Christians from believing that heaven's own music sounds curiously like what they grew up on. But I don't think I'll truly feel immortal until I hear that multitude singing "like the roar of rushing waters and like loud peals of thunder." And if I'm singing along with something approaching talent, I'll know the old life is truly o'er.

What song(s) have affected your spiritual life? Why?

_____

_____

_____

What did you feel in the music that so affected you?

_____

_____

_____

Which communicates more powerfully, singing or playing? How so?

_____

_____

_____

spirit

MERCY IS NOT STRAINED

*How then can we be saved? All of us have become like one who is unclean,
and all our righteous acts are like filthy rags.*
ISAIAH 64:5, 6

My sister and I loved visiting our honorary grandmother's house. A big backyard and cupboards full of old clothes and trinkets kept us enchanted for hours. A narrow staircase curled up from the back bedroom to a mysterious attic that stretched the entire length of the house. I giggled with horrified delight at one story she told about that attic.

The branches of a tall pine tree stretched within easy reach of that attic room's front window. One warm summer night the family cat climbed the tree, leaped through the open window, and deposited a mouse beside Grandma's young daughter. The girl shrieked in disgust at the feline trophy so lovingly offered.

Art Linkletter, known for his humorous chats with kids, told a tale of a 9-year-old girl who wanted to do something nice for her headache-ridden mother:

"Finally, Mother told the girl she could make her a cup of tea. After quite a while the girl brought it, and Mother drank it gratefully. 'You've been very helpful, dear,' said Mother. 'You did a good job of straining the tea, too.' The girl smiled proudly, 'I couldn't find the strainer, Mom, so I had to use the flyswatter.' Noticing the horrified look spreading over her mother's face, the little girl reassured her. 'Oh, don't worry. I didn't use the brand-new swatter. I used the old one!'"

You try to please your parents, impress your friends, and get that cutie's attention. But what about God? Can we earn His favor? Is anything we can offer good enough?

After wrestling with this question on bruised and bloodied knees, Martin Luther concluded that we can't. No amount of good deeds or penance will erase the sin-stains on our souls. Romans 3:22, 23 says, "This righteousness from God comes through faith in Jesus Christ to all who believe. There is no difference, for all have sinned and fall short of the glory of God, and are justified freely by his grace through the redemption that came by Christ Jesus."

Shakespeare wrote, "The quality of mercy is not strained," meaning that it is not forced or produced by effort. That's good news for anyone who has ever tried to make tea with a flyswatter.

CR

THE WORST JOB IN THE WORLD

Whatever your hand finds to do, do it with all your might.
ECCLESIASTES 9:10

I once worked the worst job in the world. No, it wasn't the summers I worked the night shift in a 90-degree warehouse bagging 700 loaves of French bread. Ten minutes of work, and I and my clothes were soaked to the skin. After hand-stapling all those bags I'd go home and soak my hands in hot water just to be able to move my fingers.

And my worst job wasn't scrubbing toilets, though I did that, too, as a dorm night watchman and janitor while in college. No, the nastiest work I ever did was cleaning tables in the academy cafeteria when I was 16 years old. Three meals a day, seven days a week—my sister and I rotated the job with another couple students.

The cutest guys turned into pigs when they sat down at those tables. They just didn't care. Squashed french fries. Squished green beans. Veggie roast flipped from a fork across the table. And the school's most popular girls, despite sparkling personalities, dazzling smiles, and their crowds of friends, dribbled their gravy and spilled their milk with the worst of them.

I hated that job. I hated how cold and dirty the water became after just a few tables. I hated the red juice the cafeteria served, how its stain resisted the strongest detergent and my hardest scrubbing with a sturdy brush. But most of all I hated the smear of green peas stuck on so many tables at least once a week. Truly, compared to the smell of old food and the effort needed to get those ridged white plastic tablecloths clean, scrubbing toilets was nothing. Toilets are supposed to be stinky and vile. Dining room tables aren't.

Five months into the job warts sprouted on my hands from spending so much time in water. Had rubber gloves been invented yet? Of course, but neither I nor my bosses thought of it. Twice a day we worked our way down the rows of tables. Skating during Tuesday evening recreation? Not till we'd finished. Baseball games? Hockey? Can't cheer them on until the last of the ground-in peas is gone.

Yet this job had one lasting benefit, and I suppose I'm lucky that I gained it when I was so young. After that year, I could work at almost anything. I'd done the worst. No job I've had since has even come close.

PW

Mission

TAKEN FOR GRANTED

So he asked Jesse, "Are these all the sons you have?"
"There is still the youngest," Jesse answered, "but he is tending the sheep."
1 SAMUEL 16:11

Being a youth or young adult in your local church can feel pretty powerless. You don't have money, so they don't listen to you. You don't have seniority, so they don't think of you. You don't have the same tastes as they do, so they don't want you involved.

A lot of churches have discovered that a family-friendly approach involving all age groups makes for the healthiest congregations, but chances are you're not so lucky as to enjoy such a church. And even if you do, you may still lack critical support.

A famous Ellen White quote declares, "With such an army of workers as our youth, rightly trained, might furnish, how soon the message of a crucified, risen, and soon-coming Saviour might be carried to the whole world!" (*Education*, p. 271). Unfortunately it hasn't always sunk in, and youth are far too often taken for granted. So how can you help your church involve its youth more?

There's strength in numbers. You may not be able to effect change in your church all by yourself, but you can with friends who feel the same way. Meet together with friends and pray and brainstorm what you feel called to do as a group. What activities would you enjoy together? What church and community needs can you meet? What talents do you have to share? What do you need that the church isn't offering? What would it take to get more youth involved with your church?

Start small. Choose three or four objectives to start with, such as more recreational activities, raising money for class or mission projects, or sharing of class talent in church worship. Let your church know what your group has come up with and what support you'll need to make it happen.

Find allies. Your parents or other adults. Your Sabbath school leader. You need support and wisdom, especially when working with a church that still doesn't "get it."

Take charge of your own spiritual life. Even a good church can stunt your spiritual life if you let its programs substitute for developing your own spirituality. Commit to studying the Bible on your own every day. Keep in touch with God through prayer. Seek out opportunities to serve God in ways that your church may not provide, whether it be a mission trip, writing and producing a skit, or mentoring younger kids.

STAND UP, STAND OUT

There is no fear in love. But perfect love drives out fear,
because fear has to do with punishment.
1 JOHN 4:18

Evil is easy. If it weren't, it wouldn't be so popular—on the battle-field, on the playground, at the movies. Evil is glamorous. Evil is fun. Evil means big bucks.

Standing up against evil. Now, that takes creativity and genuine guts. Everybody wants to save their skin. When Paul wrote, "After all, no one ever hated his own body" (Ephesians 5:29), he wasn't kidding. Until we've been pushed beyond despair, we'll do anything to keep going in the face of evil, no matter the compromise, body or soul.

Evil is second nature, and so ingrained that it's easy to forget that it truly is our second nature. God created us noble, loving, wise, but we swallowed the bitter pill, so shrewdly sugarcoated, and ever since we've either battled or embraced the buzz.

If evil is easy, if evil is big business, what does it take for someone to stand up, speak out, and defy the powerful? What makes people willing to stick their necks out? Samuel and Pearl Oliner decided to find out. They studied people who'd risked their own lives during World War II to rescue Jews. They wanted to know why, despite the authoritarian environment, they didn't just toe the line. The Oliners discovered that those courageous people all had something major in common: their parents had not physically punished them. Instead of spanking, their parents talked things out with them, encouraging them to think for themselves.

Rescuers' parents "reasoned rather than threatened," Eva Fogelman wrote in *Conscience and Courage: Rescuers of Jews During the Holocaust*. Instead of motivating their kids by fear of punishment, they taught them to think things through and to do the right thing be-cause it was the right thing.

Social psychologist Martin Hoffman has extensively studied what makes people compassionate. Hoffman found that "parents who ex-plained rules and used inductive reasoning instead of harsh punish-ment tend to have children who care for and about others. After all, parents who voluntarily relinquish the use of force in favor of reason-ing send their children a message about how the powerful should treat the weak."

Evil is easy. But love is eternal.

THE MAN WHO LOVED THE SEA
PART 1

Others went out on the sea in ships. . . .
They saw the works of the Lord, his wonderful deeds in the deep.
PSALM 107:23, 24

Growing up in the then-whaling capital of the world, New Bedford, Massachusetts, in the early 1800s, Joseph Bates obsessed about going to sea. He wanted to see the world. Finally his parents let him go along the coast on a cargo ship with his uncle. Surely seasickness and other hardships would cure him of sea fever. It didn't.

A few weeks before Joseph's fifteenth birthday, his father found a ship captain about to sail to England. Captain Terry said he'd be personally responsible his new cabin boy's welfare. The ship sailed to New York to pick up its cargo of wheat, then headed across the Atlantic. It was smooth and uneventful sailing to London, but on a Sunday morning 18 days into their return, the crew spotted a shark following them.

The sailors attached a big chunk of meat to a rope and threw it over the side of the ship, hoping to catch the beast. The shark ignored the meat and kept following the ship.

The sailors started swapping tall tales of sharks—how they'll swallow men alive, or bite them in two, or follow ships with sick crew members for days, patiently waiting to feast on the next burial at sea. As Joseph wrote in his autobiography: "Sailors are generally brave and fearless men; they dare meet their fellows in almost any conflict, and brave the raging storms of the sea; but the idea of being swallowed alive by a voracious shark . . . often causes their stout hearts to tremble."

The men finally gave up trying to catch or distract the shark, which stayed behind the ship as it sailed. That evening Joseph climbed the ship's mast to look out at the ocean and see if any other ships were in sight. Seeing nothing but open sea, he began climbing back down, but misjudged a rung. He fell backward, knocking into a rope, which kept him from falling onto the ship's deck. Instead, he fell 60 feet into the frothing sea.

Joseph struggled to keep his breath—and his head above water. The ship sailed farther and farther from his reach. Weighed down by his heavy clothes, he struggled to follow.

Captain Terry and crew rushed to the ship's stern. The first officer flung out a rope. As Joseph managed to grab it, the first officer called out, "Hold on!" *Continued.*

THE MAN WHO LOVED THE SEA
PART 2

Then they cried out to the Lord in their trouble, and he brought them out of their distress. He stilled the storm to a whisper; the waves of the sea were hushed.
PSALM 107:28, 29

Joseph hung on for his life as captain, crew, and officers strained to pull him back onboard. At last he landed on deck, and everyone breathed out again.

"Are you hurt?" someone asked.

"No," Joseph gasped, shivering in his drenched clothes.

"Where is the shark?"

Joseph suddenly remembered, and began to tremble in belated fear. The shark! He'd completely forgotten about the shark.

Joseph and the crew rushed to the other side of the ship. There was the shark, silently, serenely swimming alongside the ship. Everyone stared in amazement, and nobody bothered the creature again. But they couldn't figure out how the shark had moved to where he would miss the excitement going on behind and beside the ship.

Though he'd just gotten a little more up close and personal than comfortable, Joseph's love for the sea only grew. He kept sailing with cargo ships, a few months at a time. But when he was 17 a journey from New York to Archangel, Russia, gave him more adventure than he'd ever sought.

At midnight the ship struck ice off the coast of Newfoundland. The crash knocked Joseph across the room, momentarily dazing him. Joseph and Mr. Palmer, the man who'd been steering the ship, were trapped in the ship's forecastle. They put their arms around each other's necks and braced for the ship's plunge into the frigid Atlantic. Men screamed for mercy from the deck above them.

The hatch above them flew open. "Is there anyone below?" someone shouted into the darkness. Joseph and Mr. Palmer scrambled up to the deck, where he found the captain and second mate on their knees, praying for their lives, while the crew fought to control the ship. Ice surrounded them, and the wind rushed them forward. Palmer threatened to throw the captain overboard. It would be a rather late mutiny, but he said sending the captain to eternity a few minutes early would be nonetheless satisfying. Joseph grabbed Palmer. "Let go of him! Help me try the pump!" *Continued.*

Adventism

THE MAN WHO LOVED THE SEA
PART 3

*They mounted up to the heavens and went down to the depths;
in their peril their courage melted away. They reeled and staggered
like drunken men; they were at their wits' end.*
PSALM 107:26, 27

Somehow the pump worked. Buoyed by this turn of events, the chief mate shouted, "Let go the top-gallant and the topsail halyards! Let go the tacks and sheets! Haul up the courses! Clew down and clew up the topsails!" As Bates later described it: "The wind thrown out of the sails relieved the ship immediately, and like a lever sliding from under a rock, she broke away from her disastrous position, and settled down upon an even keel broadside to the ice."

Somehow the ship, the front of it wrecked, its mast sagging, sailed free of the ice. Fourteen days later they landed in Shannon, Ireland, and made needed repairs for their voyage to Russia. They joined a convoy of more than 200 British ships, then, after a storm, sailed off on their own to along the coast of Denmark.

Suddenly two Danish privateers started shooting cannonballs at them. The privateers captured and took them to Copenhagen, Denmark, to stand trial. The ship and its cargo were condemned, by order of Napoleon Bonaparte, for its fraternization with the British.

The cargo's owner begged the ship's crew to swear that they'd had no association with the British. Joseph insisted he could not lie. Joseph was called first to testify. "Do you know what it means to take an oath, to swear to tell the truth?" a judge asked in English. Bates said he did, and the judge motioned to a small box. "That box," said the judge, "contains a machine to cut off the two forefingers and thumb of everyone who swears falsely here. Now hold up your two forefingers and thumb on your right hand."

Joseph swore to tell the truth, and tell the truth he did. Set free, he tried to make his way back to Ireland, but in Liverpool he found himself kidnapped and forced into the British Navy. He tried to swim to freedom, but was captured. He found himself headed toward the Mediterranean to fight against Napoleon's army. Joseph tried to contact his parents. When at last a letter reached them, his father wrote President Madison for help. The president and Massachusetts governor gave assistance, but then war broke out. *Continued.*

THE MAN WHO LOVED THE SEA
PART 4

They saw the works of the Lord, his wonderful deeds in the deep.
PSALM 107:24

Joseph and his American friends chose to go to prison rather than fight their own country. They spent the war as POWs. When 18 prisoners escaped, they were sent to the infamous Dartmoor Prison in England, known as "the abode of lost and forgotten men." Joseph was released in 1815, exactly five years from the day he'd been kidnapped, and began his journey home.

Two months later his mother, siblings, and friends rejoiced to have him home. Now nearly 23, he had been gone for more than six years. When his father came home from business a few days later, he was shocked to see his long-lost son again—and amazed that Joseph hadn't become a rum-slurping reprobate.

Joseph got reacquainted with his childhood friend, Prudence Nye. "I knew you'd come back," she said. Two and a half years and several voyages later—Ireland, England, Baltimore, New Orleans, Brazil, the Amazon—they married.

Despite the hardships, Joseph Bates still loved the sea. He sailed on trip after trip, his wife, "Pru," keeping a home as he sailed to Bermuda, the West Indies, Rio de Janeiro, Montevideo, Buenos Aires. Eventually he became a ship captain. Wanting to improve himself, he gradually stopped drinking and chewing tobacco. When Pru packed him a Bible to read, he grew convicted that he should be a Christian, but felt he'd already wasted too much time. Yet hadn't God protected him through the years? He felt overweighed with guilt. Perhaps, he thought, walking the deck one night, he should just jump overboard and end it all. Shocked by the thought, he shut himself in his cabin till morning. He looked for some proof that God had forgiven him, but couldn't find it.

Back home in Massachusetts, now 34 years old, he was asked by a Christian friend about his spiritual life. He told her he'd never been converted, for surely God could not have forgiven him. But meeting with Christian friends and hearing their own stories assured him that his conversion was as genuine as anyone's. He felt like a new man.

When he sailed again, he found it much harder to leave family and friends than ever before. Pirates attacked his ship off the coast of Brazil, but didn't find the gold doubloons hidden with the ship's beef and pork, even when they grabbed themselves some supper.
Continued.

THE MAN WHO LOVED THE SEA
PART 5

The Lord your God will be with you wherever you go.
JOSHUA 1:9

On his last voyage before retiring, Bates had a surprise for the crew: no drinking, no swearing, and no shore leave on Sunday. After their shock they actually came to appreciate the new rules and wanted to sail with him again.

But from then on, Bates threw his energy into other things. At 35 he was ready to settle down—mostly. Living in New England, he soon ran across some Millerites and became excited that Christ was coming soon. He felt burdened to share the good news with slaves and their masters. People told him he'd be killed for being an abolitionist, but he'd seen and experienced too much to worry about a few irritated slaveholders. His friend H. S. Gurney went with him to provide the music.

Crossing the Chesapeake Bay, they came to Kent Island, where Bates had been shipwrecked 27 years before. Town leaders refused permission for them to speak in the meetinghouses, but the owner of a tavern invited them to use the tavern hall. The owner had been 10 when Bates had been shipwrecked there, and remembered him.

Bates and Gurney spoke to a packed hall for five days. When a man denounced their Millerite teachings and threatened to ride him out on a rail, Joseph Bates replied, "We are all ready for that, sir. If you will put a saddle on it, we would rather ride than walk." The crowd hooted and hollered as the man tried in vain to find his friends—or anything to say.

Joseph continued, "You must not think that we have come 600 miles through the ice and snow, at our own expense, to lecture to you, without first sitting down and counting the cost. And now, if the Lord has no more for us to do, we had as lief lie at the bottom of the Chesapeake Bay as anywhere else until the Lord comes. But if He has any more work for us to do, you can't touch us!"

Moving on, in Chester, Maryland, the two men found a place where they could speak to both slaves and their owners. As usual, Gurney opened the meeting with a song, this time singing, "I'm a pilgrim, and I'm a stranger . . . I can tarry but a night." After the meeting an elderly slave offered him 25 cents (perhaps all the money he had) for a copy of the song. *Continued.*

THE MAN WHO LOVED THE SEA
PART 6

And my God shall supply all your need according to His riches in glory by Christ Jesus.
PHILIPPIANS 4:19, NKJV

Gurney found paper and pencil and copied it for him—for free. The man told Gurney that he couldn't read but that someone would read it to him. Gurney knew that the song was the story of his life.

The Great Disappointment shattered Joseph's hopes. Yet he held on, joining the small group of believers who met to study the Bible further. By 1846 he had spent all his money to spread the gospel, but felt called by God to write a tract on his latest discovery: the Sabbath.

As he wrote, Pru told him she needed four pounds of flour and asked him to get that and a few other items. Back home with exactly what she'd asked for, Pru burst into tears when he confessed that he'd spent his last cent. "The Lord will provide," he said. Pru hardly found that assuring—he always said that!

A half hour later Bates felt impressed that an important letter awaited him at the post office, so he went back to town. He didn't have even the few cents for the postage due, so he asked the postmaster to open it. If money was inside, he could pay himself the postage, then give Bates the letter. It held a $10 bill! Praising God, Bates bought a barrel of flour and some more groceries, then used the rest to print the Sabbath tract.

Arriving in Battle Creek, Michigan, in 1852, he headed to the post office and asked the postmaster to tell him who was "the most honest man in town." Bates believed such a person would be interested in the Adventist message. Sure enough, Presbyterian David Hewett and his wife accepted the new truths Bates brought, and became the founding members of the Battle Creek church.

Alongside James and Ellen White, no one did more to establish the Seventh-day Adventist Church than the old sea captain. When the church floundered in the 1850s without sturdy organization, the ever-organized Bates promoted order. He helped steer the church through rocky shores to solid ground.

(Adapted from *Heartwarming Stories of Adventist Pioneers*, book 1, and *The Autobiography of Joseph Bates*.)

Innovation

THE NAZIS WITHIN

Let no debt remain outstanding, except the continuing debt to love one another,
for he who loves his fellowman has fulfilled the law. The commandments . . .
are summed up in this one rule: "Love your neighbor as yourself."
Love does no harm to its neighbor. Therefore love is the fulfillment of the law.
ROMANS 13:8-10

There's something about the Nazis. They made evil look . . . dashing. A tyrannical regime that persecutes people it fears is one thing. Doing it with such flair is another. Those uniforms. That precision marching. It was malevolence made suave.

While the world's economies prospered in the "roaring twenties," the post-World War I Weimar Republic in Germany, punished by the war's winners, spiraled into ruin. Then while the rest of the planet endured the Great Depression in the 1930s, under the Nazis Germany came roaring back to life, putting millions back to work improving the infrastructure, paving the Autobahn, and even inventing the Volkswagen Beetle.

Hitler appealed to people's innate sense of superiority. Everybody wants to hear they're better, smarter, prettier—and innately so. Yes, you've been beaten down, pushed back, and written off, but now your time has come. And you deserve a little payback. And anyone who had such low self-esteem that they didn't buy the superiority psychology just kept their heads down. Nazism took the beauty of community and family and twisted it into a hideous ideology that justified destroying anyone on the outside.

When someone tells you how superior and entitled you are, the next natural thing is to look down on those judged inferior and to blame *them* for your own problems. The terrible thing is, there's a potential Nazi in every one of us—you, me, your aunt Dee, and that cute, gurgling baby. Since the serpent told Eve she simply deserved the best, we've all been bent toward the twin evils of self-exaltation and self-preservation.

Germany marched to war with the words "*Gott Mit Uns*"—God with us—emblazoned on their belt buckles. Yet despite the religious and family rhetoric they wrapped themselves in, everything about them contradicted God's law of love. Jesus' commandment is to "love your neighbor as yourself." It's a two-sided coin. If you only love yourself, you can't show your neighbor love. If you love only your neighbor, you'll soon have no more of yourself to share.

ADVENTISTS AND SLAVERY

If a slave has taken refuge with you, do not hand him over to his master. Let him live among you wherever he likes and in whatever town he chooses. Do not oppress him.
DEUTERONOMY 23:15, 16

In the 1850s there was no hotter issue in America than slavery. While Baptist, Methodist, and Presbyterian churches split over whether or not to support slavery, Adventists stood united against it from their beginning.

Adventist abolitionism often went beyond mere words and opinions. Founding church member Joseph Bates was also a founding member of his hometown's abolitionist society. John Byington, the church's first General Conference president is said to have served as a conductor in the Underground Railroad. At his farm in Buck's Bridge, New York, in the 1850s, he helped escaped slaves from the South make it north to a free life in Canada. Battle Creek, Michigan, church member John Preston Kellogg, assisted slaves passing through his farms.

Such actions broke U.S. law, but Adventists believed they answered to a higher authority. Ellen White wrote, "When the laws of men conflict with the word and law of God, we are to obey the latter, whatever the consequences may be. The law of our land requiring us to deliver a slave to his master, we are not to obey; and we must abide the consequences of violating this law. The slave is not the property of any man. God is his rightful master, and man has no right to take God's worksmanship into his hands, and claim him as his own" (*Testimonies*, vol. 1, pp. 201, 202).

Though many thought a civil war unlikely, Adventists came to expect it, thanks to Ellen White's strong words and predictions on the subject. Though Adventists did not believe in taking up guns to fight, they saw God's hand in the war. Wrote Ellen White, "God is punishing the North, that they have so long suffered the accursed sin of slavery to exist; for in the sight of heaven it is a sin of the darkest dye. God is not with the South, and He will punish them dreadfully in the end" (*ibid.*, p. 359).

Adventism's strong stance against slavery and association with northern America delayed its progress in the South for many years. And while Adventism's history of race relations is far from spotless, it can take pride in its legacy so long as it keeps it alive.

Bible

SHEPHERD, LIAR, SCHEMER, THIEF

I am the Lord, the God of your father Abraham and the God of Isaac.
GENESIS 28:13

Jacob had the hardest time waiting, but he surely knew how to scheme. God had told Jacob's mother, Rebekah, that he would be honored above his minutes-older twin brother, Esau, a startling pronouncement in the rigid ancient world that honored firstborn men above all. The odds certainly seemed against him. His father's favorite, Esau was all muscle and fiery red hair, rampaging across the fields catching wild animals. But Jacob was a quiet kid, sticking close to home, hanging out with his mother.

Then Esau popped in one afternoon, famished and drenched in sweat from gallivanting after game, begging for a bowl of the stew Jacob was stirring. And Jacob struck. Sure you can have some, he said, but first you gotta swear that the birthright is mine. Heart racing, belly begging, Esau shrugged and made the vow—no use for a birthright if you die of starvation, right?

When their father, Isaac, tried to secretly impart the ritual blessing on Esau without Jacob getting wind of it, Rebekah overheard and began a game of deception that haunted the family for years. Isaac's eyes weren't what they used to be, so Rebekah had Jacob dress up in his brother's clothes and some hairy goatskins for good measure. And before Esau got back from hunting, Jacob had sauntered off with his father's blessing for himself.

Esau exploded with grief and anger, vowing revenge on his brother. So Rebekah suggested that now might be a good time for Jacob to find a good God-fearing wife at her brother's place, which just happened to be far, far away. As Jacob set out for Haran, alone and ashamed, God's blessing seemed further away than ever. Lying down for the night, his head on a stone, he dreamed of a stairway that stretched from heaven to earth. He saw angels ascending and descending, and God standing beside Him declared, "I am with you and will watch over you wherever you go, and I will bring you back to this land. I will not leave you until I have done what I have promised you" (Genesis 28:15).

Jacob awoke with holy fear. "What an awesome place!" he exclaimed. "This is the house of God. This is the gate of heaven!" Jacob's wanderings would teach him to wait, and to wonder, and that God loves turning schemers into dreamers.

MEXICAN PIZZA

Now Jesse said to his son David, "Take this ephah of roasted grain
and these ten loaves of bread for your brothers and hurry to their camp.
Take along these ten cheeses. . . . See how your brothers are."
1 SAMUEL 17:17, 18

I love pizza. I love Mexican food. And like chocolate and peanut butter, when you put 'em together, it's amazingly delicious. When you make this incredible—and incredibly easy—dish, you just might feel ready, like shepherd and errand boy David, to take on a giant.

You will need:
    1 12-inch premade pizza crust
    1 12-oz. can of fat-free refried beans
    1 cup of Mexican, cheddar, or shredded cheese of choice
    1/2 head of lettuce cut or shredded
    tortilla chips
    salsa
    toppings: olives, green chilies, red peppers, onion,
        or other topping of choice

How to make it:
    Your local grocery store probably sells pizza crusts in packs of two. With the directions below, you can easily make two pizzas with a 16-ounce bag of cheese and one can of refried beans.
    1. Preheat oven as directed on pizza instructions.
    2. Place pizza crust on round cookie sheet.
    3. Spread 1/2 can of refried beans evenly over crust.
    4. Scatter your toppings on the pizza, and top with cheese.
    5. Bake 8 minutes or until cheese is melted.
    6. Cut into 8 slices and top with shredded lettuce, tortilla chips, and salsa.

LH

spirit

THE AGONY AND THE GETHSEMANE

And being in anguish, he prayed more earnestly,
and his sweat was like drops of blood falling to the ground.
LUKE 22:44

I've heard a few too many Week of Prayer sermons about the Crucifixion.

Well, I should say too many *bad* sermons about that chapter of the Greatest Story Ever Told. Sermons that focus a bit too much on the gore and far too little on the glory. Sermons that try to guilt-trip you with Jesus' physical suffering.

Sitting in chapel at Andrews University, I listened as the Week of Prayer speaker, a professor from another university, launched into a grisly description of the stages of death by crucifixion, from flailing, to impaling, to body tissues swelling. By the time he got to a story about a mother cat rescuing her kittens from a fire, getting herself flambéed and charbroiled in the process, with intense descriptions of each bubbling blister, I was just glad the chapel service was before lunch and not immediately after.

The blockbuster movie *The Passion of the Christ* depicted Jesus as a superhuman masochist, capable of sustaining physical brutality that would have killed any ordinary person a dozen times over. The film exaggerated Jesus' physical suffering far beyond the realm of plausibility. The thing is, Jesus needs neither our pity nor our guilt—because it wasn't the physical torture that killed Him.

In real life, crucifixion was a long, drawn-out process that killed people over several days. The Gospels describe the Roman soldiers' surprise, before sundown Friday, when they found that Jesus was already dead and that they didn't need to speed His death by breaking his legs (which caused suffocation). Two things killed Jesus, both spiritual rather than physical: the crushing weight of our sin, and His separation from God.

The night before He died Jesus anguished in the Garden of Gethsemane about the path before Him. He despaired at the burden He had to bear, and begged God to find Him a way out. He pled, "Father, for you all things are possible; remove this cup from me; yet, not what I want, but what you want." Luke describes Jesus' agony as so intense that He sweat blood. Hanging on the cross, He cried out, "My God, my God, why have you forsaken me?" (Matthew 27:46). Jesus died not of a broken body, but of a broken heart.

DEATH

God has made everything beautiful for its own time.
He has planted eternity in the human heart, but even so,
people cannot see the whole scope of God's work from beginning to end.
ECCLESIASTES 3:11, NLT

I hate thinking about death. A friend of mine recently shared with me that her father has terminal cancer. The daughter of someone I know died at birth. After losing my own father, a grandmother, an uncle, a classmate, and others close to me, all I can conclude is: I don't understand why people have to die.

I've heard some say that it must have been just their time to die, or that it was God's will for them to die. I disagree. I don't think it was, or ever is, God's will for His kids to die. I do think death is a natural consequence of sin.

I think some people die because of the genes they happen to inherit from their family. I think people die because of their poor choices that lead to unhealthy bodies. I think people die because of other peoples' poor choices, such as drunk driving or reckless driving. I think people die because some people are angry, hateful, vengeful, insecure, or just plain mean, and take their feelings out on others.

Yet despite all these logical answers I still see death as irrational. I'm shocked whenever a person dies, because in my heart I know that God created us to live forever. I can't understand death because, from the beginning, it wasn't part of God's plan for us.

God created each and every one of us out of love. And instead of giving us up and letting us go when sin separated us from Him, Jesus chose to die. He chose to purchase our lives with His own.

If I die before Jesus returns, I know that I don't have to be scared, because my last thought will be my first thought. Jesus will come back to resurrect everyone who has accepted His salvation, and I, and billions of others, will live for Him for eternity.

One day I will look deep into Jesus' eyes and tell Him I never understood death.

And Jesus may say to me, "That's OK, my dear child. You weren't supposed to."

SP

Mission

SERVICE WITH A SHOVEL

You are the light of the world. A city on a hill cannot be hidden.
Neither do people light a lamp and put it under a bowl. Instead they put it on its stand,
and it gives light to everyone in the house. In the same way, let your light shine
before men, that they may see your good deeds and praise your Father in heaven.
MATTHEW 5:14-16

As the appetizing aroma of Sabbath lunch wafted through the house, Dad glanced absently down the basement stairs. The sight of our dog wading in a fast-deepening pool jolted his attention. A record snowfall, followed by a quick thaw and heavy rain, had proved too much for the slight embankment intended to shield the rear of the house. Cold water now poured under the back door. There was nothing to do but throw on old clothes and start bailing.

While Mom and I worked to clear the basement, Dad hurried to the backyard to dig a channel through the snowbank so the water could drain properly. With the three of us working together, we managed to quickly contain the threat. Leaning on his shovel, Dad considered the house next door. Did the neighbors have the same dilemma? The dad's business kept him away for long stretches of time, and two young children wouldn't be much help to his wife if there was a problem. Better check.

Their sump pump, which usually whisked away any extra moisture, wasn't keeping up, and the lower floor was under water. Our Italian feast a fading memory, we moved our operation down the road. This time Mom and I dug through the snow while Dad tried to figure out what was preventing the pump from working properly.

All the commotion had roused Bob, the elderly man who lived across the street, and he couldn't resist coming over for a closer look. At first he tried to lend a hand, then stood by and offered a running commentary on our progress, his excited speech punctuated by profanity. Catching himself, he apologized for swearing on "our Sabbath." A nominal Christian from another church, he quickly observed that we were "rescuing the ox from the ditch." Ankle-deep in icy slush, I pondered this witnessing opportunity. I decided it would probably never be as popular as taking literature door to door.

The pump finally repaired, the waters began to recede. Collecting our shovels and buckets, we plodded home for hot showers and lasagna redux.

CR

KALEIDOSCOPE OF BEAUTY

Don't copy the behavior and customs of this world, but let God transform you into a new person by changing the way you think. Then you will know what God wants you to do, and you will know how good and pleasing and perfect his will really is.
ROMANS 12:2, NLT

When I was in kindergarten, I loved art. No matter what I made, everyone said, "That's beautiful, Sonia; good job." I could do no wrong; whatever I created was complimented with the highest praise. I would run around beaming with joy, self-confidence, and acceptance. I felt loved.

When I was in the upper classes, art wasn't as fun. The teacher dictated step-by-step instructions, including arrows that pointed to the exact color, length, and width that our artwork should be. The students who followed the instructions, who fit the scholastic mold, received high praise. However, those of us who were free spirits striving for our own identity received, at the least, disapproving glances—or stamps of a bandaged happy face with the word "messy" printed under it.

What's wrong with coloring the sky plum and the grass brown and yellow? I grew up in California, and that's what our grass usually looked like anyway. And if you ever bothered to get up really early in the morning you might have seen that the sky was closer to shades of pink and purple than to blue. Can any crayon accurately capture the true beauty found in creation?

I believe that God needs, desires, and treasures diversity. Each of us was created unique and perfect in His image. If God needed male and female, such complicated individuals, to make up His image, then how can we measure beauty by our own standards? God's beauty goes beyond anything we could ever dream up or make with human hands. And God created our minds; minds can bring joy to others as we share the "unexplainable" images, our work of art.

Some of us will always follow instructions and end up with art that copies that of those around us. Others will go beyond the expected and create masterpieces. Don't allow the world around you or well-meaning adults to mold you in their own image. Allow God to change you into the person you were meant to be. You are a kaleidoscope of beauty. You are one of a kind.

SP

Bible

PAID BACK!
WITH JEREMIAH SMITH / PART 1

Judah then said to his daughter-in-law Tamar, "Live as a widow in your father's house until my son Shelah grows up." For he thought, "He may die too, just like his brothers."
GENESIS 38:11

Stagehand (*counting off with fingers*): "Now, in 5, 4, 3, 2, 1."

Jerry: Welcome to *Paid Back!* Today's topic: Women who kill their husbands. Let's call out our first guest. He hails from somewhere in Bible land. Let's meet . . . Judah!

Judah: Hi Jer.

Jerry: Judah, you've come on this show to confront someone. Who is that?

Judah: That would be Tamar, my daughter-in-law.

Jerry: OK, Jude, tell us your side.

Judah: Well, I'm a good father. I had three of the greatest sons you could ever ask for. And you know what a special relationship a father has with his boys. They're my pride and joy, the very core of my manhood . . . (*boasts on and on*). Anyway, they were growing up before my eyes, and I decide it's about time my oldest son Er got himself a wife. So I find this chick Tamar here, and the next thing I know, he's dead! Well, I'm a bit suspicious now, but I decide to give her another go. And so, being the nice guy I am, I give her my second son, Onan. And you know what happens next, Jerry? Go ahead and ask me what happens! Onan dies too. So I know it can be tough for widows out there, with no sons to support them or give them a sense of identity. I'm a sensitive man, Jerry. And how does she repay me? She goes and kills them. Then she has the nerve to ask me for my third son. She must think I'm a fool, Jerry. Guess what she has done now, Jerry—go ahead and just guess. Go on.

Jerry: What has she done, man?

Judah: The wench has gotten herself pregnant. She doesn't care about embarrassing me or the family at all. She deserves whatever is coming to her. She deserves the full punishment under the law. She deserves to die.

Jerry: Well, let's call out the woman of the hour. Let's hear it for Tamar! (*The crowd boos.*) Now, Tamar, what do you have to say for yourself? That is a strong accusation Judah has against you. Any words of defense? *Continued.*

SP, BS

PAID BACK!
WITH JEREMIAH SMITH / PART 2

*When Tamar was told, "Your father-in-law is on his way to Timnah to shear his sheep,"
she took off her widow's clothes, covered herself with a veil to disguise herself,
and then sat down at the entrance to Enaim, which is on the road to Timnah. For she
saw that, though Shelah had now grown up, she had not been given to him as his wife.*
GENESIS 38:13, 14

Tamar: Oh, Jerry, life has been so tough. I have been treated so wrong, Jer. I thought that I'd finally found a nice guy to marry. I even thought that maybe I could one day love Er. But far too soon I realized what a mistake I'd made. Er was an evil, evil man.

Next I marry Onan, hoping life will be better, but he was even more evil than his brother. He knew that any son we had would never carry his name but would be considered Er's, and so he refused to give me an heir. Then next thing I know, *he's* dead. So then Judah promises me that I can marry Shelah—that's his youngest boy. He just wants me to wait awhile for Shelah to get older, but somehow that day never comes. I can't believe Judah broke his promises to me. I was devastated. *(Stagehand shows "Boo" sign for crowd.)*

Meanwhile, I'm aging, Jer, and I'm hungry, Jer, and I just don't know where to turn. How much bad luck can one girl have, Jer? Does anyone understand what life is like for a poor widow? We have no respect. We're nobodies. We can't get a job, and without any sons to help support us we are forced to fend for ourselves. How are we supposed to eat, Jer? And so, well, a girl has to do what a girl has to do.

Jerry: Interesting, very interesting. *(Stagehand holds "Jerry" sign.)*

Judah: Yeah, well, ask Tamar what she did—go ahead and ask her, Jerry. Ask her why she'd embarrass the family like that. Go ahead and tell him, Tamar, how you prostituted yourself in order to get pregnant. *(Stagehand hold holds "Boo" sign.)*

Jerry: Sad. This is a sad situation. *(Stagehand holds up "Jerry" sign.)* Unlike most of my shows, this is a very confusing and complicated story. Let's see if there is someone out there who can shed some light on this situation. Ms. Lola, please, come on down. *(Stagehand holds up "Jerry" sign as crowd chants his name.)* So, Ms. Lola, what do you know about all this? *Continued.*

SP, BS

Bible

PAID BACK!
WITH JEREMIAH SMITH / PART 3

When Judah saw her, he thought she was a prostitute, for she had covered her face.
Not realizing that she was his daughter-in-law, he went over to her by the roadside
and said, "Come now, let me sleep with you." "And what will you give me to sleep with
you?" she asked. "I'll send you a young goat from my flock," he said. "Will you give me
something as a pledge until you send it?" she asked. He said, "What pledge should I give
you?" "Your seal and its cord, and the staff in your hand," she answered.
GENESIS 38:15-18

Ms. Lola: Well, Jerry, I was there from the beginning. I was the one. I was the one that Tamar came crying to. I was the one whose shoulder she leaned on when she had no other place to go. I can tell you what really happened that night. Because I followed Tamar, and I saw how she disguised herself as a prostitute. *(Stagehand holds "Boo" sign.)* And I also saw the man who picked her up. I even have his credit card and signed receipt right here—guess no one carries cash nowadays. Read the signature, Jer. You see! You see it was Judah (*points accusingly at Judah).* He's the one; he is the father of Tamar's baby! *(Stagehand holds "boo" sign.)* Judah's the person Tamar had to prostitute herself to, for he wouldn't do his duty and help her.

Jerry: You should be ashamed of yourself, man! *(Stagehand holds "Jerry" sign.)*

Judah: Oh, Tamar, you are more in the right than I am. Will you ever forgive me?

Jerry: Well, there you have it, folks. Things aren't always as they seem. It is sad to see what means some people have to go to when we don't take the time to spread love, mercy, and kindness to one another. Remember, everyone, next time you want to pay someone back, try a little compassion first. Goodbye, everyone, and be good to one another. Join us next week for "Three days in the belly of a fish. A story of true survival."

Read the whole story in Genesis 38. Ancient levirate marriage, in which a widow married her dead husband's surviving brother, was designed to provide support for women who might otherwise be left destitute. When Tamar tricked Judah into fathering her child, preserving her dead husband's family line and ultimately providing financial security for her, Judah tried to have her killed for sleeping around. When Tamar unmasked his hypocrisy, he declared, "She is more in the right than I" (verse 26, NRSV).

Thanks to Tamar, a self-righteous jerk became an ancestor of Jesus (see Matthew 1:2, 3).   SP, BS

FUTURE TENSE

*Neither death nor life, neither angels nor demons, neither the present nor the future,
nor any powers, neither height nor depth, nor anything else in all creation,
will be able to separate us from the love of God that is in Christ Jesus our Lord.*
ROMANS 8:38, 39

The future is fascinating. Nothing gets people worked up like imagining it, whether it's the next election, next year's sports car, or the possibility of intergalactic travel. Through the years people have come up with all manner of ideas about the future, both hopeful and pessimistic, secular and religious. These have included:

• Humanity and society is getting better and better, especially as technology conquers disease and makes lives easier and more efficient. This one fell out of favor a bit after a couple world wars, the discovery of antibiotic-resistant microbes and viruses such as AIDS, and the problems of urbanization and modern technology itself.

• We're headed for environmental disaster and/or catastrophic war. Everything you've seen in action films.

• Christians will be whisked away to heaven just before a great tribulation, led by the antichrist, begins on earth.

• The future holds both disaster and deliverance, peril and promise. No matter what happens, it's all in God's hands—and so are all who trust in Him.

The Bible points to the last view. The end of the world is coming, but don't base your faith on dramatic events, for until then, life will be like it was before Noah's flood, with people carrying on their normal daily business (Matthew 24:37, 38). There will be a time of trouble "such as never was" (Daniel 12:1, NKJV). But don't worry, because Jesus has promised to never leave us (Matthew 28:20).

Jesus will return to earth to rescue and resurrect all He's counted righteous, and take them home to heaven. For 1,000 years we'll bask in God's presence and the wonders of heaven, learning to truly love and studying the eternal choices people made on earth (Revelation 20:4). Then God will take us back to earth, where He'll destroy sin and Satan forever (verses 10, 14, 15). He'll re-create earth as a perfect place, and we'll live in peace and joy for eternity, at last healed from our deadly experiment with sin (Revelation 21:4).

Life

GUY + GUITAR = GIRLS

Come, my lover, let us go to the countryside.
SONG OF SOLOMON 7:11

I always wished I had a guitar so I could just sit on a bench on my college campus, strum awhile, and wait for the girls to arrive.

I wouldn't even have to know how to sing. I could just sit there, play a few chords, casually brush my hair out of my eyes, and soak up the attention. I've never figured out the secret connection between girls and guitars, but trust me, it never fails. Not every girl, I know, but definitely enough to make it worthwhile.

I once had a saxophone that I managed to play "Three Blind Mice" on before someone vandalized it. My musical career thus tragically shattered, I sold my sax to a used instrument store and used the cash to visit a friend in New York City. I'd have to attract the complementary gender with my confident attitude instead. Problem is, while "making 'em laugh" worked reasonably well, it was just so much more work than the 1-2-3 of sit down/play guitar/bask in feminine admiration.

And then there are the guys who get all the attention without even trying. I'm not even talking about your chiseled-chest sports enthusiasts, with girls lining up to watch as they crash their way across the field. I'm just talking about those guys who have "it." I think of my friend Floyd my first year of college. If you looked up "happy-go-lucky" in the dictionary, you'd find Floyd. Nothing ruffled this guy's feathers. A nuclear bomb could have gone off in the school library as he walked toward it, and he would have been momentarily surprised, then have cheerfully determined what he could do about it.

My friend Tim and I once pondered Floyd's appeal to a steady stream of female admirers. Tim summed it up: "He's goofy."

Ah. Oh. Goofy yet spiritual. Certain girls eat that stuff up. Just don't take yourself too seriously, and be friendly to everybody. It's that confidence thing again—an acoustic guitar for the soul. I shook my head. I'd moved past giving a hoot about what anybody else thought of me, and I was plenty goofy, but I suspected that while Floyd was goofy-haha, goofy-effortlessly-charming, I was goofy-off-key.

A few months later I met my match. Ten years later I married her. I never did learn to play the guitar.

THIRTEEN THINGS TO DO

Be happy, young man, while you are young,
and let your heart give you joy in the days of your youth.
ECCLESIASTES 11:9

1. Write a letter to an older relative you rarely see.

2. Volunteer! Your local church and community need your help. Find a need you'd enjoy filling and make it happen.

3. Just cook it. Talk with your Sabbath school leader about making breakfast for your class next Sabbath, or for your next class get-together.

4. Chalk the walk. Put your artistic skills to work with colorful sidewalk chalk, and brighten your neighborhood until it rains (or the neighbors turn on their sprinklers).

5. Hike to it. Scout out local trails on the Internet or at your local library, pack your bags, and get into nature. You might be surprised at how close you are to natural beauty.

6. Say "I love you." When was the last time your parents heard you say it?

7. If your family has a small yard, save money and natural resources by mowing with an old-fashioned push mower (now available in newer models) instead of a gas-powered one. You'll help the environment and tone your muscles at the same time.

8. Pray. Find a few minutes today to start a prayer journal in a notebook or on a computer. Tell God what concerns, challenges, and worries you, and write out some of the ways you've been blessed lately. Make a list of continuing prayers you want answered, and keep a record of how God answers.

9. Throw a youth rally this summer. Work with your youth leader to create the event and activities, find a speaker (perhaps people in your group), and advertise to area teens.

10. Clear out your closet. Donate what you're no longer wearing to organizations that distribute used goods.

11. Plan lunch. This Sabbath, give your elders a break and take charge of the cuisine. The best part is, there's guaranteed to be something on the table you like.

12. Get some heavenly wisdom this summer. Proverbs has 31 chapters. July has 31 days. You do the math.

13. Create a bulletin board for your youth group that highlights each member, with photographs, school newspaper clippings, quotes, and stats.

Innovation

THE BIG QUESTIONS

All the days ordained for me were written in your book before one of them came to be.
PSALM 139:16

I could ask God a million questions, but I have a feeling they'd all be the wrong ones. It seems presumptuous and a waste of time, like an unborn child pondering why life is so dark and confining, knowing nothing of fashion or art or architecture or sunsets.

So if I could just have my curiosity stirred (if not satisfied, as answers too big for my brain to hold spur more questions) on one thing, I'd ask God, "What have You done in my life that I've been too ignorant even to notice? What coincidences disguised as inevitabilities have shaped Your plan for me when I thought things just sort of happened?"

If you could have God answer any question, what would you ask?

_____

_____

_____

What do you think is the hardest part of being a Christian?

_____

_____

_____

What part of Christianity do you think people misunderstand the most?

_____

_____

_____

What are some of the biggest misconceptions about God?

_____

_____

_____

THE PIT AND THE PENDULUM

In those days Israel had no king; everyone did as he saw fit.
JUDGES 21:25

In the 1850s the Adventist Church started mushrooming (growing from 200 to 2,000 members from 1850 to 1852), but it still had no name, no schools, no way to keep track of who actually represented the church, and no way to support itself financially. Adventists had figured out their main doctrines, but if they were going to survive as a church they'd need to get their act together.

The problem was, many of the early Adventists had left churches that had kicked them out, and, well, it just didn't seem right to start another one that could be just as narrow-minded and ungodly. They did their best to avoid all manner of creeping institutionalism. They had a word for it: Babylon. They worried that organizing a structure to hammer out creeds and regulate church activity was the very spirit of the beast. They feared a self-absorbed structure that worshipped itself in place of Christ.

As the still-unnamed church hit the 1860s, members argued the topic. James White backed stronger organization so that the church could own its own businesses and church buildings. Others just as strongly disagreed, including White's colleague R. F. Cottrell. He argued that naming their denomination would make them like the people who built the Tower of Babel, who had declared, "Let us build ourselves a city, with a tower that reaches to the heavens, so that we may make a name for ourselves and not be scattered over the face of the whole earth" (Genesis 11:4).

In October 1860 the church officially chose "Seventh-day Adventist" as its name, pointing back to Creation and forward to Jesus' return. In May 1863 the Adventist Church formally organized. It had grown to 3,500 members. In the next few years it established its first schools, spread across America, baptized thousands, and sent its first missionaries outside the United States.

But only a few decades after they escaped the pit of chaotic spiritual Babylon, the pendulum swung just as far in the other direction, to a Babylon of another kind. The church moved from disorder to consolidation in the hands of too few people, a situation Ellen White condemned as "kingly power." What Cottrell and others had feared became a reality, as the church "built itself a city" that God would have to scatter.

Bible

JOSEPH REVISITED

When his brothers saw that their father loved him more than any of them,
they hated him and could not speak a kind word to him.
GENESIS 37:4

He was noble; he was clever; he was smart. But when he was a teenager, you have to admit he was still a bit of a brat.

One of only two sons born to Jacob's favorite wife, Rachel, Joseph ticked off his older brothers by different mothers with his tattletaling, know-it-all attitude. And when he told them he'd dreamed that they'd someday all bow to him—well, that didn't help either. In the family tradition of deception, they sold Joseph into slavery and told their father that a wild animal had killed him.

Stranded in Egypt, Joseph finally got his act together. Instead of becoming bitter, he held on to God and took every opportunity to improve himself. People started to notice: This guy's humble, but he gets things done. When his master Potiphar's wife took a little too much notice of him and accused him of rape, Potiphar sent him away but could not, it seems, let him be executed. Joseph hung around in prison quite awhile, itself remarkable because Egyptian prisons weren't intended for long-term storage—they were merely pit stops on the way to freedom or execution. When Joseph went from prisoner to prime minister, he was no doubt quite shocked, but I doubt Potiphar was that surprised.

Joseph soon took charge of Egypt's new command economy. And thanks to Joseph's divine advice when famine hit, Egypt was the only place still brimming with grain. At last the older brothers reappeared in Joseph's life, but now the tables were turned. Joseph had to know—were they still the same self-serving, murderous jerks? So he decided that the only way to know for certain was to mess with their minds awhile.

To Joseph's amazement, they'd changed their stripes. Even Judah, who'd suggested that selling him would be better than killing him because that way they'd at least make a few shekels, was a new man. Joseph revealed himself to his stunned brothers, and his now elderly father breathed without pain for the first time in years.

Joseph reminds me of some nice Christian guys and girls I know—a little overeager, a little Goody Two-shoes, a lot of annoying. But cut 'em some slack. Someday they just might save your life.

EGYPT: A GREAT PLACE TO LIVE

Then Pharaoh said to Joseph . . . "The Land of Egypt is before you;
settle your father and your brothers in the best part of the land."
GENESIS 47:5, 6, NRSV

To most of the people of the ancient Near East the land of Egypt would have seemed like Paradise. Farmers in Canaan depended upon the often unpredictable rains to water their crops. Their soil was stony and quickly exhausted. But the annual flooding of the Nile River replenished the valley of Egypt with rich new soil, and the extensive system of irrigation canals leading away from the river allowed farmers to water their fields easily. Frost and cold snaps never threatened tender plants. People could harvest up to three crops a year, providing ample food in a world that was often only one crop failure from starvation. The Nile itself teemed with fish, and Egyptians kept large flocks of livestock. No wonder that as the people of Israel wandered in the wilderness after the Exodus they kept longing for the foods they had left behind.

All that abundance helped Egypt to develop an impressive civilization. During June through September, when the floodwaters of the Nile covered the land, the king employed the people on massive building projects. Teams of laborers constructed large palaces and temples as well as Egypt's famous pyramids and tombs. Artists covered the walls of the temples and other public buildings with brightly painted scenes honoring kings and Egyptian gods. Some of the pyramids and temple complexes still survive.

The Egyptians were skilled in technology and were good administrators and bureaucrats. Their scribes wrote and preserved wonderful poetry and stories, and their sculptors and painters produced works of art still admired today.

Although Egypt was surrounded and protected by vast deserts, it occasionally did get invaded and conquered. One period was about the time of Joseph. Semites, the people that Joseph and his family belonged to, had migrated from Canaan into the delta region of the north. There they became numerous enough that a group of them known as the Hyksos managed to seize control and rule the region. If the pharaoh that had the dream of the seven fat and seven lean cows was a fellow Semite, it would have made him a little more willing to listen to Joseph, but only the Holy Spirit could convince him that the prophecy was true.

GW

spirit

LONG-LOST LOVE

*He remembers his covenant forever, the word he commanded,
for a thousand generations.*
1 CHRONICLES 16:15

September 1914. The war in Europe had scarcely started as Great Britain marshaled its troops. Private Thomas Hughes left behind his wife, Elizabeth, and infant daughter, Emily, for the kill-or-be-killed frontiers of battle. As his ship sailed the English Channel toward France, he wondered if he'd ever see them again. One idea struck him: write a letter, slip it into a bottle, and toss it into the frothy channel. Perhaps the current would carry it to his family, and he could tell them once more how much he loved them.

"This ninth day of September, 1914," he wrote. "Dear Wife, I am writing this note on this boat and dropping it into the sea just to see if it will reach you. . . . Ta ta, sweet." On the envelope he wrote, "Kindly forward this letter and earn the blessing of a poor British soldier on his way to the front. . . . Pvt. T. Hughes, Second Durham Light Infantry."

A few days later Hughes died on his first day in the trenches of France. His body was never recovered, but his bottle was—on March 27, 1999. When fisherman Steve Gowan found the bottle he shared what he'd found with the press. When the story ran in a London newspaper, one of Hughes' descendants told the paper that though Elizabeth died in 1979, Emily, now 86, was living in New Zealand.

The New Zealand postal service flew Gowan to Auckland to make the late but nonetheless meaningful delivery. With no memory of her father and no grave to visit, the bottle and letter were an overwhelming glimpse of her father's love.

In 1969 Norman Lewis' girlfriend, Janice, lost the class ring he'd given her. She'd last seen it at the New Smyrna, Florida, beach. Thirty years later a boy caught a four-foot shark at the same beach. When he cut it open, he found a Mount Dora High School ring bearing the initials N.L. With the help of high school officials and the 1969 yearbook, he returned the ring to Norman and Janice, now married.

A remarkable coincidence after 30 years. But not greater than the fact that a Man's death in a far-away country, 2000 years ago, can still change our lives for all eternity. Remember that the same Jesus who buries your sins at the ocean bottom isn't lost at sea. Soon your ship— or bottle, or shark—will come in.

THE SEX QUIZ
YOU'VE BEEN WAITING FOR

I am my lover's and my lover is mine.
SONG OF SOLOMON 6:3

True or false. Ready, set, go!

1. If sex weren't so overhyped, it wouldn't be such a big deal.
2. If sex weren't so important, it wouldn't get so overhyped.
3. Sex is something we do, not what we think.
4. The most important sexual organ is the brain.
5. Sex is not essential for a happy, fulfilling life.
6. If you don't marry the person, it's not premarital sex.
7. Marriage just means you'll have sex with only one person now.
8. There's more to sexuality than what you see in soda advertisements.
9. Blandness is next to godliness.
10. I'd date somebody even if I didn't think I could be good friends with him/her.
11. Sexual attraction and romantic love don't necessarily go together.
12. Opposites attract.
13. Like attracts like.
14. Any sex is good sex.
15. If it weren't for all the diseases, pregnancies, taboos, and emotional entanglements, sex would be a good time anytime.
16. Sex should be a meeting of not just skin and senses, but minds and souls.
17. Adultery is no more and no less than cheating on your spouse with another person.

What did you think of those questions? Silly? Deep? Random? Ridiculous? Pointless? Too vague? Too flippant? Irrelevant?

The truth is, when it comes to sex, there are rarely easy answers. It's confusing. It's messy. It makes you vulnerable. Because sex is more than a bowl of cherry ice cream you can jog off later. For good or not, it sticks with you.

In God's plan, sex says, "You're it. I don't ever want to be closer to anyone than I am with you right now. I will always be as close to you emotionally as I am right now. You'll always be able to lean on me the way you can right now." Because while it's not always wise to live for the moment, sex should be one moment you can live in.

Mission

"GOD LOVES YOU" / PART 1

I will never leave you or forsake you.
JOSHUA 1:5

Damaris grabbed Inez's hand as they walked up the dark street. "I feel as though something bad is going to happen," she said. The 14-year-old girls, selling Adventist books and magazines to pay for school tuition in Venezuela, had been warned about the gangs that roamed the streets, robbing and—even killing—people. They hadn't planned to be out that late. But the sun sets early in the tropics, and a Bible study that Inez was giving went much longer than expected. The woman they were visiting cautioned them about the dangerous area, and said she would be praying for them as they walked home.

Part of their way included unlit streets. They knew they'd be helpless if attacked, so before they started walking they claimed God's promise that He would never leave or forsake them. To keep up their courage, they kept talking to each other. Then suddenly they both sensed danger. In the distance they saw dark shapes. They clutched hands, stopped, and prayed.

When they opened their eyes, they saw that they were surrounded. "God is with us," Damaris whispered.

All was silent. The girls dared to look around them. Young men stared them down through ski masks. In the darkness not even their eyes were visible. "Do it!" the leader commanded, motioning to one of the guys. The boy standing behind them stepped forward, thrusting a knife toward their faces. "Drop the bag or we'll kill you," he spit. Inez put her book bag on the ground.

Then, looking up at him, she said, "God loves you." He looked around, surprised. "Get back in line!" the gang leader shouted.

With both girls silently praying that God would perform a miracle, Inez began to speak of Jesus' love. "Jesus loved you so much that He left heaven to come to this awful world and die to save you. Jesus died for you," she said.

"Why are you telling us this?" the leader demanded. "We came to rob you, not for a sermon."

"Jesus came to change you from a sinner to one of His followers, and we must tell you about Him," Inez continued. At that, the leader rushed toward her, pulled a gun from his belt, and held it against her head. "If you keep talking, I'll kill you." *Continued.*

"GOD LOVES YOU" / PART 2

The Lord is my light and my salvation—whom shall I fear?
PSALM 27:1

Even the night seemed to hold its breath. Standing in the darkness, a gun against her temple, Inez dared to cut her eyes toward the gang leader. "Even if you kill me," she said quietly, "I must tell you that Jesus loves you and wants to change you."

"You're crazy!" he shouted. "I want to kill you, but you just keep talking." Then slowly he lowered the gun and stepped back into the circle. "How can Jesus change a life?" he asked her. "What can He do for me?"

So as Damaris silently prayed, Inez explained that Jesus loved even the people who crucified Him. She looked around at the masked faces. "Jesus loves all of you," she pleaded as they looked at the girls in confusion. *Why weren't they scared for their lives?*

Then the leader spoke again. "How do we change our lives?"

"What are you doing, man?" one boy demanded. "What's happened to you? Aren't we going to kill them?"

"I can't kill these girls," came the reply. "Something strange is happening. I can't resist this feeling."

"God is in this place," Inez told him. "You are feeling God's love." Then the two girls went around the group, introducing themselves by name. "God is in this place," Inez repeated. "Jesus is calling you to follow Him."

All this time she'd been hugging her Bible, but now she held it out to the leader. Slowly, carefully, he took it. "Thank you very much," he whispered.

"Don't you remember that we came to kill these girls?" one boy demanded.

Inez turned to him. "Jesus wants to give you His new life too."

"You're crazy," he said, slapping her across the face.

"No. No," Inez countered. "Jesus loves you. He will love you no matter what you do even if you don't believe it."

"Maybe this will help you understand God's purpose for you," Damaris said. She gave each boy one of the magazines she had held all that time. "God bless you," she told them all. "We're going now." *Continued.*

Mission

"GOD LOVES YOU" / PART 3

Believe in the Lord Jesus, and you will be saved.
ACTS 16:31

Leaving the gang of boys back in the shadows, Inez and Damaris hurried through the dark streets until they came to their neighborhood and finally home. Inez's mother was waiting for them, worried sick. "Why are you so late? What happened to you?"

It took a while before they could talk. So much had happened! While they changed into dry clothes Mother fixed warm tea, and finally they could share what had happened.

As they talked they realized anew the danger God had brought them through. "But I'm sure that God has transformed their lives," Inez said. At that Mother suggested that they pray for the boys and the seeds of hope God that had planted in their hearts.

Some months later the girls, who had continued selling books and magazines to earn tuition money, were asked to come to a tiny church some distance away for a literature evangelistic seminar. As they went they wondered why they were even going. A tall young man met them at the door of the church. "I think we have met before," he said. The girls agreed that he looked familiar. He then took a Bible from under his arm and handed it to Inez. She gasped. It was the Bible she'd given to the gang leader several months before. They stared at him in disbelief.

"When you gave me the Bible, you told me that Jesus would change my life, and you were right," he said. "From that night on He has worked a miracle in my life."

Amazed and silent, they listened as he told them how he'd wanted the peace and love he'd seen in them. Then he asked, "Do you want to see the others?"

Sitting on the front row of the church were the other eight boys! They'd heard about the seminar and had come, hoping the girls would be there. Then came another surprise. After the meeting they went to meet the boys' families, who welcomed them with smiles and hugs. After their nighttime encounter the boys had changed. They'd spent hours reading the Bible and the magazines, even sending for Bible studies to an address they found in the magazine. Seeing how much they had changed, their families had joined in their quest to learn about God. Both family and friends of each of these boys had become Adventist Christians. And all because two teenage girls stood firm in their trust of God. (Adapted from *Mission,* March 1995.)

DEATHBED PROPHECY

Then Jacob called for his sons and said,
"Gather around so I can tell you what will happen to you in days to come."
GENESIS 49:1

Learning that his beloved Joseph was alive after all (never mind ruler over Egypt) left Jacob stunned. But seeing his 10 oldest sons finally become honorable men must have been the real shocker.

Jacob had lived a whale of a life. Fleeing and reconciling with his twin brother; conniving and thriving against his uncle; waking up from his wedding night to discover he'd married the wrong sister; watching his wives try to one-up each other; reeling as his sons slaughtered their neighbors for raping their sister; mourning his beloved Rachel, who died giving birth to his youngest son. And now his lost Joseph was found. It didn't change what had come before, but he'd take it.

In Egypt, father and son fell on each other and wept, holding each other until their years apart at last began to fade into the now.

Seventeen rich, rewarding years passed. At last Jacob called his sons together, to bless them and prophesy of their descendants.

Reuben, his firstborn, should have received the greatest blessing, but his attempt at usurping his father's authority by sleeping with his concubine had forfeited that. Instead Jacob told him, "Turbulent as the waters, you will no longer excel" (Genesis 49:4).

To Simeon and Levi, hotheaded instigators of the Shechemite slaughter, he predicted that their descendants would be divided and scattered. Yet Levi's descendants bucked the prophecy, for prophecy is always conditional on human choices. When only the tribe of Levi refused to worship the golden calf, only they became priests.

Zebulun, Jacob predicted, "shall settle at the shore of the sea" (verse 13, NRSV). "Asher's food shall be rich, and he shall provide royal delicacies. Naphtali is a doe let loose that bears lovely fawns" (verses 20, 21). "Issachar is a strong donkey, lying down between the sheepfolds" (verse 14, NRSV).

Yet Judah received the greatest prophecy. Jacob compares him to a lion, and declares that he will rule over his brothers and be praised. And as Jacob saw, in his mind's eye, the true Lion of the tribe of Judah to come, he must have recognized his ladder, his wrestler, his Redeemer.

Science

THE RUNNING MAN

Everyone who competes in the games goes into strict training. They do it to get a crown that will not last; but we do it to get a crown that will last forever.
1 CORINTHIANS 9:25

Dean Karnazes makes me feel kinda pathetic. And that's just reading about him. The photo of him (*Wired*, January 2007) in his running shorts, specially designed laceless shoes ("enmeshed in thin steel cables that connect to a tension dial at the back," so he never needs to stop and tie), and speed-and-elevation-monitoring watch on his ridiculously chiseled frame reminds me that not only am I not in as good a shape as I used to be, I'm never gonna be in a fifth as good condition as Karnazes is now. And he's 15 years older than I am. Then again, I don't seal my blistered feet with superglue.

They call them ultramarathons, because the puny 26.2 miles of your average marathon, on its nice paved city streets, is a stroll in the park compared to what Karnazes tackles. Think 50 marathons in 50 states in—you guessed it—50 days. Think the only-ever race to the South Pole. Then there was the time he entered a 199-mile race. Every other competitor was in a team of 12 people who took turns running. Karnazes entered all by his lonesome—and finished eighth. So if you ever see a pizza-delivery car sitting at an intersection waiting for a runner, who stops by just long enough to start rolling the slices and stuffing them in, with cheesecake and éclairs for dessert, it's probably Karnazes. He needs up to 9,000 calories a day to keep pounding the pavement.

Karnazes never really ran until after midnight on his thirtieth birthday, when he found himself staring down another bottle of tequila and a materialistic life that simply didn't satisfy. He walked home and put on some running shoes. The next thing he knew, the sun was up and he was 30 miles from home. And feeling a whole lot better about himself.

Karnazes reminds me that most things in life are a matter of perspective. *Wired* writer Joshua Davis describes how he conquered one 100-mile trek over shifting mountain terrain. "With 44 miles to go, his spirit was flagging, but he found a way to make it seem conquerable: He remembered the next checkpoint would leave only a marathon and two 10Ks left to go. He knew he could run each leg, and that helped him achieve the whole."

HOW JESUS GREW ON ME

The Son is the radiance of God's glory and the exact representation of his being,
sustaining all things by his powerful word.
HEBREWS 1:3

It took me a while to get into Jesus. About a dozen years, give or take.

Not that I had anything against Him. But when you grow up in a Christian family, sometimes it takes time for things to click. And, well, the Old Testament had so much more *action*. Granted, the Old Testament God was more cryptic and sure had a lot of rules and regulations to remember, but at least things kept moving. I know Jesus did some terrific miracles and told some cool stories, but where's the Red Sea parting? Lava raining from the sky and people turning to stone? That's good stuff. That's action, baby.

As a kid I started reading a classic series of books about the Bible written by Ellen White. I loved the one with the kicking title *Prophets and Kings*, about such dynamic people as Elijah and Hezekiah, but *The Desire of Ages*, about Jesus, just didn't hold my attention. Then one day I saw a painting of Jesus based on these words from Revelation 1: *"And when I turned I saw seven golden lampstands, and among the lampstands was someone 'like a son of man,' dressed in a robe reaching down to his feet and with a golden sash around his chest. His head and hair were white like wool, as white as snow, and his eyes were like blazing fire. His feet were like bronze glowing in a furnace, and his voice was like the sound of rushing waters. In his right hand he held seven stars, and out of his mouth came a sharp double-edged sword. His face was like the sun shining in all its brilliance"* (Revelation 1:12-16).

Wow. Jesus deserved another look.

I can't pinpoint the day Jesus finally "clicked" for me, but over the years I started wishing He'd drop by—so we could talk; so He could stand up for me when I needed an advocate; so people might change with one glance at that woolly hair and eyes of fire. Here was someone who understood the world I faced every day, a world that chews honest people up, that exalts spiritual phonies that love quoting the Bible but nonetheless miss the point. A world that needs Jesus more than ever but laps up any pale imitation of the peace and joy He's promised.

And I couldn't help wondering how much the world sees Jesus in me.

113

Life

"I'M QUITE GOOD AT NEGATIVE SELF-TALK" SOUNDS LIKE AN OXYMORON

An anxious heart weighs a man down, but a kind word cheers him up.
PROVERBS 12:25

I'd just turned 16 and gotten my braces off a few days before, so my teeth still had that weird smooth feeling. My big brother Ben and I sat outside the shoe store at the mall as I finished putting on my new sneakers. The laces were too long. I couldn't figure out why they had sold shoes with laces that looked like they could have laced the shoe up twice.

I found a loop at the back of the shoe that I tried fitting the laces through and brought back to the front. "See, that works out great," Ben assured me. Ben's affirmation was all I needed to calm my fears that this looked strange. I was all too aware of my sheltered, mostly home-schooled existence, and trusted Ben's fashion sense implicitly.

Later that summer I went on a mission trip to Chihuahua, Mexico, called the Ultimate Workout. With new glasses, my long-laced shoes, no braces, and lots of gumption I attempted to break out of my comfort zone. The work was challenging but fun, and I had a blast making mortar for the huge school our group was constructing.

"Hey, that's cool how your shoelaces go all the way around," a guy snickered, heading toward the meeting tent for supper. The way he'd said it told me he really meant the opposite. I sat down on the edge of the construction site and studied my shoes. Did they really look that stupid?

"Hey, Katy, don't worry about what that guy said. He's just being stupid." I looked up. It was Mike, the head of our mortar-making crew. From day one I had appreciated his easygoing nature and ready wit. I didn't even know anyone else had seen the incident. With a few words Mike had given me acceptance and friendship.

That trip to Mexico was a milestone in my life. Friends I made there are still my friends. Memories from that trip are very special. And none quite so special as that one moment when Mike, probably unbeknownst to him, handed me confidence in myself.

Looking back, I'm a different person today. I haven't changed 180 degrees, but I've grown in self-esteem and confidence. I wouldn't be who I am today without the support of people around me. Simple actions and words such as those Mike offered have helped me along my way.

KW

MATTHEW GAMBLE / PART 1

He will be the sure foundation for your times, a rich store of salvation and wisdom and knowledge; the fear of the Lord is the key to this treasure.

ISAIAH 33:6

Meet Matthew Gamble. He's a full-time pastor and the founder/speaker of Vagabondervant International, a nonprofit organization that you can learn more about at www.matthewgamble.com. Marcel Schwantes and I interviewed him about his spiritual journey:

Marcel: What in your background had turned you into an atheist?

Matthew: Growing up, church and religion was never a big part of my family's life. We'd go to church on occasion, but at home we never prayed, read the Bible, or talked about God. When I was 13, I moved to St. Louis, Missouri, and I attended a private Christian school. I was depressed—I'd moved away from my friends, and the school just seemed fake to me. So within a short period of time I decided, "This isn't real; God isn't real." One of my best friends taught me how to steal and we'd steal on the weekends, and then on Sunday he'd go to the confessional and be forgiven. To me it just didn't add up. The whole experience just turned me off to Christian religion. The idea that there could be a God who would allow pain and suffering just made zero sense to me.

Marcel: How in the world does a White kid from the suburbs end up in Jamaica to follow the Rastafarian religion and get into drug smuggling?

Matthew: When I was 16, I moved from St. Louis, Missouri to St. Augustine, Florida. (I think my parents knew I needed to live as close to the saints as possible.) Within days of moving I started hanging out with my cousins who had grown up there. One day we were chillin', driving around in my car, and we pulled into a secluded spot. It was there that I was first introduced to marijuana.

I immediately fell in love with the effects the plant gave me. It lifted me from my depression. I started smoking day in and day out—before school, during school, and after school. With that entire scene came listening to a lot of hip-hop and reggae. I fell in love with the message, music, and teachings of reggae legend Bob Marley. Back then I told people I was an atheist, but if there was any religion in me it was my solo times of smoking weed, relaxing, and listening to reggae on the beach. Continued.

Mission

MATTHEW GAMBLE / PART 2

For all that is in the world—the lust of the flesh, the lust of the eyes,
and the pride of life—is not of the Father, but is of the world.
1 JOHN 2:16, NKJV

Matthew: I know most people will think this was merely a fad that I was going through. The reality is that I was deeply interested in life and culture and wanted to understand more about the way the world works and what this life is all about.

After graduating from high school, I moved to Orlando to start college. I kept smoking marijuana, and when summer break hit, I decided to go to Jamaica to learn more about the Rastafarian religion. I especially wanted to know why they smoked marijuana for religious purposes. Within 24 hours of that decision I arrived in Montego Bay, Jamaica, with a backpack, a tent, and a sleeping bag. A day later I was walking down a street in the beach town of Negril when a Rasta pulled up beside me in his car and asked me to get in. And so, like any smart, White, 19-year-old American, I hopped in.

Immediately he started telling me how he could get as much ganja (marijuana) back to the States as I could get rid of. I told him I could get rid of as much ganja as he could get me, and so a relationship was born.

Two weeks later, when I boarded the plane to fly back to Miami, I had roughly two pounds of ganja hidden in two hand-carved wooden statues. (This is when this atheist turned agnostic.) After walking through customs, having passed through the X-ray machine and by the drug-sniffing dog, I realized I was free and had not been caught!

Immediately I was a believer, specifically giving praises to Haile Selassie, the Ethiopian Emperor that the Rastafarians consider to be the Messiah and God, whose birthname was Ras Tafari. I was certain that "Jah" (another name the Rastas give to their savior) was protecting my White behind from getting caught. But as I researched him I didn't find anything to make me believe he was God. My quest continued with countless hours of prayer on the beach.

That summer I returned again to fulfill a similar mission, thinking that I had found the key to life and that I was going to move to Jamaica to start a large marijuana smuggling operation. God had other plans, though.

Marcel: Tell us about your "other" conversion experience.
Continued.

MATTHEW GAMBLE / PART 3

And the world is passing away, and the lust of it,
but he who does the will of God abides forever.
1 JOHN 2:17, NKJV

Matthew: I kept praying and reading. I started going to the library and really doing some research on this religion stuff. For the life of me I could not find any reason someone would worship this Haile Selassie guy as God. Then one day, while visiting my brother up in Maryland, I met his wife's pastor, who happened to be a Seventh-day Adventist, something I had never heard of in my life. I told him my life story, and all he did in response was hand me a Bible, The Message New Testament. I started devouring that book every day and doing other research, from encyclopedias to Christian literature, on this guy Jesus of Nazareth. Now here was a guy I could believe was the Messiah.

I called the local Adventist church in Florida, because that was the only thing I knew to do. I think God knew what He was doing when he sent me to a small, all-Black, Caribbean-based church. The people of the Berea Seventh-day Adventist Church loved me as one of their own. The first Sabbath I attended I spent five or six hours straight in Bible study with the pastor after potluck. That was October, and by December I was at Andrews University.

I was so on fire and wanted to be around other on-fire Christians, and Andrews had an aviation degree and a business management degree that was very appealing to me. By the middle of my first quarter there I had switched my major to theology, because God's Word was the only thing that I wanted to study.

That spring break I went home to St. Augustine, where I was baptized in the ocean on March 23, 1996. God is good!

Tompaul: What about Jesus did you find so compelling?

Matthew: Beyond "This is a great guy" or "Wow, He did some impressive things," it was "Here's this guy who's been watching out for me, and I haven't known Him. He has a purpose for my life. Here's my Creator, the one who designed me, and now I'm reading a book about His life and His teachings that provides a way of life for me. It gives me a mind-set, a philosophy, a lifestyle of how to interact with people. I felt as though I was catching up. I had a manual for life, literally. I'm learning what life is about." *Continued.*

Mission

MATTHEW GAMBLE / PART 4

*But now that you have been set free from sin and have become slaves to God,
the benefit you reap leads to holiness, and the result is eternal life.*
ROMANS 6:22

Tompaul: So what is life about?

Matthew: Life is about figuring out what you really believe. If you believe in Jesus, do you believe in God enough to actually do what He says? To me life is about connecting to the Creator and growing to where you're willing to let your selfish life, including all of your dreams, visions, and aspirations die so that His vision for you may become fully alive.

Tompaul: What has God done for you? How has He changed your life?

Matthew: I feel that God's wiped my slate clean and given me a new start. He's taken me places I would have never in a million lifetimes dreamed. At age 20, walking into an Adventist church for the first time, I would never have imagined that I'd be a pastor preaching the good news of Jesus around the world. He's brought me into an environment in which I am living and ministering for other people on His behalf. The core of that is becoming more and more selfless. I feel closest to and most used by God when my eyes are off myself.

Of course the struggle continues. The day I was baptized I told God, "I want my sins to stop." I'm thinking, *Let my sins be dead. I want to be a new man.* Ten days later, after white-knuckling it, I'm falling back into sin again, struggling with lust and other self-centered parts of my life. As Adventists we're so truth-based, and every answer is knowledge: "If you know this, you're saved." Well, how does that help me when I've given my life to Jesus but I'm still a sinner? I believe that God allows us to wrestle through different struggles. I don't think it's God will for us to keep on sinning. But God wants to reveal His goodness to us, and He allows us to develop character through struggle.

Right now, if He wanted to, God could zap me from all my sins. But I have to say, "I'm a sinner; I recognize it. Now what's my response?" The reality is that Jesus wants me to get my eyes off me. The more I can get my eyes onto Jesus and not onto my sin or my behavior or my faults, the closer I'm growing to Him. That's where the rubber hits the road of Christianity. Are we going to look at ourselves and keep focused on how bad we are, or do we trust Jesus in spite of ourselves?

GOTTA-LOVE-IT LASAGNA

May God give you of heaven's dew and of earth's richness—
an abundance of grain and new wine.
GENESIS 27:28

This one never fails to impress, but don't worry, it only looks hard.
What you'll need:
6-8 cups water, 1 tsp. salt, 1 package lasagna noodles, 30-oz. container of ricotta cheese (part skim), 4 cups mozzarella cheese (divided), 3/4 cup parmesan cheese, 3 garlic cloves, 1-2 tbsp. Italian seasoning.* Spaghetti sauce.

How to make it:
1. In a large pot, bring to a boil 6-8 cups of water and 1 tsp. salt. Add noodles and cook 8 minutes or until al dente.† (Do not overcook.) Drain pasta, placing noodles in a single layer on a baking sheet or any flat surface so they don't stick together.
2. In a large bowl, combine ricotta cheese, 3 cups mozzarella cheese, parmesan cheese, garlic, and Italian seasoning. Mix thoroughly.

To assemble the lasagna: I like to use a ladle for the spaghetti sauce and a flat rubber spatula to spread the cheese. Clean hands work well spreading the cheese, too.
1. Evenly spread a small ladle of sauce over the bottom of a pyrex pan. It should cover the surface, but be almost translucent. Lay 3 noodles side by side on top of sauce, and spread some of the cheese mixture down the center of each noodle. Add another ladle of sauce over this layer, using the bottom of the ladle or the rubber spatula to spread evenly.
2. Next, place another layer of noodles crosswise over the first layer. Cut off ends of noodles that hang over side of pan. You can reuse the shorter pieces in this layer. Again spread cheese mixture down the center of noodles and cover in thin layer of sauce. Spread again with the rubber spatula to make sure all layers are even.
3. Keep alternating short and long layers until you get just below the top of the pan. I always try to end on a long layer, cover the long noodles with cheese and sauce, then sprinkle the remaining mozzarella over the top. You can also lightly sprinkle dried oregano or basil.
4. Cover with foil. Cook for 40 minutes at 375° F or until sauce bubbles at top.
5. Let set for 10-15 minutes to solidify. Cut into pieces and serve.

* Instead of premade Italian seasoning you can use 1/2 tsp. of rosemary, 1/2 tsp. red pepper flakes, 1 tsp. basil, and 1 tsp. oregano.
† al dente is just cooked, firm, not hard; should not stick to the teeth.

LH

spirit

REST

He makes me lie down in green pastures,
he leads me beside quiet waters, he restores my soul.
PSALM 23:2, 3

The Lord replied, "My Presence will go with you, and I will give you rest."
EXODUS 33:14

I work as a medical intern in a hospital. It's the next exciting step after eight years of college, but practically it means I don't sleep. Every fourth night I work a 30-hour shift. Sometimes I nap in a call room until my pager goes off again, but I don't *sleep.*

The first night was fine and the second night OK, but each call night left me a little more depleted, a little more drained. Finally I would come home and lie in bed. Tompaul would tuck me in, yet I didn't want to be touched because I *hurt.*

I never knew that being tired could cause physical pain. I lay in bed crying because of a pain I couldn't bandage or take an aspirin for. Pain that was untouchable. I didn't know what to do. I had to keep working, all 80 hours* every week. More than that, I had to work well. People's lives depended on my sleep-deprived brain. I was terrified of making a deadly error. I was miserable, depressed, and a beast to live with.

Pastors often tell people how Jesus can heal our wounds, and how we should call on Him and (in a booming preacher voice) claim His promises. But realistically, people, how could God give me more sleep? I can think of two times God made a day longer—for Joshua and for Hezekiah. Would He do that every fourth day for me?

"Ask, and ye shall receive." It just seemed a little presumptuous. I sat on the side of my bed, needing something and not knowing how to say it. Then it hit me, a still whisper. *I will give you rest.* Rest was what I needed. *As I slept, Tompaul often found me walking* in my sleep or giving orders to the pillow. So with Tompaul by my side I prayed for rest. I prayed hard and daily.

I'm still often tired, I still work crazy hours, and I still get cranky, but God has given me rest. When I wake up, I feel refreshed. And that's enough.

* That average was only federally mandated in the U.S. in 2003. Historically, medical residents sometimes worked 120 or more hours a week. I've eagerly participated in a nationwide survey about the effects of my manic schedule.

LH

GRIEF / PART 1

Jesus wept.
JOHN 11:35

I awoke to my sister's screams. It was 12:30 a.m.

Her fiancé, Louis, had run from his past and his pain as long as he could, while basking in the warmth of our family's love. But because he never faced his issues head-on—the lies, the abuse—he found himself in a quicksand he couldn't escape. We found his lifeless body next to the bathtub full of hot water, a needle on the floor. His skin still glowed pink, but the light in his eyes was lost, his chiseled frame turned to putty. Louis had died instantly as the cocaine-and-heroin speedball overwhelmed his heart.

His last words were "I love you." His last breath a half century too soon.

An hour later he lay in a dim hospital room, a gown on his body, a pointless oxygen mask attached, as his face and hands and arms and feet slowly turned gray, a bright flame turning to ash. My sister and a friend wrestled his *claddagh* ring—two golden hands clasping a crowned heart—from his hand. The sun rose before I slept again.

I missed his easy smile, his tender caretaking of my dying grandfather, his eagerness to please. I missed the pizza he baked at midnight while upstairs I tapped away at the computer, the aroma impossible to ignore. I missed the shrieks of Yahtzee games from another room, the S'mores and jokes and anecdotes. And I pondered the stream of deceptions designed to divert our attention from what was gouging him inside. He'd grasped for God. We could only trust that God had caught him.

Grief sneaks like a mosquito. One moment you're frolicking in the grass; the next your shoulder's smarting from an itch you just can't stop. Even years later the horror and the irrevocability overtake you, and suddenly you have wet cheeks and fresh wounds.

The odd thing about grief is that it can feel so good. No one tells you that a hearty sob can feel like a spiritual massage. *Get that knot over there . . . A little to the right . . . Up a bit . . . Yeah, right there.* You almost feel guilty for enjoying it, yet grateful for letting out some of the tension. But tears don't raise the dead. They can just help you let go of them.

And healing? That's another story. *Continued.*

life

GRIEF / PART 2

Then Jacob tore his clothes, put on sackcloth and mourned for his son many days.
GENESIS 37:34

Of all the glib things I hear on TV news, the stupidest has got to be any variation on "And now the healing can begin." The last time I heard this oh-so-insightful comment from a newscaster, bodies were still being identified from a tragic event that left dozens dead. Healing? The loved ones left behind are too numb even to feel the hurt yet.

You've just lost your leg in a car accident. Paramedics rush to stem the blood loss. As they lift you into the ambulance and you feel yourself fading, a reporter suddenly arrives and asks, "How is the healing process coming along?" How do you respond?

Hint: The blood loss has left you too weak to beat him senseless with his microphone. Which is just as well, because he's already senseless enough as it is. You'll live on, but your leg's not growing back.

Modern media demands a script for everything. The ugly duckling becomes the next top model. The abuse victim triumphs over adversity to establish an ice-cream empire. Too bad real life is more than an easy formula and oldies musical montages.

In *A Grief Observed* C. S. Lewis reflected on how he reeled from his wife's death from cancer: "No one ever told me that grief felt so like fear. I am not afraid, but the sensation is like being afraid. The same fluttering in the stomach, the same restlessness, the yawning. I keep on swallowing. . . . Perhaps, more strictly, like suspense. Or like waiting; just hinging about waiting for something to happen. It gives life a permanently provisional feeling. It doesn't seem worth starting anything. I can't settle down. I yawn, I fidget, I smoke too much. Up till this I always had too little time. Now here is nothing but time. Almost pure time, empty successiveness."

While animals often howl and cry in distress, only humans shed tears of emotion. We have three kinds of tears: basal tears that keep our eyes moistened, reflex tears that flood irritants away, and emotional tears of frustration, laughter, or grief. Though no one has a thorough explanation for emotional tears, they contain a higher level of hormones than other tears, and scientists believe this reduction may relieve depression.

Grief takes time. Grief needs touch. Some losses can't be replaced. But God isn't going anywhere. He's there no matter how sharp the pain or dark the hour.

CONFORMITY

For the Lord does not see as mortals see;
they look on the outward appearance, but the Lord looks on the heart.
1 SAMUEL 16:7, NRSV

I used to despise turtlenecks.

Not that I was some sort of fashion snob. I just remembered the Thanksgiving program in kindergarten, for which my teacher decreed that every boy had to wear a red turtleneck. Add a brown vest and a red band of construction paper around our heads to make us look like Native Americans. I was pretty sure Samoset or Squanto had never worn a turtleneck. Dab some striking red paint on my face, sure, but I was fairly certain the seventeenth-century Wampanoag didn't use sewing machines. What really got me, though, was having to look like everybody else!

I think I've worn a turtleneck maybe once since then.

In second grade I got to be fiery Miles Standish for the school Thanksgiving program. Unlike Miles, I don't have red hair (well, except one time in grad school, but that's another story), but like Miles, I had temper to spare. I got to throw a tantrum on stage and be applauded for it. Nice work if you can get it.

In fourth grade my choir teacher announced that we'd all get cummerbunds for our "Family Sabbath" performance. *Excellent*, I thought, thinking "cummerbuns" were some sort of pastry. Then I found out they were adornment: a scalped pillow we clasped around our waists. I switched to music appreciation class.

Nope, I didn't always fit in, and most of the time I didn't want to. Forced conformity just never rang my bell.

Fitting in. Individuality. It's a bit of a contradiction. We want to be unique—but not too different from everyone else. We want to stand out in a crowd—but not like a pimple.

Society is always trying to tell us how to live. Wear Levi's (just like this musician who gets all his free from the company). Drive a Lexus (all the rich people are doing it). Watch this movie (it's just like all the others). Unfortunately, as we'll explore next week, too often the church is the exact same way.

Adventism

TRUTH LOCKED IN

Wherefore I will not be negligent to put you always in remembrance of these things, though ye know them, and be established in the present truth.
2 PETER 1:12, KJV

Early Adventists passionately opposed anything that smacked of a creed—a set-in-stone statement of beliefs. They feared that they'd become smug and self-satisfied and stop growing spiritually as a community, thinking they'd learned all there was to learn. They interpreted the above text to mean that truth is progressive, that there's always much more to learn than we've yet grasped.

But the instinct to draw a line around Adventist beliefs to "protect" them proved impossible for even the earliest Adventists to resist. Ellen White practically banged her head against her Bible when people kept inventing new "fundamentals" for Adventism—fundamentals that took the focus off Jesus and the truly central issues.

Today many church members still fear that core Adventist doctrines will collapse if some small piece is adjusted. In their zeal to protect the "landmarks" they do the same thing that irked Ellen; they insist that certain points that may be interesting topics to debate, but that aren't going to save anybody, are fundamental.

In *Angry Saints* George Knight wrote, "While the motives behind such actions may be positive. . . . the process tends to point to a particular group's tradition (especially one that may be challenged or questioned at a particular moment in history) rather than to the Bible. The Bible, in fact, often becomes a threat to the traditionalists as a new generation of reformers seeks to resurrect truths that are more basic than their traditions. In the face of doctrinal change the traditionalists often lose perspective and magnify 'mere molehills' into 'mountains'" (p. 135).

Ellen White never feared the advancement of truth or the abandoning of error. She didn't worry that unresolved side issues would damage core doctrines. She wrote, "There is no excuse for anyone in taking the position that there is no more truth to be revealed, and that all our expositions of Scripture are without an error. The fact that certain doctrines have been held as truth for many years by our people is not a proof that our ideas are infallible. Age will not make error into truth, and truth can afford to be fair" (*Counsels to Writers and Editors*, p. 35).

AND GOD SAID, "CHILL"

Moses answered the people, "Do not be afraid.
Stand firm and you will see the deliverance the Lord will bring you today.
The Egyptians you see today you will never see again.
The Lord will fight for you; you need only to be still."

EXODUS 14:13, 14

A sunburned fugitive prince stands barefoot before a flaming shrub. Shepherd's rods turn into snakes. A river turns to blood. A sea divides so escaped slaves can flee, yet drowns the pursuing army. The former slaves sing and dance on the shore.

No wonder the story of the Exodus is so popular. The movie trailer writes itself.

I think about the Exodus sometimes when sweepstakes prize offers arrive in the mail. The ones I've received are purposely designed to be as complicated and labor-intensive as possible. Put this sticker here. And that one here. It's all based on a simple bit of psychology: *People think they need to work for it.* People think, *If it takes all this effort, it must be worth it.*

But when God declared an entire nation of people winners of His divine sweepstakes, His plan was totally different. There were no complicated hoops to jump through to claim their prize as chosen people in the land of milk and honey. It's simple, Moses told them: "The Lord will fight for you; you need only to be still."

It was an incredible act of grace. All they had to do was accept it. And naturally, the Israelites just couldn't figure that one out.

A lot of people today think that if we just keep enough commandments, God will save us, but the Exodus tells us that's just not how God works. God saved Israel *before* He gave them His law. As Paul wrote: "God demonstrates his own love for us in this: While we were still sinners, Christ died for us" (Romans 5:8).

God asks us to respond only to what He's already done for us. In Exodus 20 God tells Israel to keep the Sabbath because He's their creator. In Deuteronomy 5 God tells Israel to keep the Sabbath because He's their Savior: "Remember that you were slaves in Egypt and that the Lord your God brought you out of there with a mighty hand and an outstretched arm" (verse 15).

Human nature tells us that we can't get something for nothing. God says, "Chill, My children. I've got your back."

Science

ALLERGIC REACTIONS

*When an evil spirit comes out of a man, it goes through arid places seeking rest
and does not find it. Then it says, 'I will return to the house I left.'
When it arrives, it finds the house unoccupied, swept clean and put in order.
Then it goes and takes with it seven other spirits more wicked than itself,
and they go in and live there. And the final condition of that man is worse than the first.*
MATTHEW 12:43-45

As people started living longer, healthier, and cleaner lives in the twentieth century, a strange thing happened: allergies exploded.

The term *hay fever* (which has nothing to do with hay and isn't actually a fever) has been around since the early 1800s, but after World War II wealthier countries saw huge increases in such common allergies as asthma. Why? Studies suggest one major explanation: everything's so clean today.

Vacuum cleaners suck up dust and dirt. Disinfectants kill germs on our stoves, toilets, and floors. We no longer ride horses, live on farms, or stomp through mud puddles on our way to work. A German study found that children had more allergies if they grew up in a nice hygienic home than if they'd grown up on a farm. Without early exposure to the parasites and pathogens of nature, their immune systems go haywire over something else. Allergies are the body's defense reaction to something that would otherwise be harmless or even healthy, from pollen to peanuts.

An otherwise healthy newborn baby kept in a germ-free bubble for an extended period would, when released, quickly succumb to the unfamiliar germs and die. Babies need that early exposure to build immunity, so that they can live healthy lives and not need to think about germs constantly.

Too often Christians think that the best way to live in this sinful world is to shut out all signs of sin. It's a "way that seems right," but it can be deadly. Like the spick-and-span convert in today's Bible verse, we end up worse than before. It's no coincidence that some of the most sheltered kids grow up to be the most reckless. When they first crash into something from the big bad world, they don't know how to handle it. Jesus called us to be "salt," mixing it up in the world to make it a tastier place and bring out lost flavor. We may not be "of the world," but we should definitely be in it.

AFTERLIFE

Consider and answer me, O Lord my God! Give light to my eyes,
or I will sleep the sleep of death, and my enemy will say, "I have prevailed".
PSALM 13:3, 4, NRSV

Anyone who is among the living has hope—
even a live dog is better off than a dead lion!
ECCLESIASTES 9:4

You're an ancient Mesopotamian, and you're feeling kinda sick. So sick, in fact, that you just might die. And when you shuffle off this mortal coil, put on your pine pajamas, and push up a few daisies, what's next?

If you're an Egyptian (and have a bit of money) it's all about the mummification. They'll get rid of the "non-essential" organs as your brain (sliding it out through your nose), and stomach; preserve others (your heart and kidneys); and stuff your skull with sawdust or resin. After about 70 days of careful preparation they'll pack you up in a tomb with some essentials for surviving the afterlife.

Meanwhile the god Anubis weighs your heart to see if you've been mostly good or mostly bad. If it weighs less than a feather, not weighed down by wickedness, you can continue on into the afterlife. If it weighs more, sorry—your heart's chomped by Ammut, a ferocious beast that's a cross between a lion, hippo, and crocodile.

While other ancient religions had extensive teachings on the afterlife, painting vivid pictures of what dead people were up to, the Old Testament doesn't. It says the dead are in *sheol*—the grave. The Bible describes *sheol* as dusty, dark, dry, and silent. There's no mention of a flaming hell or an immediate paradise.

The book *Beyond Life: What God Says About Life, Death, and Immortality* lists seven things the Old Testament tells us about dead people: They remember nothing of their earthy life, they have no thoughts, they don't speak or praise God, they don't know what's going on among the living, they can no longer work, they no longer participate in human life or influence what takes place among the living, and humans and animals die the same way (p. 86).

Many believe that when we die, our spirits go to heaven, but you won't find that idea in the Bible. Instead the Bible describes death as sleep, and the New Testament tells us that one day a heavenly trumpet blast will be the alarm clock to end all alarm clocks.

KRISTINE'S STORY / PART 1

Ask and it will be given to you; seek and you will find;
knock and the door will be opened to you. For everyone who asks receives;
he who seeks finds; and to him who knocks, the door will be opened.
MATTHEW 7:7, 8

Growing up, I enjoyed reading more than anything else. I shut myself in my room for hours curled up with a book, devouring page after page. Books were my main source of entertainment—but I wasn't always emotionally prepared for what I read.

When I was 7, I read a book in which the main character died. Not mature enough to make sense of an abstract concept like death, I cried and cried, and grew terrified of dying myself. For several nights I feared falling asleep, afraid that I would not wake up in the morning.

That fear faded, but as I grew up another worry haunted my nights: *What if I don't wake up? Can I be sure that if I die, I'll be ready to go to heaven when Jesus comes?*

Somehow I had gotten the idea that being a Christian was all about doing the right things to make myself ready for Jesus to come. I had grown up singing songs like "Jesus Loves Me" and hearing Bible stories, including the story of Jesus' death and resurrection, but those ideas didn't stick in my mind as much as the stories I heard about what happened to disobedient kids.

I loved God—in a way—but at the same time I always feared that He was just waiting to punish me when I stepped out of line. A song I sang in Sabbath school especially reinforced this idea of God:

Oh, be careful, little eyes, what you see;
Oh, be careful, little eyes, what you see.
There's a Savior up above,
And He's looking down in love;
Oh, be careful, little eyes, what you see.

The song continued with several verses about different actions and body parts, and left me thinking that God's main concern was whether I was good enough to get into heaven. I didn't associate obedience with love—I just feared that I couldn't possibly measure up. *Continued.*

KS

KRISTINE'S STORY / PART 2

God has given us eternal life, and this life is in his Son.
He who has the Son has life; he who does not have the Son of God does not have life.
I write these things to you who believe in the name of the Son of God
so that you may know that you have eternal life.
1 JOHN 5:11-13

I turned 16, and newfound freedom—I got my driver's license. Just before Easter I started listening to Christian music on the radio, and thanks to the holiday, much of the music related to Jesus' death and resurrection.

My sister Karin and I attended several Christian concerts. At one concert the singer paused to preach a sermon about Jesus and everything He suffered for us when He died. I suddenly realized that although I had heard about Jesus for as long as I could remember, my knowledge of Him was all intellectual. I had no personal relationship with Him. The stories of His life and His death were all just stories I had heard so many times that I kinda tuned them out. They had little impact on my thinking about salvation. I just did the right thing because I was supposed to.

That night, for the first time, I really listened to the message. I had never heard it expressed so passionately and so simply. When I went home, I started reading the Bible. I had tried reading it once before, when I was 10, but I had started with Genesis and Exodus and then stalled when I came to Leviticus. I hadn't made another attempt in the six years since. This time I started with Matthew, Mark, Luke, and John—the first four books of the New Testament. I wanted to find out for myself what the Bible said about Jesus.

I read for weeks. I read the whole New Testament and then went back to the Old Testament. I spent most of my free time reading the Bible. As I read, I learned about Jesus. I learned to trust Jesus for my salvation rather than trusting myself. I learned about how all of the Bible stories I had heard as a child fit in the whole picture of salvation that God pointed to in the Bible. I learned that being a Christian isn't about doing all the right things in order to feel good enough to get into heaven; it's about loving Jesus and wanting to be like Him because we love Him. And I learned that I have nothing to fear from death because I can have assurance of salvation.

KS

TO THE TOOT

The ax is already at the root of the trees,
and every tree that does not produce good fruit will be cut down and thrown into the fire.
LUKE 3:9

In trying to be different, Christians sometimes make the same mistakes we're trying to avoid. I've watched old women corner a non-Adventist church visitor for wearing a necklace, and I've seen pop stars on TV wearing earrings that cost more than my car. The problem is that both groups are putting way too much focus on externals.

Christianity has a long history of making people conform. Cut the hair. Worship like this. Listen only to music like that. Scan the Bible, though, and nobody fits the mold. Take one of the Bible's splashiest characters: Jesus' cousin, John the Baptist.

John would have been kicked out of most of the schools I attended. Dress code violations alone would have been enough, but his mouth would have landed him in plenty of hot water as well. In a time of foreign occupation and unrest, his message of repentance and forgiveness attracted a crowd, and since he had the masses' attention, religious leaders dropped by to check it out. Perhaps they could cash in on John's popularity for their own political goals, they thought. But spotting them headed his way, John tore into 'em:

"You brood of vipers! Who warned you to flee from the coming wrath? Produce fruit in keeping with repentance. And do not begin to say to yourselves, 'We have Abraham as our father.' For I tell you that out of these stones God can raise up children for Abraham" (Luke 3:7, 8).

The religious leaders in John's day thought their family tree was a ladder to heaven. John said, "Not so fast. Where's your heart?" God had given them light, but their arrogant attitude made them worse off spiritually than people who'd never heard of their God. Their salvation depended on their love, not their lineage.

John wasn't finished with them yet. "The ax is already at the root of the trees, and every tree that does not produce good fruit will be cut down and thrown into the fire" (verse 9). That cuts deep, and that is precisely John's point. Hammering apples onto a tree doesn't make it an apple tree. It's what's on the inside that counts. Spiritual fruit must grow from within. At the same time, we can't change someone by picking off what we don't like about that person. Only the Holy Spirit can truly change us—and He always goes for the root, not the leaves.

OLD FRIENDS, NEW IDEAS
1888, PART 1

*Are you so foolish? After beginning with the Spirit,
are you now trying to attain your goal by human effort?*
GALATIANS 3:3

In the 1880s it looked as if the end-times were right around the corner. Numerous Adventists, including Ellen White's son Willie, were arrested for working on Sunday. Popular nationwide organizations, such as the National Reform Association and the American Sabbath Union, pushed for Sunday laws. In May 1888 New Hampshire senator H. W. Blair proposed a law enforcing Sunday as "the Lord's day" and "a day of religious worship."

Meanwhile, inside Adventism, the times they were a-changin'—and sparks were starting to fly. Meet our cast:

George Butler. Fiftysomething president of the Adventist Church, he considered himself a natural-born leader with "clearer views than others."

Uriah Smith. Now in his mid-50s, Smith had written and edited for the church practically from its beginning. The church's top scholar on Bible prophecy, he wasn't impressed by any new ideas that contradicted old ones. After all, he said, what would outsiders think if they saw Adventists changing their views after 40 years?

Alonzo T. Jones. A former Army sergeant in the American frontier, A. T. Jones didn't lack for confidence. The young preacher's reinterpretation of Daniel 7's "ten horns" put him at odds with Uriah Smith. When Uriah Smith told him to leave well enough alone, he argued that if people were going to examine Adventism's beliefs, they should be as solid and biblical as possible.

Ellet J. Waggoner. Young magazine editor Waggoner concluded that the church had put too much emphasis on keeping the law and too little on faith in Jesus. Smith and Butler begged to differ, arguing that keeping God's law at all costs was most important.

Ellen White. Now in her 60s, she still believed that truth was progressive, and encouraged Jones and Waggoner to keep seeking truth and proclaiming Jesus. This shocked old friends like Smith and Butler, who had been sure that she would defend their way of looking at things. She chastised Butler in particular for his bad attitude.

One thing was clear: the 1888 General Conference session (their annual church meeting) was going to be memorable. *Continued.*

Adventism

THE CALIFORNIA CONSPIRACY
1888, PART 2

So we, too, have put our faith in Christ Jesus that we may be justified by faith in Christ and not by observing the law, because by observing the law no one will be justified.
GALATIANS 2:16

When Willie White, A. T. Jones, E. J. Waggoner, and other western Adventist pastors got together to discuss issues of Bible prophecy and faith versus law in June 1888, rumors of a "California conspiracy" spread. Many older Adventists were convinced that a shady plan was afoot to change everything that made Adventism special—a plan so deep it even involved Ellen White.

When Adventists arrived in Minneapolis, Minnesota, for the 1888 General Conference session, people watched Ellen White closely to see if the rumors about her were really true. Ellen White herself was just about ready to throw up her hands at the snide, sarcastic, self-righteous attitudes of so many people.

Both traditional and progressive Adventists in 1888 were convinced that they had the church's best interests in mind. As church historian George Knight writes: *"The old guard were concerned with the distinctive truths of Adventism, while the younger men from the West were more interested in basic Christianity"* (*Angry Saints*, p. 48). Nonetheless, the old guard's mistake was to value uniqueness for its own sake, as being more important, even, than being Christian. They valued their own reputations more than they valued God's truths, especially the one that urged them to love their neighbor.

Ellen White nearly walked out of that year's meetings until, she said, a dream urged her to stay and not give up. But the damage was done. Many Adventists started ignoring any counsel she gave that contradicted their preconceived opinions.

The problem, Ellen White said, was not so much who was right and wrong. The problem was the unchristian, closed-minded attitudes that kept people from learning from each other and coming together.

The good news was that for the first time many Adventists began to see both sides of their gospel truth. Distinctly Adventist truths, so important for the world's last days, were at last united with the message of salvation through faith in Jesus that had sustained Christians for hundreds of years. *Continued.*

ICICLE HEARTS
1888, PART 3

Yet I hold this against you: You have forsaken your first love.
REVELATION 2:4

The 1888 controversy over righteousness by faith stirred up both Adventism's finest qualities and its nastiest. Ellen White expressed her frustrations with her fellow Adventists in an entry in her personal diary:

"Why, then, is there manifested in the church so great a lack of love . . .? It is because Christ is not constantly brought before the people. . . . A correct theory of the truth may be presented, and yet there may not be manifested the warmth of affection that the God of truth requires. . . . The religion of many is very much like an icicle—freezingly cold. . . . They cannot touch the hearts of others, because their own hearts are not surcharged with the blessed love that flows from the heart of Christ" (personal diary, February 27, 1891; cited in George Knight, *Angry Saints*, p. 50).

Facts alone don't save. You can have the truth about the Sabbath, the sanctuary, the state of the dead, but if you don't have Jesus—the one who declared Himself the Truth, the Way, and the Life—it's all worthless. Fallen angels know the facts, but without a relationship with Jesus, they're no better off than someone who's never heard of any of them.

Ellen White declared that some who would otherwise have joined the church were turned off because they didn't find Jesus in it. Adventists preached "in an argumentative way, . . . scarcely mentioning the saving power of the Redeemer." "Of all professed Christians, Seventh-day Adventists should be foremost in uplifting Christ before the world" (diary entry, February 27, 1891; cited in Knight, p. 50).

The Adventist community has reclaimed a wealth of neglected truths: the Sabbath, what happens when we die, principles of health. Unfortunately, a wealth of truth, out of context, can be as big a distraction as a wealth of money.

Adventism's big temptation? The same doozy that traps the rest of humanity: to think that what people do is more important than their relationship with Jesus. Adventism's unique message would never be so powerful without the right emphasis on Jesus' love and incredible power to save us when we're powerless.

BAPTISM / PART 1

*In him you were also circumcised, in the putting off of the sinful nature,
not with a circumcision done by the hands of men
but with the circumcision done by Christ, having been buried with him in baptism
and raised with him through your faith in the power of God,
who raised him from the dead.*
COLOSSIANS 2:11, 12

Much that is good is misunderstood—including baptism.

Videotaping a wedding a while ago, I also witnessed another highlight, the groom's sister's baptism. And then the pastor preached a sermon I'll never forget—for all the wrong reasons.

The topic: baptism. The implicit message: you can't be saved . . . unless you're baptized.

Lurching from one concept to another, the preacher placed immersion high on his ladder of salvation, perhaps somewhere between eating haystacks and not worshipping idols. The sermon's message was clear: if you aren't baptized, you're in deep eternal danger.

Jews in Jesus' day viewed circumcision in the same way that my friend's pastor viewed baptism: a human act necessary for God to save us. To them, circumcision and salvation were synonymous. The ancient Jewish book Jubilees put it bluntly: any man not circumcised after birth, just as God commanded Abraham, was "destined for destruction."

When Jewish Christians realized that Gentiles could be saved, they thought the ancient rite of circumcision should apply to them, too. The apostle Paul begged to differ. Paul quoted Genesis 15:6, which says that Abraham's trust in God saved him—not anything he'd done. Indeed, his relationship with God had saved him many years before he was circumcised. Circumcision was simply a "seal," a recognition of "the righteousness he had by faith while he was still uncircumcised" (Romans 4:11).

Salvation's simplicity has always confused and frightened people. It couldn't be that easy, right? People think they need to do something extra to receive God's approval—baptism, tithing, keeping the Sabbath—but such acts are only a celebration of the work God has already done. Salvation is a gift—and a transformation. *Continued.*

BAPTISM / PART 2

And now what are you waiting for?
Get up, be baptized and wash your sins away, calling on his name.
ACTS 22:16

Jessica put off being baptized for several years—but it wasn't for lack of encouragement. At night her mother often sat on her bedside, telling her that the rest of her family would be in heaven, and they sure wanted her to be there too. Finally, at 15, Jessica returned from a mission trip having made a choice. Her relationship with God had grown, and she wanted to indicate on the outside what had happened to her inside.

"My baptism was really surreal," she remembers. "I was shy, so that much attention made me squirm. On a deeper level, I also wanted to be sure that I could live up to my end of the 'bargain.' Now, I know that's a silly expectation, because there's no 'bargain' and nobody is ever perfect."

"Getting baptized is a big step," said one of Jessica's friends, but she disagreed.

"I've already made the big steps," Jessica replied. "This was just the final little hop."

Baptism is like the kiss at the end of the wedding ceremony. It's a celebration of a love that's already won you over. If a bride tells her groom, "Darrell, you know we'll have to kiss after we say our vows," it's usually flirtation, not a command.

How we view God shapes everything in life. Sermons such as the one I heard suggesting that baptism is necessary for salvation are a symptom of a larger problem of perspective. When people believe that God has conditions on His love for them, they relate to God out of guilt, not gratitude; from shuddering duty, not delight.

Baptism isn't a requirement; it's a promise. Paul tells us that if we die with Christ, we will also live with him, and sin and death no longer have power over us. With a new life through the Holy Spirit, we can focus on what really matters.

Just as a wedding kiss, baptism should celebrate a much deeper relationship. So what does baptism represent for us? Kissing burns calories, sparks endorphins, and shows affection between two people, but what does baptism do? It joins us spiritually with the experience of Christ—and promises us a new life in Him.

15 THINGS TO DO

So then, banish anxiety from your heart
and cast off the troubles of your body, for youth and vigor are meaningless.
ECCLESIASTES 11:10

1. Listen carefully this week in church. Scribble notes on your bulletin. Then drop your pastor a note telling why you appreciated today's sermon.

2. Put on some gloves, grab a bag, and pick up trash around your neighborhood.

3. Start studying another language with books and audio from your local library. It just might turn out to be useful sooner than you think.

4. Smile when you talk on the phone. People will be able to hear it in your voice.

5. Wear sunscreen today and every day, and avoid the midday sun. Eighty percent of "aging" is sun damage.

6. Make a time capsule of your life to open in 10 or 20 years. Include pictures, newspaper clippings, notes from friends, a lock of your dog's hair.

7. Give life to someone who needs it. If you're at least 17 years old, you can donate blood. Contact the Red Cross to find out where and when.

8. Ask your parents about their dating experiences. What do they wish they'd known then?

9. Listen. Pray that God will guide you to people who need a listening ear, and help you to truly give them an accepting, listening ear.

10. Start a library for your church. Have members donate their books and videos to share with other members. Make them available for checkout each week after church.

11. Read the book of Habakkuk (all 56 verses). What thoughts, feelings, and images does it bring you?

12. Stop what you're doing and pray for the person who most irritates or angers you.

13. Do something different. If you can't even boil water, try baking. Hate public speaking? Volunteer to pray during church.

14. Visit a nearby church you've never been to before this weekend. How is it similar to, and different from, your home church?

15. Sketch and draw scenes you find in the book of Revelation. What's more prominent in the book—earthly beasts, or their Creator?

WHAT REALLY MATTERS

David fastened on his sword over the tunic and tried walking around,
because he was not used to them.
1 SAMUEL 17:39

When the Pharisees asked Jesus why His disciples didn't perform the same convoluted cleansing rituals they did, Jesus called them hypocrites. "Isaiah was right when he prophesied about you," Jesus told them, quoting: 'These people honor me with their lips, but their hearts are far from me. They worship me in vain; their teachings are but rules taught by men'" (Matthew 15:7-9). Jesus explained that in holding on to their human-made traditions, the Pharisees had let go of the commands of God.

The Pharisees obsessed about staying clean—on the outside. But Jesus said their hearts were in the wrong place. Evil thoughts, greed, deceit, envy, and more all come from the inside.

What really matters to God? I think Micah says it best: "What does the Lord require of you? To act justly and to love mercy, and to walk humbly with your God" (Micah 6:8).

You won't find much about humility and mercy in the media, and they're often hard to find at church as well. But to God, they're what truly count in life.

When David stood up to fight Goliath, King Saul decked him out in his own heavy armor. David said, "Sorry, Your Majesty. Your armor just doesn't fit me. I need to wear the clothes and use the tools God gave me." By being himself he won the battle, and suddenly everybody wanted to be like him.

The Holy Spirit gives us freedom to be ourselves, and to serve God in a way truly unique to us. In Christ, we don't have to try to fit in—we are in. And with Christ in us, we've got it made.

Make a list of ways God made you unique, and what issues you struggle with as a Christian and an individual.

_____

_____

_____

_____

_____

_____

THE FALL OF BATTLE CREEK

They loved praise from men more than praise from God.
JOHN 12:43

If Adventists thought things got out of hand at their 1888 annual meeting, they hadn't seen anything yet. Fed up with the smug attitudes of church leadership, Ellen White sailed to Australia. Historians have argued whether things would have gotten so crazy if she'd stuck around, but leaving sure made her feel better. The 1888 controversy had shown the church's desperate need to know Jesus better, so she poured herself into writing such books as *The Desire of Ages* and *Christ's Object Lessons.*

News from America, especially church HQ in Battle Creek, Michigan, kept getting worse. Instead of spreading out to further the church's work, more and more Adventists were flocking to the bustling city. Meanwhile, the church was controlled by fewer and fewer people. Ellen White warned of "kingly power." Too few people were making decisions for the entire church, and she insisted that God liked variety and the devil loved power-hungry know-it-alls. White said she'd seen, in vision, "an angel standing with a sword as of fire stretched over Battle Creek."

Both the church's main publishing house and hospital in Battle Creek burned down in separate fires in 1902. The church's impressive medical work was under the command of John Harvey Kellogg, who coinvented cornflakes, pioneered surgical techniques, and, though he never consummated his more than 40-year marriage, was obsessed with sex and bodily functions. His father had been an abolitionist, but by the time the church kicked him out in 1907, Kellogg had helped found the Race Betterment Foundation, which advocated absolute segregation. Kellogg's departure also meant the loss of such members as A. T. Jones and E. J. Waggoner, who had sided with his power struggle.

When the church restructured to keep things from being so centralized, moving its headquarters to Maryland, Kellogg had kept control of the church's medical work. Cutting Kellogg loose meant losing their biggest hospital and only medical school. Kellogg had, against such advice as Ellen White's, rebuilt the Battle Creek Sanitarium bigger than ever after it burned down in 1902. (He made the place world-famous, but it went bankrupt in the 1930s.) So Adventists rebooted their medical work, including establishing a small school and hospital in Loma Linda, California, in 1905.

SANCTUARY

But will God indeed dwell on the earth? Even heaven and the highest heaven
cannot contain you, much less this house that I have built!
1 KINGS 8:27, NRSV

The Mesopotamians and other people of the ancient Near East believed that their gods needed a human staff to care for them, the same
as their kings and other rulers. The various sacrifices provided food
and drink for the gods. Human beings cooked meals, cleaned rooms,
and dusted off the idols. They washed the statues and changed the
clothing the idols wore, just as palace staffs did for human rulers. The
ancients constructed their temples as houses for their gods. They believed that if they did not make temples and sanctuaries, the deities
would have no place to live. But once a god made his home in the
statue or other image in a temple, he was trapped in the idol and had
to be carried from place to place, even to visit another god in a neigh-
boring temple.

Thanks to all this, people considered the gods as dependent upon
them. Mesopotamian myths claim that one of the highest gods created
humans to do the work that the lesser gods had refused to perform.
But that gave humanity a certain power. If the gods' human servants
stopped offering sacrifices, the deities would go hungry. If a god did
not do something a worshipper wanted, people stopped sacrificing
until the deity gave in. Kings and other rulers built magnificent sanctuaries to get on gods' good sides—not as expressions of love for them.

Not only did the people of the ancient Near East not love their
gods—the gods themselves had no special feelings toward humanity.
The relationship was one of servant and master. The highest reward a
person could expect from service to the gods was only the feeling of a
job well done.

The situation in Israel, however, was quite different. The Israelites'
various sacrifices were not food and drink for a hungry God, but expressions of repentance or thanks. Israel's wilderness sanctuary and
the Jerusalem Temple were not dwellings for God, but places He
could meet in a special way with humanity. Unlike pagan deities, the
God of Israel didn't need humans to build a house to keep Him from
being homeless. Instead, His Temple was a house of prayer and forgiveness.

GW

Science

WATER

*Jesus answered, "Everyone who drinks this water will be thirsty again,
but whoever drinks the water I give him will never thirst."*
JOHN 4:13, 14

I've never been so thirsty in my entire life! That sentence in my head was starting to take shape in my mouth and was ready to launch itself at the back of my friend's head. My mind wandered back to four hours earlier when I cheerfully agreed to go on this death march down the not-paved, longest, steepest, for-expert-hikers-only trail into the Grand Canyon.

The overwhelming dryness in my mouth and the formation of a new grand canyon on my tongue brought me back to reality—that I could quite conceivably die during spring break my freshman year in college. I recalled learning in high school that our bodies consist of 66 percent water and that a person could live a month without food but only a week without water. I also remembered reading that our brains are 75 percent water, and only a 2 percent drop in body water levels can cause short-term memory loss, trouble with basic math, and difficulty focusing. No wonder God filled most of our bodies and the earth with water.

God, if I could just get some water to drink. My thought turned prayer was interrupted by a man who could be described only as Willie Nelson meets Walker, Texas Ranger. "You folks from out of town?" he asked. As we nodded our heads in reply I wondered if it was that easy to tell.

"Got any water on ya?" he asked, as if he already knew the answer.

"No," we mumbled.

He reached into his fanny pack and pulled out a Ziploc bag full of capsules. "These here are water purification pills. There's a stream not too far from here for you to get some water to purify. It'll taste like something awful, but at least you'll get hydrated."

We thanked the man and did what we were told. I've never drunk such awful-tasting water in my entire life! The man didn't know us, but he knew what we needed to stay alive. Water gives life! It also increases energy levels and metabolism, flushes out bacteria and waste, prevents and alleviates headaches, moisturizes skin, and aids in digestion. And it can help you get out of the Grand Canyon alive.

JD

PUTTING THE AWE BACK IN
PART 1

His face was like the sun shining in all its brilliance.
When I saw him I fell at his feet as though dead.
REVELATION 1:16, 17

awesome [**aw**-suh m]:
   1. Inspiring awe: an awesome sight.
   2. Showing or characterized by awe.
   3. Slang. Very impressive: That new white convertible is totally awesome.
   "Awesome!"

It's a word you hear constantly, to describe everything from granola bars to the Grand Canyon—and now it's practically played out, drained of substance and meaning. If everything's awesome, then what truly takes our breath away, and what wonders have we forgotten in the trivia?

To assist with this unfortunate case of sapped semantics, I've compiled the following list—to sort the actually awesome from the merely [sensationalistic].

Thunderstorms and ocean waves? Awesome.

Deoxyribonucleic acid. More than awesome.

Hummingbirds in flight? Awesome.

Chugging a Mountain Dew soda? Not awesome.

Consuming 47 hot dogs in five minutes? Not even remotely.

The Crab Nebula? Awesome.

Moose Tracks ice cream? Awesome. Totally.

The problem is that a word packed with potent significance has been husked and dried. The hollow propaganda of "shock and awe" and "extreme nachos" has anesthetized us to true majesty. We're numbly satisfied with the merely thrilling, the emptily exciting sugar rush this world has to offer.

On the shores of the Red Sea the Israelites proclaimed, "Who among the gods is like you, O Lord? Who is like you—majestic in holiness, awesome in glory, working wonders?" (Exodus 15:11).

And then there's Manoah and his barren wife. *Continued.*

PUTTING THE AWE BACK IN
PART 2

"We are doomed to die!" he said. . . . "We have seen God."
JUDGES 13:22

Manoah and his wife lived in a dark time for Israel, a 40-year period when the Philistines overran the land. Then a heavenly Messenger came to Manoah's wife and promised a son, a son who must be dedicated to God, who would overthrow their oppressors. When the suddenly maternal spouse tried to describe this promise-giver, she said, "A man of God came to me. He looked like an angel of God, very awesome. I didn't ask him where he came from, and he didn't tell me his name" (Judges 13:6).

Manoah prayed that the Man would return to teach them how to raise their son. He did, and after instructing them on how to raise a son devoted to God, Manoah asked, "What is your name, so that we may honor you when your word comes true?"

The Messenger gave an answer that suggested just how extraordinary their visitor was. "Why do you ask my name?" he said. "It is too wonderful" (Judges 13:18, NRSV). When the visitor ascended heavenward in the flames of the burnt sacrifice that Manoah prepared for God that day, the couple fell on their faces in fear. "We are doomed to die!" Manoah gasped. "We have seen God!"

Even our spirituality has succumbed to pale imitations from pop culture. As C. S. Lewis noted: "In Scripture the visitation of an angel is always alarming; it has to begin by saying 'Fear not.' The Victorian angel looks as if it were going to say, 'There, there.'" And the adorable angels decorating so many things today? I won't even begin to go there.

Familiar imitations can be comforting. It's easy to say that spiritual things are spiritually discerned. It's quite another to actually open up your heart to the Almighty's blessing. Experiencing God can be downright intimidating if you haven't known Him as your friend. The Israelites begged Moses to keep his divine chats behind closed doors, saying, "Speak to us yourself and we will listen. But do not have God speak to us or we will die" (Exodus 20:19). Yet Paul promises that although we only know God in part now, "a poor reflection in a mirror," soon "we shall see face to face" (1 Corinthians 13:12).

Maybe that's why the greatest Gift we've ever gotten can't be summed up with one trite word. Wonderful. Counselor. Mighty God. Everlasting Father. The Prince of Peace. It takes all those words and hundreds more to begin to describe the incredible Gift we were given two millennia ago in a Bethlehem stable.

A STAR IS REBORN / PART 1

Remember your Creator in the days of your youth.
ECCLESIASTES 12:1

Ellen White grew to regret the way she treated her son Edson.

Henry, the oldest of James and Ellen's four sons, died of pneumonia in 1863. He was just 16. Their youngest son, John, died in 1860 at only 3 months. Number two son, James Edson, felt like he lived in a shadow. His mother's letters comparing him to his younger brother Willie didn't always help. Edson burned with endless energy, usually directed toward shenanigans. By the time he reached 16, his mother declared that his "disposition to disobedience" simply broke her heart.

His influence on five-years-younger brother Willie particularly concerned Ellen. "A gloom which I cannot express shrouds our minds in regard to your influence upon Willie," she wrote to Edson. "This influence, we have seen, has affected our noblehearted, truthful Willie. You do things and enjoin upon him strict secrecy, and when questioned, he evades it by saying, 'I don't know,' when he does know, and thus you lead him to lie in order to keep concealed your cherished, darling projects. . . . I fear your influence will ruin him."

Still, it's hard to be too tough on the guy. Think being a preacher's kid is a tough gig? Try being the son of a prophet. His older brother dead, his younger brother seemingly saintly, his dad a workaholic, and his mom recognized as God's own messenger—it's enough pressure to make anyone question their commitment and just want to vent some steam. Which might explain the reason he bought a coat worth a month's wages just to strut down the streets of Battle Creek wearing it. You gotta stand out somehow.

At age 20 Edson decided to get married. His parents threw up their hands at his impetuousness, knowing he was hardly ready to take the plunge. Still, his father officiated at his marriage to Emma McDearmon, and both parents wished him their best.

Edson spent the next 20 years working in Adventist publishing, but it's hard to say how much of his heart was in it. Then in 1893 Ellen White, now living in Australia, received a letter from Edson that stunned her. He wrote that he resented his Goody Two-shoes younger brother, was "not at all religiously inclined," was sick of the church, and was ready to jump ship and leave his Christianity behind for good.
Continued.

A STAR IS REBORN / PART 2

Listen, my son, to your father's instruction and do not forsake your mother's teaching.
PROVERBS 1:8

Reeling from the letter Edson had written her, Ellen White had a nightmare. She dreamed of Edson and four friends frolicking in the water at a beach. A deadly riptide loomed in their path, but Edson and friends were having too much fun to pay it any attention. As she wrote to Edson, "The waves were rolling up nearer and still nearer and then would roll back with a sullen roar. Gestures and warnings were given by the anxious ones looking on, but in answer to all their warnings you were presumptuous. Someone placed his hand on my shoulder. 'Did you know that is your son Edson? He cannot hear your voice, but he can see your motions. Tell him to come at once. He will not disobey his mother.'

"I reached out my hands. I did all I could do to warn. I cried with all the power of voice, 'You have not a moment to lose! The undertow! The undertow!' I knew that once you were in the power of the treacherous undertow no human power could avail. A strong rope was brought and fastened securely around the body of a strong young man who ventured to risk his own life to save you. You seemed to be making light of the whole performance. I saw the merciless undertow embrace you, and you were battling with the waves. I awoke as I heard a fearful shriek from you. I prayed most earnestly in your behalf and arose and am writing these lines" (Ellen G. White, letter 123, 1893).

Ellen's letter to Edson continued for 10 pages. She told him how in many sleepless nights she'd "review and criticize myself to ascertain where I have made a mistake" in how she had treated him.

His mother's letter hit home. Edson decided his spiritual life was in his own hands, and there was no time like the present. He wrote to his brother in Australia, "One Sabbath I decided, while listening to a very dull sermon, that I might just as well be enjoying [the] blessing of my Savior RIGHT THEN as to wait for some more favorable opportunity. . . . I took this step AT ONCE, and 'He took me.' . . . Since then HE HAS NEVER LEFT ME" (J. Edson White to William C. White, Sept. 6, 1893).

Edson decided to serve God among ex-slaves in the South. It was time to let off a different kind of steam. *Continued.*

A STAR IS REBORN / PART 3

*Now, Lord, consider their threats
and enable your servants to speak your word with great boldness.*
ACTS 4:29

For Black Americans after the Civil War, the end of slavery was one thing, but a full share of the "land of opportunity" was quite another. Reconstruction brought significant progress, but by 1880 much of it had vanished.

Southern states had passed "black codes" to limit the civil rights the Constitution's Fifteenth Amendment now guaranteed. Few Black young people were able to attend school. Whites insisted that Blacks "know their place" and always show them "proper respect" in public. Black workers were exploited and faced poverty.

From the beginning the Adventist Church had opposed slavery, supported full rights for all people, and welcomed Black Americans. But as with foreign missions and the Southern states in general, a concerted effort to reach ex-slaves was slow in coming, despite an appeal from Ellen White herself. When Edson White finally committed his life to Jesus, he felt called to work among Blacks in the Deep South.

Edson and his friend Will Palmer built a steamboat, which he named the *Morning Star.* It was 70 feet long and contained a chapel, printing press, and darkroom in addition to living quarters. A fierce storm nearly sunk it as they sailed across Lake Michigan the summer of 1894, tossing the flat-bottomed boat for some 14 hours. Six months later they'd made it all the way to Vicksburg, Mississippi. Within six months they'd built a small church for the first congregation they'd raised up there.

Edson founded the Southern Missionary Society and gathered volunteers. He published a magazine he named *Gospel Herald,* which lives on today as *Message* magazine. His society's work broke tremendous ground for Blacks, not just in evangelism, but health, education, job-training, and more. It founded numerous schools throughout the Mississippi Delta.

In 1898 angry Whites threatened to blow up the *Morning Star* and shut their schools down, and Black Adventist leaders were whipped, threatened, and imprisoned. Edson White described the racist opposition his work faced in a letter to his mother, dated May 25, 1899: "Two weeks ago tonight a mob of about 25 white men came to our church at Calmer at about midnight." *Continued.*

Mission

A STAR IS REBORN / PART 4

But even if you should suffer for what is right, you are blessed.
"Do not fear what they fear; do not be frightened."
1 PETER 3:14

"They brought out Brother Stephenson, our worker, and then looted the church, burning books, maps, charts, etc. They hunted for Brother Casey, our leading colored brother of that place, but he had escaped in time, so they did not reach him. They then went to the house of Brother Olvin, called him out, and whipped him with a cowhide. I think they would have killed him if it had not been for a friendly white man who ordered them to stop whipping after they had struck a few blows. They did not pay any attention to him at first, but he drew his revolver, and said the next man who struck a blow would hear from him, and then they stopped.

"During this time they shot at Brother Olvin's wife, and struck her in the leg, but did not hurt her seriously. They took Brother Stephenson to the nearest railway station, put him on the cars, and sent him out of the country. They posted notice on our church forbidding me to return, and forbidding the steamer *Morning Star* to land between Yazoo City and Vicksburg.

"The whole difficulty arose from our efforts to aid the colored people. We had given them clothing where in need, and food to those who were hungry, and taught them some better ideas about farming, introducing different seeds such as peanuts, beans, etc., that bring a high price, and this the whites would not stand" (James Edson White to Ellen G. White, May 25, 1899, quoted in Ron Graybill, "Historical Contexts of Ellen G. White's Statements Concerning Race Relations" [unpublished thesis, SDA Theological Seminary, 1968], p. 50).

But by now, as schools and churches multiplied, the work could not be stopped. Though prejudice persisted, the church in the South multiplied among people of all backgrounds, and countless lives were improved.

In 1900 Edson and Emma moved to Nashville, Tennessee, and set up shop in an old chicken barn. There they established what soon became the Southern Publishing Association, which supplied the church with books, magazines, and other innovative products for the next 80 years.

CHOCOLATE DREAM CAKE

Nehemiah said, "Go and enjoy choice food and sweet drinks,
and send some to those who have nothing prepared."
NEHEMIAH 8:10

Now and then a party needs an impressive dessert, and here's a recipe for one of the best. It's easy to make and have ready in the fridge, or you could invite five of your nearest and dearest to come early and have each of them whip up one of the layers. This may just be my favorite dessert ever, and one that even *I've* successfully made numerous times. My aunt taught me how to make it, so I'll let her teach you:

You'll need this:
1 1/2 cup flour
1 stick butter or margarine
8 oz. cream cheese, softened
1 cup powdered sugar
frozen whipped topping
2 packets chocolate *instant* pudding
3 cups 2 percent milk
chocolate bar
Crust: Place flour In large bowl. Cut butter into chunks and dump in with the flour. Cut the butter into flour until mixture is crumbly, then pat evenly on the bottom of a 9" x 13" pan. Bake at 350° F for 13 minutes or until firm. Cool in the freezer.
First layer: Put softened cream cheese in mixing bowl. Add powdered sugar and beat with a mixer until it's all nice and smooth. Using a spatula or big spoon, fold in 2 cups of thawed whipped topping, then spread over the cooled crust. Put back in freezer to set.
Second layer: Beat pudding powder and milk for two minutes. Be sure to turn the mixer off before licking the beaters! Pour pudding over the white layer. Put back into freezer.
Third layer: Spread remainder of whipped topping over the pudding layer, making a nice design with your spoon. I make little swirls and peaks and valleys.
Final touch: Grate chocolate bar, then sprinkle over whipped topping.

JE

Spirit

BAPTISM BY FIRE

But I have a baptism to undergo, and how distressed I am until it is completed!
LUKE 12:50

I've seen scores of baptisms in my life, but I've never seen one spruced up with ribbons, lasers, or fireworks. It's a breathtakingly simple ritual, so simple that you don't even need to wear shoes. Whether in a creek, an ocean, or a tank, it's the same: you go under water, you come back up. Add a good potluck, and you've got yourself a baptism, a life commitment symbolized by a good dunking. But oh, the pressure we put on people.

Evangelistic campaigns can include coercion and improper incentives. Kids can feel shamed into it. Something deeply personal is warped to make other people feel better. I was baptized at 12. I first wanted to be baptized at 6, but don't regret the next six years that passed before I took the plunge. I felt no pressure. My decision was my own.

To Jesus, the word "baptism" meant something else as well: His crucifixion and death. When His disciples asked what power they could look forward to, Jesus asked, "Can you drink the cup I drink or be baptized with the baptism I am baptized with?" (Mark 10:38). As He contemplated the dark journey ahead of Him, Jesus exclaimed, "But I have a baptism to undergo, and how distressed I am until it is completed!" (Luke 12:50).

Jesus' death is compared to something else, too: the Israelites' exodus from Egypt. Luke 9:31 refers to His upcoming "departure." The original word in Greek? "Exodus."

Thus baptism isn't just a hoop to jump through on our way to heaven; it's our opportunity to walk a path with our Savior. As the ancient Israelites passed through water as they escaped slavery and headed to the Promised Land, so baptism symbolizes our rescue from slavery to sin. As members of Christ's body, we have passed from death to life. We live a new life in the Spirit.

Paul wrote, "Don't you know that all of us who were baptized into Christ Jesus were baptized into his death? We were therefore buried with him through baptism into death in order that, just as Christ was raised from the dead through the glory of the Father, we too may live a new life" (Romans 6:3-4).

IS REVERENCE OVERRATED?
PART 1

Observe my Sabbaths and have reverence for my sanctuary. I am the Lord.
LEVITICUS 19:30

When I turned 10, I joined the local Pathfinder club, and soon experienced the wonders of polar bear camping—all the chill of hiking Mount McKinley with none of the thrill. I'm not going to lie and say I was Pathfinder of the Year material—I'm still not exactly the go-to guy when it comes to putting up a pup tent—but I gave it my all. Even if I didn't quite grasp the whole "pledge and law" thing.

The Pathfinder pledge and law seemed to sew up everything we needed to know and do to be good little Christians: "By the grace of God, I will be pure. I will be kind. I will be true. I will keep the Pathfinder Law. I will be a servant of God. I will be a friend to man. The Law is for me to: Keep the morning watch. Do my honest part. Care for my body. Keep a level eye. Be courteous and obedient. Walk softly in the sanctuary. Keep a song in my heart. Go on God's errands."

Whew. Our club leaders loved to have us recite it in front of large groups of people. The official explanation of each part of the pledge and law were pretty straightforward, but then there's that "Walk softly . . ." part again. Its official explanation says, "In any devotional exercise I will be quiet, careful, and reverent."

H'mm. Yeah, I know what they're trying to get at. But as you've always heard, the proverbial road to Hades is paved with good intentions. Such as this gem from the undisputed champions of meaning well—the Pharisees:

The blind and the lame came to him at the temple, and he healed them. But when the chief priests and the teachers of the law saw the wonderful things he did and the children shouting in the temple area, "Hosanna to the Son of David," they were indignant. "Do you hear what these children are saying?" they asked him.

"Yes," replied Jesus, "have you never read, 'From the lips of children and infants you have ordained praise'?" (Matthew 21:14-16).

Some of the Pharisees in the crowd said to Jesus, "Teacher, rebuke your disciples!" "I tell you," he replied, "if they keep quiet, the stones will cry out" (Luke 19:39, 40). Continued.

IS REVERENCE OVERRATED?
PART 2

"Do not come any closer," God said. *"Take off your sandals,*
for the place where you are standing is holy ground."
EXODUS 3:5

We've reduced reverence to the experience the Israelites had at Mount Sinai: scrubbing clothes, combing hair, and don't get too close to that mountain or you're gonna get zapped. But reverence goes far beyond that scene of God trying to impress His law on a mass of witless slaves. God doesn't want us stuck in fear mode forever. He wants us to experience intimacy with Him. As to how we connect and communicate with God, the experience of reverence is as rich as any relationship, and includes:

Wrestling with God in the darkness (Genesis 32:22-32).

Removing your shoes at a desert spot made sacred by God's presence (Exodus 3).

Painting your door with blood and patiently waiting for God to act (Exodus 12).

Dancing in celebration on the shores of the Red Sea (Exodus 14, 15).

Throwing Jesus a party in gratitude for resurrecting you (John 12:1-7).

Lavishing Jesus' feet with luxurious perfume (John 12:3).

Leaping and dancing in the Temple in celebration of healing (Acts 3:1-10).

When we criticize others for not relating to God the same way we do, we risk the attitude of Judas, who demanded that Jesus reprimand Mary for wasting so much money anointing His feet. For too long the church has defined reverence as a narrow, "everybody hush now" state of mind. And while truly experiencing God's majesty and your gratitude for what He's done for you can render you speechless, sometimes God's people need to express themselves as do the Hallelujah-shouting multitude in Revelation 19:6: "like the roar of rushing waters and like loud peals of thunder."

Yes, it's possible to go overboard into an anything-goes attitude. Anytime anything spiritual becomes an end in itself, it's lost its meaning. But God created us as multifaceted people, and our worship, while centered in an attitude of humble gratitude, should reflect our diversity of talents, interests, and experiences.

And one more thing: Always remember that everyone you meet is a temple of God, and how we treat others is how we treat Jesus. When you meet someone who needs God, you're treading on holy ground.

TO KILL A MOCKING SON
PART 1

Whoever curses father or mother shall be put to death.
EXODUS 21:17

OK, cursing your parents isn't exactly Christian behavior. But executing your child for doing so doesn't sound like something Jesus would do either. Remember the story Jesus told about the prodigal son? In asking for his inheritance early he effectively told his dad, "I wish you were dead." Yet the father couldn't wait to welcome back the wastrel. Should he have handed a rock to his more faithful son and said, "Here, kid, cast the first stone"? That was God's rule. Right?

The Reconstructionist movement urges Christians to enforce its interpretation of Old Testament law (with a heavy emphasis on who deserves a good stoning and a little less interest in, say, avoiding ham sandwiches and taking care of poor people). But the Bible's take on God's laws is much more flexible, always working toward the love-and-grace-centered ideal. Even in the Old Testament God mandates a rule in one book only to scrap it later. For example, take this triple whammy:

"No one whose testicles are crushed or whose penis is cut off shall be admitted to the assembly of the Lord. Those born of an illicit union shall not be admitted. . . . Even to the tenth generation none . . . shall be admitted. . . . No Ammonite or Moabite shall be admitted to the assembly of the Lord. Even to the tenth generation" (Deuteronomy 23:1-3, NRSV).

Harsh. Yet the Israelites welcomed Ruth the Moabite into the family, and she became grandma to King David. Jesus' genealogy included numerous people born out of wedlock, none of them ostracized from society. And Isaiah 56:3-5 quotes God as saying, "Do not let the foreigner joined to the Lord say, 'The Lord will surely separate me from his people'; and do not let the eunuch say, 'I am just a dry tree.' For thus says the Lord: To the eunuchs who keep my Sabbaths . . . and hold fast my covenant, I will give, in my house and within my walls, a monument and a name better than sons and daughters; I will give them an everlasting name that shall not be cut off" (NRSV).

When God first led Israel out of Egypt, He made it clear that His religion was nothing like that of the Canaanites, which included such rites as castration. Once that was understood, He opened the doors wide to include everyone who would follow Him.

But how should we relate to such laws as death for cursing? Come back tomorrow. *Continued.*

Bible

TO KILL A MOCKING SON
PART 2

*Jesus replied, "Moses permitted you to divorce your wives
because your hearts were hard. But it was not this way from the beginning."*
MATTHEW 19:8

One of the great overlooked themes of the Bible is that of "divine condescension," or how flexible God is willing to be to reach His people wherever they are. For naive, whiny, spiritually immature ancient Israel, God took a hard line in some areas that may surprise us, yet tolerated much that shocks us today. Trimming the edge of your beard? Don't do it! Slavery and polygamy? God put major restrictions on the two practices but still allowed them, even though, like divorce, "it was not this way from the beginning."

God designed the laws He gave the ancient Israelites to meet them where they were. For people who knew nothing of religion but a confusing mess of rites and regulations for gods they could never be quite sure they were pleasing, God's straightforward, here's-how-you-do-it law changed everything. While God didn't change everything back to the Adam and Eve model right away, He put them on the path toward it.

In *Who's Afraid of the Old Testament God?* Alden Thompson writes, "The facts of the matter are that divine laws are no more enduring than the human situation which makes them necessary" (p. 79). One of the greatest challenges Jesus faced was people who insisted on following God's laws to the letter—but who barely knew God at all. They added a lot to make the laws more exact, but never read between the lines.

The 176 verses of Psalm 119 celebrate the greatness and privilege of lawkeeping. "I delight in your commands because I love them," the writer exults (verse 47). For such legalists as the Pharisees, however, the law wasn't kept out of love for God or man, but out of greed and fear.

Capital punishment for people who are merely hateful clashes with Jesus' message of grace, the same as does slavery, polygamy, and everything else God tolerated for a time. Like the rules against marrying Moabites, the law ended when God's people were more secure in their faith. But for a people who knew only suffering, slavery, and swift execution, God met them where they were. Yet Jesus came to bring life, and to show that the law and love must spring from within.

CRUISING / PART 1

Instruct a wise man and he will be wiser still.

PROVERBS 9:9

EXT. SUBURBAN HOUSE—AFTERNOON

It's Sunday afternoon, the middle of summer vacation. Mike and José have just graduated from high school, and right now, part-time jobs are as much as they want to handle. Though they've been accepted at Blake University, they're just not yet ready to think about school again.

Seventeen-year-old JOSÉ pulls up in his car. MIKE is outside pushing an old mower. He is about three-fourths done and feeling the strain. The sun's blazing, and the uncut grass looks about a foot high. Even in shorts, a tank top, and a baseball cap, he's sweating it.

JOSÉ: *Dude, you're scorched. Wanna go get some burritos and shakes at Burrito Barn?*

MIKE (looking up and cutting off the mower): *Sorry, man. I'm broke.*

JOSÉ: *What? I thought you had that job at that golf course.*

MIKE: *You've been outta town for a while! What'd you do, go visit your grandma?*

JOSÉ: *Actually, yeah.*

MIKE: *Well, I was running this golf cart to pick up the golf balls and this doof hits one smack-dab in the middle of the cart windshield. I got a black eye . . . so my mom decided it wasn't "safe" for me to work there anymore.*

JOSÉ: *Well, c'mon, I'll buy you a burrito. There's a great meal deal. It'll give ya energy.*

MIKE: *Sure. I'll finish this tonight when it's not so blazing out here. I'm not in a hurry, not in this heat.*

INT. CAR

Mike hops in. We see the guys through the front windshield, with scenery changing behind them.

JOSÉ: *Dude, have you ever heard of a little thing called sunscreen? It prevents a little thing called cancer.*

MIKE: *You sound just like Rebecca on the class trip. I just ran out of the stuff.*

JOSÉ: *Rebecca! Did you hear about her?*

MIKE: *Isn't she at the Summer Start program over at Blake? That started like what, six weeks ago? Continued.*

spirit

CRUISING / PART 2

But about that day and hour no one knows,
neither the angels of heaven, nor the Son, but only the Father.
MATTHEW 24:36, NRSV

JOSÉ: Anna said that Rebecca's practically gotten herself engaged.

MIKE: Engaged? Like to a guy? She and Rich broke up just before graduation.

JOSÉ: For real, man. It's some new guy she met at Blake.

MIKE: That's whacked. Doesn't she need time to find herself or something?

JOSÉ: I guess not if she's found her man.

MIKE: Whatever. What's the hurry?

JOSÉ: You know Rebecca.

MIKE: Well, she always did look at things in her own special way. Wasn't she always seeing signs of the end of the world?

JOSÉ: Yeah. Remember when she told us that microchips were hidden in Chex Mix so the government could spy on us?

MIKE: Or that the president was going to declare war on Portugal and outlaw prayer on Sabbath?

JOSÉ: Or that the Second Coming was probably going to happen before we reached 20 because this guy in Denver discovered something new in the Dead Sea scrolls?

MIKE: Maybe that's why she's in such a hurry to get married.

JOSÉ: Hey, maybe.

MIKE: Well, I wish Jesus would hurry up and come. Then I wouldn't have to worry about asking Jailyn out.

JOSÉ: If you could choose one or the other to happen this week, which would it be?

MIKE: One or the other what?

JOSÉ: A date with Jailyn or the Second Coming.

MIKE: You mean like, which would I rather have happen this week?

JOSÉ: Exactly.

MIKE: Honestly . . . I'd probably choose Jailyn. Not that it's any more likely to happen.

JOSÉ: Why?

MIKE: 'Cause she's hot.

JOSÉ: How about 'cause she's walking this way sipping a Slushee? *Continued.*

CRUISING / PART 3

Before long, the world will not see me anymore,
but you will see me. Because I live, you also will live.
JOHN 14:19

MIKE's face registers surprise. JOSÉ slows down. We see JAILYN,
wearing sandals, shorts, and a shirt with a multipetaled daisy on it.
She looks over at the guys and smiles.
JAILYN: Hey, guys. What are you up to?
MIKE: Uh, hey, Jailyn.
JOSÉ: We were just going to the Burrito Barn. Wanna come along?
JAILYN: Sure. I was just going to Rice Gong to get some egg rolls,
but that can wait.
JOSÉ: Great. The back door's unlocked. My air-conditioning's
busted, but it's not too far.
JAILYN *(getting into back seat)*: That's OK. I've got my Slushee.
MIKE gives JOSÉ a look. JOSÉ grins. JAILYN buckles her seat belt.
JOSÉ: We were just talking about the end of the world.
JAILYN: Oh, yeah? You got some inside knowledge?
JOSÉ: We were just thinking about where it fits into our lives.
JAILYN: Well, it probably takes a pretty big chunk of it. I mean,
when the world ends, we're not gonna be the same.
MIKE: But what about all the crazy stuff first—like plagues and
earthquakes?
JOSÉ: I dunno. I always figured it'd be worth it if we're going to
end up with Jesus.
JAILYN: Me too. People are always worrying about the end-time,
or that they'll miss out on something good on earth. Most of the time
I'm just thinking, *Whatever it takes, get me out of here.*
MIKE: But some people are so obsessed with the end that they for-
get what's important.
JOSÉ: Well, Jesus is what's important now and later. The relation-
ship, you know?
JAILYN: Yeah, the relationship.
MIKE: So maybe we miss out on the point if we get too preoccu-
pied with the fireworks. We gotta enjoy the journey while it lasts.
JOSÉ: I'll eat a burrito to that.
They pull into the Burrito Barn parking lot.
JAILYN: You guys are funny.
MIKE: Well, we're just not in a hurry.

INNER SPACE / PART 1

Therefore we will not fear, though the earth give way
and the mountains fall into the heart of the sea.
PSALM 46:2.

The blue academy bus hauled its cargo of inner tubes and earli-teens down the road. I chattered amiably with my friends, excited to hit the water for some inner tube action. The bus pulled up by the dock, and my friends grabbed their tubes, waded into the water, and began floating down the cool, cool waters of the stream. Meanwhile I watched from the shore and waved. Stupid willpower . . . stupid inabil-ity to swim.

A man approached, introducing himself as Bob. "Aren't you get-ting in?"

"Uh, I can't swim very well."

"Makes no difference," Bob assured me. "C'mon, get in. You don't want to sit in the bus for the next three hours, do you?"

That proved persuasive. Before I knew it, I had entered the murky depths. I slowly maneuvered myself onto the tube.

"Just stick your tail in the middle and lie on your back," Bob ad-vised. Apparently Bob's job was to bring up the rear of our caravan. I did as Bob instructed, then let myself float out into the middle of the river.

By now my friends were merely blurry dots on the horizon. I had to find conversationalists elsewhere. Bob seemed like a good prospect. Nice guy. Pleasantly messy, wet hair; smiling face; kind, reassuring words. Unfortunately, I soon discovered one key thing about Bob—he had a son named Shannon.

"How come you're afraid of water?" Shannon asked, his face a mask of innocence.

"I just don't like water, all right?" I raised my rear to avoid a scrape from some boulders protruding from deep below. "I can't swim."

"Well, you know," commented Shannon (hey, Shannon's a girl's name, isn't it?), "there are a lot of rapids ahead. And since you're afraid of water and can't swim, well, you might get seriously injured. Some people fall off their tubes, go under, and never come back up."

This was going to be a long ride. *Continued.*

INNER SPACE / PART 2

You will not fear the terror of night, nor the arrow that flies by day.
PSALM 91:5

This guy, Shannon, was definitely getting on my nerves. Then other parts of my body got in on the fun. Goose bumps danced on my arms. My knees knocked together to the rhythm of "Michael, Row the Boat Ashore." My teeth rounded out the organ recital with a piece called "The Chatter." It was all very entertaining. To Shannon.

The creek reverberated with a few pitiful cries of "I'm going to drown. Take me to shore and let me walk. Please." After a few minutes of that I heard something that made my teeth chatter twice as fast. The unmistakable sound of . . . fast water. Very fast water. And as we came nearer, I noticed a huge waterfall with a drop of nearly 12 inches.

"You'd better watch out," Shannon warned, taking the role of helpful river guide. "Lots of people have gone over these falls and been sucked under by the current. They bash their heads on the bottom and die instantly of a skull fracture."

"Shut up, Shannon," I said. He just laughed. The waterfall loomed closer and closer. "Tow me to shore!" I begged. "Please. Aauugghh!" I nearly popped the tube with my fingernails. Then we were over it.

"Now, that wasn't too bad," Bob commented brightly.

But I would have none of that consoling talk. "Wasn't too bad?" I screamed. "I would have died if it weren't for those nice cushy rocks, and you say it *wasn't too bad?*"

The small waterfall inspired a hideous poetic stream in Shannon. He began to sing. "'Nobody knows the trouble I've seen—'"

"Nobody wants to," I suggested.

We continued our ominous journey, complete with ghostly fish in the water, stones ready to fracture your skull, bulrushes reaching out to grab your legs, the limbs of trees hanging down to grab your neck . . . and a strange moaning.

"Shannon, stop the strange moaning," I commanded. He ignored me.

Up ahead I could hear the sounds of rushing water again. Uh-oh. "Ha-ha," laughed Shannon. "Now I get to hear Tompaul scream and yell again."

Right then I made up my mind. No more bawling. (And no more ripping off Pat McManus jokes.) Our inner tubes approached the rapids. I yawned. *Continued.*

Innovation

INNER SPACE / PART 3

Nor the pestilence that stalks in the darkness, nor the plague that destroys at midday.
PSALM 91:6

Self, I instructed myself sternly, *let us be quiet.* We slid over the perilous falls, but I kept my cool.

"How come you didn't scream and yell?" Shannon asked, disappointed.

"So you wouldn't get the satisfaction," I replied, leaning back and attempting to enjoy the trip. The midafternoon sun sparkled through the trees. I had to admit the scenery was pretty magnificent out here.

"You know, a lot of water moccasins live in this creek," said you-know-who right out of the blue.

"I know," I agreed. "I've heard they'll just come up and bite you, and you'll be a goner. And the piranhas! Have you heard about them? They can rip your leg off in less than a minute."

Shannon fidgeted in his tube. But I'll give him credit: he was persistent. He told a few more tales about tubers getting sucked under to a watery grave.

I nodded, grinning wickedly to myself. "I read just the other day in the *Morning Herald* that a bunch of fishermen around here just disappeared. Not a trace. Those water moccasins can really get ya."

Shannon squirmed. *I* was beginning to enjoy the ride.

An hour and a half and several measly rapids later we reached the end of the adventure. I quickly reached dry land, wrung out my shoes, and rejoined my friends.

That evening I stood in the hall, waiting for the next camp meeting class to start. I was dry now, and in my element. Then you-know-who came down the hall.

"You're not really afraid of water," Shannon accused.

"Of course I am," I insisted. "You saw me."

"Then how come you stopped wailing in the middle of the ride?"

"So you would get frustrated." Then to prove that I was really afraid of water, I glanced at a nearby drinking fountain and yelled, "Save me!"

My friends laughed. Shannon wandered off. And I thought that was the end of that, until the unexpected happened. *Continued.*

INNER SPACE / PART 4

Wounds from a friend can be trusted, but an enemy multiplies kisses.
PROVERBS 27:6

I spotted Shannon standing on the other side of the pool, visiting with friends. It had been two years since we'd talked, but I had come to see him. I had a present. I hadn't thought much more about Shannon since our river ride, but I'd dabbled in creative writing, and submitted a humorous take on my inner tube encounter to *Guide* magazine. They published it as "Totally Tubular," and I wanted to give Shannon a copy. He saw me and snickered, remarking snidely about my sexuality for his friends' benefit. They laughed, but when I pulled out the magazine they seemed to disappear.

"Hey," I said, handing him the mag, "I wrote this story about our little inner tube trip a while back. I changed your name and details, but I thought you'd like a copy."

"Oh," he said. "Um, thanks." He riffled the pages.

"How you been?"

"Uh, I'm OK."

"Me too. See ya around."

"Yeah, see ya."

Well, it wasn't like anything I'd ever read in a "How to make friends" article, but I somehow felt better. Two years later Shannon and I ended up in the same town, and we always said hi when we saw each other, though that wasn't often. One day, though, we got to talking.

"Do you have any health problems, Tompaul?"

I shrugged. "I had asthma when I was a kid—was in the hospital several times—and still can't blow up a balloon or run a mile, but otherwise I'm good. No broken bones. Why?"

"I've got this thing," he said, looking down at the floor, then my way again. "There's something wrong with my digestive system. I have to take this nasty stuff all the time to keep everything working right."

"That's not cool," I said.

"Naah, it's OK," he said. "I'm all right."

I don't know where Shannon is these days, but I hope he's doing well. He deserves to be.

LOVING THE LAW

Your law is my delight.
PSALM 119:77, NRSV

Throughout Psalm 119 the writer expresses love for God's law, precepts, and commandments. Yet how many share the writer's enthusiasm for God's law? We think of all that we have to learn for Bible class or the seemingly endless list of things the Bible says we should or should not do. But if we understood ancient Mesopotamian culture, we could share the psalmist's appreciation.

"Law" in the Bible means more than lists of regulations that rulers might enact, lawyers interpret, and judges enforce. The Hebrew word often translated "law" was *torah*. Besides meaning "instruction, guidance, law," it also meant "revelation," that is, everything that God disclosed about Himself. Sometimes we might wish that God had not revealed so much. That way we would not be so responsible for it. After all, the God of the Bible had a lot to say to His people.

But the gods of the people around Israel were not like that at all. The problem with them was that they did not speak to those who worshipped them. If only they would communicate!

The people of the ancient world believed that as long as you had the favor of the gods, things would go well for you. But if you offended them or broke one of their commands, you'd experience suffering and catastrophe. The problem was that you never knew what deity you had made angry, or exactly what you had done wrong. (Ever had someone upset with you but no idea why?) Even worse, something that might please one god might make another angry.

People composed all-purpose prayers to seek divine forgiveness and favor with the gods. People would apologize for anything and everything. That's what Job's friends urged him to do: confess to something just so God will get off your case.

But the God of the Bible spoke to His people. Unlike the pagan gods, He didn't give them the silent treatment. Besides letting them know when they had done wrong, He also told them good things: that He loved them, what He was like, what He wanted to do for them, and how they could live wonderful, happy lives. No wonder the psalmist could proclaim his love for God's law—His revelation of His loving, wonderful self.

GW

SONNY BLUE

A wise son brings joy to his father, but a foolish son grief to his mother.
PROVERBS 10:1

I can't remember the moment the thought first struck: *Sonny would be really pretty dyed blue.* I know that I played around with it for weeks before I did anything about it. One thing that made it possible was that Sonny—with his long white fur—liked water. He'd bat at dripping water as long as you'd let him, splashing his paws in the sink. I won't go so far as to say that he liked to swim, but for a cat, he was abnormally comfortable with water.

Now, what to use? The food coloring we used in baking wouldn't work.

Diluted in a sinkful of water, it would be too weak. But laundry blue, I reasoned, would work just fine. At age 17, I'd never actually used any laundry blue, but I figured that if I didn't rinse him his fur would keep the color. The idea for laundry was to put this blue powder in your rinse water. After thoroughly rinsing it out, your white items were extra white. (Don't worry. It didn't make any sense to me, either.)

So I drove to the grocery store and bought a packet of laundry blue. And a few days later, while my mom was still at work, I took myself and the cat into the bathroom and locked the door. Filling the sink with warm water, I mixed in the coloring. The water turned a deeply satisfying blue. Then I picked up Sonny and sat him on the sink. I dipped his paws in the wet stuff and swished his fluffy tail. I dribbled blue water on his head. By the time we'd finished, I was fairly wet and Sonny was blue—and irritable. Wrapping him in a towel, I tried to dry him off and fluff his fur, but he kicked me with his strong back feet, and the instant I opened the door he shot out. I was right behind him. No one should see him just yet—not while he looked like a drowned rat, a big, blue drowned rat.

Then I heard Mom's scared voice: "What's happened to Sonny?" I tried to explain, but she didn't hear me. Her sputters had turned to tears, and she turned away. You see, Sonny wasn't my cat. He was hers.

By evening Sonny was his fluffy (blue) self. A few weeks later he was white again. He still liked playing in water, and licking off the dye didn't poison him. (I worried about that a little late.) My mother forgave me, and even said that he looked pretty. So all's well that ends well. I dyed my mom's cat. He lived through it with no ill effects. But I still wish it hadn't made her cry.

PW

FAITH IN ACTION

What good is it, my brothers, if a man claims to have faith but has no deeds?
Can such faith save him? Suppose a brother or sister is without clothes and daily food.
If one of you says to him, "Go, I wish you well; keep warm and well fed,"
but does nothing about his physical needs, what good is it? In the same way,
faith by itself, if it is not accompanied by action, is dead.
JAMES 2:14-17

When I was growing up, my church provided a lot to keep me entertained. Vacation Bible Schools. Sabbath school. Summer camp. Pathfinder campouts. Even youth rallies. I looked forward to them as opportunities to spend time with friends and yes, learn about God. But while my church did a lot to keep me entertained and ingrained about religious facts and doctrine, they didn't do nearly so much to get me *involved*.

Not that there was that much going on. Every Sabbath the church filled the same slots over and over: special music (that wasn't going to be me). Children's story. Responsive reading. But once 12:00 p.m. rolled around on a Saturday morning, there wasn't much to do church-wise but wait another 165 hours. (OK, so I did put on a killer magic act at the church talent show once.)

Churches have invested a lot of time, energy, and money studying what develops faith in young people. What they've found rebuts common practice, and affirms exactly what the Bible's told us all along. Religion is useless if it's not put into practice, and that means outside church walls. Spirituality will atrophy if it's bottled up inside.

A Baylor University study found that "involvement in community service is far more significant to the faith development of teens than involvement in worship." "The fact is that service that gives kids a sense of meaning and purpose in their lives has a profound impact on their faith," said dean Diana Garland. "Faith is deepened when they feel called out to do something. Far more than recreational activities or retreats—or even Bible study and worship—it really matures their faith."

One-time service opportunities are good, but ongoing projects that develop relationships make the biggest impact on both you and others. In outreach, people don't care how much you know until they see how much you care. Tell your church you want to take action and make a difference. Your faith will grow.

THE PHOTO THAT BROKE
A MILLION HEARTS / PART 1

My days have passed, my plans are shattered, and so are the desires of my heart.
JOB 17:11

The photograph instantly symbolized and summed up the Vietnam War, and, many believe, hastened its end.

Decades later the image has lost none of its power. Nine-year-old Kim Phuc's face is frozen in pain, her mouth wide in a silent scream as she staggers down the road. Her arms flap at her sides, a pint-size echo of a thousand Renaissance paintings of the Crucifixion. She is naked, her burning clothes tugged off and fallen away after a South Vietnamese plane dropped scorching napalm on her body. She appears about to stumble. It is June 8, 1972.

"It's hot, it's hot!" she cried. Moments after Vietnamese photojournalist Nick Ut snapped the photo, soldiers doused Kim's smoldering skin with water (which actually fueled the napalm). Third-degree burns covered a third of her body—her left arm, nearly all of her back, a splash on her chest, the back of her neck. Burns also lashed her right arm, stomach, and buttocks, and minor singes burned her ears, right hand, and cheek. Such severe injuries demanded immediate and specialized medical attention.

Nick grabbed a poncho to cover Kim, and transported her and an injured woman to the nearest hospital. Urging his driver to keep moving, he promised Kim, "We'll be at the hospital very soon."

At last they arrived, and left the two victims. Nick begged a nurse to help them and apologized for needing to run. Seeing Kim's injuries, doctors did little, for they felt she would not survive. Nick hurried to the Associated Press office in Saigon, where a technician developed his film. The images were as powerful as he'd expected. He and his colleagues knew that because of the subject's nudity the photo was unlikely to be printed, but one image was too powerful to dismiss. The next day it appeared on the front page of newspapers around the world.

After three days and desperate searching through hospital after hospital, Kim's parents found her. Only conscious enough to cry out to her cousin Danh, who had not survived the attack, she barely clung to life. The hospital did not have the resources to give her the treatment she needed to live. There seemed no hope. *Continued.*

THE PHOTO THAT BROKE A MILLION HEARTS / PART 2

Be merciful to me, Lord, for I am faint; O Lord, heal me, for my bones are in agony.
PSALM 6:2

Kim's parents begged the help of a doctor they'd met as they searched for her, and at last convinced a nonprofit hospital specializing in plastic and reconstructive surgery to admit her. There doctors rushed to give Kim the emergency treatment she'd gone so many days without: a transfusion of her mother's blood, pain relief, and daily debridement, the excruciating removal of dead skin.

Kim lingered unconscious for nearly three months, her father keeping a constant vigil at her side. Her parents prayed to the gods of Cao Dai, their Buddhist faith, believing that they'd be responsible for her care for the rest of their lives.

Gradually Kim improved and gained enough strength for skin grafting, another agonizing process. After nearly six months of constant care and physiotherapy to restore her strength, she headed home, but frequent pain sent her to a convalescent center, where her upbeat attitude impressed and inspired the nurses. When after more than a year she returned home permanently, painful stretching exercises gradually restored flexibility of her shoulder, elbow, and fingers. With her father's steady encouragement she regained feeling in her arms and legs and could lift a bowl without dropping it. Soon she could ride her bike to school and play with other children.

Kim returned to school and made up for the year she'd lost. The war continued. Twice shells exploded by her home, one wounding her uncle. When Saigon fell in 1975, Kim felt relief that the war was over, but in the chaos of the North Vietnamese takeover her family's home was destroyed. They moved to a crowded urban area, into a dwelling that made their previous modest house look lavish by comparison. Pain continued to haunt her. Damaged nerve cells left her vulnerable to heat, so her family kept ice on hand to cool her where her body could not. Painkillers helped a little. The new Communist regime controlled nearly every aspect of life, from 4:30 a.m. wakeup music to propaganda in Kim's elementary school. The government smashed much of the Cao Dai temple near her home, and Kim dreamed of escaping to a new life of freedom. *Continued.*

THE PHOTO THAT BROKE A MILLION HEARTS / PART 3

For God so loved the world that he gave his one and only Son,
that whoever believes in him shall not perish but have eternal life.
JOHN 3:16

As Kim grew into adolescence she felt stronger, and pain and headaches plagued her much less. The blemish on her cheek faded away, and with long sleeves, shoulder-length hair, and practiced mannerisms her injuries were nearly undetectable.

The day Kim turned 18 she dedicated herself to the Cao Dai religion at the nearby temple. She joined the temple choir, chanting prayers with the group each day. She enrolled in a nearby university, and life seemed nearly normal—until the day four men pulled her out of her math class. "You are the girl in the picture?" they asked. "The real Kim Phuc? But you look so normal!"

Kim pulled up her sleeve and showed her scars, and soon found herself interviewed by one foreign journalist after another. She censored her answers lest she speak of problems endured under the Communist government. The state prevented her from attending college, yet for propaganda's sake made it appear that she was a medical student. Kim grew sick of the deception. *They have destroyed my life,* she thought. *Why do they do this to me?* She prayed to the god of the Cao Dai for happiness, but felt crushed.

When Kim found a library near her home, she began exploring a section on world religions that the government had not yet censored. She read books on the major Eastern religions, then started a copy of the New Testament. She was fascinated by the stories of Jesus, yet shocked by the Bible's claims about Him. How could His death pay completely for someone's sins and thus allow that person into heaven? The Cao Dai religion gave no such guarantee, offering salvation only as an elusive goal that each person must attain on his or her own.

She became friends with a young man named Anh, an assistant pastor in the neighborhood. "God gives you salvation as a gift," he told her. "You don't have to do good things to earn it. You can't *earn* it, no matter what you do. It is God who saves you."

Kim couldn't believe it. Anh invited her to hear his pastor preach, but she told him, "If I betray my religion, my soul will wander with no resting place. Heaven has no room for followers who betray Cao Dai." *Continued.*

THE PHOTO THAT BROKE A MILLION HEARTS / PART 4

Cast all your anxiety on him because he cares for you.
1 PETER 5:7

"If you are not ready to go to church," Anh suggested, "why don't you try praying to God? Bring your burdens to God; see how you feel."

Kim prayed that God would send her a friend if she attended the Christian church. And she found one in an older woman who met daily with her to read and discuss the Bible. Then came the day the pastor told a story of someone who tried to carry his spiritual burden alone, and Kim recognized herself in his story. When he called anyone who wished to follow Jesus to come to the front of the church, Kim tearfully came forward, her mind and heart set.

Now if she could just escape her government's clutches. Again her health deteriorated under the stress, and she prayed that someone would help her. She wrote a letter to Perry Kretz, a German photojournalist who had documented her life and wounds as she recovered from the attack. He had visited her again after the government made her available for interviews. Months passed until she heard from him, and he came to take her back to West Germany for medical care. As a result of the trip Vietnam's prime minister, Pham Van Dong, invited her to meet with him, and he saw to it that she got back in school. She eventually began classes at the University of Havana, Cuba.

Not knowing Spanish isolated Kim in her new surroundings. She sought solace in a church, but could find no Christian community in the officially atheist nation. New friends gave her new confidence, but she still felt trapped by a life over which she had little control. She was studying to be a pharmacologist, but exposure to chemicals made her sick, so at 26 she started college anew to study languages. About then she was thrilled to meet, in Havana, "Uncle Ut"—the photographer who'd made her famous.

She'd been excited about the Vietnamese government sending her on a six-week tour of the United States, but suddenly the trip was canceled. Her heart broke. On a visit home, she learned why Vietnam had cancelled it. They'd snooped and read letters her brother had written her, advising her to defect to freedom in the U.S. Now Kim felt more trapped than ever. *Continued.*

THE PHOTO THAT BROKE A MILLION HEARTS / PART 5

Sing to the Lord a new song, his praise from the ends of the earth.
ISAIAH 42:10

Visiting Vietnam on leave from her studies in Cuba, Kim connected with her Christian friends there. She learned that Anh, the pastor friend who had helped her come to Christ, had just endured three years of government "reeducation." Anh took her to a house church that met in a different home each week. Kim drank in the fellowship and spirituality, though the group sang softly lest they draw outside attention.

Kim visited once more with her friend and patron Pham Van Dong, now in his 80s and retired after 35 years as prime minister. He asked of her family. After telling him of their continued poverty and struggles, she shared what lay on her heart the most: the message of salvation by Jesus Christ. He listened without interrupting, then said, "That religion is from America." Kim promised to keep praying for him. "OK," he said.

Back in Cuba, Kim grew closer to another Vietnamese student, Bui Huy Tuan. An ardent Communist, he disagreed with her on politics and religion, but still he asked her to marry him. "You are very good to me," she told him, "but I cannot decide about marriage at this moment. I have to think of my health, my studies, and my future."

At last Kim and Tuan married, celebrating their wedding in Havana with 300 guests. When they went to Moscow for their honeymoon, Kim kept a secret from Tuan until the last hour: she planned to escape. When their plane stopped in Newfoundland to refuel, Kim and Tuan asked for political asylum in Canada.

Canada granted them refugee status, and they remade their lives in Toronto. Tuan accepted Jesus as his Savior, and studied to become a minister. After a few years and further thawing of East-West relations, Kim's parents joined her in Canada as well.

On November 11, 1996 (Veterans Day in the United States), Kim Phuc spoke at a ceremony at the Vietnam Veterans Memorial in Washington, D.C. Now she works with the Kim Foundation, which aids child war victims.

Today Kim Phuc tells people how Jesus transformed her life. "It was the fire of bombs that burned my body. It was the skill of doctors that mended my skin. But it took the power of God's love to heal my heart." (Adapted in part from *The Girl in the Picture*, by Denise Chong.)

SEX AND SENSIBILITY

*Do you not know that your body is a temple of the Holy Spirit,
who is in you, whom you have received from God?*

1 CORINTHIANS 6:19

No topic inspired more discussion in my pastoral counseling class at the seminary than masturbation.

Originally scheduled for just one class period, the discussion stretched to two and a half. The class held more than 100 students, and they all seemed to have questions. One student told how his wife thinks he's not interested in sex unless he's eaten some dairy products. Another told of a talk about sex he'd given to teens that had incurred the wrath of a teacher, whose wife confessed that their sex life was pretty much in the past. The professor, a generally grave character who had at first spooked me and then, as I got to know him, earned my awe, calmly gave everyone a chance to talk while casually tossing off double entendres that few of the furiously scribbling seminarians seemed to notice.

The discussion finally concluded by emphasizing that we need to judge everything in our lives—what we eat, how we spend our time and money, what we focus on—by how it impacts our relationship with God and others. If anything becomes an idol to us, a substitution for the good things God gave us to enjoy in relationship with Him and others, it's something we need to reevaluate.

The church has wrestled with issues of sex and gender for 2,000 years. The thirteenth-century theologian Thomas Aquinas argued that masturbation was a worse sin than rape because at least rape was man plus woman the way God designed it. The church's view of women has too often reduced them to merely baby factories with cooking skills. The church's view of masculinity as a birthright to power has inspired men to worship themselves and abuse everyone else.

Our sexuality is a gift in this sinful world, and just as any gift can be broken or misused. It can be a blessing when it enhances us, uplifts us, inspires us, and motivates us to love better. It can be a curse when it defines us, limits us, distorts us into creatures living only for self and self-centered pleasure.

LOVE IN ACTION

Immediately he was cured of his leprosy.
Then Jesus said to him, "See that you don't tell anyone."
MATTHEW 8:3, 4

Which of these three texts is not like the others?

1. Today's scripture.

2. *"At this, the man's ears were opened, his tongue was loosened and he began to speak plainly. Jesus commanded them not to tell anyone" (Mark 7:35, 36).*

3. *"One Sabbath, when Jesus went to eat in the house of a prominent Pharisee, he was being carefully watched. There in front of him was a man suffering from dropsy. Jesus asked the Pharisees and experts in the law, 'Is it lawful to heal on the Sabbath or not?' But they remained silent. So taking hold of the man, he healed him and sent him away. Then he asked them, 'If one of you has a son or an ox that falls into a well on the Sabbath day, will you not immediately pull him out?' And they had nothing to say" (Luke 14:1-5).*

Jesus often told people to keep their healings secret—except when He healed them on Sabbath. Though Jesus wanted to prevent people from flocking to Him just to see a miracle, He made sure everyone paid attention to His Sabbath healings. Jesus' Sabbath miracles make clear that while we should refrain from everyday work on Sabbath, there's no better way to keep the Sabbath than to do God's business of healing and redemption.

The Pharisees, like a lot of people I've met over the years, were so intent on avoiding what they *shouldn't* do on Sabbath that they missed doing what they should. Their narrow, legalistic focus on avoiding anything that smacked of work kept them not only from enjoying their day off, it kept them from blessing others. But as Jesus asked: "Which is lawful on the Sabbath: to do good or to do evil, to save life or to kill it?" (Mark 3:4).

Jesus pointed out that the Pharisees followed the law to the letter by circumcising their boys when they were 8 days old, even on Saturday: "Now if a child can be circumcised on the Sabbath so that the law of Moses may not be broken, why are you angry with me for healing the whole man on the Sabbath?" (John 7:23). He wanted us to realize that the Sabbath wasn't an end in itself, just to be kept for its own sake. It was created to bless people. And it's our joyful duty as Christians to keep the Sabbath by blessing others.

Innovation

SIEGFRIED HORN

The Lord sets prisoners free.
PSALM 146:7

May 10, 1940. Hitler invaded the Netherlands, sending shock waves around the world. On the island of Java, in what was then the Dutch East Indies, Dutch authorities began rounding up Germans and other citizens of the Axis Powers, including missionary Siegfried Horn. Horn's only crime was being in the wrong country at the wrong time. His Dutch wife remained free, but Siegfried found himself in a series of primitive internment camps.

One day the camp authorities announced that the internees could have books from their own libraries, as long as they were not political ones. Horn wrote his wife, asking her to send him 70 books on archaeology, biblical languages, and related topics. With the help of one of Horn's friends, the head of the colonial secret police, she was able to get the list of titles approved. Shortly after Horn's 70 books arrived, the camp authorities withdrew permission for the prisoners to get books, but Siegfried had his.

Horn spent six and a half harsh years in internment camps, but he used his books to study, write articles and books, and teach courses to his fellow prisoners. Horn often wondered why God did not deliver him from the camps so that he could once again serve the church. Often he claimed the promise of Psalm 146:7. But instead of being wasted years, they prepared him to become a world-famous archaeologist.

After the war Horn came to the United States, earned a doctorate in Egyptology, and taught Old Testament and archaeology for 26 years at the Seventh-day Adventist Theological Seminary. He also wrote hundreds of articles, several books (including the *Seventh-day Adventist Bible Dictionary*), edited a scholarly journal, and founded an archaeology museum at Andrews University. But he also wanted to do one more thing: conduct an archaeological dig of his own in the Holy Land. At the age of 60 he chose what many believed to be the site of ancient Heshbon in Jordan.

Several years ago I attended an archaeology seminar at Johns Hopkins University. There I overheard William Dever, one of the world's leading archaeologists of Palestine, speaking of what he considered to be one of the best archaeological digs ever done. It was the Hesbon/Madaba Plains Project, founded by Horn.

GW

A SLIPPERY
SABBATH SITUATION

*If you keep your feet from breaking the Sabbath
and from doing as you please on my holy day, if you call the Sabbath a delight
and the Lord's holy day honorable, and if you honor it by not going your own way
and not doing as you please or speaking idle words, then you will find your joy in the Lord.*
ISAIAH 58:13, 14

After potluck one snowy Sabbath, the youth group decided to take advantage of the wintry weather and go sledding behind the church. Digging up some cardboard and an old tire from the church shed, they slipped and slid, hooted and hollered, and generally whooped it up, happy to be outside in nature.

Until one of the church elders noticed the excitement. He called the teens back inside, and, with the youth leader for backup, blasted them for breaking the Sabbath.

For Seventh-day Adventists, the Sabbath has been a controversial issue from the beginning—whether to observe it, when to observe it, how to observe it. Who was right—the teens, or their accusers? Is the Sabbath supposed to be a day of frigid dullness? What's Sabbath all about, anyway?

Today's text has always been a slippery one. Don't "do as you please," but "call the Sabbath a delight"? "Idle words"? What exactly is ol' Isaiah talking about here?

The words translated "doing as you please" refer, in Hebrew, to doing one's business—your livelihood. My *Tanakh* (a Hebrew term for what Christians call the Old Testament) Hebrew-English Bible translates it as "pursuing your affairs." Isaiah is saying "Don't work on Sabbath," not "Don't do anything pleasurable on Sabbath." Same with "idle words," which in Hebrew is literally "not speaking words," and which my *Tanakh* translates as "nor strike bargains." These verses are all about not treating the Sabbath as just another business or shopping day, not a day when fun is forbidden.

The fourth commandment tells us we have six days to work, but the Sabbath is your day to rest and refresh and remember God's work for you. Isaiah promises that if we follow that, we'll find the Sabbath joyful. And while that joy should never be an end in itself (forgetting the God who made it possible) if people get worked up about how you're enjoying the Sabbath, they're probably the ones who need to take a breather.

Bible

UNANSWERED QUESTIONS

Who is this that darkens counsel by words without knowledge? . . .
I will question you, and you shall declare to me.
JOB 38:2, 3, NRSV

For 35 chapters the patriarch Job wrestles with the question of why tragedy and suffering had devastated his life. His friends insist that he accept that he had obviously done something to deserve it. Just confess, they said, and you will regain God's favor. But Job knew that he had done nothing wrong. Yet, still sharing his friends' belief that suffering came from God, he wishes that he could confront the Lord and have a hearing about the matter. And all the time God remains silent.

Finally the Lord does respond. But He does not explain about Satan's accusation against Job or the fact that the devil is the one actually responsible for Job's disasters and suffering. Instead He begins grilling Job with a long string of impossible questions. "Where were you when I laid the foundation of the earth? Tell me, if you have understanding" (verse 4, NRSV). God asks if Job watched as He brought our planet into being. Of course Job was not a witness. No human being even existed yet.

After questioning the physical aspects of the creation of the earth and its weather, God turns to the wild creatures that dwell on it: lions, mountain goats, wild oxen, hawks. Many of the issues that God interrogates Job about are still beyond the understanding of even modern science. If the Lord were to question someone today, He might examine what we know about galaxies, black holes, and subatomic particles.

Overwhelmed by God's questions, Job acknowledges his finiteness (Job 40:3-5). But the Lord is not through yet. He talks about the mighty and dangerous creatures Behemoth and Leviathan and demands to know if Job can control them as God Himself does. At last Job declares, "I know that you can do all things, and that no purpose of yours can be thwarted" (Job 42:2).

Job realizes that if he cannot explain all of the natural world around him, how dare he think that he can understand why God does as He does when it comes to suffering and evil? And if God can control the dangerous creatures Behemoth and Leviathan, He can control every evil thing. Most important of all, if God loves and cares for all of the creatures of nature, will He not love and care for Job even more?

THE TRUTH IS OUT THERE

The heavens declare the glory of God; the skies proclaim the work of his hands.
PSALM 19:1

The inverter providing solar-powered electricity turned off for the night, I stepped off the mission station porch with my towel. I'd spent my day documenting Union College's frontier nursing class as they treated patients at makeshift clinics in Nicaragua's Mosquito Coast region, near the Wawa River. No artificial light interrupted the darkness, but thanks to a crescent moon and the night sky I could still see well enough to make my way to the shower.

The sky in Francia Sirpi, Nicaragua, blazed with stars I'd almost forgotten existed. The Big Dipper hung in the sky like a colossal amusement park ride, waiting for passengers. Orion dazzled my senses. The Milky Way Galaxy glistened like a diamond-studded stream. I pondered how earth's sun would appear in the sky viewed from some other solar system. It may have been the fog of Deet I'd sprayed on my ankles, but I felt as though I could fall upward and swim through the stars.

When my parents first moved to their current home, countless stars still twinkled above their two acres. Late at night I'd take a blanket out to the lawn and peer at the heavens through my binoculars. The Milky Way shone so fine. Cassiopeia gazed down like two friendly eyes.

Nowadays the night sky at my parents' place isn't what it used to be. The Milky Way is barely visible. I can't even find the North Star. Light that traveled trillions of miles to reach Funkstown, Maryland, is snuffed out by tiny bulbs on front porches and backyard patios. The brightest light in the night sky is no longer the Milky Way but the ever-present glow from the state prison, a few miles to the south. We're lucky to see the moon.

It's odd how we lose sight of ancient light in the artificial glow of human-made enlightenment. The truth is out there, but we miss it in a blur of fluorescents and neon. God's calling our name, but we're too distracted to notice. His love and majesty beckon us from beyond, but we can't see past the traffic light.

Stop. Whatever is driving you, whatever is blinding you, stop, pull over, and take another look at what God is showing you. With His help you'll be able to see.

spirit

DAD'S TOOLS

Endure hardship as discipline; God is treating you as sons.
For what son is not disciplined by his father?
HEBREWS 12:7

Even as I hung up the phone I could not shake the surreal feeling. In a 17-second call from my mom, I'd learned Dad was dead. Learning of my father's cancer was sudden; it started with a series of strokes that left him paralytic and potentially brain-damaged. It took less than three weeks for the strokes and the cancer to sweep in. Now my father is a box of dust barely 10 inches square.

As the realization sunk in I let big question sink its teeth in: what happens now? What chapter opens up from here; does one open up?

When the crowd watched as Christ ascended into heaven, I can imagine the disciples with that same sinking feeling. "Now what do we do? What have we got now?"

The answer is in a cardboard box and it applied to both the disciples and me. A week before the call I had driven my family from Oregon to Texas to see my dad. As we learned his condition and accepted the inevitable, I asked Mom if I could have his tools. I wanted something physical of my father, and nothing represented him more than his arsenal of eccentric tools. He had custom screwdrivers and exotic electronic meters. And when he didn't have a tool for a situation, he'd actually make one. The hallmark item was his Swiss Army knife, a gift that I helped Mom and my sister get him several years ago. It showed signs of real usage, including a scar on one corner where it came in contact with an arc welder. The plastic and metal melded into a slight bulge, but it only added to the character of the knife. The main blade had been sharpened so often that the shape was more rounded at the tip. Still, it was razor sharp.

My father was never without a tool. When we were out, he was the guy you see fixing someone else's car that's stuck in the parking lot or cutting a kid's hair free from an escalator. I learned from Dad that you never know when you're going to need a knife or a pair of pliers, so you might as well have one in your pocket. I almost always do now.

Your Father has never left you without tools either. Sure, Christ is no longer here physically with us, and neither is my earthly dad. But both left us a toolbox. After Christ ascended His disciples set out to spread the gospel. You've got that same toolbox; what are you going to do with it? Love sharpened by Jesus' example is the best tool out there.

BP

A BIRD IN THE HAND / PART 1

Honor your father and your mother,
so that you may live long in the land the Lord your God is giving you.
EXODUS 20:12

When I pet-sat Mrs. M's three cats, one dog, and two parrots for a week, it couldn't have been easier—thanks to five pages of detailed instructions from an overview of the living arrangement to all about the animals. For example:

Dog Care: Potty. If you take Shane out through the garage you can usually keep the cats from escaping. If you use the front door, try very hard to keep all the cats in. If Morris, Joey, or Bootsie escapes, they'll be back eventually.

Bird Care: Food. Molly: 3-4 peanuts. Baby Gray: 4-5 peanuts every day. If you run out of peanuts, just get dry-roasted peanuts (no salt) from any grocery store.

• OK to give them snacks. They love apples, bananas, crackers, bread, pizza crust, popcorn, etc. Be sure the food pieces are no bigger than about one inch so they can hold them in their feet. No chocolate or dried fruit—sulfur and chocolate are poisonous to them.

• Their wings are not clipped, so please don't let them out of their cage. They will fly around the house and hit the windows in an attempt to get outside.

• Spray Baby Gray at least once a day with the water in the bottle by her cage. She loves this and needs the moisture, so spray her until she is really soaked. If she comes toward you, spray gently—she likes to drink the water as it comes out of the sprayer.

With Mrs. M and her husband on their way to California, I settled in for the week. Shane liked to chill in the basement. The cats liked to chew on cell phones (oh well, I was almost done with that phone anyway, and besides, it still worked). And Molly liked to talk.

"Shower?" she squawked. "You betcha, Baby Gray," I said, blasting her with water. I was used to chatting with pets, so having one that talked back didn't seem that odd.

"Where are you going?" she peeped. "To the kitchen," said I, "where you cannot fly."

Things settled into a nice routine. But I was about to learn an important lesson: Never trust an animal with a claw for a nose. *Continued.*

life

A BIRD IN THE HAND / PART 2

"Honor your father and mother"—which is the first commandment with a promise—
"that it may go well with you and that you may enjoy long life on the earth."
EPHESIANS 6:2, 3

Thursday morning I carefully slid open the food slot in Molly and Baby Gray's cage, slid in some crackers, and shut it again. And failed to notice that I hadn't successfully latched it.

Molly was staring at me from the top of the cage. Outside it. The latch! Fortunately Baby Gray hadn't noticed her friend on the lam, but I hurriedly latched it, just in case. Which meant I'd somehow have to capture Molly, unlock the latch, and get her back into the cage.

How did I get out on a limb like this? Wait—limb! That's it! The stick! That was the solution. Just extend the Stick of Friendship, let Molly jump on it, and in a quick fluid motion, get her back into the cage.

I extended the imitation branch. Molly wasn't interested. Instead she butted my forefinger with her beak, slicing a nice hole so some blood could come out and play.

Ohhhhh-kay. I'm gonna have to call Mrs. M. I called. We talked for a minute or two. She didn't seem too worried, but that didn't make me feel too much better. Meanwhile Molly stared out at the living room, her feet firmly grasping the top of the cage.

OK. It's 11:45 a.m. It's almost lunch. Time to call . . . my parents. They worked a fairly short drive up the interstate, and surely three people could corral a bird better than one. A half hour later my mom and dad appeared. Molly hadn't yet moved, but as I let them in the front door I took no chances. The three of us crept toward the bird— which suddenly flew for the glass window over the door. Disoriented by knocking her noggin on glass, Molly winged it to the kitchen. Trying to head out a closed door, she found herself on the floor. Suddenly we had a plan. My mom grabbed a dish towel. My dad threw the towel over Molly and nabbed her while I rushed into the living room to open the cage door. My dad followed close behind, and as gently as possible placed Molly back in that cage with Baby Gray. As I locked the door I sighed with relief—and stared at my dad. The closest I'd ever come to seeing him tackle the forces of nature was mowing the lawn. Now he'd succeeded where I'd failed. I had no idea he was such a clever ol' bird.

THE BIBLE MADE BLAND

All Scripture is God-breathed and is useful for teaching,
rebuking, correcting and training in righteousness,
so that the man of God may be thoroughly equipped for every good work.
2 TIMOTHY 3:16, 17

Flying cross-country one day, I looked up to see an action movie on the screen above me. A team of scientists flew in a small plane over the jungle, seeking answers to bizarre phenomenon people had witnessed in nature. Then the airplane seemed to have some trouble, and suddenly they were on the ground, a little shaken up but with no explanation for how they'd gotten there, save for a streak of fire briefly visible in the sky.

Was it engine trouble? Had someone sabotaged their plane? Had they crash-landed? Such mysteries abounded, but since the movie was edited for showing on the airplane, and airlines don't like showing movies about airplane crashes, suddenly a potentially critical plot point was gone just so they wouldn't freak out the passengers.

Since airlines first started showing movies on board they've carefully excised anything that might upset the jittery. Movies whose plots center on aeronautical mayhem don't even stand a chance.

People do the same sort of thing with the Bible. We quote the verses that are most reassuring, ignoring ones that don't offer easy answers. Life is messy. Life is confusing. Life isn't cut and dried. And the Bible doesn't pretend it is, from the struggles of its flawed heroes to the prayers its people pray.

Next time you pick up a Bible, read a few psalms. (Unless you hit No. 119, they're not very long.) In just a few pages you'll find all kinds of prayers—praise, fear, pleading, frustration. Psalm 8:4 asks God in wonder and admiration, "What is man that you are mindful of him . . . ?" Psalm 10:1 asks, "Why, O Lord, do you stand far off? Why do you hide yourself in times of trouble?" Psalm 13:1 begs, "How long, O Lord? Will you forget me forever? How long will you hide your face from me?"

The psalms show us that we can be brutally honest with God. God doesn't want our practiced prayers, our pretty phrases we think He'd like to hear. God wants to communicate with us without barriers, uninhibited and unedited. "Come now, let us reason together," God says (Isaiah 1:18). And He means it.

Adventism

LORD OF THE SABBATH

At that time Jesus went through the grainfields on the Sabbath. His disciples were hungry and began to pick some heads of grain and eat them. When the Pharisees saw this, they said to him, "Look! Your disciples are doing what is unlawful on the Sabbath."

MATTHEW 12:1, 2

The Sabbath is controversial, and has been for at least 2000 years. In Jesus' day people argued over how to keep it. Today many Christians argue that we don't need to keep it at all, but the Bible verses they quote to prove their point actually show the opposite. The New Testament shows that Jesus kept the Sabbath the way it was meant to be kept, freeing us from the legalistic, human-made expectations imposed on it.

When the Pharisees accused Jesus' disciples of Sabbathbreaking by picking some grain to snack on, Jesus pointed them to an old story about King David and his men eating food that was reserved for the Temple priests. "Or haven't you read in the Law that on the Sabbath the priests in the temple desecrate the day and yet are innocent? I tell you that one greater than the temple is here. If you had known what these words mean, 'I desire mercy, not sacrifice,' you would not have condemned the innocent. For the Son of Man is Lord of the Sabbath" (Matthew 12:5-8).

Jesus told the Pharisees that although their zeal for the Sabbath was admirable, they'd lost its meaning. The Sabbath was made for people's blessing and so that they could *be* a blessing, but they'd turned it into a burden and a curse. Jesus' rebuke only made the Pharisees angrier. When He entered their synagogue, they brought up a man with a shriveled hand and put Jesus to the test: "Is it lawful to heal on the Sabbath?" (verse 10).

Jesus pointed to their hypocrisy. "If your sheep falls into a pit on the Sabbath, do you leave it there to get sick until the Sabbath is over, or do you rescue it? Don't you think a person is more valuable than a sheep? So yes, it is lawful to do good on the Sabbath" (see verses 11, 12). And, asking the man to hold out his hand, Jesus provided a visual aid they'd never forget, as the hand healed before their eyes.

The Pharisees sulked off and started plotting Jesus' death. If He was going to insist on breaking the Sabbath by doing good, they'd have to counter it by doing some evil.

KS; TW

BALAAM

*The donkey said to Balaam, "Am I not your own donkey,
which you have always ridden, to this day? Have I been in the habit of doing this to you?"*
NUMBERS 22:30

In 1967 archaeologists in Jordan discovered something completely unexpected—a long-lost prophecy by someone best known for smacking (and talking smack to) a talking donkey, one Balaam son of Beor. "Warnings from the Book of Balaam the son of Beor," the ancient text begins. "He was a seer of the gods." The inscription, found written on plaster in a building destroyed by an earthquake, dates to the eighth or ninth centuries B.C. The "Book of Balaam" it refers to may have dated to the prophet's lifetime. The text uses both black and red ink, with the opening lines and various dramatic portions in red.

A top prophet in his day, Balaam, though not an Israelite, had the added benefit of actually serving the right God, so his services were in particular demand. Only problem with that, of course, is that Yahweh's not for sale. As Gods go, He's a hard one to pin down—no images to tell us what He looks like, no way to keep Him in a box and convince Him to bless you. He does what He wants to do, and if you're going to say what He wants you to say, it might not make you so popular—or prosperous.

Alas, Balaam tried to have it both ways. When Balak, king of Moab, offered him big bucks to curse Israel, Balaam hemmed and hawed until his own donkey hee-hawed back. Duly chastised by his beast of burden, Balaam suddenly saw what the donkey had seen: the angel of the Lord, sword drawn, blocking their way. The message was clear: Do as you will, Balaam, but you can't go against God's will for His people.

So Balaam stood on a mountain overlooking the Israelite camp, but the curses just wouldn't come. When Balak complained that his oracles were downright complimentary, Balaam reminded Balak that he'd mentioned this might happen. Balak finally gave up when the third time was most decidedly not the charm. ("Blessed is everyone who blesses you, and cursed is everyone who curses you" [Numbers 24:9, NRSV].) Before parting ways, Balaam foresaw a scepter and a star "out of Jacob" crushing all of Israel's enemies. It wouldn't be anytime soon, though, Balaam said, and Balak said the same thing about his payment.

Science

APPLE AND BRIE BAGUETTES

Keep me as the apple of your eye; hide me in the shadow of your wings.
PSALM 17:8

A word aptly spoken is like apples of gold in settings of silver.
PROVERBS 25:11

Strengthen me with raisins, refresh me with apples, for I am faint with love.
SONG OF SOLOMON 2:5

In medical school in Charlottesville, Virginia, I had a favorite restaurant that I liked to go to during exams. It was called Hot Cakes, and my friend Kate and I would go there for studying breaks. My favorite sandwich was the apple and brie, and I always got it with a side of ginger noodles.

One day I decided I could make it for myself. It is one of the "fresh" feeling foods. It goes great with a salad, and even is good for a late-spring picnic with strawberries.

Ingredients
1 baguette
1 Granny Smith apple, thinly sliced
1 wedge of Brie or one "wheel" of the mini Brie, thinly sliced (Brie
    should be room temperature)
honey Dijon mustard
salad greens or baby spinach

Now make the sandwich.
Cut the baguette lengthwise and into 6- to 8-inch segments (fourths). If desired, after cutting lengthwise, toast the baguette in the oven at 350° F for 4 minutes.

Spread dijon mustard on bottom of baguette and honey on the top slice.

Place some salad greens on the mustard side.

Layer apple slices and brie onto the baguette, each item stacked 1 inch high.

Serve with tossed salad, potato salad, fruit salad, or macaroni salad.

LH

IF YOU THINK IT'S HOT HERE . . .

He is patient with you, not wanting anyone to perish,
but everyone to come to repentance.
2 PETER 3:9

If You Think It's Hot Here, Imagine Hell. Ever spotted that cheery message on a church sign? When eighteenth-century preacher Jonathan Edwards pounded the pulpit during his legendary sermon "Sinners in the Hands of an Angry God," Christians had been using the fear of hell as a marketing cornerstone for approximately 17 centuries.

It's as potent a message as a marketer can give—use our merchandise or suffer the consequences—but when it comes to our walk with God, it's strangely ineffective. The popular picture of ever-burning hellfire paints God as a vindictive ogre, practically delighting in punishment. It's far from the loving Father Jesus came to show us, yet many Christians fear that without constantly renewing this threat people will grow careless.

The young Ellen White was raised to believe in "an eternally burning hell, where, after the tortures of thousands upon thousands of years, the fiery billows would roll to the surface the writhing victims, who would shriek: 'How long, O Lord, how long?' Then the answer would thunder down the abyss: 'Through all eternity!'" (*Testimonies*, vol. 1, p. 24). When her mother told her that she'd come to believe that God would simply destroy the unrepentant in a moment, Ellen struggled to accept the idea. She pondered to her mother that if the threat of eternal suffering were taken away, "sinners would gather security from this belief, and never desire to seek the Lord" (*ibid.*, p. 39).

Ellen's mother answered, "If this is sound biblical truth, instead of preventing the salvation of sinners, it will be the means of winning them to Christ. If the love of God will not induce the rebel to yield, the terrors of an eternal hell will not drive him to repentance. Besides, it does not seem a proper way to win souls to Jesus, by appealing to one of the lowest attributes of the mind, abject fear. The love of Jesus attracts; it will subdue the hardest heart" (*ibid.*, pp. 39, 40).

God wants us to come to Him because of love, not fear—drawn by His grace. The Bible assures us, "There is no fear in love. But perfect love drives out fear, because fear has to do with punishment" (1 John 4:18).

17 WAYS TO KISS / PART 1

How good and pleasant it is when [sisters] live together in unity!
PSALM 133:1

My sister and I are nothing alike. I was a puny little thing at birth. Cried a lot. Judye was born with roses in her cheeks and a happy smile. I saved her life when she was just old enough to crawl up on a chair and fall facefirst into a sinkful of water. She'd already turned blue by the time I tugged our mother's skirt and led her to the bathroom.

On my first day of school she begged to come too, but I informed her that big first-graders couldn't have little kids hanging around. Some weeks later she visited for the day. It went pretty well. I taught her the correct way to eat a sandwich—in little bites, straight down from the top—but when we walked to the door to go home, she *dropped her crayons.* It was a crime beyond belief. I died a thousand deaths while she carefully picked them up, sticking them one by one into the little flat box.

I went into second grade. She entered first. She learned to corral her crayons, but there were other embarrassments. Mainly she was smarter than I was. We spent grade school in multigrade classrooms, and inevitably had to call our grades aloud for the teacher to record. Most often hers were higher. It sort of hurt my pride, but then I never cared enough to study hard enough to change it. Besides, as I discovered much later, I learned through stories while her logical mind was much more adapted to how teachers taught.

At 16 I went away to boarding school. I'd spent the whole summer planning for the big event, working out details of dorm life with my chosen roommate while Judye looked on. No special trip to Sears for towels and washcloths for her. No carefully chosen bedspread and curtains. Not even as many new clothes. But two weeks later Judye came too. She'd been so miserable, so lonesome, that my folks brought her to join me. Not to actually join *me,* but to enjoy the relative freedom and fun of academy life.

Well, she had her friends, and I had mine. *Her* friends were silly and juvenile. No brains at all. And the guys she dated! The one that stuck out his tongue. The one that went to town to buy her toothache medicine. The one that, off campus, rolled a package of cigarettes in the sleeve of his T-shirt. She thought my friends were stuffy and snobbish. And the boys I dated . . . well, I didn't date all that much.
Continued.

PW

17 WAYS TO KISS / PART 2

There is a time for everything . . . a time to mourn and a time to dance.
ECCLESIASTES 3:1-4

At academy Judye was always in the middle of a gaggle of girls, their eyes rolling toward this guy or that. And she wasn't above hopping into a car with one of the village guys and going off for a short spin. Not me! I would have been terrified of being caught.

But we maintained a cheerful truce, keeping tabs on each other's lives but not hanging in the same crowd. She went down all by herself and got a job in the campus cabinet shop. I was impressed, even if they were a wild bunch—staple fights and all. I worked in the registrar's office. Sometimes it was my awkward duty to track down a chronic class skipper and haul them to the dean of students. Occasionally the principal asked me to escort a student to the dorm for what was, in effect, house arrest. I enjoyed my work—mostly typing and recordkeeping. Kids called me "Judye's bossy sister," but I just laughed. I didn't want to be like her and her crazy friends. That I and *my* friends could seem less than desirable never entered my mind.

Then she did it! She sent off for, and in due time received, a little booklet titled *Seventeen Ways to Kiss.* I didn't even know there were 17 (count them) ways to kiss. But Judye paid a solid dollar for the information, and because such news is too good to keep secret, she showed it to me. Naturally I read it. Hunched over, scared of being seen, I read on. The butterfly kiss—fluttering one's eyelashes against the cheek of one's beloved . . . the little peck at the corner of the mouth . . . a brush of lips across the forehead. Page after page this sweet little booklet painted romantic pictures of kisses. I read them all.

If we're lucky, with the passing of time comes tolerance. I learned that different didn't necessarily mean bad. That some of Judye's friends as well as mine grew into decent, loving, churchgoing adults. And some of my friends, as well as hers, became no-count, unfeeling slobs. Life has a way of leveling things out. We are much more alike as adults than we were growing up. We share the same values. I admire her sparkling personality. And, boy, can she throw a party! She's lots more fun than I am. I realize that I could have loosened up. It was foolish to enjoy my snobbery so much.

And besides, without her, never in a million years would I have learned 17 ways to kiss!

PW

Innovation

TALENTS

*To one he gave five talents of money, to another two talents,
and to another one talent, each according to his ability.*
MATTHEW 25:15

I always imagined the talents in Jesus' parable as little slabs of gold and silver. Maybe that's some sort of image implanted from Uncle Arthur or Sabbath school felts—who knows. In any event, I never really "got" talents, how they multiply and grow. In high school I barely recognized any talents in myself at all. Sure, I played the clarinet, but I'm sure no one would have minded if I'd buried that in the backyard (and it wouldn't have just been for safekeeping).

In the cult classic film *Napoleon Dynamite*, the title character intones, "Girls only want boyfriends who have great skills." Now, skills I understand. But do I have skills? I'm a doctor, which impresses people, but will my skills save anybody in the sense that really counts?

Or how about my cooking? As I experimented and progressed in cooking I noticed I was developing "hostess with the mostest" skills. From that I began to develop skills to put people at ease, which made me a better doctor. I guess talents do multiply.

What do you think your talent is?

_____

_____

_____

How do you show it?

_____

_____

_____

What keeps you from using it?

_____

_____

_____

How could it be multiplied into more talents?

_____

_____

_____

SABBATH CONTROVERSY

Blessed is the man who does this, the man who holds it fast, who keeps the Sabbath without desecrating it, and keeps his hand from doing any evil.

ISAIAH 56:2

By the time Jesus came to earth, religious leaders had added so many traditions to the Sabbath that its restful purpose had long been forgotten. Keeping the Sabbath became a burden in itself as the new rules went far beyond what God ever intended. Laws dictated how far a person could walk on the Sabbath. Laws said that if you buried food ahead of time at intervals, you could consider those places home and thus walk farther. They had laws about connecting homes with planks so that they'd be considered one house and you could carry food between them. Handkerchiefs could be sewn to your clothing so you wouldn't actually be carrying it. They even had laws prohibiting picking up a child on the Sabbath.

When Jesus called the Pharisees on their legalism for accusing Him of breaking the Sabbath by healing, He did not tell them the Sabbath was about to be canceled. Instead, He told them they had the wrong idea about it. He told them that the Sabbath was made for people's blessing, and not the other way around (Mark 2:27). God created the Sabbath to bless us. He gave us a day to rest from our work and to focus on Him, to remember His work of creation and, once Adam and Eve sinned, His work of redemption. Jesus would not have put so much effort into restoring the Sabbath's true meaning if He was just going to abolish or replace it. (The fact that the Gospels, written several decades after Jesus' resurrection, emphasize Jesus' Sabbath-keeping tells us that keeping it holy was still a major issue for its original Christian readers.)

Jesus also mentioned that the priests in the Temple "broke" the Sabbath every week by working. Did they really? Only by legalistic definitions. Their work of ministry had to be done, even on the Sabbath. Likewise, Jesus couldn't take the day off from His ministry. The work of salvation was more important than even the requirements of the Sabbath. Jesus uplifted the Sabbath as a day especially suited for helping others.

Jesus claimed the title Lord of the Sabbath, for He made the Sabbath and gave it to humans before they even sinned. He wants us to remember it—not legalistically as the Pharisees did, but as a day to experience joy in Him.

KS; TW

Bible

THE DEAD SEA SCROLLS

For out of Zion shall go forth instruction, and the word of the Lord from Jerusalem.
ISAIAH 2:3, NRSV

No one knows for certain how the Dead Sea scrolls were actually found. The most popular story tells about an Arab boy searching for a lost goat in 1947. Throwing a stone into a dark cave, he heard the sound of shattering pottery. Later he returned to see if the cave might have something valuable in it. Whatever his reason for entering the cave, the lad discovered one of the most important archaeological finds of the twentieth century.

The collection of scrolls scattered among several caves in the area known as Khirbet Qumran included both biblical and nonbiblical manuscripts. The 2,000-year-old documents contained at least parts of every book of the Old Testament except Esther. Scholars are especially interested in them because they are 1,000 years earlier than the manuscripts that Bible translators used until recently.

Before the invention of the printing press people had to copy books laboriously by hand. No matter how careful one is, though, errors still creep in. People wondered how accurate our Bibles could be after so many centuries of hand copying. Before the Dead Sea scrolls were found, the oldest Old Testament manuscripts were a little more than 1,000 years old. The Dead Sea scrolls, dating back to before Jesus was born, allowed scholars to see how much the biblical text might have changed during a 1,000-year period. While they did find some variations (such as spelling and word form and order), the Dead Sea scrolls were surprisingly close to the Masoretic text that most modern language versions of the Bible have been translated from. Those who copied Bible manuscripts down through the centuries had been extremely careful.

The Dead Sea scrolls not only testify to the reliability of our present Bible—they sometimes help us to understand things that puzzled us. For example, a Dead Sea copy of 1 Samuel contains a piece of the story of Nahash, king of the Ammonites, that got dropped out of the later Bible manuscripts. It explains that Nahash attacked Jabesh-gilead because 7,000 refugees from his earlier cruelty had fled there. The translators of the New Revised Standard Version of the Bible have placed the missing material after 1 Samuel 10:27 and before 1 Samuel 11:1.

GW

DOUGHNUTS AND DISCIPLINE

Therefore, since we are surrounded by such a great cloud of witnesses,
let us throw off everything that hinders and the sin that so easily entangles,
and let us run with perseverance the race marked out for us.
HEBREWS 12:1

I've never been an athlete. While my grade school friends counted down the hours till gym class, I thought of ways to get out of it. Most of my friends had soccer or softball practice after school, but I headed to the city library.

Being home-schooled made it possible to avoid PE for a while. Then I started high school. My high school had a strong guys-and-girls basketball team, golf, soccer, and cross country, and required four years of physical education. I fumbled through volleyball, fouled out in basketball, and struck out in softball.

And then there was the one-mile run. Our PE teacher trusted us to practice the one-mile run during two of the three PE classes a week. To pass the class, we had to run a mile in under seven minutes.

My friend Katye and I would walk—you know, a form of running—to the local doughnut store for an after-school snack or to the gas station for pop at least once a week. We figured, A mile in less than seven minutes? We were young and healthy. It'd be a piece of cake.

Then came Judgment day. I arrived on time, ready to roll. I stretched, lined up, and took off. *I got this,* I thought satisfactorily—for the first two minutes. I got a stomach cramp after the first four blocks, my breathing became labored, and my calf muscles began complaining. All those glazed doughnuts and Sunkist orange sodas were laughing at my every step.

God, please don't let me pass out . . .

As I approached the last four blocks I realized that I wasn't going to pass out but had absolutely no clue how I was doing on time. *God, carry me to the finish line . . .*

The last four blocks blurred. Someone called out "six minutes, 59 seconds." I coughed and tried not to vomit on the sidewalk.

One second to spare. One short mile that wouldn't have been such a death-defying feat if I hadn't swapped soda and doughnuts for dedication and discipline.

JD

spirit

SEX AND SELF

Just because something is technically legal doesn't mean that it's spiritually appropriate.
If I went around doing whatever I thought I could get by with,
I'd be a slave to my whims. You know the old saying, "First you eat to live,
and then you live to eat"? Well, it may be true that the body is only a temporary thing,
but that's no excuse for stuffing your body with food, or indulging it with sex.
Since the Master honors you with a body, honor him with your body!
1 CORINTHIANS 6:12, 13, MESSAGE

There's something missing in our lives, and we try to fill it with sex.

And why not? We're here because two people had sex in the first place. Our bodies are designed for it. Our brains are wired for it. Sex is thrilling, fun, and tantalizingly otherworldly.

And yet sex betrays us. As the Rolling Stones sang: "I can't get no satisfaction." Fulfillment is always just out of reach—and a good thing, too, or we might stop buying the media that tells us what's wrong and promises to fix us in three easy steps.

In *Rumors of Another World* Philip Yancey writes, "When a society loses faith in its gods, or God, lesser powers arise to take their place. Blocked longings seek new routes. 'Every man who knocks on the door of a brothel is looking for God,' said G. K. Chesterton. In modern Europe and the U.S., sex has a near-sacred quality of mythic, numinous power. We select our sexiest individuals and accord them the status of gods and goddesses, fawning over the details of their lives, broadcasting their bodily statistics, surrounding them with paparazzi, rewarding them with money and status. Sex no longer points to something beyond; it becomes the thing itself, the substitute sacred" (pp. 78, 79).

People wrestle with how to approach sex, and they soon find themselves tied up in knots. Conservatives who preach "personal responsibility," and who would never rationalize an enemy's attack on their country, nonetheless blame an abused woman for, in their opinion, flirting too much or showing too much skin—*she was asking for it.* And for all the lifesaving power of "safe sex," we trivialize our humanity if we ignore that whole persons are more than their sex-specific organs and addictions.

God designed sex and sexuality to enhance and inspire us, but it crumbles when mixed with that most ancient of sins—the love of self.

ANNA / PART 1

Dear friends, since God so loved us, we also ought to love one another.
1 JOHN 4:11

"Gentlemen—and I use the term loosely—"

Mr. Jackson, the Bible teacher at my Christian high school, called my senior Bible class to order. One of the more anticipated parts of the curriculum had arrived: the marriage project. I think Jackson claimed that real-life marriages had resulted from past classes, but I figured most of us knew each other too well for that.

Granted, it wasn't the most ambitious marriage project I'd seen— no Monopoly money or custody battles over crying robot babies. But it did make most of us think about the nitty-gritty reality of preparing for our futures, which surely did us some good. We quieted down, if only momentarily, to await the ceremonial reading of the spouses. With more girls than guys in the class, a little polygamy made that Bible class a bit more biblical than expected. I soon learned, though, that my virtual life would be strictly monogamous: "Tompaul Wheeler, you are betrothed to—Anna Brooks!"

Oh. Kay. We were a tight-knit class of about 45 students, many of us having attended all four high school years together, and some of us going back even further. Only a few had joined us that year, including Lynelle, who'd come all the way from England (we'd become instant friends), and Anna, who I'd barely interacted with at all.

Which is not to say anything bad about Anna. All I knew of her was that she was a quiet person who liked to read. But there was a picture of her on my parents' refrigerator. On a trip with her previous school, she'd ended up in the same group photo in England as my world-traveling oldest sister, so it seemed fateful enough.

One highlight of the project was a Monday morning breakfast prepared by the guys. I pitched in making waffles, while a couple guys went all out serving exquisite cuisine with crystal stemware, and the lazier ones brought cereal and milk. Prospective brides Kim and Veronica showed up in bathrobes with pillows stuffed under their shirts.

Together Anna and I plotted out our budgets, and I planned our virtual honeymoon to Costa Rica. We barely discussed the details, and I barely got to know Anna, except to confirm that she was just as nice, and quiet, as she seemed. When we turned in our final project, we thanked each other, and got our As. *Continued.*

ANNA / PART 2

Dear friend, I pray that you may enjoy good health
and that all may go well with you, even as your soul is getting along well.
3 JOHN 2

Our bus pulled out on a Saturday night, barreling down Interstate 95 toward Florida. The senior trip gave our class one more chance to make memories.

From the aquatic splashes of "the blob" and go-karting to Universal Studios theme park, waterslides, and a lazy inner-tube ride down some river, we all let loose for a week. Greg sang constantly. Heather got roasted by the sun at St. Augustine beach, and had to wear about nine inches of sunblock on her skin and carry an umbrella the rest of the trip. We annoyed the neighbors with one water fight showdown after another.

The memory of Anna that sticks out in my memory, though, is her sitting by herself outside the bus at the water park, reading a novel. We invited her to join us in the water, but she stuck with her book. Whatever floats your boat, as they say; or in this case, whatever doesn't.

After graduation weekend I didn't see most of my old classmates for years. I stayed in touch with a handful of my closest friends, and even went to college with my friend Tom out west in Walla Walla, Washington, but unfortunately, most of 'em left my radar. And none more so than Anna.

Which is why I got such a shock at our 10-year reunion.

"Hey, Tompaul! How are you?"

The sparkling young woman throwing her arms around me acted like she knew me, so I returned the embrace. Once we let go of each other, I said, "I'm good. How are you . . . Anna?"

"I'm doing great!" she said. She pointed to a yawning blond toddler in a stroller. "This is my little boy, Bobby."

We stood around and talked for a while. If I'd passed her on the sidewalk I wouldn't have recognized her. She was a new person, outgoing, funny, and out of her shell. I asked her why she'd made the long drive back to Maryland. "People weren't very friendly at my old school, just really snobby, so I decided to change schools my senior year. And you guys just welcomed me and were really friendly."

I'd had no idea.

THE MAGIC BULLET / PART 1

Do not forsake wisdom, and she will protect you;
love her, and she will watch over you.
PROVERBS 4:6

Education is the magic bullet.

The more education you have, the likelier you are to make better choices. You're more likely to have a successful marriage. And studies the world over have shown something particularly stunning: *the longer you stay in school, the longer you'll live.*

Check out some recent stats on American women under the age of 30 who gave birth. For women who had not graduated from high school, 62.2 percent of them were unmarried. If a woman had a high school diploma, the number dropped to 51.3 percent. If they had gone to college, the number plummeted to 12.6 percent. And if they'd earned a master's degree or higher, only 4.3 percent were unmarried when they gave birth.

Meanwhile, people who graduate are half as likely to divorce as high school dropouts. As Bill Belew writes: "Clearly, the more education a person has, the more likely it is they will have children *after* making a commitment to forming a family. . . not just reproducing."

Unfortunately, only about 25 percent of Americans over age 25 have a college degree. Imagine the difference if we could double or triple that. Prisons turned into parks. Crime rates dropping dramatically. And millions more children growing up in intact families.

The more education people experience, the healthier choices they make. This goes right along with stats that show that a teen whose parents both graduated from college is half as likely to engage in risk behavior (drugs, sex, etc.) as a teen whose parents did not graduate from high school. Education changes people.

Unfortunately, higher education doesn't come cheap. While the rate of college education has risen in the past few decades, marriage rates among the people who can't afford it have dropped. People with lower incomes often think they can't afford to marry, so they're far more likely just to live together.

And that bit about education increasing your life span? We'll look at that tomorrow. *Continued.*

THE MAGIC BULLET / PART 2

He who gets wisdom loves his own soul; he who cherishes understanding prospers.
PROVERBS 19:86

Doctoral student Adriana Lleras-Muney was trying to find a unique, unexplored topic to focus on for her economics degree dissertation. She ran across an old economics paper that suggested that as far as improving a society's overall health goes, it's smarter to spend money on education than medicine.

Finally she came up with the perfect way to test it. Around the 1890s certain states in America started requiring kids to attend school for more and more years. What would she find if she compared their census and health records?

"The idea was," Dr. Lleras-Muney later told reporter Gina Kolata ("A Surprising Secret to a Long Life: Stay in School," New York *Times*, Jan. 3, 2007), "when a state changed compulsory schooling from, say, six years to seven years, would the people who were forced to go to school for six years live as long as the people the next year who had to go for seven years?"

Digging up the data was no picnic, but the results were astonishing. For every extra year someone had attended school, their life expectancy at age 35 increased by as much as 18 months. Since Lleras-Muney's initial research in America, similar studies in other countries have shown the same results: more school equals a healthier life.

To make things even more impressive, the effect never diminished, but kept right on working as long as people stayed in school. Analysts were left to ponder why. Was it because, for instance, a lengthy education teaches delayed gratification?

Scientists can only guess at the ultimate reasons, but the significance is clear. They've also found another critical part of staying young: stay connected. When Harvard professor Lisa Berkman was a graduate student, she studied Seventh-day Adventists, long known for their exceptional health. Their vegetarian diet was considered key, but she noticed that they were less likely to get ill from things that had nothing to do with diet—and they aged slower than most people. The reason, she concluded? They're socially connected.

She might also have noted that for many years Adventists have strongly emphasized education.

INSIDER/OUTSIDER

By faith the prostitute Rahab, because she welcomed the spies,
was not killed with those who were disobedient.
HEBREWS 11:31

Maybe the Holy Spirit told them where to go, and it just took them awhile to catch on. Maybe the two spies could have cared less about their reputations. Maybe they thought they'd go to a place so often visited by men that no one would think twice about two strangers walking through its door. For whatever reason the two spies landed at the home of Rahab, a prostitute in Jericho, they were going to be glad they had.

When the rumor reached Jericho's ruler that the fearsome Israelites were scoping out their very city, he demanded that Rahab turn the guys in. But she was no fool. She'd heard the stories about the miracles and victories the Israelites had enjoyed in their sweep across the land, and she knew that as thick as Jericho's walls might be, they were ripe for Yahweh's wrath. She told Jericho's authorities that, sure, she'd seen those spies, but they were long gone—so hurry up and track 'em down.

Of course, the spies were hiding under the straw on Rahab's roof. She tried to level with them. "I know that the Lord has given this land to you and that a great fear of you has fallen on us, so that all who live in this country are melting in fear because of you," she said. "We have heard how the Lord dried up the water of the Red Sea for you when you came out of Egypt, and what you did to Sihon and Og, the two kings of the Amorites east of the Jordan, whom you completely destroyed. When we heard of it, our hearts melted and everyone's courage failed because of you, for the Lord your God is God in heaven above and on the earth below" (Joshua 2:9-11). She begged them to save her life and that of her family, and asked for a sign that they would do so.

The spies looked at each other. With faith like this, the Israelites would have been enjoying honey milk shakes in Canaan decades ago. "Our lives for your lives!" they vowed (verse 14), promising to return for her if she'd keep her lips sealed.

A few weeks later trumpets blasted, walls fell, and Rahab hung a scarlet cord from her room on the city wall so Israel's soldiers would know where to spare her. And thus the ultimate outsider became an insider, marrying an Israelite and becoming an ancestor of Jesus, all because two spies cared more for people than for reputations.

HEALTHIER THAN EVER?

*Dear friend, I pray that you may enjoy good health
and that all may go well with you, even as your soul is getting along well.*
3 JOHN 2

In the 1860s 5 percent of Americans suffered from paralysis. Today, scarcely 1 percent do. In 1850 the average American man stood 5 feet, 7.4 inches and weighed 147 pounds. Today's average height is a full two inches taller—and thanks to our less physically active lifestyles the average man weighs 191 pounds.

In the 1800s a person had a 48 percent chance of living to age 60. Today the chance is nearly 90 percent. In the 1800s people could expect ailments such as heart disease or arthritis to strike as early as their 30s. Today such conditions don't appear until decades later (Gina Kolata, "So Big and Healthy Grandpa Wouldn't Even Know You," New York *Times*, July 30, 2006).

This book has told quite a few stories about early Adventists, but what always gets me in those tales is how much they accomplished despite such wretched health. The Whites lost two of their four sons— one in infancy, the other at age 16 from pneumonia. People were constantly catching cholera, diphtheria, tuberculosis . . . you name it. They accepted stress, pain, loss, and grief as a normal part of everyday life.

When the American Civil War broke out, 80 percent of males in the Union States tried to join the army. Of that group, 13 percent were rejected for health reasons. "And the Union Army was not very picky," Kolata writes. "'Incontinence of urine alone is not grounds for dismissal,' said Dora Costa, an MIT economist . . . quoting from the regulations. A man who was blind in his right eye was disqualified from serving because that was his musket eye. But, Dr. Costa said, 'blindness in the left eye was OK'" (*Ibid.*).

Healthier diets. Antibiotics. Many more years of education. Vaccines. And when you reach adulthood without having early childhood diseases (and their untold long-term effects), your body doesn't come down with chronic diseases as early or often as those who had the diseases. You're even, studies have shown, less likely to get cancer.

Science has added decades of healthy years to our lives. How you spend them, and whether you want to live forever, is up to you.

PREMATURE AUTOPSY

He replied: "Watch out that you are not deceived. For many will come in my name, claiming, 'I am he,' and, 'The time is near.' Do not follow them."
LUKE 21:8

The *Weekly World News* calls itself the world's only reliable newspaper. With headlines such as "Bigfoot Tracks Indicate Salsa Lessons [the creature's footprints reveal mastery of the spot turn, open break, and enchufla—ballroom-mambo style]" and "God's To-Do List Revealed," as well as regular updates on fang-toothed, winged-eared Bat Boy, and which politicians are having dinner with space aliens, it covers news that other publications won't touch—because they're not willing to just make crazy stuff up. Their off-the-wall stories are designed to make you laugh, raise your eyebrows, and think, *Well, maybe it's true . . .*

One week, though, the real world caught the tabloid off guard. Visiting my sister in New York, I spotted a checkout-line headline that didn't take faith or even common sense to know was a lie. That week's tabloid cover proclaimed a world exclusive: "DEAD McVEIGH ON MORGUE SLAB!" The face of a man similar to the decorated Gulf-War-veteran-turned-Oklahoma-City-bomber rested his apparently lifeless eyes next to the headline.

Thing was, Timothy McVeigh's original date of execution had been pushed back a month, and the terrorist was still alive. The publishers had counted on McVeigh stopping breathing by the time their paper hit the grocery stores, but the slow-grinding wheels of the justice system had thwarted their hoax.

Before His crucifixion, Jesus warned His disciples to beware of similar trickery and chicanery in the world's last days. People would claim to be Him, or that they knew where He was, somewhere on the earth. Don't buy it, Jesus said, because I will come back the same way I left—in the sky. If someone says Jesus is making an early appearance, they're just trying to make a buck.

Recently on the Internet I saw a guy who says that one day late in life he realized that, what do you know, he's Jesus. Then I saw all the bodyguards he pays to surround himself. Since when does Jesus need a bodyguard, or luxury cars and houses? Which just goes to show that if you don't want to be deceived about Jesus, you need to know the real deal.

NO ONE UNDERSTANDS

For we do not have a high priest who is unable to sympathize with our weaknesses, but we have one who has been tempted in every way, just as we are—yet was without sin.
HEBREWS 4:15

Ever thought that no one understands you? Well, the truth is: No one really understands you. It's true. You can marry the love of your life; you may have a great pastor or even an awesome understanding friend. But no one on this planet really, truly knows you.

You try to communicate something, but it's misinterpreted. Your ideas slam against the pavement of public opinion, and don't seem as strong as you know they are. That spark of brilliance in your head comes out flapping around like a widemouthed bass on concrete. No one understands you, the real person inside, your intent.

Now imagine how the Son of God felt. In the Garden of Gethsemane He needed time to pray and prepare Himself as the sacrificial lamb that dissolves sin for all eternity. He asked His disciples to pray for Him and to stay up with Him. These men saw Him heal the incurable, raise the dead, and even control the weather. You'd think they would understand that when Jesus asked them to be with Him, He was desperate. Instead, they napped it out while He roiled with the pain of being separated from God. Going back to His friends, He found them snoozing, and said to Peter, "Simon, are you sleeping? Could you not watch one hour?" (Mark 14:37, NKJV). Jesus wasn't mad, but He was disappointed. We can imagine Him asking, "Don't you get it? Don't you understand Me?"

Most of Jesus' followers misunderstood Him. Sound familiar? But here's where things pick up. You now have an advocate who actually understands you. In fact, He's gone through the same things. When you feel isolated, know that He's been through it already. Have you ever felt alone, rejected, or let down? Jesus knows how it is.

Here's where it gets really interesting. Once you know that Jesus understands you, you'll begin to understand people yourself. Jesus is all about relationships. And after establishing a firm base with Him, starting the same relationship with others comes naturally.

You may stop seeing yourself as the person nobody understands and become the person who understands everybody. You're not just being yourself; you're being the person in Christ being yourself. That makes a huge difference in who you are, or how you are understood.

BP

INTERCESSORY PRAYER

*Pray also for me, that whenever I open my mouth, words may be given me
so that I will fearlessly make known the mystery of the gospel. . . .
Pray that I may declare it fearlessly, as I should.*
EPHESIANS 6:19, 20

The phone rang, and I impatiently lifted the receiver. It was a
friend—with a problem. A big problem that I didn't have time to hear.
I listened, of course, as her words ran together and she began crying.
The situation seemed hopeless. There was nothing I could do for her.
Actually, I couldn't think of anything that could be done for her. Well,
there was one thing, but I didn't want to do it. I didn't have time to do
it. I didn't *feel* like doing it. But finally I drew a deep breath and asked,
"Do you want me to pray for you?"

I'll never forget her answer. "Oh, *yes!*" she cried. "Yes!"

So I took a deep breath. "Dear God, we don't know the answer. We
can't see any solution. But You do. You can. We put this in Your hands."

Praying calmed and blessed me at least as much as it did her.

From Moses interceding with God for the rebellious children of
Israel to Paul repeatedly asking Christian friends to pray for him
(Ephesians 6:19; Colossians 4:3, 4; Hebrews 13:18, 19), the Bible tells
us to pray for each other. And here's the catch: we should pray especially for people who seem the most distant from God. People who ag-
gravate us. People who think they don't need God. People who think
they're God's gift to Planet Earth, but who you really wish had stayed
home. And people who need the help that only God can give.

Our witnessing gets off course when we try to do the Holy Spirit's
job—convincing people to believe and act as we think they should.
Our job is to do what Jesus did here on earth—love people, set a good
example, and pray, pray, pray.

Prayer is powerful. A few minutes ago a friend I hadn't heard from
in a while e-mailed to say he was praying for me. It meant more to me
than he could know. But even beyond the good feeling, God loves using
our prayers to bless other people. Somehow prayer enables the Holy
Spirit to impact people in new ways. God never forces Himself on us,
but because He's chosen to reach others through us, He uses our
prayers as a supernatural way to touch people. James 5:15, 16, says,
"And the prayer offered in faith will make the sick person well; the Lord
will raise him up. If he has sinned, he will be forgiven. Therefore confess your sins to each other and pray for each other so that you may be
healed. The prayer of a righteous man is powerful and effective."

Innovation

WHAT DO YOU WANT TO BE?

We have different gifts, according to the grace given us.
ROMANS 12:6

My age: 20. My class: college junior. My problem: I was still ambling through college, having not yet decided what I wanted to be when I grew up. A freshman encounter with home economics classes introduced me to microbiology, and I was hooked. I took so many "ologies" that I ended up with a second major in biology. But those classes were for fun; they had little to do with preparing myself for a career. Then, because I'd always liked to write, I took as many writing classes as I could.

The problem was that in the midsixties there were few career options for women, at least among the people I knew. Secretary. Nurse. Teacher. I'd be a terrible secretary. Nursing didn't interest me. Teaching? Well, OK. So I finally settled on elementary ed, and got my tardy self graduated.

Today it's the large number of options that make settling on a career difficult. Recently I heard an interesting question: Can the Bible help you choose a career? My answer would be yes, in a broad sense, as you draw on texts about the value of hard work and the importance of integrity. More to the point is to consider such things as your interests, abilities, and the kinds of things that excite you. Then ask God to open your mind to the possibilities and go for it with the assurance that "God will be with you wherever you go" (Joshua 1:9).

Today most people change careers three times. As for me, I loved teaching elementary school. I was crazy about my kids, and I incorporated my own interests into the curriculum. I created a unit on Harriet Tubman, for instance, and taught the kids the fascinating beauty inside leaves and stems, and the importance of healthful choices because of what they do to your blood and brain. Then when I stopped teaching, I started writing stories, which led to writing books, which led to writing Sabbath school lessons, which led to . . . lots more writing!

Eventually I rejoined the actual work force, this time as an editor. Over the years I organized a half dozen writers' workshops, and have taught creative writing more times than I can remember. Guess what! All those classes I took paid off—as I used both my writing skills and my teaching skills to teach people how to write.

What should you be when you grow up? Ask God to lead, and use your common sense. It's a winning combination.

PW

JAMES WHITE

O God, from my youth you have taught me, and I still proclaim your wondrous deeds.
PSALM 71:17, NRSV

James White, the middle of nine siblings, was a sickly child. At the age of 2 or 3 he came down with what someone at the time diagnosed as "worm fever." Whatever the condition, it caused seizures, and he was sick for weeks. After he recovered he suffered from crossed eyes. Family members described him as a feeble, nervous, and partially blind child.

When James was 7, he accompanied his brothers to the primitive local school. But, whether because of vision difficulties, dyslexia, or some other problem, he seemed unable to learn to read. He said that the letters of printed words seemed to blur together in his vision. Frustrated, and concluding that he would always remain illiterate, he left school to work on his family's farm.

But as the years went by, his eyesight improved, and while James had dropped out of school he had not lost a desire to learn. Finally, at age 19 and six feet tall, he enrolled as a beginning student at a boarding school in St. Albans, Maine. He towered over his young classmates, but he was determined to learn, and though many advised him to stick to farming, he studied up to 18 hours a day. Twelve weeks later he received a certificate that allowed him to teach elementary grade subjects. Wanting more education, the next year he enrolled for a three-month term at a Methodist Episcopal school in Reedfield, Maine. Altogether he had only 41 weeks of formal education.

James White had hoped to start college the next year. But he reluctantly gave that up to become a Millerite preacher. And he never did get a chance to attend college. What could he possibly accomplish with so limited an education?

God can do marvelous things with any life devoted to Him. White continued to study on his own, and God used him to begin four journals, two publishing houses, and a college that eventually became Andrews University. He organized the Seventh-day Adventist Church, served as its president, and wrote countless periodical articles and several books. The Adventist Church is what it is today because of his intellect and drive.

GW

Bible

CIRCLE OF ERROR

The angel of the Lord went up from Gilgal to Bokim and said,
"I brought you up out of Egypt and led you into the land
that I swore to give to your forefathers.
I said, 'I will never break my covenant with you,
and you shall not make a covenant with the people of this land,
but you shall break down their altars.' Yet you have disobeyed me."
JUDGES 2:1, 2

One would think that people rescued from slavery, protected through a generation in the wilderness, and swept into power in a land they'd never known would stick with the winning formula. One would think they'd be so grateful for every incredible thing their God had done for them that they'd work every day, or at least on alternate Tuesdays, to make sure their God got the props.

One would be wrong.

Once the Israelites had conquered a bit of Canaan, they started getting complacent. It seemed easier—and much more profitable—to tax their new neighbors instead of driving them out, as God had requested. But that was far from God's plan. God had promised to give them the entire planet if they'd just stay faithful to Him. Canaan would have been just the beginning:

"The Lord will drive out all these nations before you, and you will dispossess nations larger and stronger than you. Every place where you set your foot will be yours: Your territory will extend from the desert to Lebanon, and from the Euphrates River to the western sea. No man will be able to stand against you. The Lord your God, as he promised you, will put the terror and fear of you on the whole land, wherever you go" (Deuteronomy 11:23-25).

But instead of trusting in the God who'd gotten them so far already, the Israelites trusted in their own get-rich-quick schemes. From idol worship to compromising with the Canaanites, they neglected God until He gradually withdrew His blessing and protection—and the people they should have conquered, defeated them instead.

That would finally get their attention, so they'd remember their old God and beg for His help. So God raised up people like Deborah, Barak, Gideon, and Samson to come to their rescue, until people got lazy all over again.

MEXICAN CORN BREAD

They devoted themselves . . . to the fellowship, to the breaking of bread and to prayer.
ACTS 2:42

I come from a long line of letter writers. My mother wrote daily letters home from college. When all of my sibs were scattered, my aunt wrote a biweekly update that always left me laughing. My grandmother wrote frequent letters to my mother, and in 1969 one such letter (which included the story of a family mishap and her comment, "It's a bad scene, just a bad scene") contained the recipe I share here. "You'll say this is the best thing you've had in years," she wrote. "It is delicious, hot or cold, for supper or breakfast." A new family favorite was born.

Here's how you make it.
Thoroughly mix the following ingredients together to form batter:
1 cup cornmeal
2 eggs
1/21 cup milk
1/2 cup flour
1/2 cup oil
1/2 tsp. baking soda
3/4 tsp. salt
1 can creamed corn

Pour half of the batter into a 9" by 13" pan.

Now you need: 1 can vegetarian burger, 1 onion (chopped),
4 jalapeño peppers (diced), and 8 oz. grated cheese.
Brown the **vegetarian burger** in a skillet, and layer over the batter.
Over that layer, add **chopped onion** and **jalapeño peppers** (if desired)
Sprinkle with the **grated cheese**, and cover with remaining batter.
Bake at 450°F for 25-30 minutes or until done.
My family has served this at lots of potlucks and lots of family meals.
If you like Mexican food—and maybe even if you don't—you'll like this.

WHAT'S IN A NAME?

The nations will see your righteousness, and all kings your glory;
you will be called by a new name that the mouth of the Lord will bestow.
ISAIAH 62:2

When I was 4, my 11-year-old sister had a cat she named Princess. That made no sense to me. After all, as I helpfully pointed out: "He's a boy!" I suggested another name I thought far more fitting: Stick Bean.

A year later my family moved from Tennessee to Maryland, from four acres of deep woods (where my dad had built for us a barn-shaped treehouse complete with its own electricity) to a former woods turned D.C. suburb. I hated this move even more than the winter we spent in Michigan that put me in a hospital for a week with asthma. When my dad introduced me to his new coworkers, he'd say, "Tell them your name."

I'd shake my head. "No name," I always said, then more emphatically, "No name!"

A few months later I decided, having rejected (thanks to the move) the nickname my parents had imposed upon my first name, to go by my middle name instead: Tompaul. Somehow it worked for me.

Baby names go in waves. Parents have taken names from classic novels, soap operas, and famous people. It's part fad, part competition, as people try to nab a name before their friends and family do. When I was in grade school, except for my buddy Matthew, almost none of my classmates had biblical names. I never played kickball with a Judah, Noah, or Mephibosheth. Today biblical names are wildly popular again. Why? I have no idea. Maybe people like their Internet-surfing, cell phone-packing preschoolers to have something classic and timeless about them.

Reading the Bible, we see that God liked to give people new names that He found more fitting, names that told how much God valued them and how much potential lived inside each one. Abram becomes Abraham: father of many nations. Sarai becomes Sarah: mother of multitudes. Jacob becomes Israel: the striver. The disciple Simon becomes Peter: the rock. What's in a name? The Bible suggests that in the world to come God will give each of us a new name—a name without stigma, a name that's both classic and eternal. A name proclaiming that our broken relationship with God is at last fully restored.

SKIPPING SABBATH SCHOOL

I will instruct you and teach you in the way you should go.
PSALM 32:8

I loved my junior Sabbath school—until it all went downhill.

With Ms. Jay as our teacher, Sabbath school was fun, energetic, playful, and colorful. Ms. Jay made Sabbath school the highlight of our week. We laughed, we learned, and we loved it. She made sure we learned that God loved us and that there was nothing we could do to change that. As I once heard Ms. Jay say, "You can't fool kids," and she never tried. She never talked down to us. And as she was heard to say, "If something doesn't work, I say, 'Ooooh-kay. We'll do something else.'"

I brought my camera to class and photographed blindfolded classmates guessing objects placed in their hands. Ms. Jay's teenage daughter brought the injured bird she was nursing back to health for us to see and learn from.

But just to prove that good things don't last forever, Ms. Jay retired from teaching us, and suddenly I dreaded going to class each Sabbath. We went from one teacher to several, each one of them wildly out of touch with the junior psyche.

The new teachers tried to ram religion down our throats. They discussed obscure theological points that had nothing to do with our lives. When we sat silently, staring at our hands, hoping not to be called on (as opposed to eagerly jumping in, as we had when Ms. Jay taught us), one teacher would zoom his long, bony index finger at a chosen student, demanding that they speak.

And finally I'd had enough. I informed my parents I'd come back to Sabbath school at some later date. For now, I'd spend my hour with my headphones and some choice reading material in the church lobby, or, depending on how the mood struck me on a given morning, the back seat of the car. And my parents said OK.

They didn't try to reason with me or convince me. They didn't tell me I needed to be in class. They just trusted me to make my own choices for my spiritual health. A few months later a class leader apologized, and asked if I'd consider coming to class again. I did, and things went better. Shortly thereafter I moved on to earliteen class, and enjoyed another fantastic Sabbath school teacher who loved us just the way we were. And I was ever grateful that my parents let me make my faith my own.

Mission

NOTES FROM A NATIVE

I have become all things to all men so that by all possible means I might save some.
1 CORINTHIANS 9:22

Growing up in Guam meant that although I was American, I was a foreigner to a lot of people from the States. I was raised to understand and respect the 10 predominant nationalities on the island. I grew up assuming that all North American teens had the same cultural knowledge I'd learned. But just in case, if you plan to be a student missionary, this is what you should know.

First, we are also children of God. True, we may not necessarily know that. Some may not even know this "Jesus." I might have traditional views that may seem thoroughly strange. Please do not assert your beliefs as correct and demean our beliefs in front of us. That just drives a wedge between us from the get-go. It didn't work for the Spaniards; it's not going to work for you. Why not try that "love and service" Jesus used?

Yes, we may have Western toilets, but it does not mean that everyone here grew up with them. Some may not have customs such as keeping track of and celebrating birthdays. Please don't try to celebrate them unless the person has an interest in it. Otherwise, you'll end up with a roomful of confused kids. Hey, here's a thought. Why not study up a bit on the people that you are going to be with? Consider having a local give you some pointers.

Don't congregate only with other missionaries. It's cliquish. You came pretty far to work with us, so why not follow through? We don't bite. Keeping in our own groups breaks down the community we could be building around a relationship in Christ.

Stop acting leary of us locals. Honestly, it freaks us out. It's hard for me to open up to you when you're still preoccupied about whether my ancestors were cannibals. They might very well have been. But don't encourage that urge in me by acting scared when I'm around. By the way, everyone has machetes here; it's called a garden tool. If your backyard consisted of old growth forest, you'd understand.

Lose your label-lust. You may think we're impressed by your knowledge of American brand names, but we've got other things on our mind, such as avoiding impetigo, managing typhoons, and earning a livable wage. Show us Psalm 96:3: "Declare his glory among the nations, his marvelous deeds among all peoples." We need to hear the message. We need to see you living and doing what you are declaring. Thanks.

BP

VIVE LA DIFFÉRENCE

*There is neither Jew nor Greek, slave nor free, male nor female,
for you are all one in Christ Jesus.*
GALATIANS 3:28

E Pluribus Unum: Out of many, one. The Latin phrase is one of America's mottoes, and makes a great goal for the body of Christ, too. But does unity mean uniformity? Should our religion make us all alike?

Whether it's race, culture, or age, we're too often uninterested in anything that doesn't match our tastes, our outlook, our experiences. And while there's no rule that says I have to enjoy bluegrass as much as I enjoy R & B, everybody loses when we're antagonistic to something simply because it's not what we're used to. The dividing lines between people are perhaps no more stark than those between different cultures and ethnic backgrounds, the lines distorted by presumptions and presuppositions.

Reflecting specifically on racial issues, hip-hop musical artist Toby Mac says, "I understand philosophically what people mean when they say they're color blind, but I think what we really need is to learn to appreciate each other's cultures, the colors of our skin, the differences each of us brings to a group of people.

"Let me put it another way. Would I want to say that Black gospel shouldn't exist anymore because we should come together? No, 'cause that's a rich tradition that I enjoy and I love. Those differences are what make us beautiful together. Not pretending we're all alike, but embracing the fact that we all have different shades of skin, and we feel and respond to things differently. I think there's a time when we even have to be willing to have the kinds of conversations where we're asking questions of one another that, in the short run, can stir up feelings of anger and bitterness . . . sometimes you have to stir that up before the healing begins" (*CCM Magazine,* May 2007).

Vive la differénce! The French phrase means "Long live the difference!" I find nothing more tragic as I travel than to find that everything's become homogenized, paved and glossed over, and that the view from my hotel is no different than the view from any street corner at home. Where's the fun in that? Whether caused by age, taste, or culture, our differences should be celebrated, embraced, and appreciated. As long as we respect and uplift each other, it's good to be different—because God's character and personality is too vast to be reflected in just one uniform brand.

Adventism

THE ORIGINAL
WHEELER-DEALER / PART 1

A generous person will be enriched.
PROVERBS 11:25, NRSV

James White not only founded much of the Seventh-day Adventist Church, but helped support it financially during his lifetime. He donated $100 to this project, $500 to another, $1,000 to something else. In addition to church projects, he helped widows and struggling ministers, and gave down payments to people needing to buy homes. Each year he contributed thousands of dollars during a period of American history when the average income was $300 to $500 a year. Where did he get all that money?

It certainly wasn't from his salary as editor of the *Review and Herald* or as president of the General Conference. In 1881 James wrote his son Willie that for the past two years he had not even collected his pay as editor. But God blessed James with a talent for making money that he then used to support the Lord's cause.

White personally sold Bibles and other religious books and used his earnings to keep the church's first publishing house afloat. He bought the inventory of a stationery store during the Civil War for $1,200, used part of it at the Review and Herald Publishing Association, and sold the rest for $2,400, and he showed a real skill with real estate. For several years he ran a plant nursery with the help of his sons. Later he acted as agent between the denomination's two publishing associations and different paper manufacturing companies. But perhaps the most interesting project occurred when he lived for a time in Texas.

A number of Adventists had moved to northern Texas, but unfortunately they were soon struck with malaria, which was still common there. Unable to work, they faced starvation. When James White heard of their plight, he decided to aid them.

Calling on his entrepreneurial skills, he bought buffalo and wildcat skins, shipped them northeast at a profit, and purchased Michigan butter, nuts, beans, and other items that he sold in Texas for more profit. Then James discovered that he could buy mules for $80 each in Texas and sell them for $200 each in Colorado. He decided to collect a herd of mules and ponies and organize a wagon train to take the ill church members to Colorado's healthier climate. *Continued.*

GW

THE ORIGINAL
WHEELER-DEALER / PART 2

Do not be like a horse or a mule, without understanding,
whose temper must be curbed with bit and bridle.
PSALM 32:9, NRSV

James White hired someone to buy the mules for his expedition to Colorado and bring them to a corral in Denison, Texas, until he could start the drive north. Unfortunately, the animals escaped and fled across the rolling plains. A young minister from Iowa, Arthur G. Daniells, tracked them down. Daniells would later become the longest serving General Conference president. Perhaps rounding up the mules gave him practice for dealing with difficult people as church leader.

The first group of 15 Adventists started from Dallas in two heavily loaded wagons, two two-seated wagons, and the Whites' family carriage. Two days later they arrived at Denison, where they met the others. But problems delayed them. One man came down with food poisoning—from eating bear—and flooding along the Red River blocked their crossing. Finally, because the Whites planned to speak at a May 15 camp meeting in Emporia, Kansas, they had no choice but to get going. The 30 Adventists in their eight wagons and the Whites' carriage headed 45 miles upriver to where they could haul the mules and wagons to the Indian Territory (Oklahoma) side on a pole-propelled ferry. Once across the river, the wagons had to hurry to avoid getting trapped in quicksand.

The mule drive struggled with broken-down wagons, cloudbursts that flooded rivers, sickness, accidents, and other delays. At dark the wagons formed a circle with the horses to protect them from marauders. Armed guards took two-hour shifts all night. They knew that White men sometimes hired Indians to stampede the herds crossing the Oklahoma territory.

Despite the hardships, for James the trip was a dream come true. He was getting to be a real cowboy. His wife, Ellen, wrote to her family that "Father rides horseback a considerable part of the time. . . . He is enjoying the journey much." In fact, he had told his family that he planned "this long, slow journey to save [prevent] a breakdown and improve health."

James White needed the break from his arduous responsibilities. Everyone needs a change of pace. *Continued.*

GW

THE ORIGINAL
WHEELER-DEALER / PART 3

Then they were glad because they had quiet,
and he brought them to their desired haven.
PSALM 107:30, NRSV

James White's mule drive to Colorado was no picnic. Many of the Adventists were still suffering from the malaria they had contracted in Texas. One man, James Cornell, had been so sick that the others felt it would be best if they left him behind. When someone told him what they had decided, Cornell replied in a raspy whisper, "You can dig a hole and bury me by the side of the road as easy as they can in Texas." After thinking about it, the members of wagon train agreed to take him.

Ellen White and her assistant, Marian Davis, were in charge of feeding everyone. "No rest, not a bit of it, for poor Marian," Mrs. White later wrote to her daughter-in-law Mary White. "We have worked like slaves. We cooked repeatedly half the night, Marian the entire night. . . . Unpack and pack, hurry, cook, set table, has been the order of the day." Not only did Ellen do cooking, she also had to find whatever she could to stretch their limited supplies. Early in the morning she'd go out to pick wild strawberries and greens.

Because of the many delays, James White decided to send a message to Battle Creek, Michigan, telling church leaders that he and Ellen would not get to Emporia, Kansas, in time to preach at the camp meeting. But when he learned from the next issue of the *Review* that Kansas had postponed camp meeting a week, he thought he might make it there by the new date. When they reached a railroad line in Kansas, he and Ellen had less than an hour to unload and catch a train. At Emporia they hired a coach and raced to the campground.

Ellen had lost 12 pounds. "I am worn and feel as though I was about one hundred years old," she wrote to Mary White. "This journey has nearly killed me."

That same day James also sent a letter to his children and reported that his health was the best it had been in four years. He felt so much better that he decided to speak at even more camp meetings than he had planned previously for that year.

Two days after the Whites arrived, the rest of the wagon train reached the campground. When the camp meeting ended, the wagon train continued on to Colorado, where its members found work, and their health soon improved in the mountain climate.

GW

YOU CAN HANDLE THE TRUTH

"There is so much more I want to tell you, but you can't bear it now."
JOHN 16:12, NLT

You want to think you are ready, but you aren't. Some people can barely spell the word "eternity," much less have a faint concept of it. You may think you've got a full handle of the gospel and all the deeper intrinsic truths. There is a truckload of realization yet to be dumped on you.

The cross is just a pair of beams with a person nailed to it. Thieves, rebels, terrorists, and martyrs all fell victim to this punishment. And for most, this process took days, not hours.

You see a body impaled on a cross. It's a Passion play, a stunt with an actor in full beard and sandals. You're seeing just a picture of a picture. You'll see only the surface of broken skin and a worn body.

Meanwhile, we don't realize the awesome pain of Jesus drawing all the evil in the world into His body. Neither you nor I could handle that. So forget the beatings, Via Dolorosa, and the crown of thorns. Those were just the pathetic attempts of men trying to belittle a Man with far greater things on his mind—such as making sure you get home.

Here's the truth: you may mess up today and either hurt others or yourself. You may not even know it. Something you did a while ago will impact others today. It will cause pain. It may even come back sometime in the future. Now take that wickedness and combine it with all the other days of your sin-speckled life.

Think of the thousands of days, the millions of minutes, that you have lost to feeling the misery of sin. Now multiply that feeling by everyone who has ever lived.

Getting the picture yet? Next, take that massive pile of sin and try to imagine a human mind having to process it all. Seem unbearable? It is. All of this was rammed through your Savior while He was stuck on that cross. And that's what took His life that gray afternoon.

Sometimes I wonder how we are going to be able to sing all those praises in heaven. Could it be that when we eventually realize the truth of our salvation, the only way to express how we feel will be to start singing?

BP

life

DEAL WITH IT

I have no peace, no quietness; I have no rest, but only turmoil.
JOB 3:26

It was just as Mom and I had planned—a full house for my graduation party, sparkling with balloons, music, cake, good food, and my favorite people. All but one: my mom. She lay in the hospital with a fever no one could explain, a potentially deadly reaction to chemotherapy. I mingled and mixed, but deep down I just wanted to cancel the party and crawl under my covers.

Mom was the one who made the family run smoothly. Everything just seemed to fall in place—until the one day it didn't. When I was 17 my mom was diagnosed with breast cancer, and suddenly everything in my life changed. My mom wasn't my mother anymore. The one who comforted me needed comforting. She was afraid, afraid she would die from breast cancer, as her mother had died.

Things changed for me at school as well. Instead of rallying around me, my friends didn't know what to do, and many became distant. Eventually some friends grew even closer, and I found a new routine, one with more responsibility and that required me to become an adult. I still went out at night, hung out downtown with friends, and went shopping at the mall. But at home I fixed meals and helped my brothers with their schoolwork. I applied to several colleges, but I still had a safety school at home, just in case the worst happened. It looked as though I was handling it all very well, except I wasn't.

I dealt with all the details while not recognizing the problem. Instead of crying and dealing with my fear of losing my mom, I dealt with getting my brothers to school on time. I never talked to my friends, parents, brothers, or even God about my fears, hopes, and dreams. I became totally self-reliant. Isn't that what we're supposed to do?

The Bible's book of Job is the quintessential "Why do bad things happen to good people?" story. But underneath all of the lamenting we find hints on how to deal with tragedy. Job took time to mourn in silence, but he was willing to talk about it. He talked to his wife and his friends about his troubles. Granted, neither were particularly helpful, but he talked. Finally Job took it up with God. They worked it out together.

So when life deals you lemons, don't make lemonade. Instead, give God a call and see if He thinks you should make lemon pasta. I am sure He would give you a hand.

LH

OWKWA'S ANGEL / PART 1
Ask and it will be given to you; seek and you will find.
LUKE 11:9

"Great Spirit, show me how to make my people good."

Time and time again the chief prayed. While his village in a remote region of British Guiana slept and the night animals prowled, the chief begged the only god he knew for wisdom to change the lives of the people under his care into something different from those of other tribes.

It was a wild, undeveloped country, dangerous in a thousand ways. In the 1880s people still lived in fear of the spirits, though often calling upon them for help. Murder was simple. From a swift poison dart shot from a blowgun to a potent poison brewed from insects, placed under the thumb of the prettiest girl in the village, then stirred into the drink of any enemy . . . it was easy to eliminate troublemakers.

Even the nationals living in Georgetown considered the jungle interior a death trap, a vast uncharted area of treacherous rapids and waterfalls, quicksand, insects, wild animals and wild people. The government could offer no protection for visitors who planned to go there. But deep in the jungle a chief continued to pray that he'd know how to make his people good. How to make them different from other tribes. How to help them have a better life.

Then one day, while in a meeting with other villagers, something happened. He was standing and suddenly went silent. Men spoke to him, but he did not answer. His eyes gazed upward, but He did not breathe or move a muscle. He stood like a statue, and when men tried to lay him on the floor he could not be moved.

The villagers freaked out. Some cried. Some thought he was dead. Hours passed. The sun rose high above the jungle. Then, as quickly as he had gone into the trance, he blinked and took a deep breath. "Papa!" his 10-year-old son gasped, "you sick?"

The man looked around. "No, Promi. No. But I have seen wonderful things." As a crowd gathered around he began to paint word pictures of the place he had been. "It's a bright place," he said, describing heaven and the long table where the saved would eat with God. "It's a beautiful place, not bad like here. I did not want to come back." *Continued.*

These readings are adapted in part from Betty Cott, *Jewels From Green Hell.*

OWKWA'S ANGEL / PART 2

I will pour out my Spirit on all people. . . .
Your old men will dream dreams, your young men will see visions.
JOEL 2:28

The angel came again to the chief, and changed his name to Owkwa, which meant "great light." People in the village grew accustomed to seeing their leader in a trance, unspeaking, unseeing, without breath. But sometimes the dreams came at night, the angel instructing him in yet another biblical truth to enrich their understanding of God or a lifestyle principle that would make the lives of the villagers better.

The angel explained passages of Revelation, and seemingly showed Owkwa such things as the long table set before the redeemed in heaven. Years later Owkwa's grandson recalled his grandfather telling him that in heaven "the tiger and lamb will lie down together." (Tigers were common there in the jungle, and dangerous.) The angel taught Owkwa a number of English words and phrases, such as Holy Bible, hallelujah, New Jerusalem, heavenly Father, "body is the temple," Satan, sorrow, and trial. The angel told Owkwa about the final judgment and the seven last plagues.

Until a church could be built Owkwa opened his house to the village for worship—on the seventh day of the week. The angel had explained that God's holy day began at sundown of the sixth day of the week and lasted until sundown of the seventh. It was holy time, the angel said, so the people must not work. They should eat simply on that day, for too much food would make them sleepy. Villagers kept track of the weekly cycle by tying six knots in a string, then making a large knot for the seventh.

Under Chief Owkwa's leadership the village changed. The people bathed. They washed their vegetables before eating, and started to keep the village clean—just as the angel had said they should. Then a missionary to British Guiana, O. E. Davis, learned of a village whose people looked forward to Christ's return. Word of Davis had filtered in to them, too, and the villagers sent a message, asking him to come and teach them more. It was a treacherous journey, but his love for the Indians and for the Lord drove him on. He taught them from God's Word, and he taught them some Christian songs. And when he died there, from blackwater fever, the Indians buried him and carefully tended his grave. *Continued.*

OWKWA'S ANGEL / PART 3

*Then I heard a voice from heaven say, "Write: Blessed are the dead
who die in the Lord from now on." "Yes," says the Spirit,
"they will rest from their labor, for their deeds will follow them."*
REVELATION 14:13

Sixteen years after O. E. Davis' death, missionaries Alfred and
Betty Cott made the treacherous monthlong trip to Chief Owkwa's village. It was now 1927, and Owkwa's son Promi was chief.

The Cotts projected slides on a sheet hung above the church's rostrum. At the first picture, a painting of Jesus and the angels, a woman
jumped up. "That's just what Grandfather said you would show us!"
she cried. The next picture was of the table set up in the New
Jerusalem. "Ah, that table Owkwa saw!" Promi said. "Plenty, plenty
long."

When the last slide, a painting of the Second Coming, shone on
the wall the people cried out, "Okwka tell us this."

It seemed that no matter what the Cotts told these people, they
already knew it. The angel had explained it first, and Owkwa had
taught them. Unlike other Indians, they did not drink the blood of their
kills. They did not eat pig, rabbit, rats, or fish without scales. They did
not drink beer, and men had only one wife. They washed their food
before eating it.

All this, and more, the angel had instructed them. And years
before when they'd built their church, someone was appointed to keep
it clean—unheard-of in their culture. Again, the angel had said to do it.

They sang hymns that Davis had taught them, and still sing many
of them today.

The angel had told Owkwa that he would die without seeing the
missionaries come. The chief urged his people to stay faithful, but
added that the angel had said some would not.

Eighty years have passed since the Cotts were amazed by this village. Their descendants remain strong in the faith. Active churches still
nurture and teach, and the self-supporting Davis Indian Industrial
College in Guyana trains young men and women in practical skills,
general education, and God's Word. Student missionaries make up
much of its staff. Perhaps you'd like to serve there.

Bible

GOD IN A BOX / PART 1

*When the ark of the Lord's covenant came into the camp,
all Israel raised such a great shout that the ground shook. Hearing the uproar,
the Philistines asked, "What's all this shouting in the Hebrew camp?"*
1 SAMUEL 4:5, 6

It had, like most bad ideas, seemed like a good idea at the time. The Israelites had just gotten slaughtered in an ill-advised battle against the Philistines, and despite a corrupt priesthood and general unfaithfulness, they just couldn't imagine why. Then someone suggested a plan that would surely give them the victory: Let's take the ark of covenant into battle with us!

When the Israelite army saw the ark coming their way, they flipped out with excitement. The ark had led Israel in victory before, and now they were gonna kick the Philistines back into the sea. When the Philistines learned of it, they flipped out in fear, exclaiming, "Their gods have come to their camp! Nothing like this has ever happened before. We're done for! Who can save us from the clutches of these supergods? These are the same gods who hit the Egyptians with all kinds of plagues out in the wilderness. On your feet, Philistines! Courage! We're about to become slaves to the Hebrews, just as they have been slaves to us. Show what you're made of! Fight for your lives!" (1 Samuel 4:7-9, Message).

The Philistines' theology and history was a little fuzzy, but they fought like never before, and the Israelites suffered defeat like they'd never seen. When Eli, the indulgent and complicit high priest, learned that his two sons were dead, his heart broke. But then came the news that was truly a killer. When Eli learned that the Philistines had captured the ark, he died of a heart attack, his neck snapping as he fell backward.

The Philistines' giddiness knew no bounds. They'd captured Israel's god and won an incredible victory. Still, since it was a god after all, they knew they'd have to give it proper respect, so they took the ark and placed it in the temple of their god Dagon in Ashdod. The next morning the Philistines found Dagon's idol fallen (bowing?) before the ark. They put Dagon back in its place, but the next morning the same thing had happened again—except this time the idol's hands and feet had fallen off.

It was time for an amazing game of hot potato. *Continued.*

GOD IN A BOX / PART 2

*Those who did not die were afflicted with tumors,
and the outcry of the city went up to heaven.*
1 SAMUEL 5:12

The ark consisted of a wooden chest covered with solid gold, a golden angel on each end. The Ten Commandments, written on tablets of stone, were stored inside, along with manna and Moses' brother Aaron's walking staff that had flowered as a sign of God's approval.

The people of Ashdod came down with a plague, and tumors broke out in their bodies. "It's the Israelite's ark!" the people exclaimed, remembering the now centuries-old tales about Yahweh striking Egypt with plagues. "We can't keep the ark of the god of Israel here," they said, "because His hand is heavy on us and upon our god Dagon." So the Philistines sent the ark to Gath.

Any excitement the good people of Gath might have felt about the Israelites' ark coming to town vanished quickly when tumors broke out there, too, and rats started rampaging everywhere. When they tried to pass the ark on to Ekron, the Ekronites begged for mercy.

Ekron called Philistine leaders together to figure out what to do. "Send the ark of the god of Israel away," they pleaded, panicked. "Let it go back to its own place, or it will kill us and our people."

By now seven months had passed. Philistine magicians recommended they send the ark back, but not without a guilt offering: five gold tumors and five gold rats. They hooked the ark up to two oxen and let the oxen carry it back to Israel. They followed behind as, without human guidance, the oxen returned the ark to the Israelites.

The Israelites tried to use the ark as a magical talisman, but God refuses to allow people to box Him in and manipulate Him. Today many Christians still think there's something inherently virtuous about waving around the Ten Commandments (the tablets of which were stored inside the ark), but I don't think God is any more impressed now than He was then. Or than He was when He told King Saul, "To obey is better than sacrifice" (1 Samuel 15:22). Or when He told the people of Judah, "The multitude of your sacrifices—what are they to me? I have more than enough of burnt offerings" (see Isaiah 1:11). He'd much rather see the law written on our hearts (Jeremiah 31:33).

SELECTIVE LISTENING

If anyone has ears to hear, let him hear.
MARK 4:23

It's funny how we hear what we want to hear.

My father is a classic early-to-bed, early-to-rise kinda guy. He's also a pretty heavy sleeper. He'd have to be, with a couple cats criss-crossing his mattress all the time.

One night after I'd gotten back from a solo road trip that included a visit to my father's hometown, my mom and older sister stayed up late chatting with me in my sister's room while my dad slept across the hall. My mom asked if I'd stopped by the Country Bakeshop, one of his favorite places to pick up a cookie or pastry, and bought anything tasty for him. "Well," I said with mock sorrow and sincerity, "I would have, but it had burned down."

Laughing inside, I remembered the unfortunate time my parents and I had tried to visit a favorite restaurant on a trip down South, only to learn that it had recently gone up in flames.

It was late, and I was positive my dad had been sleeping for at least an hour. But a voice called out in the darkness. "What? The Country Bakeshop burned down?"

My sister, mother, and I looked at each other and laughed. I quickly reassured my father's disembodied voice that his nightmare was not real. The bakery was safe and sound. He notified me that certain things just aren't funny.

If I had to admit it, I probably have some selective listening skills of my own. Sure, I love my Jesus and would drop everything for the Second Coming, but in the meantime I'm a little . . . preoccupied. Distracted. When the Holy Spirit broadcasts, "Great concert coming up" or "Snow cones!" I'm all over it. When the Holy Spirit whispers, nudges, "Take a quick second and say something encouraging to that person you've never seen before," suddenly my sanguine ways evaporate—or at least want to stay in their nice cozy sphere. When the Holy Spirit suggests I be a little friendlier, a little more—Christlike?—to the smug jerk who thinks he's God's gift to my spiritual walk, it's sure easier to use him as a writing illustration than to embrace him as my brother.

This world hasn't burned down yet. That day's coming, but in the meantime, keep your ears open. There might just be something you need to hear.

LEAP OF FAITH

Taste and see that the Lord is good; blessed is the man who takes refuge in him.
PSALM 34:8

Sometimes you need to take a flying leap.

Try something you're not sure you can actually do. Volunteer for the job nobody else wants. Sign up for that mission trip when you don't know where the money's coming from. Put yourself out there.

Because if you don't try something once in a while that you're not totally certain you can do, how will you grow, and how will you discover what you're really made of?

If you haven't stretched yourself spiritually lately, ask God to give you just such an opportunity. It may be scary, but it can be exhilarating. It may seem impossible, but that's God's area of expertise.

Are you satisfied with your spiritual life today? If not, why not?

_____

_____

_____

What would it take for you to take a leap of faith, to stretch your wings and give God a chance to do something incredible in your life?

_____

_____

_____

How would you like to see your spiritual life grow? If you could challenge God to do something for you, what would you say to Him?

_____

_____

_____

What would you do for God if you knew that He would always bless you?

_____

_____

_____

Mission

ANNA KNIGHT / PART 1

For everyone who asks receives.
LUKE 11:10

Anna rode her pony over the Mississippi hills, revolver in hand, practicing hitting targets. Soon she could hit a knot on a tree from 50 or 100 yards away, and her pony knew when to stop, turn, or run at a wave of her hand. Such careless free time didn't come often, but when it did, she made the most of it.

Something inside young Anna Knight made her long for an education. By careful planning her mother, a freed slave, had managed to buy 80 acres of land in rural Mississippi. The family grew food for themselves and cotton for cash, but it was never enough to cover all their needs. Anna's days were filled with work, from plowing in the field to cooking in the kitchen, yet she bargained with White neighbor girls to help do their work, too, if they'd let her look at their books and even teach her some of the words.

Her prized possessions were a Webster's speller and a *McGuffey's Reader*. She carried her books with her when she visited her neighbors and lead the neighbor kids in spelling bees. Then one day a magazine ad changed her life. The ad said that for 10 cents the reader's name would be put on a list to receive free books and magazines. That was all Anna needed to know. It took time and effort, but at last she sent her dime for the free samples. And in one of them she read a column, The Cousin's Exchange, where readers could make requests.

Using her best handwriting, Anna carefully wrote, "Will some of the cousins please send me some nice reading matter? I would like to correspond with those of my own age."

Forty people answered, and books, papers, and letters poured in. Anna devoured the material at every spare moment. An Adventist woman, Edith Embree, began sending a copy of *Signs of the Times* every week. The woman in California and the girl in Mississippi began corresponding, and Edith taught her about the Bible and Jesus' love. Anna's mind spun with questions—about life after death, the Sabbath, the investigative judgment—and Edith would simply reply, "I am sending you a tract on that very subject which will tell you all about what you want to know. If you don't understand it, ask me again; and I will be very glad to help you understand." *Continued.*

(These readings are based on *Heartwarming Stories of Adventist Pioneers*, Book Two; and Anna Knight, *Mississippi Girl*.)

ANNA KNIGHT / PART 2

God . . . desires everyone to be saved and to come to the knowledge of the truth.
1 TIMOTHY 2:3, 4, NRSV

Anna slowly digested everything she learned from the Adventist magazines and her long-distance friend Edith. But when Anna began keeping the Sabbath, her mother became outraged. Why should she "lie around" all day when they were working!

Anna spent her Sabbaths in the woods or barn, reading, thinking, and praying. When Edith sent *Steps to Christ*, Anna embraced every word. It brought her peace and happiness, and put in her heart another longing—to be baptized into the Seventh-day Adventist Church. She poured out her heart's desire in a letter to Edith, who wrote to the secretary of the Southern Missionary Tract Society in Tennessee. She told him about the girl who had grown to love Jesus and wanted to be baptized. But there were no Adventist conferences in the South at that time and not many organized churches. The closest church was in Grayson, Tennessee, 382 miles away.

When Anna told her family that she was about to head east to be baptized, they tried to convince her to stay. "You're crazy!" they told her. "All your reading is making you lose your mind. You've never even met these people. They're not going to be like they seem in their magazines."

"If you'll let me go," Anna promised, "I'll help you make a crop next year." By now her family knew better than to try to keep her from something she had her mind set on, so they decided they'd let her be disappointed. By the time she came back, she'd be over this fanaticism.

Anna sold half a cotton bale and bought a ticket to Chattanooga, a 382-mile ride. Elder L. D. Chambers arranged to meet her at the train station in Chattanooga. He sent a picture so she'd recognize him, and told her to hold an Adventist magazine so he'd recognize her. Anna could scarcely believe how her dreams were coming true. She attended a Week of Prayer at the Graysville school, and at the end she was baptized.

A 10-week school term started the following Monday, and the Chambers had arranged for her to go to school. She would sit in a real classroom with a teacher and classmates and books. In Mississippi she had gathered small children around her and taught them reading and math, but now it was her turn to be a student. *Continued.*

Mission

ANNA KNIGHT / PART 3

*Six days you shall labor and do all your work,
but the seventh day is a Sabbath to the Lord your God.*
EXODUS 20:9, 10

Anna awoke early the first day of school, excited and eager to begin. The teacher and students were glad to have her for Anna was bright and clever—and fun.

But people in the neighborhood soon caught wind of the latest gossip: *There's a---at the Adventists' school.* So Anna moved into the school matron's home where she could be taught privately, unthreatened by militant local racists. In those 10 weeks Anna learned so much that her family never had any idea that she had attended only one day of class. Perhaps because she was so hurt, Anna never told them.

Back home, people saw that Anna's time away had only intensified her commitment to her strange church. When she finished preparing Saturday morning breakfast for her family she took off by herself for the woods, with her dog, revolver, Bible, and magazines.

Things finally came to a head when the cotton harvest came in. A beautiful Saturday morning dawned, and her mother insisted, "You go plow that cotton."

Anna stood her ground. Her brother chimed in, "You sit and lie around every Saturday and let the work go. I'll not work unless you do."

At that, Anna's mother exploded. "You will plow cotton today!"

Anna's back straightened. *Fine!* she thought. "I'll go and do the work," she announced, "and if I don't get through this day, I'll finish it on Sunday or die. But if I can't keep the Sabbath, *I will not keep Sunday.*"

Feeling lost, hurt, and angry, Anna and an equally irritated horse plowed four acres at record speed. She put the horse away and returned home as the sun began to set, but the next morning, instead of putting on her Sunday best, she grabbed her hoe and started working in the flower garden. Appalled, her family left home all day. Anna felt wretched. She'd been such a good witness in the weeks since returning home. People had been so impressed by the change in her attitude. The Holy Spirit had helped her keep her temper in check that whole time. Now all seemed lost. She poured out a letter to Mr. Chambers. Was there any hope for such a backslider? *Continued.*

ANNA KNIGHT / PART 4

I will teach you the way that is good and right.
1 SAMUEL 12:23

Mr. Chambers sent back a letter encouraging her to know that God forgave her, and that God would give her strength to follow Him in the future. Anna never worked on the Sabbath again, but her mother never understood. "You can't teach me anything!" she stormed. "I'm your mother! You stop this Saturday-for-Sunday foolishness—or leave!"

Anna waited until her mother began to wind down. Somehow she found the grace to calmly say, "All right, I can leave; but I can't give up the Sabbath and my hope of eternal life." She waited until she'd kept her promise to help with the harvest then took what little money she had and cried her way back to Chattanooga and the Chambers' home. But now her course was set, and she was excited. She was going to go to school and become a teacher.

For some time Anna assisted Mrs. Chambers with her baking business, but soon they helped her enroll in the first real school of her life, Mount Vernon Academy in Ohio. Her classmates laughed at someone so countrified and "green," and so uneducated, but when she caught them mocking her one day, she left them speechless as she passed by, saying, "Never mind, green things grow." She soon made strong friends who helped her in her studies and appreciated all the interesting things she knew about nature.

After a year at Mount Vernon Anna needed further education, and the place to get it was Battle Creek College. There she attended classes, worked most of her days in the laundry, and did private ironing. All this income helped her pay her school expenses. And by the end of the year she was ready to begin nurses' training at Battle Creek Sanitarium.

One experience became a highlight of Anna's nurses' training. A Mrs. Henry was admitted to the hospital with heart failure, and decided to stay for long-term care. Doctors said that although she had previously been very active, now only a miracle could save her. One day she asked the hospital chaplain if she could be anointed as outlined in James 5. She would ask God to heal her.

Her friends were asked to pray at a specific time. Mrs. Henry was taken to the chapel in a wheelchair. The service was quiet and spiritual, and when it concluded, Mrs. Henry had been healed. She *walked* back up the stairs to her room, and upon examination, doctors found no signs of the heart disease that had previously ruled her life. *Continued.*

ANNA KNIGHT / PART 5

When I called, you answered me; you made me bold and stouthearted.
PSALM 138:3

Anna stood in an old log cabin on her uncle's farm. The roof was fairly sound and two long log benches had been made for the students to sit on. There was a homemade chair and table for the teacher. After graduating from nursing, Anna returned to her hometown, where family and neighbors welcomed her back, their ill-feelings forgotten. One of the first things she did was to start a school for their children, setting up a building fund for a new schoolhouse. Women and children picked cotton on the four acres she'd planted, selling it for the building fund. Almost everyone was proud of the new school—it had been a true community effort.

Anna taught two different schools each Sunday, about six miles apart. She also taught reading, writing, and math for adults, as well as lifestyle changes for better health. The local moonshiners didn't like what she said about whiskey, and after several threats, to make her friends feel better, Anna started carrying a revolver. Then one Sunday afternoon on her way home from school, she saw several of the men who'd threatened her life some distance ahead. She was on a horse in a lane that was fenced on both sides. There was nowhere to flee.

Riding on as if she hadn't seen them, Anna suddenly dropped the reins and slapped the horse on its sides. He took off, running like the wind. She leaned against his neck, urging him to go faster. The mob fired again and again, but missed both her and the horse. At last free of danger, Anna patted the horse. He slowed to a walk. They were safe.

The day's second session had hardly begun when three of the same men—now drunk—came in and sat in the back. After a confrontation they strode out, but Anna saw that they'd slipped into the nearby woods, so she ended the lessons and left. However, two of the men in her family stayed by. When the three men returned, the two were ready, and the troublemakers discovered that two Knights were two too many! After that, guards watched the school every night, but that was the end of Anna's trouble.

Anna started Adventist health work in Atlanta and pioneered and supervised Adventist education for Blacks in the South and Southeast. When the church needed a missionary to India, she sailed there to serve. Her carefully kept records show that in her work in schools and churches she traveled the equivalent of 23 trips around the world. Her influence on the lives that she touched cannot be calculated.

YES, I DO ALL MY OWN STUNTS

I came that they may have life, and have it abundantly.
JOHN 10:10, NRSV

There's nothing cooler than walking sideways down a steep cliff. And yes, I'm quite happy to say, I speak from personal experience.

Unfortunately, I was 11 years old the last time I rappelled down 90 feet of rock, so one of these days I need to call up my friend Tom (who's been known to rappel down mountainsides, the local water tower, the side of a college dorm, whatever) and find the nearest precipice. Fortunately, living in mid-Tennessee, they're not hard to find, so hey, it could happen.

There's something oddly exhilarating about pushing the world's limits. And when I see an ad for an action movie, I have to admit, no matter how ludicrous the premise or how much I know the mayhem is totally computer-generated, a part of me still wants to see the world from 90 degrees. I'd probably draw the line at piloting a canoe over a raging waterfall, but deep inside I want to leap chasms on a motorcycle. I want to clash swords on a mountain ledge. I want to outrun fireballs.

OK, not really. Well, maybe the fireballs. I'm a pretty good jumper, so I'm confident I could time my leap to safety just right. And I'm hardly what you'd call an extreme sports enthusiast (wasn't bad at skiing, though; wasn't great, either). But I love to see the world from every vantage point I can.

Sitting in a sinking canoe once (albeit sinking in about two feet of water) in, the Amazon River, I suddenly pictured my potentially waterlogged camera and the 1,000-plus photos I'd just shot ruined forever. Nothing thrills me more than picking up a camera or videocamera and capturing the world around me. (And yes, I got a fantastic shot of us pushing the canoe back into the flow of things.)

I read recently that of the top highest-grossing movies, nearly every one of them has at least one explosion in it somewhere. All these movies tap into that sense in us that we were made for more than the mundane.

So maybe there's something to all that talk of destiny. Ready to grab on and see where God takes you?

SLIPPERY COMMITMENT

So they are no longer two, but one.
Therefore what God has joined together, let man not separate.
MATTHEW 19:6

Debbie and Joe had a large, beautiful church wedding. As part of the service they took Communion, and the congregation was invited to make that recommitment too. The bride and her friends had used all their creativity to make a wonderland of flowers and tulle. A full meal was catered, and each guest received a small silver picture frame to take home as a remembrance.

The groom, a man of few words, was all smiles, but he didn't say much. That was OK—Debbie schmoozed the crowd for them both. After many years of friendship-turned-love, she understood him. She knew that she thrived with lots of friends, while Joe was content with one or two. Or maybe none at all. He didn't need, nor did he even want, a lot of people around. But Debbie knew that, too.

But somehow, after they married, Debbie began to feel different about Joe's lack of social skills. It began to irritate her, his disinterest in having friends, and as the months went by, her feelings changed into something far worse. She didn't like him anymore. In fact, she didn't want him around.

And the promise she'd made, to love Joe for better and for worse, didn't seem nearly as important as how she now felt. She wanted out. She didn't want to live with this sphinx for the rest of her life.

The problem is—and it *is* a problem—is that opposites attract. The outgoing guy with a million friends, who always has a dozen irons in the fire, with his phone ringing all day, is attracted to a quiet, introspective woman. In the spinning vortex of his life, she is calm. In the bland sameness of her days, he's excitement. But living together 24/7, without a lot of understanding, and yes, commitment, they can drive each other nuts.

You can't blame someone for being who they are. Much of it is in the DNA. Yes, we all need to stretch and grow. Yes, we can learn—actually learn, sometimes—how to be different. But never marry with the thought that you can change your partner into the person you want them to be. It's not fair to either one of you. And your commitment to love, honor, and cherish is, in truth, a holy promise to your mate and to God.

THE SCANDAL OF THE INCARNATION

And the Word became flesh and lived among us.
JOHN 1:14, NRSV

It's part of Christianity's foundational truth, and still, it offends a whole lot of people.

The Incarnation. It's the fantastic fact that the ultimate Missionary utterly transformed Himself so that He could reach humans on their level. It's also a principle that Christians have used ever since to communicate Jesus to people who don't even know where to begin to get to know Him. But even in Jesus' day a lot of powerful people didn't like it. After all, if Jesus had to condescend Himself to reach them, that meant they weren't quite as great as they already thought they were. They were too busy acting condescending to everybody else to accept that.

Jesus' incarnation—from all-powerful deity to squalling infant and executed criminal—was the greatest condescension of all. And for the past 2,000 years the very idea has scandalized people. Today rigid-minded Christians are still offended by the idea of what we call "incarnational ministry"—translating the gospel's age-old truths into modern lingo and style.

A fellow student in my seminary anthropology class shared a striking experience. He'd been a missionary to an island in the Southern Hemisphere, and the people at the American church he now attended loved to hear tales of how he'd adapted Christianity so that people in a vastly different culture could grasp and understand it. But when my classmate used the very same principles to communicate to teens in the Sabbath school class he now taught, they accused him of introducing worldliness.

An incarnational attitude requires humility. It requires people who realize that they still have a lot to learn about God, about love, and about life. It requires people who are patient and teachable, open and giving. Missionaries, evangelists, and everyday Christians have done incalculable damage to Christianity and the world when they've forced others to blindly accept their culture, their attitudes, and their methods—even when those traits have nothing to do with the heart of the gospel.

If you're a public Christian, you're the only Jesus a lot of people see. Do people see a Jesus who's willing to meet them where they are?

Innovation

SAFE

Whoever trusts in the Lord is kept safe.
PROVERBS 29:25

I just don't get it.

Living in Nashville, I can find no less than three different local radio stations playing Christian music. They each have their own slogans, programs, and personalities. But one of them has an ad campaign that always strikes me as off-tune. The slogan? "Safe for the whole family!" (plastered on billboards around the city, and exclaimed in the radio commercial by a high-pitched 6-year-old voice).

I see the appeal, targeting parents driving their kids around town who don't want to have to quickly turn the station when somebody starts telling a dirty joke. But . . . why? If you're the kind of person who listens to Christian radio, you're not expecting raunchiness anyway, so it's really a moot point. It's preaching to the choir, and that's not going to grow your audience.

The message is basically, "Come on in: We're bland and inoffensive." Is that really the best witness? Why not something that *defies* expectations, or at least has some fun with them? Like, I dunno. Try these.

Christian Radio: The Most Joy Available Without a Prescription.
Christian Radio: The Best Music You've Never Heard.
Christian Radio: Not Tested on Party Animals.
Christian Radio: Our Music Can Beat Up Your Music.
Christian Radio: Not Been Proven to Regrow Hair.

My sister once attended an Adventist college that advertised itself as "spiritually safe." I guess that sounded reassuring to some people, especially parents who want to see their children grow up, but not grow out of their religion. But without risk, which includes testing your faith, there's no growth. As the old saying goes, A ship is safe in a harbor, but that's not what a ship is for.

It's tempting to think that Christianity simply involves sealing yourself in a bubble of blandness and hoping a few fed-up people will drop in for detoxing. But that's not what we're called to do. We're called to bang a drum in the highways and byways.

What's your life advertising?

THE FUNDAMENTALIST PARADOX

You strain out a gnat but swallow a camel.
MATTHEW 23:24

When nobody's challenging their doctrines, religious groups tend to take them for granted. When people start attacking or questioning their beliefs, though, all bets are off. Before Charles Darwin and company publicized their theory of evolution, Christians didn't talk that much about creation. Christians didn't talk a lot about how the Bible was inspired—until nineteenth-century scholars started questioning it. Suddenly they took a hard line, making much stronger claims about the Bible than before.

I call it the fundamentalist paradox, sacrificing part of a belief to defend the honor of another. As people try to defend a doctrine, they actually undermine it.

Adventists have been particularly tempted by fundamentalism on the issues of prophecy and inspiration. With unique views on prophecy and a famous church member, Ellen White, whom they believe God specifically inspired, discussions have gotten heated.

After writing about prophecy and history for more than 40 years, Ellen White summed it all up in her 1888 book *The Great Controversy*. In a special intro she wrote about how the Holy Spirit worked with people to create the Bible. The book tells the story of the Christian church throughout history, and predicts that in the last days we'll see intolerance and persecution disguising itself as Christianity.

White wanted to correct two misconceptions: that some parts of the Bible are more inspired than others, and verbal inspiration, which says that God dictated the Bible word by word. Verbal inspiration spelled double trouble for Adventists. If they believed that the Bible was verbally inspired, it was a simple extension of logic that the same held true for Ellen White. Dr. David Paulson suffered a crisis of faith when White made mention of 40 rooms in the 38-room Paradise Valley Sanitarium. He wrote to White in 1906, "I was led to conclude and most firmly believe that every word you ever spoke, in public or private, was as inspired as the Ten Commandments."

Ellen White described the Holy Spirit working through people, not God simply handing down the words. Replying to Dr. Paulson, she wrote that inspiration was "a union of the divine and the human." She told him that though "the testimony is conveyed through the imperfect expression of human language, yet it is the testimony of God" (*Selected Messages*, book 1, pp. 25, 26).

Bible

SAMUEL AND SAUL

But now your kingdom will not endure;
the Lord has sought out a man after his own heart
and appointed him leader of his people,
because you have not kept the Lord's command.

1 SAMUEL 13:14

It's hard to imagine a longstanding kingdom of Saul, but that's what could have been if Saul hadn't become so full of himself. Things started out so well: Saul could scarcely believe that he was worthy of such an honor; Saul prophesied along with the prophets, making his old friends wonder just what was going on; Saul sheepishly hid himself among the baggage and the prophet Samuel had to call him out.

One thinks of Saul's fearless and noble son Jonathan, who would surely have made as good a king as anyone. Perhaps the kingdom could have stayed together far longer. We'll never know, except as much as we always know that the destinies of nations lie in the choices of each one of us.

The years passed, and Saul's shyness swung into rashness. When Saul insisted on sacrificing to God without Samuel's blessing, Samuel told him that God was already looking for another ruler, one who, though as fallible as Saul, would acknowledge his sins and love God completely.

When Saul demanded that no one in his army eat, under penalty of death, until they'd defeated the Philistines, he unwittingly condemned his own son Jonathan, who'd enjoyed some honey in between knocking down a few enemies. When Saul found out what his son had done, he vowed to carry out his rash decree, caring more for his reputation than his son. Only the people's outraged insistence stopped Saul from doing it.

When Saul claimed that his failure to eradicate the Amalekites and their goods was really just a misunderstanding (for, you see, he'd really been wanting to save some good sacrifices for God, and besides, it was the people's fault), Samuel told him that his fate was sealed: "For rebellion is like the sin of divination, and arrogance like the evil of idolatry."

The desperate king grabbed Samuel's garment as he turned away. Never at a loss for words, Samuel underlined that Saul's kingdom was torn from his hands for good. For when it comes to following God, self-righteousness is the one sin that's always deadly.

STOP THE MUSIC

I will give you a new heart and put a new spirit in you.
EZEKIEL 36:26

For heart patients and their families, waiting for a donor heart can be a long and emotionally draining process. Days, weeks, and months pass by, their lives on hold as they wait for the phone call that could change everything—and that means instant prepping for transplant surgery.

John-Paul had received his first donor heart at only 10 months of age, but coronary artery disease had ravaged it, leaving his body starving for a fresh start. When a heart finally became available at the Children's Hospital in Pittsburgh, Pennyslvania, doctors had only four hours to complete the transplant before the heart would no longer be viable. Trouble was, John-Paul was nowhere to be found.

He'd gone with his mother to a jazz concert at Slippery Rock University. As usual, his mother, Sue May, had put her cell phone on vibrate and put it in her purse, but no matter how many times the doctors or her husband called, she just didn't notice.

Cardiologists contacted police for assistance in tracking down Sue May and John-Paul. Police officers from five counties searched every shopping mall and movie theater in the area. Then an officer sitting at a desk had an idea: track Sue May's cell phone through a satellite global positioning system. The practice is illegal without a judge's warrant unless police are searching for a homicide suspect or the situation is life-or-death.

GPS soon pinpointed the cell phone's location, and police sped to the university concert auditorium. There was only one thing to do: stop the music. State police corporal James Green rushed into the building. Finding the music conductor's wife, he breathlessly informed her of the situation, then strode on stage, motioning the conductor to stop midsong. Taking the microphone, he asked, "Is there a Mrs. Sue May in the audience?" Stunned, Sue May tentatively raised her hand from her seat in the back row.

"Mrs. Sue May, please come forward. A heart has been found for your son. We need to get you and your son to Children's Hospital in Pittsburgh."

As John-Paul and his mother came to the front, the crowd burst into applause. Police rushed the Mays to the hospital, where surgeons successfully gave John-Paul a new heart.

Spirit

INTIMACY / PART 1

A new command I give you: Love one another. As I have loved you, so you must love one another. By this all men will know that you are my disciples, if you love one another.
JOHN 13:34, 35

When my friends and I describe what we like about our home church, one word comes up again and again: *Intimacy*. Close at its heels is *family*.

Words not used to describe my church? *Boring. Bland. Rigid. Repetitious. Same o' same o'*. Sure, we've got a great pastor, great music, and the most engrossing sermons I've ever heard, but the best part is that people feel comfortable to come and be themselves. No pretenses. No phony conformity. My Sabbath school class is made up of a varied group of people, but we accept one another. Sometimes we shake our heads at some of our friends' opinions and perspectives, but, as they say, *vive la différence*. We tease one another and laugh with and about one another, but we still accept one another. And we're always eager to pull new people in.

The thing is, we actually like hanging out with one another, after church and at one another's homes. Right now we're planning to go spend a week living with one another in Jamaica (where two of our group grew up), working together to serve others. (Granted, we'll be staying on the beach, but, hey, it's Jamaica—you're never far from the beach.)

That sense of connection keeps us coming back week after week. We don't always see eye to eye, but that's OK—we're side by side.

The sense of intimacy we enjoy at my church is the fulfillment of Jesus' promise that He'd send the Holy Spirit to guide us and unite us. And—stay with me now—it's what the world promises us about sex, but never truly delivers. As Rob Bell writes in *Sex God: the Endless Connections Between Sexuality and Spirituality*: "Our sexuality is all of the ways we strive to reconnect with our world, with each other, and with God" (p. 42).

Most of the time the world looks like a happening, sexually charged place, while the church looks like a sterile, austere environment. But while the church has too often deserved its reputation as cold and unforgiving, the world's sexuality is nonetheless an illusion, a song and dance that never goes the distance. *Continued.*

INTIMACY / PART 2

This is the message you heard from the beginning: We should love one another.
1 JOHN 3:11

The world is good at fetishizing, finding things that remind us of intimacy and flashing them before our eyes at every turn. But the world never delivers. It's the same as sitting down to watch a new video and finding that no matter how much you fast-forward, it's just one unending stream of trailers with no movie in sight. Fixations may be exciting, but they're unfulfilling. (Of course, churches have displayed the same gimmicky attitude in other areas, from worship styles to exactly where the pulpit should stand in the sanctuary.)

The original meaning of the word *fetish* was anthropological: an object believed to have supernatural power. It's a shortcut to connection that ultimately connects to nothing. Describing Amsterdam's infamous red-light district, where prostitution is openly advertised and available, Rob Bell writes, "What is so striking is how unsexual that whole section of the city is. There are lots of people 'having sex' night and day, but that's all it is. There's no connection. . . . There are lots of people having lots of physical sex—for some it's their job—and yet it's not a very sexual place at all" (*Sex God: the Endless Connections Between Sexuality and Spirituality*, p. 43).

Hit movies often follow a simple formula: A person moves from one level of connectedness to another. Romantic comedies celebrate two lonely people connecting. In *The Christmas Carol* Ebenezer Scrooge goes from a miserly, self-centered jerk to a selfless man in touch with all of humanity. There's a reason why people keep making new versions of *The Christmas Carol* and *It's a Wonderful Life*—they tap into our innermost longings for connection.

Describing the emotional power of attending a concert with hundreds of other people, Bell writes that it connects us. "The experience of a great concert . . . has a significant sexual dimension to it. We don't know each other, . . . we disagree on hundreds of issues, but for an evening, we gather around this artist and these songs and we get along. The experience moves us so deeply because it taps into how things were meant to be, and we have so few places where we can experience what God intended on such a large scale. . . . What we're experiencing in these moments of connection is what God created us to experience all of the time. It's our natural state. It's how things are supposed to be" (p. 42).

Mission

SMOOTH THINGS

They say to the seers, "See no more visions!" and to the prophets,
"Give us no more visions of what is right! Tell us pleasant things, prophesy illusions."
ISAIAH 30:10

If there's one Bible text I used to get sick of, it's Philippians 4:8: "Finally, brothers, whatever is true, whatever is noble, whatever is right, whatever is pure, whatever is lovely, whatever is admirable—if anything is excellent or praiseworthy—think about such things."

The problem was that the people quoting it implied it to mean whatever they wanted it to. Which generally defended their own habit of ignoring real problems, often ones they'd caused themselves. More to the point, these same people may have prided themselves in ignoring the evil in the world around them (when they weren't harping about something they'd seen on TV), but they surely were good at pointing it out in their fellow Christians.

That's why I'm mighty grateful for Isaiah 30. In that chapter God faces down a crowd of people who want to hear only nice, pleasant, smooth talk. Nothing to offend their sensibilities, rock the boat, or make their children ask pesky questions. They'd self-righteously laughed off the threat of destruction. God had told them to chill and trust in Him rather than in themselves. "But," He adds, "you would have none of it. You said, 'No, we will flee on horses.' Therefore you will flee! You said, 'We will ride off on swift horses.' Therefore your pursuers will be swift!" (verses 15, 16).

If anyone knows how to cut to the chase, it's God. Again and again in the Bible He asks cutting questions: Where are you? Where are you going? What are you doing here? And with God, there's no smooth-talking your way out of it.

In everyday life "pleasant things" are a huge temptation. TV news covers celebrity fluff instead of anything viewers can really chew on. Schools fear upsetting parents if their classes dig too deeply into serious issues. And churches fear that God's truths can't stand close inspection.

So what will you say when someone asks your opinion of the new girl? when a teacher tries to smooth over a controversial issue? when people are dying inside because no one will speak out?

THE LEGEND OF XENIA

"The alien living with you must be treated as one of your native-born.
Love him as yourself, for you were aliens in Egypt. I am the Lord your God."
LEVITICUS 19:34

Love makes the world go round. It's a quaint old saying, but for too many people love doesn't make it past the front sidewalk.

Borrowing from the ancient Greeks, C. S. Lewis wrote a book about the four loves: *agape, philos, storge, eros.* But he left out a major one, xenia: the love of strangers.

The other loves are easy to understand—all-encompassing agape, familial philos, affectionate and ticklish storge, and sizzling eros. But loving strangers? That's hardly human nature, is it? At least not in this modern world of immigration fears, border fences, and ethnic cleansing. You've probably heard the word *xenophobia*—but *xenophilia*? Stranger means danger, baby.

But for the ancient Greeks, living in a world without hotels or hospitals, xenia was essential. They considered xenia the noblest, purest, most essential form of love.

It's easy to love people who are similar to us, who enjoy the same music, share the same sense of fashion, cheer for the same football team, and vote for the same political party. People who are different, though—who laugh at jokes that aren't funny, wear clothes that offend our taste, or just plain get on our nerves—stretch our patience, and our love, mighty thin.

Which brings us to one of the most ignored parts of the Bible. These lonely verses pop up here and there in the Old Testament and the New, especially the good ol' Mosaic law. They tell us to watch over the strangers and aliens in our midst.

"Do not go over your vineyard a second time or pick up the grapes that have fallen. Leave them for the poor and the alien" (Leviticus 19:10).

"And you are to love those who are aliens, for you yourselves were aliens in Egypt" (Deuteronomy 10:19).

"Do not deprive the alien or the fatherless of justice, or take the cloak of the widow as a pledge" (Deuteronomy 24:17).

It's easy to love people just like us. To love a stranger? That's divine.

Adventism

REVELATION AND INSPIRATION

*But we have this treasure in jars of clay to show
that this all-surpassing power is from God and not from us.*
2 CORINTHIANS 4:7

In 1911 Ellen White shocked a lot of people by making corrections and clarifications to *The Great Controversy*. How could she do that? people wondered. Wasn't she inspired by God? Why would something she wrote need any changes, let alone so many? For example, on page 65 of the 1888 edition White had written, "The Waldenses were the first of all the peoples of Europe to obtain a translation of the Holy Scriptures." The 1911 edition clarified, "The Waldenses were *among* the first . . ." (italics supplied).

Though the changes did not affect the book's overall message, they were still enough to get people talking. No one was more shocked than the editor that Ellen White asked to help her, W. W. Prescott. Prescott had himself believed in "verbal inspiration," that God had told the Bible writers exactly what to write, and he figured that White's inspiration worked much the same way. On April 26, 1910, Prescott wrote to W. C. White, Ellen's son, that "it has been quite a shock to me to find in this book so many loose and inaccurate statements; and what I have submitted for your consideration will indicate how much of an undertaking it will be to revise this book so that it will be in harmony with historical facts."

Ellen White had a two-sided problem. Some people said that only the things she wrote that they agreed with were inspired. And some people took everything she ever said or wrote as infallible, making an idol of her words.

A lot of confusion could have been avoided if people had just paid attention to the book's introduction, where White described a fusion of divine inspiration and human effort. "The Bible points to God as its author; yet it was written by human hands;" she wrote, "and in the varied style of its different books it presents the characteristics of the several writers. The truths revealed are all 'given by inspiration of God' (2 Timothy 3:16, KJV); yet they are expressed in the words of men. The Infinite One by His Holy Spirit has shed light into the minds and hearts of His servants. He has given dreams and visions, symbols and figures; and those to whom the truth was thus revealed have themselves embodied the thought in human language. . . . The Bible, with its God-given truths expressed in the language of men, presents a union of the divine and the human."

DAVID

The Lord has sought out a man after his own heart.
1 SAMUEL 13:14

Poet. Philanderer. Shepherd. King. Murderer. Commander. Man after God's own heart.

King David is a wonder, and an enigma. He loved God immensely yet sinned devastatingly. He loved his sons—yet not always enough to discipline them. His life still grips and amazes us today, because despite his dramatic imperfections, his passion for life and God has never been topped.

We meet David as the youngest of eight sons of Jesse in Bethlehem. Samuel, having mourned good and hard for wayward King Saul, is reluctant to anoint a new king over Israel, but God tells him it's time to get moving. The people of Bethlehem are a bit unnerved to see God's man in their midst, but he assures them, "I come in peace." But since his mission is a secret one, he skips saying, "Take me to your leader," and assures them instead that he's just come to sacrifice to God.

When Samuel sets eyes on Jesse's oldest son, Eliab, his height and features remind Samuel of the towering Saul, and he thinks, "This has got to be the guy." But God tells him nope. "Looks aren't everything. Don't be impressed with his looks and stature. I've already eliminated him. God judges persons differently than humans do. Men and women look at the face; God looks into the heart" (1 Samuel 16:7, Message).

Six more sons pass before the prophet, but God keeps telling him to hold his horses. Finally, perplexed yet again at God's mysterious ways, Samuel asks, "Is this all ya got?"

"There's still the youngest," Jesse says apologetically, "but he's out with the sheep."

A few minutes later David arrives on the scene as one of the few people the Bible specifically points to as good-looking. And God says, "Rise and anoint him; he is the one."

The Bible tells us that from then on, the Spirit of God "came upon David in power." Sometimes that Spirit gave him bravery. Sometimes strength. And sometimes the Spirit simply reminded him not to take himself so seriously.

Science

MILLIONAIRE SALAD

*Then God said, "I give you [to eat] every seed-bearing plant
on the face of the whole earth and every tree that has fruit with seed in it."*
GENESIS 1:29

Are you tired of chewing your way through the same old salad of iceburg lettuce, carrots, and cucumbers? It's time to try something new, and it's fun to use the field greens that we find in today's supermarkets. (I always knew those cows were on to something.)

Unfortunately, dollar bills aren't handed out with the millionaire salad, but it's so easy to make that it might make you feel like a million bucks. And I guarantee that your friends and family will ask you to serve this again.

Ingredients:
a big bowl of mixed lettuce and/or field greens
crasins (dried, sweetened cranberries)
feta cheese

Dressing:
1/2 cup apple cider vinegar
1/2 cup olive oil
1/2 cup sugar or sugar substitute
1 packet Good Seasonings Italian dressing mix (dry)

Directions:
Toss the green stuff with the craisins. Add crumbled feta cheese on top. Beat dressing ingredients with a fork or wire whisk. Pour over salad just before serving.

It's the dressing that makes this salad extra special. Experiment with the amount of sweetening. This recipe makes a lot of dressing, so for a smaller salad, use only half of it.

LH

ANGELIC ENTERTAINMENT

Do not neglect to show hospitality to strangers,
for by doing that some have entertained angels without knowing it.
HEBREWS 13:2, NRSV

I was on my way to do an errand when I first noticed the elderly woman hobbling painfully along the shoulder of the road. She leaned on a staff, and one leg seemed quite twisted. Obviously she had just arrived by bus at the little Greyhound station behind the McDonald's. When I finished with my business at the credit union, about a half mile farther down the road, she was just then walking by it. Thunder rumbled in the distance.

Suddenly having an idea where she might be heading, I hurried to my car and pulled alongside her. At first she declined my offer of a ride, explaining that she had walked to where she was going several times in the past. The weather bureau had predicted the possibility of rain, I said. Well, if it did rain, she would dry off, she replied. Besides, her destination would be out of my way. She was headed for the regional prison, three miles or more down the road. Telling her that it would be no problem, I insisted that I would be glad to take her there.

After much physical effort she managed to slide into the passenger's seat of my car. As we drove along she told how she had changed buses in Baltimore. Another passenger who had been on the previous bus had asked where she was going, and when she told the other woman, that person called her minister, who was not too far away. When he arrived, the two of them prayed that God would send her a ride from the Hagerstown bus station to the prison. I had become the answer to that prayer.

The Hebrew and Greek words translated into English as "angel" both mean "messenger." That messenger can be either supernatural or human. But when God sends "angels," He seems to prefer working through human beings. Perhaps that is why some prayers seem to take a while to get answered, or never get answered at all. God waits until someone responds to the Spirit's convicting to serve as His agent in the answering of that prayer. Sadly, sometimes no one will get involved, and the prayer may never get fulfilled at all (see, for example, Ezekiel 22:30).

All of us can be God's "messenger," witnessing for the gospel or helping others in countless ways. Give someone today an opportunity to entertain an "angel" unawares.

GW

SPRING CHICKENS / PART 1

*In those days people will no longer say, "The fathers have eaten sour grapes,
and the children's teeth are set on edge."*
JEREMIAH 31:29

My father once drove a Ford service van, the kind you'd often see used by plumbers and electricians. It was far from clean, its origins unknown. Dad just came home with it. At least 10 years old by the time my dad got it, it was more a dingy gray than white. But it had four tires and could be controlled via a steering wheel, so it met my father's main criteria.

Because the van lacked any rear seats, my dad took a bench from an old school bus and tack-welded it behind the driver's seat. Voilà, a four-seater! For anyone brave enough to open its panel doors they'd see an interior scattered with engine parts, electronics, and tools while their nose was assaulted by the sharp stink of engine oil, solvents, and gasoline. In the string of cars my father owned, this one caused the most embarrassment when he dropped us kids off at school.

And then the hen dropped in.

It happened right after Dad picked my sister and me up after school. Jessica and I slunk into the bowels of Dad's auto terror, and we headed home. My mother sat in the front seat while we two kids huddled on the red vinyl bus seat. I remember how I abhorred its smell as we bumped along, how much it reeked on that hot day, and how it stuck out among the regular cars picking up the normal kids. In my van-induced funk I failed to realize that a hen had taken flight moments before and was headed our way.

The van turned a corner by a patch of farmland. At the crest of the curve a huge white hen zoomed toward it. Flying! Apparently no one had told the hen that she was excused from such commitments. Dad made a dramatic swerve, but it was too late. The bird slammed into the van's mirror at 40 miles an hour. The metal arms snapped, and shards of mirror filled the cabin. Fast on its tail came the mirror's housing—then the chicken itself. The van rocked back and forth as Dad struggled to steer while a broken mirror slammed into his chest and a frenzied chicken flapped madly in his face. *Continued.*

BP

SPRING CHICKENS / PART 2

He will turn the hearts of the fathers to their children,
and the hearts of the children to their fathers.
MALACHI 4:6

Tires screeched as Dad regained control, finally letting one hand off the wheel to commandeer the flapping bird. Still very much alive, it screamed. Gone was the classic clucking one usually hears from chickens. Instead, a droning baaawk filled the van. With his left hand Dad smacked the hen down from his face and into the crevice between him and the driver's door. Using his left knee, he clamped down on the chicken as he coasted the van onto the road's shoulder.

The van stopped. The hen went silent. No one spoke while the engine idled and the chicken moaned a final cluck. In the silence countless white feathers drifted peacefully in the cabin. My mother looked in quiet shock at her husband. He sat covered in feathers and bits of reflective glass, a bloody mirror in his lap. More distressing were his black sunglasses. His Ray-Bans were askew to the point that half of them rested on top of his scalp.

"Is everybody OK?" Dad asked in a low tone.

"We're OK."

With pale knuckles resting back on the steering wheel, Dad looked down at the chicken and then checked us for damage. Among the victims of the fowl assault, he had suffered the brunt of it. I made off with just a few scratches and feathers in my hair. As a *Far Side* comic once put it, the scene was "grisly, yet strangely hilarious."

Romans 5:3, 4 says it best: "Not only so, but we also rejoice in our sufferings, because we know that suffering produces perseverance; perseverance, character; and character, hope."

I thought I was "suffering" in that van; then I really got it. And through it all—the nasty van and the fowl that struck it—I persevered. I made it through with my family intact. They mattered. The look of the vehicle that took me to school did not. God has your heart in mind with every trial.

And trust me, if a head-on collision with a chicken doesn't build your character, little else will.

BP

LISTEN

Pay attention to him and listen to what he says.
EXODUS 23:21

The role play in my pastoral counseling class was a simple one. I would be the emotionally distraught church member; my classmate would be the pastoral counselor. I'd share my problem, and he would share gentle wisdom. The teacher handed me a slip of paper describing why I'd sought a pastor's help, and . . . "Go."

We started with pleasantries, then moved on to a polite "What can I do for you?"

"Well, Pastor," I began to explain, "I'm just not feeling God's presence in my life anymore. I used to. I mean, I've felt God leading me all my life, even when things were rough, but lately God's just been invisible . . ."

He didn't interrupt me, but he was definitely right on my heels when I finished my opener. He then whammed me with a Bible text. I couldn't for the life of me tell you what it was, but then again, if this had been a real pastoral counseling session, I have a hunch it wouldn't have stuck long in the parishioner's memory either.

"Well, thanks, Pastor," I said, "but I don't know. I still pray and read my Bible practically every day, but something's just—missing."

Robo-pastor didn't miss a beat. His right hook ineffective, he hit me with an uppercut (probably something from the Epistles). We went back and forth a few more times, my classmate offering platitudes for my problems while I tried to explain that my dilemma needed more than a biblical adhesive bandage.

It took a few minutes, but by the time our teacher called time, I think the guy was beginning to catch on. Just like someone seeking a pastor's support and wisdom for real, I didn't need his amazing instant recall of 2 Thessalonians. I needed his sympathetic ear. I needed a friend, not a fortune cookie.

Listening. It's an essential skill for anyone, but too often those who should be most skilled know how to listen to only one person—themselves. We think we understand where someone else is coming from, but we haven't a clue. We offer advice that only makes our friends feel more disconnected. As for my classmate, I was just glad that he got to practice his techniques on a test subject before he could do any real damage.

Because everybody just wants to be understood.

INSPIRATION ON TRIAL / PART 1

Dear friends, do not believe every spirit, but test the spirits to see whether they are from God, because many false prophets have gone out into the world.
1 JOHN 4:1

Exploring the authenticity of a self-proclaimed messenger of God is a tricky issue, because one can claim many unverifiable things. If I announced today that God had told me He now wants everyone to wear purple plaid jackets with yellow galoshes, there's no scientific way to assess my claims. Ellen White's writings on health, however, are a different story. She wrote in the 1800s, a time of general medical ignorance. Medical science has advanced exponentially since then, so the principles she and other nineteenth century health reformers proposed can be evaluated by modern science. This brings us to some critical questions:

1. How accurate was Ellen White on matters of health?

2. If she got her ideas just from strictly human sources, how accurate were those other writers?

3. How does the accuracy of those other writers compare to Ellen White's?

Researchers Leonard Brand and Don S. McMahon explored those questions. In *The Prophet and Her Critics: A Striking New Analysis Refutes the Charges That Ellen G. White "Borrowed" the Health Message*, Brand and McMahon present the results of their research, lining up Ellen White's writings on health, as verified by modern science, against those of her contemporaries. The results are remarkable and compelling. In short, their answers to the above questions are:

1. Incredibly so. While her explanations—the "whys"—are not always as accurate or verifiable, the principles she espoused were overwhelmingly reliable.

2. The accuracy of her nineteenth-century contemporaries is mixed, including numerous principles we would consider kooky that White never passed along to her readers. If she merely borrowed her ideas from other writers, with no supernatural assistance, she had an uncanny ability to pick the right ones and ignore the bad ones.

3. Their level of accuracy pales in comparison with that of White's. There's clearly more going on here than an author simply researching what other writers have to say. On August 22 we'll take a closer look at what these findings tell us. *Continued.*

Science

INSPIRATION ON TRIAL / PART 2

Teach me your way, O Lord, and I will walk in your truth.
PSALM 86:11

In the early 1800s it was a lot easier to become a doctor than it is today, because there was so much less for doctors to learn. From draining blood with leeches to poisonous cure-alls, most of medical science was not only wrong; it left patients worse off than before.

Ellen White claimed to have received her messages on health in visions from God, yet she also read books by such health reformers as Sylvester Graham (who thought everybody should eat crackers). Her critics have said, "See, she wasn't inspired by God after all; she was only copying what other writers had already written." The problem with this argument is that it emphasizes the similarities between White's writings and those of other health reformers, yet ignores the critical differences that set White apart.

In addition to saying some of the same things that Ellen White did, the health writers Ellen White quoted said plenty of things she ignored. For example:

Don't heat your house.

Don't cut your hair.

Don't drink water—get your liquids from fruit.

Don't comfort children, because crying is good for them.

Don't sweat.

Don't let children eat fruit.

Don't eat breakfast.

Don't have sex more than once a month.

Don't eat cucumbers.

While Ellen White's advice is overwhelmingly verified by modern science, the same can't be said for other nineteenth-century writers. Their accuracy pales in comparison. Take Jackson's *Laws of Life*. Alongside some good health principles, it told readers not to wear black or to use soap, and advised children not to eat potatoes.

If Ellen White's writings were merely dependent on other authors', they should have included a significant amount of such bogus advice. Instead, her writings consistently offer sound medical counsel, including much that no other writer in her day had come up with, and include little that modern science has not verified. *Continued.*

INSPIRATION ON TRIAL / PART 3

Put your hope in God, for I will yet praise him, my Savior and my God.
PSALM 42:11

In comparing Ellen White's writings on health to modern medical knowledge and the writings of other nineteenth-century health reformers, Leonard Brand and Don McMahon found that though Ellen White's writings demonstrated accuracy far beyond what one could reasonably expect of someone in her time, there was one area where her accuracy slipped. While the principles for good health she advocated were consistently on the mark, she sometimes gave explanations for them that don't make much sense today. As they put it, her "whats" were spot on, but the "whys" were less so.

Brand and McMahon suggest that "the 'whats' and 'whys' came from different sources of information. Perhaps God gave us the health principles to follow and left it for us to figure out the reasons why they work. Indeed, God could not have explained some of the 'whys' correctly at that time without inventing medical vocabulary and revealing psychological concepts that were not known until decades after Ellen White wrote. Even in a prescientific era, saying, 'Don't eat meat,' or 'Drink lots of water,' or 'Get plenty of sleep' didn't require any special vocabulary or advanced knowledge. . . . However, it would be another matter to explain the reasons for these instructions when no one knew about bacteria or viruses, to say nothing of our immune and endocrine systems. . . .

"Interestingly, when people are troubled by apparent medical errors that Ellen White made, it's usually the 'whys' that trouble them. . . . But the correctness, or lack thereof, of the 'whys' is not a good test of whether Ellen White's health principles were inspired. It's her principles for living—the 'whats'—that can affect our health. As long as we follow these principles, it doesn't matter whether or not we understand the physiological reasons for them—or even whether or not the reasons given, the 'whys,' are erroneous. . . . God has communicated the truths we need" (*The Prophet and Her Critics*, pp. 73, 74).

God gave Ellen White insights to share so that people could understand Him better and live healthier while they were at it. A careful analysis reveals that she, though lacking a medical education and living in a time of medical ignorance, shared medical wisdom that cannot be convincingly explained without accepting her claim of divine assistance. And that assures us of something even more important: that God can be trusted.

Bible

THE WITCH OF ENDOR

When Saul inquired of the Lord, the Lord did not answer him,
not by dreams, or by Urim, or by prophets.
1 SAMUEL 28:6, NRSV

Saul, the first king of Israel, found his kingdom collapsing about him. Step by step he had substituted his own judgment for God's wisdom and ignored the prophet Samuel's counsel. At last God announced that He would give the kingdom to another king. Saul felt frantic. Both the upstart David and his old nemesis, the Philistines, defeated him at every turn. And when Saul sought help from God through all the legitimate channels, He remained silent—or so it seemed. And Samuel was now dead.

At last, feeling that he had no other option, Saul decided to seek aid through a source that God had explicitly forbidden. The rejected king would find a sorcerer to get him in touch with the dead prophet. Canaanites believed that the dead could persuade the gods on their behalf. Perhaps Saul hoped for the same thing.

Saul sneaked into Philistine territory to find the witch of Endor. After he managed to persuade her to accept his request, she claimed to have summoned up Samuel's spirit. (Saul saw nothing himself, but accepted her description.) Did the witch bring the prophet from the dead? Many theologians and preachers think so. As is so frequent in Scripture, the author makes no direct comment on what is going on. But the biblical writer does provide clues if the reader will pay careful attention. Notice that in 1 Samuel 28:15 Saul himself echoes what the narrator said in verse 6. Biblical writers were always terse, and when they repeat something, it means that we must pay special attention to it.

If God would not speak to Saul through the regular channels of divine/human communication, why would He now employ one that He had expressly commanded against? Alexander Heidel, in his comparison of Old Testament descriptions of the dead with those of other Mesopotamian cultures, concluded about the Endor story: "I believe that the whole affair was a demonic delusion, reminding one of 2 Thessalonians 2:9-12" (*The Gilgamesh Epic and Old Testament Parallels*, p. 189).

While the being that called itself Samuel accurately forecast Saul's fate, Satan already knew the logical outcome of the king's actions. The devil is willing to use even truth if it serves his purposes.

GW

BUT I WANT IT

You shall not covet your neighbor's house.
EXODUS 20:17

The tenth commandment has always been my bane. I frequently break it more than the others. Don't kill? No problem. Tell the truth? Check. Do not covet . . . Oh. H'mmm . . . but it is so hard.

Let's take my car, for example. God has blessed my car. If you ever saw it, you would understand. In my senior year of college I needed a car of my very own. I had done OK without a car up to that point. That doesn't mean I didn't *want* my own car before then, but now things had changed, and I *needed* a car. I had a clinical rotation 30 miles from campus, and I needed wheels. I traded $750 for my best friend's car. The lucky model? An 11-year-old ratty Plymouth.

My parents didn't think it would last longer than the six months I needed it, but I had a different plan. As soon as that car came my way I sat in it and blessed the car. I prayed that God would give my car long life, and in return I would name it Miles and always be thankful. I would always attribute its long life to God's blessing.

Now five years and 60,000 miles later it still comes roaring to life every time I need it. Usually I keep my promise. I am thankful every time I get in the driver's-side door (so what if the passenger-side door no longer opens). Every time I turn on the air and blast the radio I say, "Thank You."

But sometimes I look at other cars and desire a newer, nicer, more respectable automobile. Shiny, with paint. So what is the big deal? Every time I wish for someone else's car I remember my promise to be thankful.

Coveting is an ungrateful act. God gives only good gifts, and we must recognize those and in return attribute all good things to Him. So what is the "thing" you covet most often?

_____

_____

_____

How might God be blessing you without it?

_____

_____

_____

LH

Mission

ORDINATION FOR DUMMIES

He appointed twelve—designating them apostles.
MARK 3:14

Here's how you too can become a full-fledged, legitimate, and legal minister: Find yourself a few minutes with a computer with Internet access. Head for www.ulc.org. You're in the right place when you see a dove. Next, click on the "Free Online Ordination" link and follow the on-screen instructions. And last, be sure to print out your "Credentials of Ministry" certificate.

Ta-daa! You are now a minister. Forget about that stuffy cloister or being able to read Aramaic. The Universal Life Church (ULC) has only two core beliefs: "to promote freedom of religion" and "to do that which is right." It's so easy you could ordain your cat. I just did! Pastor Cheyenne (a domestic shorthair) and I now share a ministry.

The Universal Life Church has been around since 1959, when it was started by a disgruntled Baptist who felt that every person should find his or her own walk with faith and religion. However, the ULC has been in hot water with its gratis ordinations, as some have used them improperly as a tax shield.

According to the site, you *could* be eligible to perform marriages in some states. Funerals, baptisms, and even last rites are now your forté. You can do almost anything a person of the cloth does.

But what does it do for your ministry? Do you change lives? Did you answer a call, or a dare? Consider John the Baptist. John 10:41 tells us, "Though John never performed a miraculous sign, all that John said about [Jesus] was true."

John scarcely had a last name, much less ministerial credentials from any church. But he had the most important asset to lead a ministry: he presented the truth as he knew it. No tricks, no healings, no problem. John made his best effort to spread the gospel.

Sure, there is a seemingly long-drawn-out process that requires years of study to get you into being a pastor. However, John seemingly had no trouble without ordination. And the last I read, he did not have 501(c)(3) nonprofit organizations or a degree in divinity.

And quite possibly, neither do you. Which means one thing: you are in the same boat as John. Are you making your best effort?

BP

THINKING OF MARRIAGE? THINK AGAIN.

*For this reason a man will leave his father and mother
and be united to his wife, and they will become one flesh.*
GENESIS 2:24, NIV

Think you'll get married someday? Here are some points to ponder.

Have fun. Don't take life so seriously that you exclude from your circle people who might make good friends.

What ideals are you willing to go to the mat for? What things do you cherish (believe in, clutch to yourself) that you'd be willing to give up if you had to?

If you've only dated--or been friends with--a certain kind of person, are you willing to branch out in the interest of enlarging your own world?

Look into yourself (or ask your friends to help) and discover the kinds of people you always date. Are you a fixer, a helper? Do you only date people who need you? Do you "choose" your friends for the same reason?

Do you crave excitement? Do you like living on the edge? What's good about this? What are the weaknesses of it? Do you only date those who add to that sense of danger?

Take time to grow first. Don't rush into marriage while you're still young. Enjoy the possibilities and opportunities that being single provides. Your late teens and early twenties are times to discover who you really are and what your life is going to be about. Marriages established at older ages are far more likely to succeed. So in the meantime learn who you are. Examine yourself. What do you truly enjoy? What do you dislike? We're not talking here about loving chocolate and hating bluegrass but what you truly value.

Tackle your own issues. Intimate relationships bring everything unresolved to the surface. Terrific people can find themselves acting in unexpectedly hurtful ways because of issues they've been able to ignore all their lives. If your life—and your head—have problems that you know you should untangle, seek the assistance of a trained counselor.

Make sure you share the same view of God. This goes beyond issues of doctrines or denominations, significant as those are. Do you and your future spouse have a similar perspective on God's character? How we view God—joyful, joyless; exacting, embracing—colors everything in our lives, from careers to relationships to parenting. Do they follow God out of fear or out of love and gratitude? If you marry someone whose attitude toward God, and whose perception of God's character, is radically different from yours, you'll never see eye to eye.

Adventism

HOW JESUS CHANGED EVERYTHING

For this reason he had to be made like his brothers in every way,
in order that he might become a merciful and faithful high priest.
HEBREWS 2:17

Over thousands of years countless lambs, bulls, goats, and doves lost their lives in sacrifice to God. Each was a bloody reminder that sin is severe, yet atonement is available. Still, bleeding lambs, goats, or doves had no saving value of their own, and so the ghastly ritual had to be repeated, and the high priest made an annual sacrifice as well.

But when Jesus died as a perfect sacrifice, the jig was up. There was no more need for proxy, stopgap sacrifices. Jesus' death accomplished it all. His sacrifice had staying power.

So what now? Now, instead of human priests swinging a metal ball holding incense in an earthly Temple, we have none other than Jesus Himself interceding for us in heaven. The book of Hebrews presents Jesus, front and center, as the answer to everything in our lives. What the prophets hinted, Jesus revealed. What the sacrifices pointed to, Jesus fulfilled.

Reading Hebrews is a dazzling experience. In 13 short chapters this book is a tour-de-force exploration of the difference Jesus makes. We learn that because Jesus actually lived the down-and-dirty life of a human, He knows just what we're going through. His experience qualifies Him to serve as our priest in heaven and to help us with our every need. When we speak of our struggles in prayer, He understands, and knows just how to help. When we ask forgiveness for sins, He jumps at the chance to forgive us.

Hebrews emphasizes that Jesus made everything better. He's a better revelation, a better priest with a better name. He's a better leader; He brings a better covenant, offers better blood, and points us to a better country and a better city, a better resurrection, and a better way of looking at life. He ministers in a sanctuary built by God Himself.

The work performed in the earthly sanctuary taught people about Jesus, but it wasn't enough. Only Jesus' ministry could bring about the better covenant, where we can rest on His victory rather than our own. Only Jesus' offering "has made perfect forever those who are being made holy" (Hebrews 10:14). Nothing we could ever do can make us right with God, but Jesus' sacrifice has made it possible. Though we're not perfect and may still be drawn to sin, through the merits of Jesus' blood we are already counted perfect in God's sight.

ABSALOM / PART 1

Amnon became frustrated to the point of illness on account of his sister Tamar,
for she was a virgin, and it seemed impossible for him to do anything to her.
2 SAMUEL 13:2

Lust makes fools of us all.

The fallout from his theft and seduction of Bathsheba and murder of her husband, Uriah, haunted King David the rest of his life. He lost respect from his people and within his own family. Looking into the future at how David's sin would affect those around him, Nathan the prophet said, "Why did you despise the word of the Lord by doing what is evil in his eyes? You struck down Uriah the Hittite with the sword and took his wife to be your own. You killed him with the sword of the Ammonites. Now, therefore, the sword will never depart from your house, because you despised me and took the wife of Uriah the Hittite to be your own" (2 Samuel 12:9, 10).

Up first: David's son Amnon fell in lust with his half sister Tamar.

Gazing at her from across the palace and around Jerusalem, he obsessed about her. Her beauty stunned him afresh every time he set eyes on her, and he could think of nothing else but getting his hands on her as well.

His cousin Jonadab saw that Amnon was tripping. "What's wrong?" he asked him. "You're the king's son. How come you look so wretched? You can confide in me."

Amnon hung his head, then locked Jonadab in a mad gaze. "I'm in love with Tamar, my brother Absalom's sister."

Jonadab cackled. He knew it. It had to be a woman! And half sister or not, he could certainly understand why Amnon would be so fixated on someone as delicious as Tamar. "Ah," Jonadab said, "here's what you've got to do! Go to bed and pretend to be ill. Then when the king comes by, tell him you simply must have Tamar fix your next meal — while you watch."

So Amnon lay on his bed and whimpered until Tamar came in. As he watched feverishly, she kneaded, then baked, bread and set it before him. Then, moaning as if in pain, Amnon ordered everyone out. "Now, Tamar, bring the food to me in my bedroom," he said, "so I can eat from your hand." And when she did, Amnon grabbed her, saying, "Come, lie with me, my sister." Jerking her onto his bed, he pushed aside the food. He didn't want bread; he wanted her. *Continued.*

ABSALOM / PART 2

*Absalom ordered his men, "Listen! When Amnon is in high spirits from drinking wine
and I say to you, 'Strike Amnon down,' then kill him. Don't be afraid.
Have not I given you this order? Be strong and brave."*
2 SAMUEL 13:28

Tamar trembled in fear and pain outside Amnon's door. Her own
half brother had violated her. Then, his lust mutating into loathing,
he'd thrown her out in spite and disgust. Expressing how she felt inside, Tamar ripped her lavish robe, crumbled ashes onto her head,
and, crying out in anguish, staggered home, finally falling into her
brother Absalom's arms.

He hugged his shaking sister close. "Has Amnon your brother
been with you?" he asked. Inside he was seething, but his tone
soothed. Tamar's fogged eyes were all the answer he needed. "Be
quiet for now, my sister. He is your brother; don't take this to heart."
So Tamar moved in with Absalom as a "desolate woman." The law of
Moses demanded that a rapist marry the victim. Unlike the practices in
other ancient societies in which assaulted women were regarded simply as damaged goods (an attitude still seen in certain societies today),
Israelite law took a step forward and ensured that such women were
taken care of. It was a long way from the justice we seek today, but a
far cry from the lawless world around them.

David was outraged. From the Dead Sea scrolls the New Revised
Standard Version adds to 2 Samuel 13:21 a line lacking in other trans-
lations: "but he would not punish his son Amnon, because he loved
him, for he was his firstborn."

And so while David drifted numbly with misplaced love, Absalom
plotted his revenge. He waited two years before he struck. Reeling
Amnon into a sumptuous feast, Absalom watched until his brother
was good and drunk, then ordered his servants to strike him down.

Horrified at Amnon's brutal death, David's other sons hopped on
their mules and fled. When the rumor reached David that all his sons
were dead, he writhed on the ground, tearing his garments in grief.
When David's sons returned to Jerusalem, king, sons, and servants all
wept together.

In the meantime Absalom raced to the home of his mother's
father, Talmai, king of Geshur, for sanctuary.

Conflicted and broken, David mourned his fallen and his prodigal
son. *Continued.*

ABSALOM / PART 3

Joab son of Zeruiah knew that the king's heart longed for Absalom.
So Joab sent someone to Tekoa and had a wise woman brought from there.
2 SAMUEL 14:1, 2

"The play's the thing wherein I'll catch the conscience of the King."—Shakespeare, Hamlet.

One son was dead, another had fled, and David felt paralyzed. Guilt for his own past sins ever stabbed at him. He had not held Amnon to account for raping his sister, and now Amnon was dead. David had lost both of his oldest living sons. David loved and longed for Absalom, yet he could hardly permit him to return from exile after committing such a crime. Neither Absalom nor King David's subjects should think that such a crime should be overlooked.

Then one day a woman appeared before the king. She appeared haggard, and dressed like one in mourning. "Help me, O king!" she exclaimed, pressing her face to the ground before him.

David leaned forward on his throne. "What is troubling you?"

The woman looked up. "I am indeed a widow; my husband is dead. I your servant had two sons." She explained that her sons had quarreled alone in a field, and one son had struck and killed the other. "Now the whole clan has risen up against your servant; they say, 'Hand over the one who struck his brother down, so that we may put him to death for the life of his brother whom he killed; then we will get rid of the heir as well'" (2 Samuel 14:7). She brushed a tear from her weary eyes. "They would put out the only burning coal I have left, leaving my husband neither name nor descendant on the face of the earth."

David's heart was moved at this woman's tale. He pledged to use his royal authority to resolve the issue. But the woman protested, "My lord the king, let the blame rest on me and on my father's family, and let the king and his throne be without guilt" (verse 9).

David replied, "If anyone says anything to you, bring him to me, and he will not bother you again."

The woman tightened the knot: "Then let the king invoke the Lord his God to prevent the avenger of blood from adding to the destruction, so that my son will not be destroyed."

"As surely as the Lord lives," he said, "not one hair of your son's head will fall to the ground" (verse 11). *Continued.*

ABSALOM / PART 4

In all Israel there was not a man so highly praised for his handsome appearance
as Absalom. From the top of his head to the sole of his foot
there was no blemish in him. Whenever he cut the hair of his head—
he used to cut his hair from time to time when it became too heavy for him—
he would weigh it, and its weight was two hundred shekels by the royal standard.
2 SAMUEL 14:25, 26

The woman moved in for the kill. "Let your servant speak a word to my lord the king."

"Speak," said the king.

"Why then," said the woman, "have you devised a thing like this against the people of God? When the king says this, does he not convict himself, for the king has not brought back his banished son? Like water spilled on the ground, which cannot be recovered, so we must die. But God does not take away life; instead, he devises ways so that a banished person may not remain estranged from him."

She had more to say, but David knew the jig was up. When she finished, he said, "My servant Joab put you up to this, didn't he?"

With flattering words she confessed that it was so. At last, having heard her out, David said, "Very well, I will do it. Go, bring back the young man Absalom." Joab bowed to David in gratitude, but David put down one condition: "He must go to his own house; he must not see my face."

So Absalom returned. He married and had three sons and one daughter, whom he named Tamar. But for two years he never saw his father. Frustrated, he decided to get Joab's attention—and had his servants set Joab's barley field on fire. When Joab inquired as to why, precisely, Absalom had done that, the prince vented. "Look, I sent word to you and said, 'Come here so I can send you to the king to ask, "Why have I come from Geshur? It would be better for me if I were still there!"' Now then, I want to see the king's face, and if I am guilty of anything, let him put me to death."

Joab told David, David summoned Absalom, Absalom knelt before the king, and David kissed his son. David felt great relief at seeing his beloved son again, but Absalom took it as his cue to start planning his takeover of his father's throne. *Continued.*

ABSALOM / PART 5

In the course of time, Absalom provided himself with a chariot and horses and with fifty men to run ahead of him.

2 SAMUEL 15:1

"Good morning!"

The irate man, stomping his way toward Jerusalem, turned his head. Why, it was Absalom, the prince! The man's face cracked a smile for the first time in days. "Great prince, good day!"

Absalom's face beamed. "What brings you to Jerusalem?"

The man's face tightened. "I've been wronged! I seek justice! I . . ." The prince nodded sagely as the man poured out his complaint, but his thoughts wandered elsewhere. The particulars were hardly important. When the man finished, Absalom took him by his shoulders. "Look," the prince said, "your claims are valid and proper, but there is no representative of the king to hear you." He let out a long sigh. "If only I were appointed judge in the land! Then everyone who has a complaint or case could come to me and I would see that he gets justice" (2 Samuel 15:3, 4).

As far as Absalom was concerned, everyone he met was in the right—because everyone he met was a potential supporter for his rebellion.

Absalom pulled the man forward and kissed him. Overcome, the man thanked him profusely and went home to tell everyone he knew about how kind and understanding Prince Absalom had been.

Absalom schmoozed and sweet-talked and schemed until, as 2 Samuel 15:6 says, "he stole the hearts of the men of Israel." But his father saw only what he wanted to see. When Absalom told his father he wanted to travel to Hebron to worship God there, David suspected nothing. "Go in peace," David said, but peace was the last thing on Absalom's mind. The first? Taking over the throne.

As trumpets blasted, messengers proclaimed: "Absalom is king in Hebron!"

David summoned his loyal officials. "Come! We must flee, or none of us will escape from Absalom. We must leave immediately, or he will move quickly to overtake us and bring ruin upon us and put the city to the sword."

Now David, once a fugitive from King Saul, went on the run from his own son. *Continued.*

Bible

ABSALOM / PART 6

But David continued up the Mount of Olives, weeping as he went.
2 SAMUEL 15:30

As David traveled with his entourage away from the capital city, he encountered friends and foes alike. Ittai the Gittite, a Philistine convert to Yahweh, declared the unwavering support of himself and his 600 men. People wept to see their king fleeing for his life. David trudged up the Mount of Olives, head covered as a sign of mourning and distress, weeping alongside his servants and friends. And having learned that his servant Ahithophel was actually helping Absalom, David prayed, "O Lord, turn Ahithophel's counsel into foolishness" (2 Samuel 15:31).

As David traveled farther, he met one of Saul's relatives, Shimei son of Gera. "Get out, get out, you man of blood, you scoundrel!" Shimei jeered at the king, hurling rocks at him. "The Lord has repaid you for all the blood you shed in the household of Saul, in whose place you have reigned. The Lord has handed the kingdom over to your son Absalom. You have come to ruin because you are a man of blood!" (2 Samuel 16:7, 8).

David's servant Abishai grasped his sword. "Why should this dead dog curse my lord the king?" he snarled. "Let me go over and cut off his head" (verse 9).

But David shook his weary head. Perhaps, David suggested, God Himself had told Shimei to curse. "My own son is trying to kill me, so let this man curse! Perhaps God will see my distress and repay me with blessings for these curses."

Back in Jerusalem, Absalom and his entourage swept in to a royal welcome. There Ahithophel gave him some truly wretched advice: demonstrate his royal authority by lying with the king's concubines.

That deed done, Absalom and his men discussed strategy. Ahithophel advised immediately attacking David while he was still weak. Just kill David, he recommended, and everyone else will scatter. But Hushai the Arkite, playing double agent for David, recommended a true showdown. After all, he said, David was a legendary fighter, and he'd be hiding out in some cave or such apart from his troops. Nothing short of all-out war, he said, would win Absalom the kingdom.

Ahimaaz and Jonathan, sons of the priests Zadok and Abiathar, rushed to inform David of Absalom's plans. Then spotted by a young man loyal to Absalom, they hid in a well. *Continued.*

ABSALOM / PART 7

Christ redeemed us from the curse of the law by becoming a curse for us,
for it is written: "Cursed is everyone who is hung on a tree."
GALATIANS 3:13

Absalom's men hammered on the door of the house. "Where are Ahimaaz and Jonathan?"

The woman of the house answered. She had covered the well, in which the priests' sons had hidden, with grain, so that it was no longer noticeable. "They crossed over the brook," she told them, and the prince's men hurried off.

Once it was safe to leave, Ahimaaz and Jonathan sped toward David to inform him of Absalom's plans. But when Ahithophel learned that his advice to attack the king alone had not been followed, he "put his house in order" and hanged himself.

The armies gathered, and as the brokenhearted father watched his troops ready for departure, he had one more plea. "Be gentle with the young man Absalom for my sake," he commanded.

The battle raged in a thick forest, and David's men won a decisive victory. Then as Absalom rode his mule under an oak tree, his head caught in the branches, and he hung there while the mule ran on. A young man spotted the prince there and informed Joab. "What!" Joab roared. "Why didn't you strike him down? I would have rewarded you with 10 shekels of silver and a warrior's belt!"

The soldier clung to principle. He'd heard the king's command to spare his son. But Joab had no patience for the king's moody madness, and plunged a javelin into Absalom's heart.

When David learned of his son's death, he lost all hope. "O my son Absalom!" he cried. "My son, my son Absalom! If only I had died instead of you—O Absalom, my son, my son!"

The king was inconsolable, so it's just as well that Joab was in no mood to console. Approaching the grieving king, he tore into him. "You've insulted your men!" he charged. "You love those who hate you and hate those who love you. . . . Now go out and encourage your men." And so the king did, but his mind was far away.

A thousand years later another Son of David hung from a tree, begging to know where His Father had gone. And a King at last died in the place of His children.

Bible

SIBLINGS, SLINGS, AND HONOR

Guide me in your truth and teach me, for you are God my Savior.
PSALM 25:5

I never appreciated the passing reference to going down to Jericho from Jerusalem in Jesus' parable of the good Samaritan (Luke 10: 30) until I came up from the ancient city. A small group of us entered the West Bank from the country of Jordan. After crossing the wide plain west of Jericho we started up the road to Jerusalem. We climbed and climbed and after what seemed like a long time we saw a roadside sign stating that we had finally reached sea level. Jericho is 740 feet below sea level, and Jerusalem is 2,300 to 2,500 feet above sea level. It really is a long way down to Jericho.

Nor did I catch the biblical writers' sense of pride when they referred to the slingers in Israelite military forces (Judges 20:16; 2 Kings 3:25) until I held one of the baseball-sized sling stones in my hand. A good slinger could hurl a stone 100 miles per hour. Slingers were the heavy artillery of the Israelite military forces.

Sociologists who study the Middle East tell us that the most important relationship to its people has always been that between siblings—brothers and sisters. Even today many brothers and sisters feel closer to each other than to anyone else. Siblings were expected to honor and uphold each other. So consider how shocking it must have seemed to find the Bible filled with stories about estranged brothers such as Jacob and Esau. Even today Middle East society expects brothers to be responsible for and to take care of their sisters, even if the brother is still only a child and the sister is older. A girl often asks her brother for permission to do something, while the boy will be especially protective of her. How does the special sibling relationship help us to understand why Absalom reacted as he did when Amnon disgraced Absalom's sister Tamar (2 Samuel 13)?

People in the Middle East are greatly concerned about honor. They believe that there is only a limited supply. The only way a person can get more is to take it from someone else. One way to do that is to challenge others in public and shame them. The Pharisees would often confront Jesus, asking Him questions they thought He couldn't answer or putting Him in positions they assumed He couldn't get out of. But when He did, they were the ones shamed, and He, to their horror, gained more honor.

GW

THE MYSTERIOUS WORLD OF SLEEP

At this I awoke and looked around. My sleep had been pleasant to me.
JEREMIAH 31:26

Sleep. Everyone wants you to go to sleep when you're awake and wants to wake you up when you're asleep. When school starts in the morning, you can't wake up to pay attention, and when school is over, you have enough energy to run a marathon. Why is sleep such a royal pain for teens?

News flash: The teenage body naturally needs more sleep than an adult's: a grand total of 9 1/4 hours. Teens are naturally inclined to go to sleep around 11:00 p.m., waking up a little after 8:00 a.m. Their first class starts about the time they should be waking. This is all determined by circadian rhythms, an internal clock shaped by melatonin and sunlight. Sleep patterns also change our circadian rhythms. Weekends lead to late nights, which lead to sleeping in late. Then when Monday rolls around it's difficult to get moving.

All mammals need sleep to survive—some more than others. Housecats sleep up to 16 hours a day. Dolphins, on the other hand, never appear to sleep, but this is trickery. Half of their brain sleeps while the other maintains minimum functioning, and then they switch.

Sleep is an intricate process with multiple levels. The first is rapid eye movement (REM) and nonrapid eye movement (NREM). NREM is the biggest chunk of sleep, about 75 percent, and has four stages. Stage 1 is drowsiness, in which your brain is slowing down and you start to nod.

You lose consciousness in stage 2. In stages 3 and 4 sleepwalking, bedwetting, and night terrors are likely to occur. During REM sleep the good stuff occurs: dreams. Your entire body is paralyzed, but your eyes dart about. Throughout the night you rotate through the various cycles.

So why do we sleep? There are different theories, but one is that NREM sleep is useful for the body. It uses this time to build up the immune system, neurons, hormones, and protein. It is also thought that during REM sleep our brain takes information in short-term memory and stores it into long-term memory—which means that pulling an all-nighter before a test won't help you remember stuff in the long term.

LH

NEW WINE,
OLD COOKIE DOUGH / PART 1

Then Levi held a great banquet for Jesus at his house,
and a large crowd of tax collectors and others were eating with them.

LUKE 5:29

We meant to send some cookies in a care package, but, well, we just got too busy. So a big chunk of our double batch of cookie dough sat in a plastic container in our fridge for about two weeks.

About an hour ago I thought, *Hey, I should run a few cookies through the oven.* Nothing smells better in a late afternoon, sunshine or rain, than fresh-baked chocolate-chip cookies. Wash it down with a glass of milk, and what you have is a slice of heaven.

Still, since it was two weeks old, I resisted my usual inclination to eat raw dough. The first batch I baked came out burnt after only eight minutes. I tried the next one for a little more than seven minutes, and it came out a bit too gooey, so I put it back in for a little longer.

What came out of the oven looked like cookies. They felt like cookies. They even mostly smelled like cookies. But when I took my first bite, something just wasn't right. The taste was . . . off. I couldn't place it, but what should have been sweet, chocolatey, and refreshing tasted gummy and sour. After my first swallow, my stomach turned ever so slightly. The dough hadn't baked right, didn't taste right, and a few bites made me feel kinda ill.

As Jesus feasted with a crowd of tax collectors and other people of poor reputation, hosted by His tax-collector-turned-disciple Levi Matthew, Pharisees and other religious leaders started pestering Him. Didn't He know the company He was keeping? they demanded. "Why do you eat and drink with tax collectors and 'sinners'?"

"It is not the healthy who need a doctor," Jesus replied, "but the sick. I have not come to call the righteous, but sinners to repentance" (Luke 5:30-32).

It was an ironic statement if there ever was one, for the people the Pharisees called sinners were counted righteous the moment they acknowledged their need for Jesus. But the Pharisees, who thought themselves so righteous, so spiritually healthy, were, on the inside, nothing but rotten. Like cookies cooked too late. Even when they looked fresh, they left a nasty taste in your mouth. *Continued.*

NEW WINE, OLD COOKIE DOUGH / PART 2

No one tears a patch from a new garment and sews it on an old one. If he does,
he will have torn the new garment, and the patch from the new will not match the old.
LUKE 5:36

Riding through Pennsylvania with my parents as a kid, I came down with a bad cough. I needed to take some medicine, but I knew I couldn't stand the taste. Then I had a brainstorm. What if I mixed a little cough syrup with a lot of Slurpee? My dad pulled over at the next 7-Eleven, and I eagerly mixed several frothy flavors, then added the spoonful of medicine to the cupful of sugar.

Let's just say there's a reason a cherry Robitussin Slurpee has never been a big hit. The vile medicinal taste infected the entire once-delicious Slurpee. I should have just downed the medicine, and then enjoyed the sugary sweetness.

When Jesus told the Pharisees that He ate with so-called sinners because they were the ones who needed Him most, the church leaders were ready with another question. How come, they asked, Jesus and His disciples ate and drank and celebrated constantly, and never fasted, as they did?

"Can you make the guests of the bridegroom fast while he is with them?" Jesus asked (Luke 5:34). The answer was obvious. As long as the wedding party is at the party, it's time to celebrate! Then, for a moment, Jesus looked to His future death, perhaps hoping they'd yet catch on to what He had to offer when the time was ripe: "But the time will come when the bridegroom will be taken from them; in those days they will fast."

Jesus continued with one of His usual brain-stretching parables. Would you, He asked, repair an old garment with a piece torn from a new one? Of course not—then both garments would be ruined. "And no one pours new wine into old wineskins," Jesus elaborated. "If he does, the new wine will burst the skins, the wine will run out and the wineskins will be ruined. No, new wine must be poured into new wineskins. "

Jesus' message could not be combined with the superstitious self-righteousness of the Pharisees. The Pharisees' empty rituals left their spirituality as dried up as an old wineskin. The vibrant spirituality that Jesus offered was simply incompatible with their formulaic traditions.

If we want to taste the new wine that Jesus offers, we have to be willing to let go of old attitudes.

Mission

THE GREATEST MIRACLE
PART 1

Hear my voice when I call, O Lord; be merciful to me.
PSALM 27:7

"We're hit! We're hit!" There was nothing for flight engineer James Harris to do but hang on for the ride as German aircraft scored eight direct hits on the B-17 during a bombing raid over Berlin. Two shells hit the nose, one the fuselage. Another shell hit the left wing, releasing 500 gallons of fuel. The pilot flying their P-38 escort radioed: "I don't know how you fellows are staying in the air. You look like a kitchen sieve!"

It was June 21, 1944. On just one engine they kept the plane going for another 90 minutes. Then, taking more flack, it went into a dive, and the soldiers bailed out. James was spinning headfirst toward the ground. At his parachute's opening his shoulders took the force, cracking vertebrae in his neck. A walnut tree cushioned his fall, but the moment they reached him three civilians began beating him with clubs. Having had their towns and farms devastated by Allied bombs, the men took out their anger on the first enemies that fell into their hands.

These were the first GIs they'd captured, and the farmers made the best of it. Quickly sending for the town's burgonmaster, they forced James and a buddy to stand about 25 feet ahead of 10 men. Each held a gun, and it didn't take a rocket scientist to know what would happen next. James was terrified. Growing up, he'd had no religious education. He hadn't even seen a Bible until he was 19. As he was standing there the bits and pieces of religion that he'd picked up raced through his mind—when you died, if you weren't saved, you went to hell, where you burned for eternity. James was 20, and he was afraid to die.

"Ready. Aim. FIRE!"

Ten guns clicked, but not a single one fired.

"Reload!" the burgonmaster commanded. The farmers pulled back the chambers of their guns. Ten bullets fell to the ground. They reloaded. Again came the shout: "Ready. Aim. FIRE!"

Ten guns clicked again, but none fired. As the two American soldiers stood weak and sweating in the June sun, the command came a third time. Again, no report. Then six soldiers came up and ordered the firing squad to drop their guns. And James and another crew member were taken to a stalag in Frankfurt. Now James was a prisoner of war. *Continued.*

THE GREATEST MIRACLE
PART 2

[God] is able to do immeasurably more than all we ask or imagine.
EPHESIANS 3:20

A prisoner of war in Germany, James Harris lived in a tiny gray-walled cell that had no windows, no ventilation, and no toilet. A lightbulb hanging from the ceiling burned continually. The little food that the prisoners received was hardly enough to keep a child alive. Mornings the men were awakened at 4:00 a.m. and marched to a cemetery a few miles away for interrogation. Once, they were given shovels and ordered to dig a 2' by 6' pit. They dug as slowly as they dared, but by evening the grave-shaped pit was almost six feet deep. Commanded to stand on its edge, the men faced a firing squad. This was psychological warfare, for after threats the men were marched back to camp. But during those terrible hours James had a strange strength that brought peace.

Months passed. With the Russian army nearing the prison 10,000 prisoners were evacuated, marched out in columns of 1,800. Walking was extremely difficult for James, as his injuries had not healed properly. Of course, the men were literally starving. In 91 days they walked 550 miles, stumbling along in snow, ice, and sleet. One day as James painfully dragged one foot in front of the other he cried to God, "If You exist, if You'll save me, I'll seek and serve You." Of the 1,850 men in his section, only 250 lived to be liberated.

Back in the United States James began visiting churches, only to be convinced that God was a myth. Then one day the man he worked with called out a taunt to a tall man walking toward them: "Get ready to meet your Lord."

"I'm ready!" the man replied in a deep voice. "You'd better get ready."

"Don't listen to him," James' partner whispered, "or you'll be as crazy as he is. He's a Seventh-day Adventist." James looked in the stranger's face and saw peace and power.

"You go to church on Saturday?" he asked, puzzled.

"Yes. On what day do you go to church?"

"I don't go," James replied. "I don't know anything about religion."

The big man took a Bible from his pocket. "This is what God says," he began.

James Harris became an SDA pastor, a missionary, and a popular speaker for youth and young adults. "Learning about Christ brought even greater miracles than I'd seen during the war," he'd say as he told his life story. (Adapted from *Adventist Review*, May 24, 2007.)

Adventism

HOLDING UNSWERVINGLY TO THE HOPE

Let us throw off everything that hinders and the sin that so easily entangles,
and let us run with perseverance the race marked out for us.
Let us fix our eyes on Jesus, the author and perfecter of our faith.
HEBREWS 12:1, 2

Faith. Covenants. The Bible's jargon isn't always so easy to follow. We think we finally understand one tricky word, and another comes along and confuses us all over again. But once we start to get the hang of things, an incredible picture and promise becomes clear.

The book of Hebrews talks about the "new covenant" offered to us by Jesus. What is it? It's the same one that the Holy Spirit promised back in Jeremiah's day, while the Israelites were rebelling their way into captivity in Babylon.

Hebrews 10:16 quotes Jeremiah 31:33: "This is the covenant I will make with them after that time, says the Lord. I will put my laws in their hearts, and I will write them on their minds. . . . Their sins and lawless acts I will remember no more."

If you truly think about it, it's hard to believe that we have this relationship with the Being that rules the universe. This new heart-centered relationship with God means we no longer spend our lives tiptoeing around rules. It means that we no longer have to be afraid, "held in slavery by [our] fear of death" (Hebrews 2:15). Indeed, *our relationship with God makes us bold*. Hebrews 10:19-23 paints an amazing picture: "since we have confidence to enter the Most Holy Place by the blood of Jesus, by a new and living way opened for us through the curtain, that is, his body, and since we have a great priest over the house of God, let us draw near to God with a sincere heart in full assurance of faith, having our hearts sprinkled to cleanse us from a guilty conscience and having our bodies washed with pure water. Let us hold unswervingly to the hope we profess, for he who promised is faithful."

We hear people talk a lot about hope, but faith goes infinitely beyond it. Faith is more than simply belief; it's more than just hope. If it were merely one or the other, it would simply be a feeling with uncertain foundations. But faith is hope and belief multiplied by each other. Faith is certainty and assurance, based on what Jesus has done for you and me. It is what helps us endure as we look ahead to something better—not just hoping, not just feeling, but with assurance and conviction.

KINGDOM DONE

*Any kingdom divided against itself will be ruined,
and a house divided against itself will fall."*
LUKE 11:17

United we stand—but divided we fall.

Approximately 800 years had passed from the Israelites' crossing of the Jordan River to King Nebuchadnezzar's dragging them off to Babylon (a century after the Assyrians had walloped 10 tribes out of their 12). We tend to think of the 12 tribes as a united people most of those years, but the century of monarchy ruled by Saul, David, and Solomon was about as good as it got.

Before the prophet Samuel anointed and crowned Saul the Benjamite, civil war had nearly wiped out his tribe. Even the legendary David faced numerous dissenters challenging his grip on the throne— first members of other tribes and Saul loyalists, then members of his own family. Solomon, the second son of David and Bathsheba, and their choice for the throne, took over while his dad still lived, just to jump the slingshot on his scheming half brother Adonijah.

Solomon's reign is remarkable not only for Israel's peace with its neighbors, but for its peace within. Before losing his horse and his life in battle, big brother Absalom "stole the hearts of the men of Israel" (2 Samuel 15:6) with his good looks and charisma, but for young Sol it would take more than looks or luck. No doubt, having to get by on wits alone contributed to his asking God for wisdom above everything else.

When two prostitutes came to Solomon's court for judgment after one's newborn son died and the other tried to claim the remaining son as her own, he solved the custody dispute by suggesting the baby be shared—by slicing it in two with the closest sword. The true mother tearfully offered to give up her son, while the faker spitefully agreed to the split. So King Sol awarded the child to the one who was willing to lose him to save him. When the people heard how cleverly Solomon had deduced the truth, "all Israel . . . held the king in awe, because they saw that he had wisdom from God to administer justice" (1 Kings 3:28).

Perhaps today we should be awed that he held a country together for so long, for at his death it was torn, and no king's horses or men ever put it together again.

Science

HUMMUS

Take wheat and barley, beans and lentils, millet and spelt;
put them in a storage jar and use them to make bread for yourself.
EZEKIEL 4:9

First, a language lesson. "Hummus," what you know as the name of a tan-colored dip, is actually the Arabic word for chickpeas. (So, hey, now you know some Arabic.) OK, what are those small round things in the can labeled "garbanzos"? They're chickpeas too. The Spanish word for them is "garbanzo." Where did hummus, the dip, originate? It's fair to say that way, way back in Old Testament times some clever person ground up chickpeas, added a little salt, garlic, and oil olive, then dipped their bread in it.

Hummus is amazingly simple to make, though you might be confused by the many variations. Here's a basic recipe.

Ingredients:
2 cans chickpeas, drain and save liquid
2/3 cups tahini paste (found in a can at the grocers)
3 tbsp. olive oil
1/4 cup lemon or lime juice
2 cloves garlic
Salt to taste
1 tbsp. chopped fresh parsley (optional)

In food processor, puree the chickpeas, tahini, olive oil, lemon juice, and garlic until smooth. Add a little of the chickpea liquid if mixture is too thick. Garnish with chopped parsley. Makes about 3 cups. Recipe can be halved.

White bean hummus: Drain and rinse 2 cans of white beans. Proceed as with above recipe.
Peanut butter hummus: Halve above recipe, substituting 4 tablespoon peanut butter for the tahini paste. As needed, thin with 1/3 cup warm water; do **not** use liquid from the can.
To serve: Because the color is so light, it's nice to serve hummus in a bright-colored bowl. A sprinkle with paprika adds color too.

This makes a great appetizer. Or just eat it 'cause you like it. Serve with raw veggies or triangles of warmed pita bread.

THE POOR IN WHAT?

Blessed are the poor in spirit, for theirs is the kingdom of heaven.
MATTHEW 5:3

I can't say poverty has ever been one of my ambitions. My financial goals have generally tended more along the lines of "More money than I know what to do with." That always sounded pretty good to me, thanks. I'd make sure I had a nice, sturdy, nonleaking house, a functioning, energy-efficient car, and that I could see every bit of the world that I wanted to.

I've never been big on flashy clothes or hotels or anything that's cool just because it's expensive, so I figured I'd be a happy philanthropist. C. S. Lewis (who never even learned to drive a car) made plenty of loot from all his books, but gave his wealth away to people who needed the money more than he did. That sounds like fun. But being "poor in spirit" sounds like something I'd really rather pass on.

Yet Jesus says the "poor in spirit" are "blessed." The word translated "blessed" from the Greek, *makarios*, means "happy"—even "fortunate." What's going on here? What's wrong with being self-sufficient?

Self-sufficiency is a spiritual killer. In the book of Revelation, Jesus tells self-satisfied Christians, "You say, 'I am rich; I have acquired wealth and do not need a thing.' But you do not realize that you are wretched, pitiful, poor, blind and naked" (3:17).

But the "poor in spirit" know that without Jesus, they're nothing. They sense how much they need God's grace. Though the spiritually self-sufficient think they've already got it made, if they could see themselves as God sees them they'd be horrified to see how shallow and pathetic they really are.

To keep us from thinking we can—or should—do everything ourselves, God gave us the Sabbath, (So what if you haven't finished your homework? God wants you to take a break.) To keep us from feeling that we have to earn our own salvation, Jesus earned it for us on a bloody cross.

Most of the people listening to Jesus' mountainside sermon looked for a political kingdom on earth, but the "kingdom of heaven" Jesus refers to in today's verse begins in our hearts. From there it spreads from person to person, changing the world with the power of love.

HABIT-FORMING

Let us not give up meeting together, as some are in the habit of doing,
but let us encourage one another.
HEBREWS 10:25

In the mid-twentieth century, reconstructive cosmetic surgeon Maxwell Maltz noticed something intriguing again and again: it took 21 days for amputee patients to stop feeling phantom limb sensations.

Maltz's epiphany suggested something that subsequent tests have confirmed. It takes 21 days to form a habit. If you want to rewire your brain to do something new, to commit to a new way of thinking or living until it comes "naturally," you should commit to doing it daily for three straight weeks.

This bit of psychology explains why good habits are so hard to make and bad ones so hard to break. From eating habits to controlling your temper, staying the way you've always been is way too easy. Getting out of bed early to go jogging? Rolling over is easy; shaking the fog out of your eyes is hard. But commitment and discipline can make all the difference in personal growth.

What habit do you wish you could develop?

_____

_____

_____

How would this habit improve your life and your walk with God?

_____

_____

_____

What obstacles or distractions prevent you from making it a habit?

_____

_____

_____

What will you do to commit to developing your new habit?

_____

_____

_____

STEWARDSHIP

For where your treasure is, there your heart will be also.
MATTHEW 6:21

Stewardship. It's a stuffy word if there ever was one, and it's another one of those vague biblical terms that gets tossed around, politely batted at, and then forgotten as we get back to our real lives.

So what does it actually mean, and what difference should it make in your life? I'd sum it up like this: *You need only to have faith in Jesus to be saved forever, but until He returns to rescue you, it's also important to be faithful.*

Stewardship is how we relate to every gift God's given us. Our health, our wealth, our time, our talents—God has blessed us in various ways so that we might enjoy life and glorify Him through our lives. Some people have incredible talents for athletics, for selling things, for making money, for speaking, for listening, for leading. Whatever your talents may be, make sure you use them for God. Be open to opportunities to share your gifts in ministry for God.

We should always trust in God, not the gifts He's given us. It's easy—and human nature—to think we can give God a break. *That's OK, God,* we think, *I'll take it from here.* While God definitely wants us to develop our gifts and resources, we should always remember that without Him, we've got and are—nothing.

Our responsibility includes the whole world. God gave us an incredible planet to live on, fine-tuned to our every need. Take time to get out and appreciate it, and take care of it.

We need to control our money before it controls us. Jesus told parable after parable about managing our resources. When it came to money, though, Jesus' words were particularly sharp: "No servant can serve two masters. Either he will hate the one and love the other, or he will be devoted to the one and despise the other. You cannot serve both God and Money" (Luke 16:13). Christians need to remember that ultimately, all the wealth on earth is God's. As Christians we need to put God first when it comes to our money, giving him a tenth of our income and freewill offerings. In return, God will bless us financially and spiritually in ways we'd miss out on if we weren't faithful.

Stewardship always pays.

Innovation

TO MAKE GENTLE
THE LIFE OF THIS WORLD / PART 1

Blessed are the peacemakers, for they will be called sons of God.
MATTHEW 5:9

A thousand people cheered as Robert Kennedy stepped out of his vehicle in the inner-city ghetto. But the young presidential candidate would not be all sheepish smiles this night. Civil rights leader Martin Luther King had just died in Memphis.

As U.S. attorney general in his brother John's presidential administration, Robert Kennedy had worked tirelessly to promote civil rights, from desegregation to voting rights. Though his relationship with King began with mutual suspicion (he had allowed FBI director J. Edgar Hoover to wiretap King's home phone), as the years went by, King and Kennedy grew to trust each other as allies in a greater cause.

His brother's assassination in 1963 devastated Kennedy and refocused his priorities. A year later he successfully ran for the Senate, and used his new position to champion the causes he believed in. In 1966 he visited South Africa. Speaking out against South Africa's oppressive policy of apartheid at the University of Capetown, he told the audience, "Each time a man stands up for an ideal, or acts to improve the lot of others, or strikes out against injustice, he sends forth a tiny ripple of hope."

When President Lyndon Johnson announced in 1968 that he would not run for reelection, Kennedy decided to enter the presidential race himself. He centered his campaign on social justice, campaigning in impoverished cities, coal mining communities, and to teeming crowds of young people at colleges.

The evening of April 4, Kennedy was scheduled to speak in a ghetto in Indianapolis, an area notorious for its poverty and crime. Then news of Martin Luther King's death came. Kennedy recoiled as if punched in the gut.

Indianapolis' mayor begged Kennedy to cancel his appearance. The police chief said he wouldn't be held responsible for anything that happened in his city if Kennedy persisted. When Kennedy's vehicle entered the ghetto, his police escort disappeared into the rainy night. As he stepped on to the street, the crowd cheered, warming themselves by waving hand-painted banners. Without mobile phones or round-the-clock news channels, few had yet heard the news of King's death. Then discarding any prepared speech, Kennedy faced the crowd and softly began to speak. *Continued.*

TO MAKE GENTLE
THE LIFE OF THIS WORLD / PART 2

The Lord God has given me the tongue of a teacher,
that I may know how to sustain the weary with a word.
ISAIAH 50:4, NRSV

"Could you lower those signs, please?" Kennedy asked. "I have some very sad news for all of you, and that is that Martin Luther King was shot and killed tonight in Memphis."

As one, the crowd cried out in shock and pain. "Martin Luther King dedicated his life to love and to justice between fellow human beings. He died in the cause of that effort. In this difficult day, in this difficult time for the United States, it is perhaps well to ask what kind of a nation we are and what direction we want to move in. For those of you who are black—considering the evidence evidently is that there were white people who were responsible—you can be filled with bitterness, and with hatred, and a desire for revenge. We can move in that direction as a country, in greater polarization—black people amongst blacks, and white amongst white, and filled with hatred toward one another. Or we can make an effort, as Martin Luther King did, to understand and to comprehend, and to replace that violence, that stain of bloodshed that has spread across our land, with an effort to understand, with compassion and love. . . .

"My favorite poet was Aeschylus. He once wrote: 'In our sleep, pain which cannot forget falls drop by drop upon the heart until, in our own despair, against our will, comes wisdom through the awful grace of God.'

"What we need in the United States is not division; what we need in the United States is not hatred; what we need in the United States is not violence and lawlessness; but is love and wisdom, and compassion toward one another, and a feeling of justice toward those who still suffer within our country, whether they be white or whether they be black.

"So I ask you tonight to return home, to say a prayer for the family of Martin Luther King, yeah, that's true, but more importantly to say a prayer for our own country, which all of us love—a prayer for understanding and that compassion of which I spoke. . . .

"Let us dedicate ourselves to what the Greeks wrote so many years ago: to tame the savageness of man and make gentle the life of this world. Let us dedicate ourselves to that, and say a prayer for our country and for our people."

That night riots broke out in more than 60 U. S. cities, but the streets of Indianapolis stayed calm.

Bible

THE RISE AND FALL
OF JEROBOAM / PART 1

Also, Jeroboam son of Nebat rebelled against the king.
1 KINGS 11:26

"Greetings, Jeroboam, son of Nebat."

The prophet's fierce gaze stopped the ambitious young government official in his tracks along the road outside Jerusalem. Jeroboam was a man on the move, it was true, entrusted by King Solomon to oversee construction work in Jerusalem. The man greeting him was, he knew, Ahijah the prophet. What would such a man want with him?

Ahijah stepped forward, then suddenly began to rip the garment he wore into a dozen pieces. Handing 10 of them to Jeroboam, he declared, "Take ten pieces, for that's how many tribes God's going to give you to rule."

Jeroboam stared in shock as Ahijah pointed out the obvious—idolatry, corruption, a king and people forsaking God. God's love for the late, great David meant that his grandson Rehoboam would still reign in Jerusalem over the tribes of Judah and Benjamin, but the other ten tribes were now Jeroboam's baby. The usual catch, of course, was that if he wanted God's blessing, Jeroboam needed to honor God in everything.

Now, why is that always easier said than done?

When Solomon got wind of his potential usurper, he tried to have Jeroboam killed, so Jeroboam fled to Egypt until the king died. When Rehoboam promised to squeeze the people even harder than Solomon, 10 tribes said, "No, thanks; we're outta here," and Jeroboam took command of the new kingdom of Israel.

"This means war," Rehoboam decided, and assembled his troops. But another prophet, Shemaiah, charged Rehoboam and his people, "Don't fight against your kindred, the people of Israel. Let everyone go home, for what has happened is My will." And, in one of those rare moments that bucks even the worst of trends, that is just what king and people did. The kingdoms lived in tension that often spilled into violence, but the devastation would be limited.

But now that he'd been handed the kingdom, Jeroboam floundered. How, he wondered, would he keep his people from going back to the house of David if they kept on worshipping in Jerusalem? The plan: The Israelites' original sin. *Continued.*

THE RISE AND FALL
OF JEROBOAM / PART 2

A man of God . . . proclaimed against the altar.
1 KINGS 13:1, NRSV

The people of Israel gathered in Bethel before their new ruler as he prepared to make his announcement of a plan that, he hoped, would solidify their commitment to the kingdom. "Israel!" Jeroboam shouted, his arms raised in emphasis. "It's time to stop wearing yourself out going all the way to Jerusalem to worship. That's just too much to ask, don't you think? So here, here are your gods, O Israel, who brought you up out of the land of Egypt!"

Murmurs swept the crowd as Jeroboam presented a golden calf and prepared to offer incense upon its altar. The murmurs turned to shouts of exaltation. It went against everything their religion had ever stood for, but if it meant they wouldn't have to travel so far from home to make sacrifices, they figured, Count us in.

A prophet from Judah emerged from the crowd. Sweeping toward the king, the prophet started pronouncing doom upon the altar itself. "O altar, altar," he uttered. "Someday a king named Josiah, a descendant of David, will sacrifice not animals but humans on you—he'll burn the bones of the false priests on you. This altar will be destroyed with fire and ashes!"

"Seize him!" Jeroboam demanded, stretching out his hand toward the prophet. Suddenly Jeroboam's hand withered. Jeroboam panicked. "Please!" he shrieked. "I beg you, pray to God that my hand will be healed!"

And so it was done. A grateful—yet politically conniving—Jeroboam invited the prophet to dine with him that night, but the prophet refused, for it would indicate acceptance of Jeroboam's illegitimate actions. "You can offer me half your kingdom," the prophet intoned, "and I'll still pass on your offer. God commanded me to not eat, drink, or return by the way I came."

But as the prophet traveled home a man heard that he'd refused Jeroboam and decided to snooker him. He convinced the prophet that an angel had told him to feed him at his house. As they ate, God suddenly sent a message: Death awaited the prophet for misrepresenting God's message against Jeroboam's abomination in Bethel. As the prophet traveled home a lion killed him, but left his donkey alive, and lay down beside them both. Now everyone knew that God condemned the false altar. *Continued.*

Bible

THE RISE AND FALL
OF JEROBOAM / PART 3

You have provoked me to anger and thrust me behind your back.
1 KINGS 14:9

But while many people were impressed to follow God by the startling scene they'd witnessed in Bethel—including some who moved to Jerusalem to live and worship with the people of Judah—Jeroboam kept right on doing his thing.

His plan left him with a practical problem: he needed priests. So Jeroboam hired whoever applied, and Israel sunk deeper and deeper into sin, worshipping other gods. Jeroboam established temples for the worship of the Canaanite fertility goddess Asherah, where poles were dedicated in her honor.

Back in Jerusalem, in the kingdom of Judah, Rehoboam started out well, but soon slipped back into idolatry. In the fifth year of his reign the Egyptian pharaoh Shishak attacked and plundered Jerusalem. Rehoboam and his officers and people acknowledged that they had forgotten God, and God promised to preserve them from future assaults.

Then one day Jeroboam's son Abijah became deathly sick. Jeroboam told his wife to seek out Ahijah, the prophet who had promised him the kingdom so many years before. "Go, disguise yourself," Jeroboam said, "so that no one recognizes you. Give him these gifts of loaves and cakes and honey, and he'll tell you whether our boy will live or die."

Jeroboam's wife headed to Shiloh with a heavy heart. But though Ahijah was now blind with old age, you just can't fool a prophet.

"Come in, wife of Jeroboam!" Ahijah greeted the startled spouse. "What's with the disguise?" Jeroboam's wife's mouth dropped, but he continued. "I'm afraid I have to give it to you straight. Tell Jeroboam that God entrusted him with power, but he's been the worst king yet! So here's what's going to happen: Dogs will eat any of his people who dies in the city, and birds will devour anybody else. So go on home, and when you set foot in the city, your son will die. All Israel will mourn for him and bury him, but he's the only one of Jeroboam's family who'll get a decent burial, because he's the only one God has anything good to say about."

And so it happened. After Jeroboam's death his son Nadab reigned only two years before Baasha overthrew him. Three hundred years later King Josiah shattered Jeroboam's altar—and left the bones of false prophets smoldering on it.

SWEET LITTLE LIE

A good name is more desirable than great riches.
PROVERBS 22:1

Frustrated that my family's computer had broken right before my class deadline, I sat in my high school's computer lab, working on a science project. But as I looked up I decided that being stuck after school had its advantages. My boyfriend Sam stood before me. "Hey, wanna go for a walk?" he asked.

"Sure," I said, jumping up. "Let's go."

Sam took my hand as we found some privacy behind a building outside. "You looked really good at homecoming," he said. I tried to return his compliment, but his lips kept getting in the way.

Minutes passed. Suddenly I pulled back and disentangled myself as I spotted Mr. Inglesworth, our math teacher, in the distance. Trying to quickly adjust my now-rumpled shirt, I whispered, "We should go back!"

"What were you guys doing behind the building?" Mr. Inglesworth asked.

Then, before my very ears, Sam told the stupidest lie I'd ever heard. "Well, sir, a dollar bill fell out of my pocket, and Jill was helping me look for it."

What on earth? I thought to myself. *A simple "Walking" would have sufficed!*

Mr. Inglesworth turned to me, as I became acutely aware that a button in the middle of my shirt was still undone. "Is that what happened, Jill?" he asked.

My arm folded across my chest, I tried to decide the better option: to tell the truth and point out that my boyfriend was a liar, or join him in his folly. "Yes, that's it," I said, trashing the trust I'd spent a year developing with one of my favorite teachers.

The look that Mr. Inglesworth gave me broke my heart. "Well, I'm glad you found it," he said. "Have a good afternoon." He walked away.

I didn't say much as Sam and I walked back to the computer lab— or much to Sam ever again. A half hour later I was in Mr. Inglesworth's office, telling him the truth.

"I knew you weren't looking for a dollar," he said. "The worst part, though, is that I knew you were lying to me."

I felt horrible for lying to my teacher. And I couldn't believe I'd taken the side of a silly boy who couldn't even make up a decent lie, instead of being true to myself.

JP

INVESTMENT

Each of you must give as you have made up your mind,
not reluctantly or under compulsion, for God loves a cheerful giver.
2 CORINTHIANS 9:7, NRSV

Maybe your church promotes this (I hope it does), a quaint notion that if we ask God to be our partner in just about anything, He will bless us. It's called the Investment offering—money for missions that you earned, found, or just committed to give—and the best way to explain it is to give you some examples.

Zeph was excited about his diesel car until, one after the other, two engines burned out. The car's body was decent, and Zeph didn't have the money for a new car, so he decided to partner with God. With yet another engine in place he promised God one cent for every mile that the car continued to run. It ran nearly 100,000 more miles before its tired body gave out. The engine was still purring along.

Lori likes to walk and run and has a knack for finding money, so she decided to give whatever change she spied on the ground to Investment. After several weeks she had a whole 38 cents. It seemed silly, but she put in the Investment Offering, and continued to keep her eyes open. Then she hit the jackpot—an edge of green tucked in a crevice. It was a $20 bill. Sure, she could have reminded God that she'd promised Him all the change that she found, but she didn't. Once she got over the pain, it felt good to give that $20.

Here are some ideas you can try for Investment.

Commit to give a certain amount of money for every basket you score, or every point your basketball team makes. Do the same for other sports that you play.

Do you cut and style hair for your friends? Hit them up for a donation for Investment.

Do you have a cookie or brownie specialty? Bake them, and sell to friends and family. Give all or a percentage of the money to your church's mission offering.

Are you into running or weight lifting? Commit to giving a certain amount for every fourth pound or mile that you improve.

Give a thank offering for good grades, an answered prayer, your dog's birthday, or your adorable niece or nephew.

Be creative. Your ideas will be better than these.

WISDOM

Take my instruction instead of silver, and knowledge rather than choice gold;
for wisdom is better than jewels, and all that you may desire cannot compare with her.
PROVERBS 8:10, 11, NRSV

Whenever Marguerite's family made excuses why they hadn't yet gotten around to doing something or protested that it was impossible to do, she would quote Proverbs 22:13: "The lazy person says, 'There is a lion outside! I shall be killed in the streets!'" (NRSV). People quickly got the point, and some wished they never had to hear that verse again.

The book of Proverbs is one of several in the Bible that scholars call wisdom literature. Wisdom literature is not unique to the Bible. The people of ancient Egypt, Palestine, and Mesopotamia liked to study nature and the rest of the world around them to see what practical lessons they could learn to live a more successful life. Some of these proverbs and maxims are almost word-for-word similar to ones we find in the Bible. (We should not be surprised. No one group has a lock on common sense, and God is the ultimate source of all truth anyway.)

Centuries before the Bible was written sages collected practical advice and compiled such books as the Instruction of Amenemope, the Instruction of Ptahhotep, and the Words of Ahiqar. But they did it not to make people more intelligent, but to enable them to advance in their careers and gain influential friends. Follow these sayings, such books said, and your success is guaranteed. Wisdom was selfish and self-centered.

But the Bible's wisdom literature has a different goal in mind. In the Bible, wisdom isn't knowing how to negotiate your way through the world of power and prestige, but seeking a relationship with God. Notice that the first few chapters of Proverbs describe wisdom as if it's a person. True wisdom is not what you know, but whom you know—God. Wisdom is not what you know how to do, but what you are as a person. Interestingly, the New Testament applies to Jesus many of the images that Proverbs uses to depict wisdom. If you have a relationship with Jesus, He will transform you into the kind of person that will be a success in all that you do in life. Jesus is infinitely more valuable than gold, silver, or jewels of any kind.

GW

Adventism

THE DAY OF ATONEMENT
PART 1

For on this day atonement shall be made for you, to cleanse you;
from all your sins you shall be clean before the Lord.
LEVITICUS 16:30, NRSV

The smell of burning flesh still lingered in the air, though the smoke from the sacrifice had long drifted into the brilliant blue desert sky. The crowd of worshippers stood in hushed anticipation, listening for the tinkling of the little bells on the hem of the high priest's robe. Would he return safely from inside the tabernacle tent?

Shimron wiped the sweat trickling down his forehead away from his eyes and stared at the entrance to the tabernacle. As memories of his life in Egypt flashed through his mind, he realized that he had never been this close to a sacred shrine before. Egyptian priests conducted all their rituals deep within the dark recesses of the sprawling temple complexes. Such worship was not meant for ordinary mortals. Today Aaron had gone into the inner chamber. Moses had said that the high priest could do that only once a year. Strange. Egyptian priests entered the sanctuaries of their gods every day. What was special about this day?

Moses had said that Aaron would be cleansing the tabernacle of sin. What did that mean? Shimron had once met a merchant from Mesopotamia who had told him about a yearly rite in which a priest had a sheep beheaded and used its body to wipe and purify the most important temple in the city. Usually the sacrifices offered in Egypt as well as elsewhere were meant as meals for the gods (of course, the priests and their families got to eat them afterward) and not to purify anything. But Moses said that Israel's sacrifices in the tabernacle were for forgiveness of sin and as gifts of thankfulness to its God. Scratching at his beard, Shimron thought a moment. *What did it mean to purify a holy place?*

Again he listened for any tinkling of bells. Before the ceremony began, Moses had said that Aaron must be clean. To do that, the Egyptian priests would shave all the hair from their bodies and then wash. That made them ritually pure. But Moses had also said something once about Israel's priests avoiding sin. Egyptian priests could do anything they wanted when off duty. And sadly, some of them had been pretty corrupt. Moses, though, had given the Israelites the impression that their God expected more of His priests than the Egyptians did. Why did He demand so much more than the Egyptian gods did? *Continued.*

GW

THE DAY OF ATONEMENT
PART 2

[The priest] shall make atonement for the sanctuary,
and he shall make atonement for the . . . priests and for all the people of the assembly.
LEVITICUS 16:32, 33, NRSV

A goat bleated in the tabernacle courtyard. Earlier there had been two of them. Moses had said that one had been for the Lord and the other for something named Azazel. Aaron had slaughtered one of the goats as well as a bull for a sin offering. What was an offering if it was not meant to feed God? Shimron shook his head in puzzlement.

He had an idea what sins were, but what did that have to do with an offering? Sins were wrong things you did. What did God care about them? The Egyptian gods did not worry about how their worshippers lived. His Mesopotamian merchant friend had once said that his gods were unconcerned about what human beings did as long as they fed the deities, clothed and washed their cult images, and kept up their temples. After all, the merchant explained, the gods had created humanity to be their servants in the first place. As long as people were good servants, the gods didn't care how they behaved off duty.

The crowd of Israelites outside the tabernacle was getting restless. Was Aaron still sprinkling blood on the mercy seat of the ark of the covenant in the Most Holy Place, as Moses had explained he would? Aaron had created a cloud of incense around him before he entered the Most Holy. That way he would not see God and die. Strange. The Egyptian priests could look at their gods any time they wanted.

Moses had explained that Aaron would be cleansing the sanctuary of defilement. Shimron could understand that. The Egyptians also cleansed their temples of ritual contamination. But Aaron as high priest would be doing more than cleansing the tabernacle—he would also be cleansing the people of Israel of their sins. Egypt had nothing like that. And Shimron was sure his merchant friend would say the same thing about his home country.

What deity had ever cared enough about his worshippers to do anything about their failings? After all, what master paid any attention to his servants as long as they did their job well? But the God of Israel seemed to be concerned about what His people were like as men and women all the time. He wanted them to do and be good every moment. And if they were bad, He had a way of dealing with it. And that was what Aaron was doing right now—on the Day of Atonement.

GW

Science

FEAR

He leads me beside quiet waters, he restores my soul.
PSALM 23:2, 3

Sauntering down the sidewalk, Monique laughs as Anna jokes about their crazy PE teacher. "If he'd just stop doing those stretches and shut up with that whistle—"

"GrrPhhhGrrrPhhffffftttGrrrrr!"

For an instant, Monique freezes, a Doberman's slobbery face mere inches from her own. The dog's teeth glisten in the late-afternoon sun, and though he's separated from her by a tall chain-link fence, somewhere deep inside Monique can already feel his teeth. Grabbing hands, the two girls stampede down the sidewalk, nearly tripping over their own flip-flops. They finally collapse under an oak tree on the nearby playground, its friendly, spreading branches offering them protection.

Sprawled against the tree, the girls wait for their adrenaline rush to subside. Monique lays her hand on her chest, as if to keep her heart from bouncing out of her tank-top. "Did you"—she's at last able to breathe—"see that thing?"

Drifting off to sleep that night, Monique suddenly jerks wide awake. A dog's bark lingers in the distance, still echoing in her skull. She tells herself she's being stupid.

In the early 1900s Swiss psychologist Edouard Claparede treated a woman experiencing severe amnesia after brain damage. She remembered most of her life and could still reason and navigate her world without difficulty, but she could no longer form new memories. They met every day, and each time the doctor reintroduced himself. If he left her alone for 15 minutes she didn't know him when he returned. But one day he tried something different. He introduced himself as usual, but as he shook her hand he jabbed her with a pin. The next day when Dr. Claparede came by, his patient looked at him as blankly as ever, but when he reached to shake her hand she refused—and had no idea why.

Our brains store at least three different kinds of memories: descriptive memories, procedural memories (such as how to ride a bike), and emotional memories. Emotional memories, from how it felt to curl up in your grandfather's lap to the alcohol on your mother's breath when she smacked you, trace a deep groove in your brain. The memories you make with God—listening, praising, the answered prayers—will stay deep in your heart. That's why it's so important to build strong memories with Him.

DIGGING DEEPER

Be still, and know that I am God.
PSALM 46:10

As you grow as a Christian, it's important to dedicate regular time to your relationship with God. Here's some ideas on how to do it.

Meet with friends. My freshman year of college, I met in the dorm every weeknight at 11:00 with my friends Tim, Kris, and Dave, and occasional other friends. We shared prayer requests, praises, and whatever else was on our mind. It provided an anchor to our hectic schedules and cemented our friendships with each other and with God.

Find quiet time with God on your own. Today's world wraps you in sound from the radio that buzzes you awake, to the weather report while you get dressed, to the speakers that rock your car. Find a quiet place, and take time to hear what you're missing.

Try 10 minutes at first. That's not long. It will pass in a heartbeat. Go to some place you can be alone. It's nice to be outside if you can. A park, a woods (lucky you if you're near a beach), your backyard deck, or even your front steps. Sit down and invite God to sit with you. Imagine that He is there, and just sit with Him. Don't try to think. Concentrate on "being with" God. Thoughts will come to you. You might bring a pad and pen to jot down the things that come to mind that you need to do. Written down, you can forget them and turn your mind back to God.

Make this a habit, a vital part of your worship. It takes a little practice, keeping your mind open to God. A certain text that gives a key to a problem may come to mind. A person may come to mind, with a nudge to do something for them. Some days you'll find that your worries fade to the background and that this 10 or 15 minutes with God is as refreshing/rejuvenating as a nap.

Rewrite a familiar Bible verse or even a psalm as if you were writing about yourself or a friend. For example: For God loved Tamara so much that He dropped everything to save her from death.

Serve others. Find something or someone in your neighborhood who needs help. Cook a meal for a single mother who never gets home before 8:00 p.m. Pull the weeds in your favorite old person's garden. Repair a broken toy, or volunteer for Vacation Bible School.

Memorize. Memorize your favorite chapters in the Bible. It's one skill that gets easier with practice.

THE DREAM / PART 1

Fear not, for I have redeemed you;
I have summoned you by name; you are mine.
ISAIAH 43:1

I hear the dull thud as my skull connects with the road. My body is a rag doll as the force sends me reeling. As I roll along, views of sky and asphalt flip in front of my eyes. I come to a shuddering stop, my arms and legs sprawled across the road. I cannot move. Tendons are stretched, muscles have been ripped, and a warm wet sensation is pooling beneath my head. It's blood. And as the weight of my injuries pin my body to the highway, a small but stern voice gives a two-word order: Get up.

Then I woke up. I sat straight up in bed. I felt sure that I was bashed and bloody on a road a moment before. But no, I'm in my bed, ready for another day in high school. But it was the voice, the deep and stern voice, which took me out of my dream and back into my bedroom. It was sudden, something akin to that "falling dream" in which you jerk awake before you hit the bottom.

The voice stayed stuck in my head for three weeks. I could feel everything, down to the surface of the road. I smelled the tar and felt the heat of the sun. I felt the sticky consistency of blood and sweat. And three weeks later my vivid dream came true.

My father brought his work truck that day. The truck had a toolbox bed, complete with pipes that held 20-pound spools of wire and cable. Being the cool sophomore, I had to ride in the back. I sat on the smooth surface of the toolbox bed and braced my back against the pipe that held the spools of wire. My sister, admiring my prime spot, wanted to sit up on the edge too. In brotherly authority, I commanded that she sit in the dead middle of the truck's bed, with her back against the truck's rear window. She reluctantly conceded, and we headed home.

As we turned a blind corner, a woman speeding in her Buick roared into our lane, hitting the truck head-on. I remember seeing the dazed face of the woman as her car rammed into the front of the truck. I watched as if in slow motion the crumpling of the truck's front. The two vehicles seemed to melt into each other. Then I felt the force. My head slammed into the pipe that suspended the wire spools, and the force of the impact threw me from the truck bed. It was all familiar— the sky, the asphalt, and the same sudden stop that I'd had in my dream. I was lying on the road, and I could not stay awake. *Continued.*

BP

THE DREAM / PART 2

How great is the love the Father has lavished upon us,
that we should be called children of God.
1 JOHN 3:1

My body shattered, and all I wanted to do was sleep. Yes, sleep sounded good. After being jettisoned from a head-on collision, my body wanted to take a nap. I felt my surroundings grow distant, my vision began to tunnel. But I remembered the voice. I remembered what it said. Instead of going to sleep, I sat straight up on the road. I got up and tried to help my sister and father from the wreck. After they were free from the wreck, my body shook violently and everything beneath my lower back could no longer move. Good thing ambulances are quick to these events.

The doctor in the ER stitched shut the two-inch gouge in the back of my head. She gently touched the two spots, one where my head crashed through the PVC pipe, and the place where the back of my head hit the road. According to her, the level of blunt trauma was supposed to earn me a coma. I was supposed to be passed out, with brain swelling. I should be losing brain cells. Instead she talked me up while she stitched, surprised that I was responsive at all. I told her that I was a good dreamer, and a good listener as well.

"Your young men will see visions, and your old men will dream dreams" (Acts 2:17, NLT). I thought about that verse as I spent the next three weeks trying to coerce my lower body to move. Was it God's voice that told me to get up when I was thrown out of the truck? Was this a premonition? Was I psychic? Should I start a new line of work and maybe get a nice spot on a talk show as "resident prophet" or something? I was only 17.

Then I read about Joseph in Genesis 37. I discovered that Joseph was also 17 when he had his first dream. His dream set him on a path of exile and slavery. His dreams assured him that no matter what happened, God had a plan for his life. Ever wonder what would have happened if he'd lost sight of his dreams? It would have been as bad as me having gone to sleep on that road. God piloted Joseph on the path that he needed to be on.

As for me, why do I still walk upright? I've not interpreted dreams for anyone lately. But I have witnessed to others. I've helped others better understand Jesus' love—a particularly interesting development since, at the time of my accident, I was not yet a Christian.

BP

Innovation

CRUSADE / PART 1

But I tell you: Love your enemies and pray for those who persecute you.
MATTHEW 5:44

It seemed like a good idea at the time. But then again, it always does. Constantinople, 1094. Emperor Alexius I Comnenus felt cornered. The Byzantine Empire had been almost entirely consumed. Turks hovered ominously to the east. He needed allies, but Europe was too splintered. If he was to get sufficient help, he'd have to call on something a little deeper, something that could stir and unite them all: religion.

The emperor contacted Pope Urban II, and the two hatched a plan. They'd drum up an army to assist the citizens of Constantinople, and while they were at it, they'd overthrow the Muslims who'd recently started harassing Christian pilgrims in Jerusalem. Pilgrimages to Jerusalem, the trip of a lifetime for an eleventh-century European, had gotten increasingly popular over the years, but pilgrims sure didn't think it made any sense to show up in the Holy Land and find non-Christians in charge.

Thronged by expectant townspeople, Urban announced the plan in a rural field in France in November 1095. He thrilled the crowd with promises of glory, valor, and an instant ticket to heaven if they should be so unfortunate as to die in battle. His war offered liberation, salvation, and a pretty nifty fashion accessory: a red cross worn on your chest, thus making all who joined the world's first "crusaders."

Here's part of how one historian remembered Urban's speech: "For your brethren who live in the east are in urgent need of your help, and you must hasten to give them the aid which has often been promised them. For, as the most of you have heard, the Turks and Arabs have attacked them and have conquered. . . . They have occupied more and more of the lands of those Christians, and have overcome them in seven battles. They have killed and captured many, and have destroyed the churches and devastated the empire. If you permit them to continue thus for a while with impurity, the faithful of God will be much more widely attacked by them. On this account I, or rather the Lord, beseech you as Christ's heralds to publish this everywhere and to persuade all people of whatever rank, foot-soldiers and knights, poor and rich, to carry aid promptly to those Christians and to destroy that vile race from the lands of our friends. I say this to those who are present, it meant also for those who are absent. Moreover, Christ commands it." *Continued.*

CRUSADE / PART 2

*When . . . James and John saw this, they asked, "Lord, do you want us
to call fire down from heaven to destroy them?" But Jesus turned and rebuked them.*
LUKE 9:54, 55

The crowd now snuggled firmly in the palm of his hand, Urban continued:

"All who die by the way, whether by land or by sea, or in battle against the pagans, shall have immediate remission of sins. This I grant them through the power of God with which I am invested. O what a disgrace if such a despised and base race, which worships demons, should conquer a people which has the faith of omnipotent God and is made glorious with the name of Christ! With what reproaches will the Lord overwhelm us if you do not aid those who, with us, profess the Christian religion! Let those who have been accustomed unjustly to wage private warfare against the faithful now go against the infidels and end with victory this war which should have been begun long ago. Let those who for a long time have been robbers now become knights."

"But if you are hindered by love of children, parents and wives, remember what the Lord says in the Gospel, 'He that loveth father or mother more than me, is not worthy of me.' 'Every one that hath forsaken houses, or brethren, or sisters, or father, or mother, or wife, or children, or lands for my name's sake shall receive an hundredfold and shall inherit everlasting life.' Let none of your possessions detain you. . . ."

"Let therefore hatred depart from among you, let your quarrels end, let wars cease, and let all dissensions and controversies slumber. Enter upon the road to the Holy Sepulchre; wrest that land from the wicked race, and subject it to yourselves. That land which as the Scripture says 'floweth with milk and honey' was given by God into the possession of the children of Israel. Jerusalem is the navel of the world; the land is fruitful above others, like another paradise of delights. This the Redeemer of the human race has made illustrious by His advent, has beautified by residence, has consecrated by suffering, has redeemed by death, has glorified by burial. This royal city, therefore, situated at the centre of the world, is now held captive by His enemies, and is in subjection to those who do not know God, to the worship of the heathens. She . . . desires to be liberated, and does not cease to implore you to come to her aid."

"It is God's will!" the people cried. "It's God's will!" Urban's speech had set their imaginations ablaze, and soon that fire would consume nearly all it touched. *Continued.*

Innovation

CRUSADE / PART 3

All who draw the sword will die by the sword.

MATTHEW 26:52

If Urban's crusade was going to be a ticket to glory, soon everybody wanted a piece. Urban had hoped to rally a few thousand skilled knights to his cause, but one particularly skillful rabble-rouser named Peter the Hermit rode his donkey throughout France and Germany, encouraging everybody who was nobody to get on board. Soon tens of thousands of men, women, and even children headed out under Peter's command—while Urban was still busy organizing his knights.

However fun things may have been at the get-go, Peter's ragtag horde soon found itself in need of food and supplies in the midst of startled Eastern Europeans who hadn't planned to feed an army that suddenly dropped by. In Hungary an argument over the proper price for a pair of shoes led to a riot and then an all-out attack on the city of Semlin—and the deaths of 4,000 people.

Others reasoned that if one was going to travel all the way to Jerusalem to kill non-Christians, they might as well knock off non-Christians that happened to live nearby, too. Count Emicho claimed that Jesus had told him he'd soon become emperor and would help him convert Europe's Jews. With his own dedicated mob he declared that hundreds of Jews throughout Germany needed to convert or die, and he massacred hundreds who chose the latter. Emicho's army finally disbanded after they reached Hungary, where the king didn't appreciate their raping and pillaging, and executed every one of them he got his hands on.

Peter lost about a quarter of his army when it started fighting with locals in Serbia. The rest finally reached Constantinople August 1, 1096, much to the locals' dismay. They'd expected a real army, not these bloodthirsty clowns. The emperor shipped them to Asia Minor while he waited for more competent help, but the restless mob still managed to keep them busy. They attacked Nicaea, the technicality that the Nicaeans were Christians not stopping them from slicing babies and roasting prisoners on spits.

After a group of German Crusaders found themselves trapped inside city walls without water in an eight-day siege, the Turks proved they could play the "convert or die" game as well as anyone. Meanwhile the Turks ambushed the French group, and that was the end of that. For the main group of Crusaders, however, Jerusalem awaited. *Continued.*

CRUSADE / PART 4

A time is coming when anyone who kills you will think he is offering a service to God.
JOHN 16:2

In 1097 the "official" Crusaders at last headed through the blistering desert toward Jerusalem, stopping by Antioch along the way. Antioch had been captured by the Turks only a dozen years earlier, so the Byzantines were eager to get it back. The well-protected and fortified city was so large that the Crusader army could not entirely surround it. Their siege started well enough—nothing gets a crowd going like chucking 200 Turkish heads over a city wall—but after eight months of famine, attacks from two outside armies, and cannibalism, things looked bleak, and another Turkish army was on its way.

Then a knight named Bohemund bribed the captain of the Antioch guard, and the Crusaders streamed in, slaughtering Turks left and right. But now, as a massive Turkish army arrived, the Crusaders found themselves trapped in the city they'd just conquered. There was only one way to win: mad religious fervor. One Peter Bartholomew declared that he'd had a vision of the sword that pierced Jesus' side, the "Holy Lance," buried in the city's cathedral. Initial excavations found nothing. Then Peter himself took a look, and voilà—a spear point! Never mind that it was already on display elsewhere. Truly God must be on their side! The Crusaders rallied and vanquished the Turkish army. (Peter Bartholomew, on the other hand, attempted not long afterward, to convince his skeptics that he was no crank by passing unharmed through a fiery furnace. A few days later he died from his burns.)

At this point most of the Crusaders were ready to go home. Jerusalem was already back in the hands of more gracious Arab hosts than were there a few years earlier, and Jerusalem's Christians weren't enthused about being conquered again either. But a group of Crusaders headed on anyway. The siege of Jerusalem started out no better than Antioch's had, and before long Crusaders were dying of starvation. After an inspirational, Joshua-style march around the city walls, however, they managed to burst in.

The Crusaders slaughtered every Jew and Muslim they found, and soon the streets flowed with blood. (City rulers had already expelled the Christians, so they didn't need to worry about sorting out their victims.) After four and a half centuries, Jerusalem was now back in the hands of people who called themselves Christians.

MOURNFUL ANTICIPATION

Blessed are those who mourn, for they will be comforted.
MATTHEW 5:4

I once heard dynamic and renowned speaker José Rojas draw out the syllables in the word "beatitudes"—the Be-Attitudes, he called them. Jesus' soul-bending introductory lines to the Sermon on the Mount present a counterintuitive way of looking at life, a new attitude that defied self-centeredness and self-justification, shortcuts and short-sightedness.

The word "beatitude" is from the Latin word *beatitudo*: blessed. Happy. Fortunate. Yet Jesus' second beatitude, "Blessed are those who mourn," sounds more like a slap in the face than a pat on the back or a shot in the arm. What's next? Blessed are those who are insulted and victimized?

Well, yeah, but that's not for another six verses.

Blessed are those who mourn, for they will be comforted. Jesus' words promise consolation, restoration, for all who've suffered on this shattered planet, but they go far beyond that. They promise that the loss we can't even place will be repaid.

I feel it sometimes, that aching for a phantom piece of my soul, behind the locked door that no earthly key ever fits. Sometimes I feel it in a haunting melody, or taste it in sugared peaches, or hear it in blurred laughter from some distant playground. Sometimes I see it in a faded photograph of long ago, or the latest snapshot of a distant galaxy. Sometimes I hear it in a prayer that only those who've wrestled with sin and loss and love and fear and grief and pain and numbness and shock and joy can pray, their voices as scratched as their hearts.

It's a strange awareness that feels peculiarly like mourning. It tells us that every good thing we may encounter is scarcely a taste of the joy yet to come, a joy made sweeter only by the anticipation.

"Therefore we do not lose heart. Though outwardly we are wasting away, yet inwardly we are being renewed day by day. For our light and momentary troubles are achieving for us an eternal glory that far outweighs them all. So we fix our eyes not on what is seen, but on what is unseen. For what is seen is temporary, but what is unseen is eternal" (2 Corinthians 4:16-18).

HONEYMOON / PART 1

Take me away with you—let us hurry!
SONG OF SOLOMON 1:4

Lisa and I both grinned as our plane landed in Belize City, Belize, just after noon. We'd spent the first two days after our wedding visiting with family who'd flown in from Africa. Next we'd checked into an inexpensive motel near the Baltimore airport, slept a few hours, then a little after 3:00 a.m. we'd dragged our weary bodies up to catch our early-morning flight. We'd rested on the plane, and now we were ready to roll.

I'd booked three nights for us at an ecolodge outside San Ignacio. We rented a vehicle and set out along the highway across the skinny little country. As we passed a sign that read "Welcome to Belize" I slipped a recording of our wedding into the car's CD player. The countryside rolled by and we laughed and sang and played "pair of pants on a clothesline," the object of which is to be the first to spot . . . a pair of pants on a clothesline.

We stopped by a gift shop along the way to pick up our directions to the ecolodge. It was a bit sketchy, drawn by someone only slightly more artistic than me, and was, it admitted, "not drawn to scale." Turn left at this street, cross the one-way wooden bridge, right at the cemetery, past the gas station, left at the mansion, drive two miles, then right onto the one-lane road. Drive a few miles through the orange plantation, then past the cows, on by the one house on the right, then turn right at the home of the bare-bottomed baby (he always seemed so happy to see us). We knew we were getting close when a steep ledge (marked only by yellow caution tape) pointed to a river on the left, and a steep hill, thick with vegetation, rose on the right. Keep driving, and you'll soon arrive at the ecolodge. Along the way you've enjoyed spectacular views equal to anything you might see in a fantasy film.

"I think we're the only people here," Lisa whispered. "That works for me," I replied.

Since it was midweek in the low season, that night we were indeed the only guests. We pulled our luggage down the stone path to our cabana to the sound of jungle birds tweeting in the distance, and could hardly believe our good fortune.

That night we dined on delicious food prepared there at the lodge—burgers, absolutely heavenly mashed potatoes, and *tres leche* that permanently rewired my taste buds. As a cool breeze soothed us to sleep that night, we looked forward to a week of exploration, relaxation, and tropical inspiration. *Continued.*

life

HONEYMOON / PART 2

He has taken me to the banquet hall, and his banner over me is love.
SONG OF SOLOMON 2:4

"Birding. Caving. Horses. Canoes. Tubing. Night Hike," the sign proclaimed.

The possibilities were practically endless at our jungle destination, but we decided to start our first morning there off right with some birding with Tommy, the resident tour guide. Neither of us knew much of anything about birds and absolutely nothing about jungle plants and trees, so what better time to learn?

After breakfast Tommy led us on a five-mile hike through the surrounding hillsides, along jungle trails, into a pottery-strewn cave (where Lisa discovered she's not too keen on bats), and to the site of an ancient Mayan shrine (about which time I discovered I'd not brought enough water). I photographed a massive termite mound and got some close-ups of leaf-cutter ants on the job. We spent the afternoon exploring some much larger Mayan ruins in town, and made plans to cross the border into Guatemala the next morning and visit the pyramids of Tikal.

Tikal was absolutely spectacular. The ceiba trees looked like something out of a Dr. Seuss book, and the friendly howler monkeys dwelling in them decided to greet Lisa in typical howler monkey fashion—by knocking an acorn off her arm. That night we kicked back at the lodge, looking forward to the next day when we'd fly to the town of San Pedro on the island of Ambergris Caye, just off the coast from Belize City.

"We just got back from there," a woman told us. "You'll love it." The lodge at last had other guests, and a middle-aged couple from the U.S. had joined us for supper. Apparently girlfriend and boyfriend, they shared a few details of their trip to the island, and began to extol the merits of a "great restaurant" they'd found on one of the smaller islands nearby. "We got fresh lobster and wine for only $50—that's not a bad deal at all," the woman burbled.

Lisa and I looked at each other. Could this be us in 25 years—well, us if we were divorced and seeing other people—looking strangely soulless underneath our sun-leathered skin, spending nearly as much on a meal as we were on our lodging (that ecolodge was a terrific deal)? We sure hoped not. We only knew two things: we loved each other, and "unless the Lord builds the house, its builders labor in vain" (Psalm 127:1).

FORGIVENESS

Father, forgive them, for they do not know what they are doing.
LUKE 23:34

Nothing tells you more about your spirituality than how you feel when someone who's hurt you, or a loved one, dies.

My friends and I had a teacher who, though well-intended, failed to endear himself to most of his students. A few years later word went around that he'd died. When a pastor contacted his wife to offer condolences, it turned out that he was alive and well. And parents were shocked at how glad their kids had celebrated someone's (merely imagined) death.

A few years ago I read that someone who'd hurt a friend of mine had died. And I had to confess to God that I was kinda the opposite of sad to find that out. I figured I didn't necessarily have to cry at the news, but my satisfaction at the death was definitely not the Holy Spirit's doing.

Forgiveness may be the hardest Christian discipline to master.

In the movie *Catch a Fire*, based on the true story of Black South African Patrick Chamusso, Chamusso is falsely accused of participating in terrorist attacks against the government during the apartheid era. A police officer tortures him to force him to confess, and he is tempted to confess when the officer threatens his family, but he is at last released without charges. Chamusso then decides to become exactly what he was accused of being, and travels to Mozambique to join the militant anti-apartheid group Umkhonto we Sizwe.

Back in South Africa he coordinates a partly successful bombing of an oil refinery, and, once captured and tortured again, is sentenced to 24 years in prison on desolate Robben Island, off the coast of Cape Town.

A few years into his prison sentence, apartheid at last falls, and Chamusso is released. He'd served only 10 years. The film depicts Chamusso crossing paths by chance with the police officer who had tortured him. He considers taking his revenge, but decides that would solve nothing and only deepen his own pain.

In a brief epilogue the movie touches on what, to me, is the most remarkable part of Chamusso's story—a development made possible by his ability to forgive. Remarried, Chamusso and his wife have taken care of dozens of AIDS orphans. His forgiveness gave him the emotional strength to give back.

Adventism

REVELATION: BEHIND THE SCENES

The revelation of Jesus Christ, which God gave him to show his servants.
REVELATION 1:1

Reading Revelation is like listening to the waiter at an amazing restaurant reel off the day's specials. They all sound exquisite and delicious—not least because the words are all in French or Italian and you have no idea what he's talking about.

If you could peek into the kitchen, you'd spy servers dashing about, balancing plates on their arms. Between the steam you'd see cooks slicing and dicing, fussing and arranging, chopping and shredding. You'd wonder how many times a day that fire jets up from beneath the sizzling pot.

Revelation gives you a drive-by tour of God's kitchen—and what's happening behind the scenes of earth's history.

But back to the amazing writing. The dirty little secret is that in the written Greek the grammar is a bit convoluted. It's quite evident that Greek is not the writer's first language. And if John the revelator is, as most believe, the same as John the apostle from Galilee, writing in exile from an island where he has no access to editorial help, the fractured Greek makes a lot of sense.

So wrap your mind around verses 4 and 5 of chapter 1:

"John, To the seven churches in the province of Asia: Grace and peace to you from him who is, and who was, and who is to come, and from the seven spirits before his throne, and from Jesus Christ, who is the faithful witness, the firstborn from the dead, and the ruler of the kings of the earth."

In one brilliant run-on sentence we've learned the author (John), the original audience (the members of seven churches in what is now Turkey), and a feast of flashpoint insights about Jesus. You'll find that richness of detail throughout the book—and then when you step back and look at the book as a whole, you'll find new details you'd miss if you only looked at it close up.

Revelation fascinates readers just as much for its construction as for its content. It's written in an intricate chiastic pattern—that is, not just A-B-C, as we'd be used to today, but A-B-C-B-A. Scholars continue to argue about how to group its scenes and themes. But for the patient, prayerful reader, one thing is sure: It's all about Jesus' love.

UNWARRANTED FUGITIVE
PART 1

Then Elijah said to the people, "I, even I only, am left a prophet of the Lord;
but Baal's prophets number four hundred fifty."
1 KINGS 18:22, NRSV.

There's nothing like false humility.

Elijah had just pulled off a faith-driven victory like few in history. Having declared a famine to an evil king, hidden out during a massive manhunt for him, witnessed a few miracles, and undeclared the famine after three years, Elijah had presided over an incredible display of God's power. Mocking the priests of Baal that now infested the nation of Israel, Elijah challenged them to a down-and-dirty "Who's Your God?" contest on Mount Carmel.

Four hundred fifty prophets of Baal and 400 prophets of Asherah gathered before the people on Mount Carmel. Elijah laid out the rules of the game: they'd each sacrifice a bull on an altar, but it would be up to their deities to roast the steak.

Elijah courteously gave the Baalites first go, but after they'd spent all morning begging and cajoling the old storm god to throw 'em some thunder, Elijah took off the proverbial gloves. "Cry louder! Maybe he's meditating! Maybe he's taking care of some personal business! Maybe he's on vacation to Six Gods Over Samaria! Or maybe he's snoozing, and you need to wake him up!"

The prophets screamed and swung and slashed themselves, but to no avail. So finally, when they'd worn themselves out, Elijah decided it was time to show them who the boss of them really was. He built an altar of 12 stones, sliced up the bull, and laid it on top, then proved that when it came to showmanship the shrieking Baalites had nothing on him. He had jar after jar after jar of water poured over the altar until the trench around it was completely filled. If God was going to do a miracle today, there'd be absolutely no excuse to doubt it.

Elijah called out to God, "O Lord, God of Abraham, Isaac, and Israel, let it be known this day that you are God in Israel!" (1 Kings 18:36, NRSV). The crowd watched stunned as fire fell from the sky, its flames devouring the wood, the stones, the bull, and even the water around the altar. And the people fell on their faces, exclaiming, "Yahweh is God!" *Continued.*

UNWARRANTED FUGITIVE
PART 2

"It is enough; now, O Lord, take away my life, for I am not better than my fathers."
1 KINGS 19:4, KJV

Everything looked smoking. Elijah stood at the top of his game. Rain began to fall, just as Elijah had prayed. Under God's power Elijah raced on foot before King Ahab's speeding chariot—an adrenaline rush if there ever was one. But then Ahab told Elijah that Jezebel had murdered all of God's prophets, and a messenger said that Jezebel had vowed that, come hell or high water, she'd see that he met the same grisly fate. And despite the heavenly fire and everything else he'd witnessed that day, everything that shouted "God's got your back!" and "Onward and upward!" Elijah freaked out.

So Elijah found himself a 40 days' journey into the wilderness, at a cave in Mount Sinai. And somehow the conquering hero found himself . . . sulking.

His route had retraced the Israelites' route through the wilderness, from Sinai to Canaan, only in reverse. He'd gone where Ahab and Jezebel could not touch him—but also where God could not make him a blessing.

Then God spoke, with yet another one of His rhetorical Are-you-man-or-mouse questions: "What are you doing here, Elijah?"

Elijah leaped up from the rocks where he'd been relaxing and yelled into the mountainside, his words echoing off the walls. "I've been zealous for God, that's what I've been doing! The Israelites have broken Your covenant, thrown down Your altar, and murdered Your prophets, and now it's just me, and they want to kill me, too!"

The voice said, "Go out and stand on the mountain before the Lord, for the Lord is about to pass by" (1 Kings 19:11, NRSV).

A wind stampeded by, shredding boulders, but it was not God. An earthquake sent Elijah surfing, but it was not God. A fire threatened to consume him, but that was not God either. And then Elijah heard the unmistakable sound of God whispering through the silence. Some versions of the Bible translate it as "a gentle whisper," others as "a still small voice." I wonder if it might be described best as . . . a sigh.

Then: "Go." God had kings for him to anoint. A new prophet to call. And 7,000 faithful Israelites to back him up.

MEEK TO ME

Blessed are the meek, for they will inherit the earth.
MATTHEW 5:5

Meekness is one of those mysterious virtues that we hardly even ponder. We may gossip that some blowhard is hardly humble, but we don't think, *You know, what that guy needs is a little more meekness.*

Meekness sounds wimpy, almost negative. If someone's meek, it sounds like they're a pushover. A doormat. A wimp.

But here's the reality: true meekness exerts incredible power. Meekness is not weakness. Meekness is strength. It has softened hearts and toppled empires. It's a power that can't be countered.

I think of my grandfather, a pillar of quiet strength and a mighty rock in my young life, whom I could always count on to stand up for me. I think of Gandhi, who won independence from England for India through a radical commitment to nonviolence, which he steadfastly believed would prove superior to, and longer-lasting than, any armed opposition. His struggle took a lifetime, he often found himself in jail, and his opponents frequently responded with violence. Yet he said, "When I despair, I remember that all through history the way of truth and love has always won. There have been tyrants and murderers and for a time they seem invincible, but in the end, they always fall—think of it, always."

In meekness, happiness doesn't come from possessions, circumstances, or accomplishments. Meekness is not cowardice or spinelessness, but springs from an indomitable commitment to reflecting God's love and grace to everyone, no matter how they treat you.

In a culture that worships tough-talking, butt-kicking, get-out-of-my-way self-reliance, meekness is a rare trait. But with the Holy Spirit's blessing, it can change the world.

It's hard to think of meekness ruling the planet, but it's the commitment of the meek to a better world to come, and their determination to live by its rules rather than the self-destructive fads around them, that gives them their power. Meekness may not be popular, but for the meek, the future is now.

THE END OF THE WORLD

And surely I am with you always, to the very end of the age.
MATTHEW 28:20

For Seventh-day Adventists, end-time expectation is right in the name. Adventists believe that while God's prophecies are conditional, God will nonetheless soon return to rescue and redeem His children. People generally take that as good news. It's what happens in the meantime, however, that Adventists have always worried about. What's going to happen in the infamous "time of trouble"? If Jesus came right now, would I be saved? What about my loved ones? Will I be deceived?

When it comes to the end-times, Adventists have been notorious for hyping the crisis but ignoring the Christ. A close look at the Bible assures us that God will always be with us, no matter what happens, and provides clear guidance to the turbulent times ahead. Though the end-times simmer with uncertainty, we can know that if we hold on to Jesus, everything is going to be all right.

What thoughts come to your mind when someone mentions the last days?

_____

_____

_____

What about the end-times might make you nervous?

_____

_____

_____

How do you think you'd feel if you realized that you were unmistakably living at the end of the world?

_____

_____

_____

What are you most looking forward to about the end-times?

_____

_____

_____

NEXT DOOR OR BUST

So I was afraid and went out and hid your talent in the ground.
MATTHEW 25:25

The stereotype of the missionary often precedes the actual job. Their name is usually Todd or Amy, and they stick out like a record in a CD collection. They're probably a doctor, teacher, or preacher, and have contracted the alphabet list of jungle diseases. And yet to a lot of people this very scenario is attractive. And it's not because the one job God gave him or her is to serve as Christ's ambassador. It's more because they wanted to escape Minnesota.

Going to Haiti and feeding the orphans will not make you a missionary. If you are not using your talents and spiritual gifts in the here and now, a trip to some faraway land won't necessarily flip the switch. What are you doing currently to employ your talents? You'll find that a lot of missionaries first sharpened their skills at home.

Look at your neighborhood. Have you witnessed to anyone there? Have you ever served people in your community? Contrary to popular belief, the missionary field is not limited to the tropics. It starts just outside your front door. True, there are few to no cannibals in North America, and the continent as a whole has tackled that nasty malaria stuff, but it is still a mission field. Going out on a mission is about leaving your comfort zone. That can be just a block away. Being a missionary is not a position, it's a practice.

"We are therefore Christ's ambassadors, as though God were making his appeal through us. We implore you on Christ's behalf: Be reconciled to God"(2 Corinthians 5:20). Your job as a Christian is to bring the message of the gospel, to reconcile others with Christ. If you get a souvenir machete, that's just a perk, not the focus.

Even so, there are those few who are convinced that when they "get there," when they arrived at that far off mission locale, they are going to engage their talents and spiritual skills. That's like saying you'll be an expert swordsman once you get stabbed. Sadly, some missionaries miss this point and end up overwhelmed. The result is a poor experience for the missionary *and* for those who needed an honest servant.

When you have an opportunity to mission, don't balk. Don't bury your talent and take the lame way out. Start by applying your talents around you now. And realize that these opportunities are ignorant of the time, place, and location. You'll be surprised how a soul saved in Iran will look just like a soul saved in Canada when both are with you in heaven.

BP

Innovation

DEATH BY SCREENPLAY

Our gospel came to you not simply with words, but also with power,
with the Holy Spirit and with deep conviction.
1 THESSALONIANS 1:5

Trying to pick a mutually interesting flick at the video rental shop, Lisa and I came to an impasse over one title in particular. I argued that everything about the movie screamed "Flee! Flee for your life!" but Lisa wanted to give it a chance.

Then a woman came by. "My husband really enjoyed that movie," she said.

That woman was a filthy liar. I bet she'd never even seen it. If she had, she wouldn't have tried to side with a fellow female by recommending it—she'd have urged Lisa and I to avoid it at all costs, while covering up a nervous tic. The movie should have come with warnings: Do not watch while operating heavy machinery. Do not induce vomiting. Do not watch before taking your SATs.

It was the kind of movie that screenplay classes would show as an example of everything *not* to do. I'll spare you its name (looking it up on the Internet, I discovered I remembered the name wrong; guess I'd blanked it out), lest someone experiencing clinical depression be tempted to view it. Just remember the lamest movie you've ever seen, and try to imagine something far, far worse. Or just start jamming your house keys at your eyes.

It starred famous actors who've appeared in actual blockbusters, but the only way even the most talented could have made this self-important movie entertaining would have been to stop taking it so seriously. Any given scene could have made for some hilarious sketch comedy, but the issues addressed were just so very significant, you see. Until, that is, an out-of-the-blue ending that left Lisa and I staring at the screen, and then at each other, asking, "Were the filmmakers out of their minds?"

It featured a ridiculous attempt at special effects, twin characters who didn't even look the same age, encyclopedia entries disguised as dialogue (utterly fake example: "Hey, I was just reading that blue cheese is made from cows that eat blue grass—mind if I spend the next two minutes telling you all about it?") and character motivations that made no sense.

The sad thing was that the issues the movie tried to illuminate are important ones that most people are totally ignorant of. But just as with the gospel, people don't care how much you know until you make them glad they met you in the first place.

ASK THEM

Children's children are a crown to the aged, and parents are the pride of their children.
PROVERBS 17:6

It was an arranged marriage. I imagine the groom in his Sunday suit and the bride in her best dress. My guess is that Josef, at age 44, had a bit of a strut about him, but Karolina surely blinked away tears. She was 17 and in love with a young soldier. At best, they were very poor, and life was hard. Some years later—with four children—they immigrated to America from Austria-Hungary. They were my grandmother's parents.

"Mama," my grandmother, grew up in central Texas. I loved the few stories she told of her childhood, and always asked to hear them again. She described building playhouses of stones by the Bosque River. She recalled her father's loud wails as, leaning on his hoe in the cotton fields, he wept for the green hills he'd left behind in Europe. Mama often hoed and picked cotton instead of going to school, and her father would slip cotton in her bag to help her reach the 200-pound minimum required even for kids. Once she was so thirsty she drank vinegar. With these stories, and a few others, I wove a faint picture of her as a child. Her mother died before she was 10; her father, a few years later.

Mutti—my grandmother's grandmother, who forced her daughter to marry a widow with nearly a dozen grown children—reluctantly accepted care of the orphans. She measured the bread with a string so she'd know if they cut a slice. She gave her other grandchildren apples; the orphans ate their cores.

There are so many things I long to know today, but I never asked. My grandmother and I were very close, and still, I never thought to ask. "Tell me about the sharecropper cabin. Was your mother pretty? What was she like? Was she sick a long time? Who taught you how to make pierogies? Tell me about your father."

Go to your grandparents, your aunts and uncles. Ask them about their lives when they were young. Ask your parents, too. They may say they don't remember, but don't give up. If some things are painful, let it go, but continue to coax them to share with you. What were their schools like? Who were their friends when they were teens? What did they do for fun? How did they meet their husband or wife? You are the sum of many things, including the lives of your ancestors. Find out all you can about them. Whether good or not so good, it influences who you are today.

PW

Bible

JUST WHERE DID THOSE SAMARITANS COME FROM, ANYWAY?

The king of Assyria brought people from Babylon, Cuthah, Avva, Hamath and Sepharvaim and settled them in the towns of Samaria to replace the Israelites. They took over Samaria and lived in its towns.

2 KINGS 17:24

Welcome to another episode of "Things You Never Learned in Vacation Bible School."

So you're reading your Bible and suddenly these folks the Samaritans show up. And for some reason everybody looks down on them. What gives?

Their story begins in 2 Kings 17. After the ever-idolatrous 10 tribes of the northern kingdom of Israel get hauled off from Samaria to Assyria in the 720s B.C., the land's left pretty empty. Without shepherds to knock 'em off with a slingshot, wild animals (such as lions) roam free. But then, being thoughtful conquerors, the Assyrians send people from five different cities (who happen to worship five different gods) to Samaria.

Things don't go that well, though, for the new residents. When lions come and kill a few of the residents, they get a little spooked. So someone sends a message to the king of Assyria: "The people you deported and resettled in the towns of Samaria do not know what the god of that country requires. He has sent lions among them, which are killing them off, because the people do not know what he requires" (2 Kings 17:26).

So the king grabs a few Israelite priests (evidently of Jereboam's sketchy variety) he's had exiled to Assyria and sends them back to Samaria to teach the new immigrants "what the god of the land requires" (verse 27). So they learned about Yahweh and started worshipping Him—right alongside their own gods. They learned about all the incredible things God had done for the people of Israel, but they still kept worshipping, and even, say, sacrificing their children to, other gods.

As the centuries passed, they gradually gave up their idolatry and formed their own Samaritan religion, very similar to Judaism but with a number of little twists, including a belief that Mount Gerizim was a much holier place than ol' Jerusalem.

When Jesus met the Samaritan woman at the well, He told her, "You've had five husbands, and you're not married to the husband you're now with." That description just as accurately described their religious history—their ancestors had worshipped a lot of different gods, and though they worshipped Yahweh now, they were not fully committed to Him spiritually.

FRIED RICE FANTASTIC

I commend the enjoyment of life, because nothing is better . . .
than to eat and drink and be glad.
ECCLESIASTES 8:15

One of the jobs that got me through college was night watch and janitor in the ancient dorm where I lived. My roommate, Andi, and I alternated each night, enabling us to sleep every other night. Every hour we checked the second and third floors in the unlikely case that something had caught fire there. The third floor was empty, and I dreaded its dark halls. The one thing I really enjoyed was Thursdays, when Andi and I both worked. We gave the dorm a good cleaning, including scrubbing down the kitchen. The grand finale was fixing fried rice. We never used a recipe—so here's my best try. By the way, you want your rice to be fairly dry, the kernels separate. Unless you're really good at cooking rice, it's best to use the five-minute instant.

Ingredients:
    6 cups cooked rice, cooled
    2 tbsp. oil (olive is best)
    1 medium onion, chopped
    2 carrots, cut in matchstick strips
    1 can bean sprouts, drained
    1 can sliced water chestnuts, drained
    1 or 2 eggs, optional
    soy sauce

How to create this masterpiece:
Sauté onion over medium-low heat until translucent, then add carrots and cook 2 minutes. Add cooled rice, stirring to mix in the onion and carrots. Increase heat slightly so that the rice will brown, but watch it carefully, stirring so that it doesn't burn. After approximately 10 minutes, add bean sprouts and water chestnuts. Stir occasionally as they heat. (The sprouts will wilt.) With the spoon, make a hole in the center of the rice and drop in the egg. Let cook a moment; then, using a fork, quickly stir it into the rice until done. Add soy sauce and enjoy.

What's most fun about this is that you can create your own masterpiece. Except for the onion and carrot, everything else was optional for us. Nowadays I'd replace the egg with flavored tofu. Vegetarian chicken would be a tasty change too.

PW

Spirit

THINGS I KNOW NOW

Get wisdom, get understanding.
PROVERBS 4:5

There's no time like the present. Take advantage of opportunities to travel, serve as a student missionary, or take a class just because it sounds interesting.

God's leading is often easier to see when you're looking backwards.

The more I study and get to know Jesus, the more fascinating He gets.

On earth there's nothing more fascinating than other people—and nothing more important than getting to know them.

Scholarships: apply early, apply often.

The Bible can be read in less than 40 hours—but take your time and savor every page. (OK, you have my permission to hum your way through the genealogies as quickly as possible, but trust me, they're important too.)

People who love God know how to love people.

You should marry someone who shares similar values.

You should marry someone who has the same picture of God that you do.

Praying—and knowing you're being prayed for—works wonders, helping keep life focused and tolerable.

Take lots of pictures.

It's fun to be spontaneous. It's wise to be well grounded. A lot of both makes for a very happy life—and relationships.

If you're not contributing your spiritual gifts to the world, you're not enjoying life as much as you could.

Sometimes your best friends start out as really aggravating people.

It's generally a waste of time to worry about what people you'll never get to know think about you.

The people who mind don't matter. The people who matter don't mind.

God gets excited every time He thinks of you.

The Holy Spirit is far more powerful than I could ever imagine.

So is love.

Hug often.

SELF-IMAGE

O Lord, you have searched me and you know me.
PSALM 139:1

Ray loves basketball, loves soccer, and is pretty good at tennis if it comes to it—and he has the six-pack abs to prove it. He's happy to take his shirt off at any occasion he thinks might be improved by his doing so.

Dani just got invited to Ramona's pool party. She prides herself on cute outfits that hide most things she considers a flaw, but the last time she tried to buy a swimsuit every single one made her feel like a freak of nature.

Tyrone enjoys working behind the scenes, but for some reason one of the school music teachers thinks he'd have a great singing voice. Tyrone sometimes sings to his girlfriend when nobody else is around, but in front of hundreds of people? Not a chance.

Everybody knows that Laura is an overachiever. People think all she's interested in is good grades and showing how much she knows, but what she really wants is for people to see her more relaxed sometime.

Self-image. How we see ourselves shapes how other people see us, though the two aren't necessarily the same thing. How would you describe yourself?

_____

_____

How do you think other people would describe you?

_____

_____

How would you like other people to see you?

_____

_____

What traits do you admire in other people?

_____

_____

How do you think God sees you?

_____

_____

Mission

VISIONARY MISSIONARIES
PART 1

*They trample on the heads of the poor as upon the dust of the ground
and deny justice to the oppressed.*
AMOS 2:7

The impoverished people of Peru loved Fernando and Ana Stahl. The people who were living the good life while others suffered—not so much.

Fernando and Ana became Seventh-day Adventists in 1902 and received nursing certification from the Battle Creek Sanitarium. They did various medical work around the Midwest, but they couldn't shake the conviction that they had a greater work to do. Then in 1909 they met J. W. Wesphal, president of the church's South American Union. He told them that Bolivia had incredible needs, but the church couldn't afford to send anyone. So Fernando made him an offer: He'd sell his home in Ohio to pay the way to Bolivia if Westphal could support Fernando and Ana and their two children once they got there.

Arriving in Peru, the family traveled by train to Lake Titicaca in the Andes Mountains, 12,500 feet above sea level. They then took another train to La Paz, Bolivia, to live and work. They established a clinic available to anyone who needed help, and Fernando spent much of his time traveling to various villages, getting to know the indigenous people and selling literature. He soon discovered a major hurdle: Almost no one knew how to read—and that was exactly how the people in power liked it.

Indigenous people made up 95 percent of the Andean population, but they held almost none of its power. Landowners wanted a submissive workforce for their farms, judges oppressed people who didn't know how to fight back, and village priests exploited worshippers. So the Stahls started school after school after school to offer basic education. Soon the people could better stand up for themselves and were able to avoid being ripped off by shopkeepers. Newly infused with self-worth, they began to demand their rights from the government.

In 1915 an Adventist convert tried to get justice for her husband's murder. When no one would help her, she cut the head off her husband's corpse, put it in a basket, and, alongside Manuel Camacho, another Adventist convert and a major civil rights activist, traveled to Lima, Peru to demand official action. The gospel that the Stahls had brought to her people had empowered her. *Continued.*

VISIONARY MISSIONARIES
PART 2

The angel of the Lord encamps around those who fear him, and he delivers them.
PSALM 34:7

The Stahls worked tirelessly to bring the gospel to the Andes' indigenous people, and the work took its toll. As the wealthy and powerful realized they could no longer rip off the uneducated lower classes, they began to violently oppose the Stahls. Offended by how the Stahls treated everyone as an equal, thus weakening their political power, in 1913 the bishop of Puno stirred up a mob to attack them. Though they found no one home, they smashed the Stahl and Camacho homes, and dragged eight Adventists 21 miles to jail.

The prisoners were acquitted and set free, and in 1915 the event helped inspire passage of an amendment to the Peruvian constitution, guaranteeing religious liberty. But opposition hardly ended then. The more the Stahls built schools, the more they and fellow believers were attacked. Mobs set fire to schools and attacked teachers; numerous Adventists were murdered; and people repeatedly came after the Stahls.

One day as they treated patients in their clinic, a mob led by village priests arrived with threats to kill them. The priests set off fireworks as a signal to attack—then rushed forward, hurling stones. A rock smashed into Fernando's forehead, and blood poured down his face. Stumbling, he made his way toward a hut for safety. Ana pulled him inside and barred the door.

Rocks continued to shake the structure, and the Stahls knew they had no way out. As they prayed together Ana treated Fernando's wounds. Suddenly a priest yelled, "Set the roof on fire!" The roar of the crowd threatened to deafen them. Then the Stahls heard the mob's voice change. It turned from rage to panic.

As they stood trembling with fear, the Stahls heard the voices fading and the sound of running feet. Their attackers had fled. But why? At last they ventured a look outside. All was quiet. They stepped out. "What happened?" they wondered. Their friends pointed to an army of Indians in the distance, come to rescue them. This army had frightened the attackers away. The Stahls saw nothing, yet knew that God had sent angels to protect them.

After many years in the Andes the Stahls moved to the Amazon River basin to continue their missionary work. Their legacy lives on in hearts—and a culture—transformed.

Adventism

SO HOW DO WE FIGURE OUT REVELATION? / PART 1

Blessed is he who keeps the words of the prophecy in this book.
REVELATION 22:7

Say what you want about the book of Revelation, if you go in without a map you'll soon get lost. Revelation rewards the careful reader, but it has sent many a reader off the deep end.

In the commentary *Revelation of Jesus Christ* (Andrews University Press, 2002), Ranko Stefanovic notes (pp. 25-45) some of the many patterns that researchers have found in Revelation. Each sheds a bit of light on what's really going on behind the scenes and how its original readers would have understood it. Yet because Revelation's structure is so incredibly complex, and even though its order of scenes is essential for interpreting it, scholars still debate just how John outlined it.

One intriguing thing to note is that the last words of each section of the book give a clue to the deeper meaning of the next section. For example, 3:21, "To him who overcomes, I will give the right to sit with me on my throne, just as I overcame and sat down with my Father on his throne" "seems to provide the interpretive outline for chapters 4-7" (Stefvanovic, p. 26). Another helpful tip is that whenever the book introduces a major new character, a short description sums up what he or she is about. For example, Revelation 12:9 instantly clues us into who we're dealing with: "The great dragon was hurled down—that ancient serpent called the devil, or Satan, who leads the whole world astray."

The number 7 pops up again and again throughout Revelation: seven churches, seven seals, seven trumpets, seven plagues. Looking at this, some scholars argue that Revelation consists of four groups of seven events. Others suggest that the book should really be divided into six sections of seven things. Others suggest the book consists of six sections: "the churches, the seals, the trumpets, the bowls, seven personages (woman, dragon, child, Michael, Lamb, the beast from the sea, and the beast from the earth), and seven new things (new heaven, new earth, new peoples, new Jerusalem, new temple, new light, new paradise)" (Stefanovic, p. 29).

Revelation is, at heart, a very Jewish book. It constantly echoes passages from the Old Testament, which should be studied on their own to discover the context of what Revelation is referring to. *Continued.*

SO HOW DO WE FIGURE OUT REVELATION? / PART 2

Do not seal up the words of the prophecy of this book.
REVELATION 22:10

Soaked in Old Testament ideas and imagery, Revelation is, in part, a companion to the New Testament book of Hebrews. Both focus on Jesus in the context of the sanctuary.

Jewish Adventist author Jacques Doukhan sees each section of Revelation as corresponding to a different Jewish religious festival: the seven churches to Passover, the seven seals to the Feast of Weeks (Pentecost), the seven trumpets to Rosh Hashanah (the Jewish new year), the seven signs to Yom Kippur (the Day of Atonement), and the seven victories and seven wonders of Jerusalem at the end to the Feast of Tabernacles.

Ranko Stefanovic notes that the first half of Revelation is modeled on daily ceremonies of the ancient Jewish temple, but the second half (starting in chapter 12) repeatedly reflects the Day of Atonement. Like the book of Daniel, some parts of Revelation repeat and develop themes, while others explore completely new territory.

Stefanovic suggests that one of the most useful ways of looking at Revelation is to divide it into three sections: messages to the seven churches (Christ as high priest), opening of the sealed scroll (Christ as prophetic ruler), and the contents of the sealed scroll (Christ as apocalyptic warrior) (pp. 40-42). However you slice it, Revelation is an intricate work that has no equal. The more you study it, the more it will lead you into the rest of the Bible, and the more it will reveal about God and His plans for this world.

Imagine if you took the first 65 books of the Bible—creation, Exodus, law, covenants, Psalms, serpent, sanctuary, prophets, kings, etc.—and swirled them in a kaleidoscope. That's Revelation. Far from being some sort of zany, acid-tripping tagalong to the rest of the Bible, Revelation is a carefully composed performance of all of the Bible's major themes.

So if Revelation gets bewildering; if it makes you want to rub your eyes and not look again for at least 12 years; if it gets hijacked by people who think Revelation was written yesterday on their back porch with notes from tomorrow's newspaper—remember that you can always dip back into the rest of the Bible for a while. When you return, something new will become clear.

Science

LIGHT

Light is sweet, and it pleases the eyes to see the sun.
ECCLESIASTES 11:7

I love light. Our house has skylights that brighten everything up. I love summer days that last forever, and I get saddened when we move toward winter and the nights get longer. If I ever had to move into the northern latitudes I would need the special lights that simulate the sun. When night comes, I try to turn on all of the lights that I see. When I was younger, my dad always complained that I left on lights that I was not using. Now I have a job and live in my own house, but there's still someone asking me to please conserve some electricity.

Truth be told, though, I do use less light now. Not to save money or because I like the dark, but because I love the earth. I believe that we have a responsibility to take care of what God has given us. My way of doing that? I try to be more energy-efficient. Tompaul and I have changed our old-fashioned lightbulbs for new energy-efficient ones. We keep our air-conditioning set higher than I want and the heat lower than I desire. Here are some facts to gnaw on:

• A standard lightbulb uses 10 percent of its energy for light; 90 percent is wasted by heat.

• In the lifetime of one energy-efficient compact fluorescent lightbulb, 200 fewer pounds of coal will be burned.

• On average, one house emits twice the greenhouse gas emissions of one car every year.

• Unplug! Even when an appliance such as a TV, DVD player, or computer is turned off, it continues to use electricity if it's still plugged in. In fact, as much as 75 percent of energy used by appliances is used when they're turned off.

• Drive slower. Each five miles over 60 mph adds 6 percent to your fuel costs.

Some companies and families are trying to become carbon neutral, meaning that they do positive things to offset their emissions load. You can help in many ways, such as planting trees or purchasing green power. In 30 years of growth one tree will offset 320 kilograms of carbon, prevent erosion, reduce pollution, and add to the environment.

Most important, we must be aware of what our actions cost. It's difficult to see how our individual choices affect the world. This is true in how we treat the environment. We are caretakers of God's earth.

LH

GOD NEVER EVEN THOUGHT OF IT / PART 1

"The people of Judah have done evil in my eyes," declares the Lord.
"They have built the high places . . . to burn their sons and daughters in the fire—
something I did not command nor did it enter my mind."
JEREMIAH 7:30, 31

Uriel squatted down at the edge of field, yanked up a few stalks of sun-charred grain, then scraped up a handful of soil. Rubbing the dust between his fingers, he let it sift back to earth, then stood up with a grunt. "Going on three years without the rains," the man standing next to him muttered. Unlike Uriel, his skin rippled in a thousand wrinkles. "I've seen this before. Baal is angry." He lifted his hands in helplessness. "Only one thing . . ."

"I have made sacrifices," Uriel said, thinking of the sin that he feared had brought this on. "Grain offerings. My first pressing of oil. My best lamb." He sighed. "I have sacrificed to El."

"Ah, yes." The laugh was derisive. "Your Hebrew god. But does he hear you?"

Wordless, Uriel turned away. His *best*, of course. Even he could understand that. El, the God of Israel—who could say that He, the same as Baal, did not demand your best—the fruit of a man's body for the sin of his soul? The challenge now lay in the open, flung there by the old man. Others had done it for the good of them all. Uriel's feet slapped the hard ground as he walked toward the village. In the distance, the high place of sacrifice blurred into the brass sky.

Home, he sat against an outside wall, his mind on the terrible challenge. The gods were different, theirs and his. El rarely spoke, but when He did the earth trembled. As did the Canaanite gods, He asked for sacrifices. At times Uriel felt a pull to the raucous worship of his neighbors, but he had not bowed to the pagan gods. Just then his son, Jakim, toddled by, hands filled with small stones. Uriel winced. *The fruit of my body for . . . that secret wrong.* The Festival would be soon—food, dance, prayers. Had he courage enough to make *the* sacrifice? He thought of the boy's mother, shuddered, then tossed the thought aside. Dina was only a woman. She knew nothing of the weight of guilt.

One day burned into another. He made his heart hard when Jakim climbed into his lap or his wife scooped up the giggling child. He had no choice. Not even El could forgive, he reasoned. Not without the highest sacrifice. Then came the day Dina made cakes for the gods, her hands expertly kneading the dough. He picked up his son and for a moment drew him close. Tomorrow fire would blaze on the high place. *The fruit of my body for the sin of my soul.* Continued.   PW

GOD NEVER EVEN THOUGHT OF IT / PART 2

Will the Lord be pleased with thousands of rams, with ten thousand rivers of oil?
Shall I offer my firstborn for my transgression, the fruit of my body for the sin of my soul?
He has showed you, O man, what is good. And what does the Lord require of you?
To act justly and to love mercy and to walk humbly with your God.
MICAH 6:7, 8

Uriel slept little that night. Despite the drought and the real threat of starvation, the Festival was exciting. The Hebrews had few places of their own for community worship, so sometimes they used for their own worship the low hills where their neighbors sacrificed to Baal and other of the Canaanite gods. He could not have put it into words, but he was attracted to the small clay and stone figures one could hold in the hand—gods you could actually touch. Dina had some, the ugly little statues that promised to bring babies. What was the harm?

Just then Jakim's small body rolled against him, and reality hit like a slap in the face. Could he do it? Must he do it? He vowed that he would not, but even then he didn't know the truth of his own heart.

A read through the book of Jeremiah could break your heart. "What fault did your fathers find in me, that they strayed so far from me?" God asks. "They followed worthless idols and became worthless themselves" (2:5). "How can you say, 'I am not defiled; I have not run after the Baals'? See how you behaved in the valley. . . . You said, 'It's no use! I love foreign gods, and I must go after them'" (verses 23-25).

In chapters 2 through 5 God says, "A horrible and shocking thing has happened in the land: the prophets prophesy lies . . . and my people love it this way" (5:30, 31). Keep on reading. Nothing changes. "For they have forsaken me and made this a place of foreign gods; . . . they have filled this place with the blood of the innocent. They have built the high places of Baal to burn their sons" (19:4, 5).

If someone betrayed you in the way God's chosen betrayed Him, your friends would say, "Don't be a fool. Forget him!" But God doesn't give up. Can't you hear the tears in His voice: "'I know the plans I have for you,' declares the Lord, 'plans to prosper you and not to harm you'" (29:11). "I have loved you with an everlasting love; I have drawn you with loving-kindness. I will build you up again" (31:3, 4).

PW

THE FACE OF LOVE / PART 1

"O unbelieving generation," Jesus replied, "how long shall I stay with you? How long shall I put up with you? Bring the boy to me."
MARK 9:19

I grew up with a lapsed-Catholic father and a Jewish mother. As the joke goes, I had twice the holidays and double the guilt. For years my Bible stopped at the book of Malachi. The rest was just additional stuff that the crazies (read: Christians) read to make it through their Sunday sessions. I had the classical non-Christian view of Christ; a historically relevant figure who was a good teacher, but a poor candidate for Son of God. The latter was impossible, for "God is one"—that is, not accessorized. There were no levels of God in Judaism.

We lived in Guam, and, ironically, I spent 11 years at an Adventist school with this very belief in mind. At one point in the eighth grade I refused to complete Bible class assignments solely because I felt they lionized negative Jewish stereotypes. My teacher understood, but my grade still tanked. In high school I aggressively confronted my Bible teachers, going verse-by-verse, in an attempt to trounce Adventist doctrine and Christianity itself.

Why? It was largely because of the people who claimed themselves "Christian." I could not see Christians as people who grew. I expected the perfection in them that they claimed. Each year at the academy, naive missionaries came swooping in with condescending tones, legalist views, and lives that didn't always match their talk. Some teachers were barely fit to instruct; the church and school board had to routinely reprimand or fire student missionaries and instructors. Amid all the politics and craziness, I was supposed to find Christ?

For 11 years I watched the Adventist school in all of its phases. Amazingly, several teachers who met me where I was and helped me to grow came into my path. There was Mrs. Costello, an import from Oklahoma who taught a drama class, and Mrs. Masilamony, a demure woman from Sri Lanka with a British accent. They didn't talk about the Great Commission; they worked in it. I learned what made a Christian, but still was not going to be one.

In my senior year I looked desperately for a college or university to call home. I found an Adventist university in Texas that offered a decent communications program, but I was living on Guam, thousands of miles from Texas. I had no money even to get there. Even with the obvious impediment, I still applied and got my financial aid in order. The first day of class came, and I was still on Guam, and deeply depressed. Then Mrs. Masilamony knocked on my door. *Continued.*

BP

innovation

THE FACE OF LOVE / PART 2

Then he said to Thomas, "Put your finger here; see my hands.
Reach out your hand and put it into my side. Stop doubting and believe."
JOHN 20:27

My English teacher and her husband had told their small church on the south part of the island about my trying to get to college. A ticket straight to Texas was donated on my behalf. The only catch was that I had to be ready to leave the next morning. They'd also collected money for me—precisely enough for my books and necessities for the first semester. The Christians of which I was so wary had just sent me to college.

The year sped by, and I looked at my options for the summer. Just when I had conceded to an expensive stay on campus, I got a letter inviting me to serve as a counselor for Camp Yorktown Bay. The funny thing was that I hadn't even applied. I didn't even know where the place was, but my girlfriend, Kimberly, had recommended me. It seemed that once again God wanted me to go where He wanted me to go.

For the next few months I was supposed to show kids how to make smores and to introduce them to Jesus. I realized the job was providential, so I was willing to play the game and teach the kids about Christ. I mean, far be it from me to mess with kids; I'll tell them what their parents sent them there to learn. But that's when the pieces started to fall together for me.

Every night I had to share the gospel to a handful of wide-eyed children. Every night I told a story out of Mark or Acts. Every night I had to read that once off-limits New Testament for material to use the next night, and the next. And so I was forced into the Testament I had written off, and the Holy Spirit started His slow and steady work on my heart. Meanwhile, Kimberly was praying for me. She always kindly and consistently presented Jesus, even while I sneered at her earnestness.

One evening during an agape feast on the shore of Lake Ouachita, Kimberly sat quietly and prayed for me. It worked. I felt the call to be baptized. I realized what I had been trying to explain to all those children: Jesus had gotten me free airfare, bought my books, and introduced me to Kimberly. His acts weren't hypocrisy, but love. Once I understood that Jesus is the face of that love, I wanted to be a part of it.

That summer I was baptized. I've been a part of that love ever since.

SEVEN LETTERS TO SEVEN CHURCHES / PART 1

He who has an ear, let him hear what the Spirit says to the churches.
REVELATION 2:7

After a stunning vision of Jesus, Revelation starts something deceptively simple: short notes to seven churches in Asia Minor (today's Turkey). But these are no mere "Tell Mrs. Lumpkins to go easy on the cheese doodle casserole, and be sure to pick up the dry cleaning" notes. These are crucial messages of counsel and warning, charging church members to live life wholeheartedly for God.

The words are directly from Jesus to the churches. Each letter begins with a unique description of Jesus: He "who holds the seven stars in his right hand and walks among the seven golden lampstands" (2:1, Ephesus); "the First and the Last, who died and came to life again" (2:8, Smyrna); "who has the sharp, double-edged sword" (2:12, Pergamum); "whose eyes are like blazing fire and whose feet are like burnished bronze" (2:18, Thyatira); "the Amen, the faithful and true witness, the ruler of God's creation" (3:14, Laodicea).

Each contains a blunt evaluation of the church's spiritual condition or circumstances: "I know your deeds, your hard work and your perseverance" (2:12, Ephesus); "I know your afflictions and your poverty—yet you are rich!" (2:9, Smyrna); "I know where you live—where Satan has his throne. Yet you remain true to my name" (2:13, Pergamum); "you tolerate that woman Jezebel" (2:20, Thyatira); "you have little strength, yet you have kept my word" (3:8, Philadelphia); "you are neither cold nor hot" (3:15, Laodicea).

Each contains counsel: "repent" (2:5, Ephesus); "do not be afraid" (2:10, Smyrna); "hold on" (2:25, Thyatira); "wake up!" (3:2, Sardis); "buy from me gold refined in the fire" (3:18, Laodicea).

Jesus urges each faith community to listen to the Spirit's advice. And each message offers spectacular promises to all who hold on and overcome. To the listless people of Ephesus, Jesus promises "the right to eat from the tree of life" (2:7). To the persecuted people of Smyrna, Jesus promises victory over eternal death (2:11). To the compromising members of Pergamum, Jesus promises "hidden manna" and a "white stone" printed with a new name known only to its receiver (2:17). To the few in Sardis who haven't compromised their faith, Jesus promises to walk alongside (3:4). To the persevering people of Philadelphia, Jesus promises protection from trial and an ultimate reward as pillars in God's temple (3:12). And to the lackadaisical Laodiceans, Jesus offers the most extravagant promise of all: "the right to sit with me on my throne" (3:21). *Continued.*

SEVEN LETTERS TO SEVEN CHURCHES / PART 2

Then all the churches will know that I am he who searches hearts and minds.
REVELATION 2:23

So what should we make of these mysterious and cryptic messages to long-gone churches? Are they just historical curiosities? Do they merely make nice devotional reading? Or do they have potent relevance to us today?

In the metaphorical realm, Bible students have noticed that when connected on a map, the seven churches form what looks distinctly like a candlestick. The letters follow an A-B-C-D-C-B-A pattern—rebuke for legalism to first and last churches Ephesus and Laodicea, praise for faithfulness to the second and sixth churches, sharp condemnation to the idolatrous third and fifth churches, and both condemnation and praise for the good and the bad to be found in Thyatira.

Many scholars have noted that the sequence of churches and their descriptions seems to describe the Christian church through the ages. Ephesus, suggested to represent the church in John's day, starts out strong but has lost its "first love" of Jesus and the truth. Smyrna typifies the experience of the impoverished Christians in the second and third centuries, surviving persecution both social and physical. Jesus says they'll endure "ten days" of persecution, and the most extreme persecution from the Roman Empire, under Emperor Diocletian, lasted 10 years.

Pergamum reminds readers of the church after Roman emperor Constantine's conversion to Christianity, which went from a persecuted minority to state religion violently enforcing itself on others. The church continued to mingle its doctrines with paganism, as, for example, Constantine declared Sunday the church's day of rest.

Things go from bad to worse in Thyatira, corresponding prophetically to what we now know as the Dark Ages. Jesus says that "Jezebel" runs amuck in Thyatira, suggesting that, like King Ahab of old, this church has joined itself with idolatry. "Heresy has become official and coincides with the church's power elite. The church has now established itself as a political power and clad itself with robes of royalty" (Jacques Doukhan, *Secrets of Revelation*, p. 37). This is the era of the Crusades and of numerous false doctrines and distortions, yet while Thyatira's leadership is corrupt, the church itself still contains many faithful believers (Revelation 2:24) who are urged to hold on. *Continued.*

SEVEN LETTERS TO SEVEN CHURCHES / PART 3

I know your deeds.
REVELATION 3:15

Jesus urges the people of Sardis to return to pure faith. Their experience mirrors that of Christianity in sixteenth and seventeenth centuries, which went from a dynamic rediscovery of Bible truths to lifeless arguments and legalism. They have a lively reputation, but they've become spiritually dead (Revelation 3:1), and, like the medieval church, even persecute people. Jesus urges them to remember what they used to be. Jesus urges them to "remember," "obey," "repent," and "wake up!" At the same time, Jesus encourages a faithful remnant who've held on to a pure faith.

On the other hand, Jesus says all sorts of good things about the Asia Minor church of Philadelphia—and no wonder, for its very name means "city of brotherly love." This, many scholars believe, parallels the church of the great awakenings of the 1700s and early 1800s, when people embraced Christianity more often than almost any other time in history, and missionaries spread throughout the world to share the gospel. Jesus praises this church for its faithful works, and declares, "Since you have kept my command to endure patiently, I will also keep you from the hour of trial that is going to come upon the whole world to test those who live on the earth" (Revelation 3:10). Though this church, prophetically speaking, comes near the end of time, it is spared the turmoil of the last days.

Yet, like all the other messages, the message to Philadelphia contains meaning for people living at any time. For those facing the trouble that the end of time brings, Jesus' words here tell us that His followers will be spared the judgment on the wicked. As Jesus prayed in John 17:15: "My prayer is not that you take them out of the world but that you protect them from the evil one."

These days the church of Laodicea gets the most press, and for good reason—it sounds remarkably familiar. Laodicea is a prosperous place, yet spiritually its people are pathetic. Jesus describes them as "lukewarm"—not flagrantly wicked, but not on fire for God, either. Worst of all, they think they're all right: "You say, 'I am rich; I have acquired wealth and do not need a thing.' But you do not realize that you are wretched, pitiful, poor, blind and naked" (Revelation 3:17). Jesus urges them to hear His knocking on their hearts, because He hasn't given up on them: "Those whom I love I rebuke and discipline" (verse19).

Are you ready for a new pair of honest eyes? Is your church?

spirit

13 MORE THINGS TO DO

Be imitators of God, therefore, as dearly loved children and live a life of love,
just as Christ loved us and gave himself up for us as a fragrant offering and sacrifice to God.
EPHESIANS 5:1, 2

1. Nothing sparks fun (and even learning) like charades. Burn off your lunch this afternoon with a laughter-inducing round of spontaneous skits.

2. Spread the thankfulness around. Surprise those who've helped you this year with personalized thank-you notes.

3. Pray for God's work in countries difficult to reach with the gospel. Research a country in which Christians are currently persecuted.

4. Explore ways you could translate God's love into something that the culture around you may understand. What would the biggest challenge be?

5. Figure out the chore your parent hates the most, and do it for them. (Well, maybe not if it's doing their taxes.)

6. Write a song about what God's done for you so far this year.

7. Dream about what you'd like to do for God in your life. Do you think your role will be in front or behind the scenes? Do you think you'll be comfortable with God's plan for your life? Write down what you think it will take to get there.

8. Ask your parents or grandparents what they did for fun at your age.

9. Paint a picture or shoot a short film of the most intriguing Bible story you can find.

10. After researching their country and the challenges they face, write a letter to a missionary family serving overseas.

11. Pick a word the Bible uses often, such as "light," "salvation," "hope," "faith," "grace," or "trust," and use a concordance (at the back of some Bibles and available on the Internet—www.biblegateway.com) to research its meaning throughout Scripture.

12. Pray about your greatest weakness, that God can turn the underlying issue into a true strength.

13. Write your own devotional and share it.

FOOLISH GENIUS

Instead, God deliberately chose things the world considers foolish
in order to shame those who think they are wise.
And he chose those who are powerless to shame those who are powerful.
1 CORINTHIANS 1:27, NLT

A teenager armed with rocks. That's about it. The exhausted hopes of the chosen people of God rested on a young guy and his slingshot. Amid the sweaty smell of a hot battlefield and metal-clad warriors, a whippersnapper approached a giant who towered over him with mockery and contempt.

You know who won. Again and again it seems as if God delights in consistently turning our perception of the world on its head. The weak are invincible, the strong are delicate, and the poor are wealthy. God delights in poetic justice. And in the process he'll use gawky teenage sheepherders to do it.

That is perhaps the most encouraging verse to me. You see, I've tripped on painted stripes on the road. I've dressed up as a "Magic Chicken" to entertain a room of kindergarteners, and I enjoyed it. I've worn jester hats and bright-blue skater pants—at the same time. I still watch cartoons as an adult. I still want to get a prize when I buy cereal. I am no perfect being—I'm really quite the fool; just ask my wife. I've even worked against God's will for me in my life. That's the epitome of foolishness. And even with all this junk in my repertoire, I am still very much in the running to be a part of God's plan.

If you've ever felt ridiculous or ridiculed, take heart—God's got a use for you. Picked last in gym class consistently? Great, Jesus wants you on His team—and you're the captain. You say you've never fit in? Perfect. The Holy Spirit has a lesson to teach, and you'll be the corner-stone.

As it turns out, God doesn't want the proud marines; He wants the awkward goonies. An old Yiddish expression says, "With God, even the broom can shoot." As long as you are a willing servant, God is going to use you.

God does not want your interpretation of perfect, nor does He want to hear what this cruel world considers "wise." God-given quirki-ness beats self-made know-it-alls any day.

BP

Mission

FORMING, STORMING, NORMING, AND PERFORMING

You diligently study the Scriptures because you think that by them you possess eternal life. These are the Scriptures that testify about me.

JOHN 5:39

I sat in a trendy coffee shop one afternoon, the kind where the baristas listen to jazz and talk about the finer points in abstract cubism. It was so chic I wondered if it would collapse under the weight of its own ego. But they had a really good orange creamsicle frappuccino, so I stayed.

Within seven feet of me a handful of high school girls were having a "Bible study." A circle of girls sat quiet and doe-eyed while the leader in the middle rattled on about what she thought about the passage she had just read. The girls could barely keep their heads bowed; they were as far from a spiritual mood as possible. Each one seemed alone. The study wound down, and the leader still rambled on. "You know, it's like no one talks at all," she said. "So, like, let's have a, like, a talk more and better next time, and, like stuff," she said. I wondered if maybe the coffee shop's ego had taken its first mental hostage.

Before the leader could leave, I talked with her a bit. I told her about the work of Bruce Tuckman, a psychologist who in 1965 had developed a four-stage model of group development: forming, storming, norming, and performing.

Forming is about getting to know one another and forming a group. If it's a Bible study, you meet like-minded people, you share common beliefs, and you build friendships at the beginning even before you start reading together.

The girl's eyes glittered with the faint glimmer of realization. Her solemn group was quiet because she had not connected the people and the format together first. She just thought that telling girls to come was going to just make the magic happen.

Then comes the storming, during which you figure out what's going to happen and who will lead. In forming, people finally get into the groove of how the group operates. And finally there's performing. Performing means more than just meeting regularly. A good Bible study has a central focus. As it turned out, even this girl was nervous, which explained the high-pitched Valley Girl accent. As for my frappuccino, it was finished, just like my lecture, and I left the coffee shop praying that their next meeting would produce more revelations than reservations.

BP

HAPPINESS IS A WARM PUPPY

*Keep falsehood and lies far from me; give me neither poverty nor riches,
but give me only my daily bread. Otherwise, I may have too much
and disown you and say, "Who is the Lord?" Or I may become poor and steal,
and so dishonor the name of my God.*
PROVERBS 30:8, 9

Happiness is a warm puppy. So said Charlie Brown. And since he didn't mention money, maybe he was on to something. Today's text goes against much of the attitudes we see in the world today. What, money doesn't buy happiness? It buys plane tickets and Toyotas and projection TVs, so close enough, right?

Studies have found that today's verse is, shall we say, right on the money. Some money does indeed make people happy—but only to a certain point. In fact, richer countries are no happier than moderately well-off ones. For example, the people of Vietnam, with a per capita (divided evenly among everybody, man, woman, and child) income of about $700, are just as happy as the people of France, where the average per capita is more than $25,000.

In America, the average income has risen significantly since 1970 (though the average wage in real dollars has dropped), but people aren't any happier than they were years before, when they lived in smaller houses and had "rabbit ears" attached to their remoteless TVs. And though America's gross domestic product has more than tripled since 1980, people are, you guessed it, not any happier now than they were then. The number of people who said they were "very happy" was highest in 1974, when America faced major economic problems. Today the number hovers around a mere 33 percent.

Over in Japan, income quadrupled between 1958 and 1986, and today's Japanese, similar to Americans, own far more stuff than a generation or two ago, but they're no happier or satisfied with their lives than they ever were.

So what's the magic number? About $10,000 per capita. When poor countries grow more developed and people start enjoying such luxuries as running water, indoor plumbing, and better health, their happiness does rise. But as people start investing more time and energy in their stuff and less in enjoying rich relationships with other people, the amount of happiness they report drops.

Adventism

CORONATION

God has raised this Jesus to life, and we are all witnesses of the fact.
Exalted to the right hand of God, he has received from the Father
the promised Holy Spirit and has poured out what you now see and hear.
ACTS 2:32, 33

After the letters to the seven churches, Revelation sweeps us into the very throne room of God in heaven. A dazzling scene awaits. Twenty-four elders, dressed in purest white and wearing crowns, sit on their own thrones around God's royal seat. Four creatures surround God's throne, one like a lion, one like an ox, one like an eagle, and one with a face like a man. The creatures live to praise, "Holy, holy, holy is the Lord God Almighty, who was, and is, and is to come" (Revelation 4:8).

As for God Himself, John cannot find words to describe Him. He can only compare Him to precious jewels: He "had the appearance of jasper and carnelian" (verse 3) and sat surrounded by a rainbow.

Yet suddenly a mysterious dilemma intrudes on this world of majesty and harmony. A powerful angel inquires, "Who is worthy to break the seals and open the scroll?" (Revelation 5:2). John reports that he weeps, for no one is worthy, but then an elder tells him, "Do not weep! See, the Lion of the tribe of Judah, the Root of David, has triumphed. He is able to open the scroll and its seven seals" (verse 5).

Wait up. Hold on a minute. What's going on here? Surely there's more going on than meets the eye. And there is. The scene itself follows the imagery of a royal coronation and enthronement. We are witnessing nothing less than Jesus' exaltation in heaven after His death and resurrection on earth. As Ranko Stefanovic notes: "In the Old Testament, the enthronement ceremony had two stages: the coronation, which was performed in the temple, was followed by the enthronement, which was performed in the royal palace" (*Revelation of Jesus Christ*, p. 161). Here, though, the temple and the palace are one place.

The mighty "Lion of the tribe of Judah" about to be crowned and celebrated doesn't look like a typical king. He appears as a lamb who has been sacrificed. Yet for Jesus, His moment of greatest weakness is nonetheless His greatest triumph. As today's text notes, with Christ on His throne, the Holy Spirit is now active in human hearts.

HEZEKIAH VERSUS SENNACHERIB / PART 1

While King Sennacherib of Assyria was at Lachish with all his forces, he sent his servants to Jerusalem to King Hezekiah of Judah.
2 CHRONICLES 32:9, NRSV

The hearts of the people of Jerusalem sank. The dreaded Assyrian invaders had made their appearance before the holy city itself. They knew Sennacherib must be confident of his soon capture of Lachish to spare such high officers as the Tartan, the Rabsaris, and the Rabshakeh, as well as a large portion of his army. Everyone knew that the siege would now begin. The Assyrian forces would surround Jerusalem, dig fortified trenches, and begin building ramps against the city walls. Escape from the city would quickly become impossible. Slingers and archers would bombard its defenders with stones and ar-rows. Sappers would dig tunnels under the walls. After the Assyrians set fire to the wooden supports propping up the roofs of the tunnels, the tunnels would collapse and the walls above them would crack and tumble.

Other troops would assemble the siege engines. The siege ma-chines were heavily armored four-wheeled vehicles with a long iron-headed ram on the front. Mobile towers would be moved in place near them. As the machines hammered at the city walls and gates, archers stationed on the towers would protect the siege engines as the frantic defenders struggled to set the wooden devices on fire.

Raids both day and night would keep the defenders constantly on edge. Few would be able to sleep because of the blaring of trumpets, the clashing of swords, and the screams of dying soldiers and civil-ians. As each sling stone or arrow found its mark, Jerusalem would lose another soldier it could not spare. And with each death the morale of its people would weaken.

In addition to the military forces surrounding the doomed city, Assyria had other weapons at work. Jerusalem's food would eventu-ally run out, and starvation would weaken and kill its inhabitants. The crowded conditions and poor sanitation in Jerusalem would breed dis-ease that would cause even more death. Human waste and garbage would pile up until the city became a reeking sewage pit. Sometimes a besieging army would deliberately catapult dead bodies into a city to produce more illness.

Would God allow the Assyrian Empire to devastate His beloved city? Would He not come to their aid? *Continued.*

GW

Bible

HEZEKIAH VERSUS SENNACHERIB / PART 2

Hear the word of the great king, the king of Assyria!
2 KINGS 18:28, NRSV

To Jerusalem's surprise, the Assyrians did not immediately begin their siege. Instead, they seemed interested in another kind of warfare—one that they were just as skilled at.

As Hezekiah's representatives approached Sennacherib's emissaries, the Rabshakeh (perhaps an Assyrian regional governor) delivered his message to Hezekiah. How could the Judahite king possibly imagine that he could resist the might of the Assyrian Empire, he demanded in a loud voice. Did they expect help from Egypt? Pharaoh was nothing more than a broken reed.

As for the God of Judah, what aid would He be? Especially since Hezekiah had destroyed the high places where the ordinary people worshipped. The Rabshakeh implied that they could never expect a deity to support anyone who had removed his holy places. (He either did not know or ignored the fact that God wanted them destroyed because the people were imitating the rites of their pagan neighbors.) But it seemed a good argument to use in the hearing of the people of Jerusalem. After all, Hezekiah's religious reforms had not seemed to have done any good in protecting Judah so far. The inhabitants of the city stood silently listening to the encounter from their positions on the walls. Perhaps the Rabshakeh could drive a wedge between Hezekiah and his people.

Hezekiah could not possibly stand up to the power of Assyria. Why, Judah was so weak, the Assyrian taunted, that if he gave Hezekiah 2,000 horses, the king would not have anybody to ride them. The horse and chariot was one of the most technologically sophisticated weapons of their day, so the suggestion was really an insult. It would be like a modern nation offering its enemy a fleet of stealth fighter aircraft, knowing that the other country was just too backward to fly and maintain them.

Then the official made an even crueler claim: Assyria had been able to attack Jerusalem *because Judah's own God had appointed the empire as His special agent to destroy them* (2 Kings 18:25). Was he right? After all, God had earlier announced through His prophets that He had allowed Assyria to destroy the northern kingdom of Israel. *Continued.*

GW

HEZEKIAH VERSUS
SENNACHERIB / PART 3

Where are the gods of Sepharvaim, Hena, and Ivvah?
Have they delivered Samaria out of my hand?"
2 KINGS 18:34, NRSV

By now Hezekiah's officials were becoming extremely concerned about the impact that the Rabshakeh's taunts might be having on the people of Jerusalem. The Assyrian leader spoke in Hebrew instead of Aramaic (which was his own language and the one used in international diplomacy). Desperately Hezekiah's envoys asked him to stick to Aramaic so that the people would not know what was going on. But he refused. He was going to use every advantage to the fullest. One of the main weapons that Assyria had employed to create its empire was terror. It would flay prisoners alive or impale them on stakes to fright their conquests into submission, but in this case words were almost as effective.

Sennacherib had sent the Rabshakeh to announce his intentions. The people needed to know their fate if they continued to resist—and it was not a pretty one (2 Kings 18:27). Shouting up at the people lining the walls, he declared, "Do not let Hezekiah deceive you, for he will not be able to deliver you out of my hand. Do not let Hezekiah make you rely on the Lord by saying, The Lord will surely deliver us, and this city will not be given into the hand of the king of Assyria" (verses 29, 30, NRSV).

The deities of every other nation had failed to protect their peoples from the power of the Assyrian armies, he told them. "Who among all the gods of the countries have delivered their countries out of my hand, that the Lord should deliver Jerusalem out of my hand?" the official quoted his king as declaring (verse 35, NRSV). No, he said, your only choice is to capitulate. Neither military might nor divine intervention can save you. Your situation is absolutely hopeless.

Sennacherib not only challenged the God of Israel; he acted like a rival god. When he promised that the people of Judah would eat of their own vine and fig tree and drink from their own cistern, he parodied Deuteronomy 8:7-9. They are symbols of security, life, and land—things that only God can supply. Well, he boasted, your God can't give them to you, but I can.

The situation seemed utterly hopeless. Tearing their garments, Hezekiah's officials reluctantly trudged back to report to their king. What could they possibly tell him? Had their God abandoned them? *Continued.*

GW

Bible

HEZEKIAH VERSUS SENNACHERIB / PART 4

Thus says the Lord: Do not be afraid because of the words that you have heard, with which the servants of the king of Assyria have reviled me.
2 KINGS 19:6, NRSV.

When Hezekiah's envoys gave their report, the king could only react in horror. Not only did he rend his own garments (because clothes were extremely valuable in the ancient world, one did not do that lightly); he also covered himself with sackcloth, another symbol of extreme grief.

Perhaps his prophet friend Isaiah would know what to do. He sent a message outlining the tragedy that faced Jerusalem, and asked Isaiah to pray for what was left of Judah. But God had given a response to the prophet even before the royal servants arrived. Don't worry, Isaiah told them. Sennacherib has been having delusions of Godhood, but I will put him in his place. The Lord Himself "will put a spirit in him, so that he shall hear a rumor and return to his own land." Even beyond that, "I will cause him to fall by the sword in his own land" (verse 7, NRSV).

When the Rabshakeh returned to Assyrian headquarters at Lachish, he discovered that Sennacherib had moved on to attack the city of Libnah. But Assyria's spies had brought disturbing news. Tirhakah, king of the Cushite dynasty currently ruling Egypt, had started north to confront the Assyrian invaders. Even though he needed to deal with the potential Egyptian menace, Sennacherib did not forget Hezekiah. He sent the king of Judah a letter detailing how he had overcome the gods of all the nations he had already conquered. Even worse, he sharpened his attack on the God of Judah. At his command he had the Rabshakeh call Hezekiah a deceiver (2 Kings 18:29). But now he declared that God was the deceiver (2 Kings 19:10). The Assyrian king labeled God a liar.

As soon as he received the letter, Hezekiah took it to the Temple and spread it before God. *Lord, You alone are the true God, the Creator of everything,* he prayed. *Hear what Sennacherib has been saying about You. He has been mocking You. Assyria has been destroying other nations right and left.* "So now, O Lord our God, save us, I pray you, from his hand, so that all the kingdoms of the earth may know that you, O Lord, are God alone" (verse 19, NRSV).

Then Hezekiah waited for God's answer to his prayer. *Continued.*

GW

HEZEKIAH VERSUS SENNACHERIB / PART 5

That very night the angel of the Lord set out and struck down one hundred eighty-five thousand in the camp of the Assyrians.
2 KINGS 19:35, NRSV

Hezekiah did not have long to wait before he received God's answer to his prayer for deliverance from Sennacherib.

Yes, God acknowledged through His prophet Isaiah, Sennacherib is partly right when he claims that he has been My agent of destruction. He brags about all the devastation he has done. While I may use him to fulfill My will, he must not employ that fact to mock Me. It is no excuse for pride and arrogance. I am quite aware of what the Assyrian king is doing. And he cannot go unpunished. Just as he does to his own prisoners, I will put my hook in his nose and my bit in his mouth and drag him back to Assyria. He will have no chance to set a siege against Jerusalem (see 2 Kings 19:21-34).

And then God quickly fulfilled His promise to deliver Jerusalem from the Assyrians. Disease was a constant danger to the armies besieging a city, as well as those inside it. Whenever large groups of people congregated in the ancient world, the primitive sanitary conditions soon led to outbreaks of disease. But the death of almost the entire Assyrian army was more than that. Sennacherib was forced to abandon Jerusalem in defeat.

The Assyrian king loved to brag about his conquests. The walls of an entire room of his palace in Nineveh were carved with scenes of his destruction of Lachish. His annals record in great detail the capture of "all the fortified cities of Judah." But when it comes to Jerusalem, he only says that he imprisoned Hezekiah like "a bird in a cage," but says nothing about the outcome of any siege or even if he started one. Although he gloats about all the tribute he received from the Judahite king, it is as if he were trying to obscure the fact that he really didn't take the city.

God had prophesied that Sennacherib would die by the sword in his own land. Eventually two of his sons assassinated him while he was praying at his god's temple.

Sennacherib was a cruel tyrant, but perhaps his worst trait in the Bible's eyes was his arrogance. His arrogance led him to mock God and even claim divine attributes. It was the trait that led to Lucifer's downfall. And it threatens to destroy anyone—even those who serve God out of love.

GW

Innovation

NO THANKS, I'M STUFFED

As goods increase, so do those who consume them. And what benefit are they to the owner
except to feast his eyes on them? The sleep of a laborer is sweet, whether he eats little or
much, but the abundance of a rich man permits him no sleep.
ECCLESIASTES 5:11, 12

Stuff. We like it—especially shinier, fresher, and more of it. The problem is, while a little bit of stuff can perk things up, too much more just adds to the clutter. And so we're never satisfied.

Writes Bill McKibben, "When the Irish were making two thirds as much as Americans they were reporting higher levels of satisfaction, as were the Swedes, the Danes, the Dutch. Mexicans score higher than the Japanese; the French are about as satisfied with their lives as the Venezuelans. In fact, once basic needs are met, the 'satisfaction' data scrambles in mind-bending ways. A sampling of *Forbes* magazine's 'richest Americans' have identical happiness scores with Pennsylvania Amish, and are only a whisker above Swedes taken as a whole, not to mention the Masai. The 'life satisfaction' of pavement dwellers— homeless people—in Calcutta is among the lowest recorded, but it almost doubles when they move into a slum, at which point they are basically as satisfied with their lives as a sample of college students drawn from 47 nations" ("Reversal of Fortune," *Mother Jones*, March/April 2007).

Life—and happiness—is about priorities. Do we want to end up with the most toys, or the closest friends? Will we focus on what we can give, or what we can take? The problem is that people and countries have assumed that the more money and possessions they have, the happier they'll be. And that's just not how life works.

A few months ago I heard a story on the radio about a man who worked with lottery winners. While they'd enjoyed purchasing power they could only dream of before their big payday, in the end 80 percent of the big winners felt that winning the lottery had been a curse. Why? Because all that money just intensified their worst tendencies. If they were selfish, they grew more selfish. Suspicious of people? Now they had a lot more reason to distrust. And perhaps when you have far more than you ever dreamed, there's no longer anything to dream of. If you want it, you can buy it. And money will buy pretty much anything except—you knew this already, didn't you—happiness.

Just remember one thing: You can never have too many books.

WHITE, RED, AND BLACK

Who is worthy to break the seals and open the scroll?
REVELATION 5:2

When Jesus takes the scroll in Revelation 5, everyone bows and sings His praises. Their words proclaim the gospel—what Jesus has done, and what He will do through His people: "You are worthy to take the scroll and to open its seals, because you were slain, and with your blood you purchased men for God from every tribe and language and people and nation. You have made them to be a kingdom and priests to serve our God, and they will reign on the earth" (Revelation 5:9, 10).

So far, so good. Jesus is celebrated and glorified for having saved and uplifted humanity. Now for the opening of the seals that have gotten such a dramatic buildup the past two chapters. They're bound to be something fantastic, right? Some "good news" equal to Jesus' death and resurrection?

Well, yes and no. The seven seals cover the same prophetic time period as the seven letters. As Jacques Doukhan explains: "They recount the same story but with a different emphasis. While the seven letters denounced the heresies of the churches, the seven seals condemn their oppression, violence, and persecution" (*Secrets of Revelation*, p. 59).

This prophecy of church history won't be a pretty one. Nonetheless we're beckoned, "Come!" We see a rider on a white horse, wearing a crown and holding a bow, galloping out to conquer. A close study reveals that this scene represents the initial spread of the gospel, a time of celebration. Now that Jesus has been glorified, the Holy Spirit has been given (John 7:39). This white-horse-riding conqueror is not a violent one, for His victory is "given" and accomplished through the peaceful persuasion of the Holy Spirit.

But after the first three centuries of Christianity, times changed. When the second seal is broken, the horse we see is not white, but red—the color of blood. The originally peaceful and humble church has sold out and become violent and controlling. It has achieved political power, and now uses political force to get its way.

A black horse emerges at the opening of the third seal. A voice is heard proclaiming, "A quart of wheat for a day's wages, and three quarts of barley for a day's wages, and do not damage the oil and the wine!" (Revelation 6:6). The words tell us that (in the Dark Ages) a spiritual famine has come, but the "oil and the wine"—salvation and the Holy Spirit—are still available.

Bible

BELSHAZZAR'S BASH / PART 1

"Fallen, fallen is Babylon the great!"
REVELATION 14:8, NRSV

October 12, 539 B.C.

Belshazzar's bacchanalia got off to a roaring start. A thousand guests slurped wine, guzzled beer, feasted on royal delicacies, and partied like it was their last day on earth. Which, for their host at least, that's exactly what it was.

The party swung to laughter and music. Yet Belshazzar felt that he needed to kick his bash up a notch, to somehow ratchet up the revelry.

Perhaps it was the alcohol. Perhaps it was his own sense of insecurity. The mighty, legendary King Nebuchadnezzar had died 23 years before. Nebuchadnezzar's son Amel-Marduk reigned just two years before his brother-in-law Neriglissar murdered him and took over. When Neriglassar died four years later, his son Labashi-Marduk was too young to rule properly, and a conspiracy killed him nine months later. Belshazzar's father Nabonidus came to power in 556, but he was far more interested in studying history and religion than actually running the country. In 549 he packed his bags and headed a few hundred miles away to the city of Tayma (in modern-day Saudi Arabia) to worship the moon god Sin. Though he was still considered king of Babylon, he declared Belshazzar his second-in-command and left Babylon in his hands.

For whatever reason inspired him, Belshazzar ordered his servants to bring him the sacred goblets Nebuchadnezzar had captured from the Temple in Jerusalem. Taunting the true God, the partygoers drank wine from gold and silver cups and praised their pagan deities. Belshazzar felt a buzz no artificial stimulant could provide. He felt like no mere coregent working for his father, but the true emperor—a master of the universe.

Then a gasp swept across the room.

Belshazzar turned and stared. Disembodied fingers—a hand?—traced words on the plaster walls of the royal chamber. The blood rushed from Belshazzar's face. His legs wobbled, and he struggled to remain upright. Every tale of palace prophecies slammed into his brain. Such things had driven even Nebuchadnezzar mad, so he did what Nebuchadnezzar would have done: called the astrologers. And they told him what they would have told his predecessor—absolutely nothing useful. *Continued.*

BELSHAZZAR'S BASH / PART 2

Mene, Mene, Tekel, Parsin.
DANIEL 5:25

It was up to the older and wiser queen mother to point out the obvious. Only Daniel could help them now.

Belshazzar offered Daniel a purple robe, a gold chain, and the position of third-highest ruler in the kingdom, behind only himself and Nabonidus. Daniel politely declined.

First, Daniel reviewed the relevant history, then turned to the words on the wall—*Mene. Tekel. Peres. Numbered. Weighed. Divided.* Yahweh, the God of that distant land, whoseTemple goods they'd so casually swigged from, had numbered Belshazzar's days, and now his number was up. The king had been weighed in the scales of judgment, and now his kingdom would be divided and handed to the Medes and the Persians. And so it came to pass.

Babylon became one of the most forceful symbols the Bible used to depict everything opposed to God and His people. But the danger is that we too can become too impressed with the power of the various agencies of evil at work in the world. We can become more in awe of the might of evil than we trust the infinite power of God. Listening to some people, you would think the forces of the devil are stronger than those of Jesus.

Evil is always a hollow power—it contains the seeds of its own destruction. We see this fact even in the terrifying biblical image of Babylon itself. One thing the Bible doesn't mention is that Belshazzar held his banquet in a besieged city. Who in their right mind would hold a celebration while surrounded by their enemies? Belshazzar believed that his city was unconquerable. Babylon had massive defensive walls and enough food supplies to outlast any siege.

Yet Babylon still fell. Two ancient traditions explain why. One says that the Medo-Persian forces attacking the city dug a canal to divert the Euphrates River flowing through the midst of the city, and then marched under the exposed water gates. The other tradition claims that the people, disgusted by their rulers, themselves opened the city gates to the invaders. But either way, the city fell because of forces within itself.

Sin is always self-destructive. It cannot hold anything together long. Like the former Soviet empire, nothing evil in this world can ever win against God.

GW; TW

LAMB OF GOD

The next day John saw Jesus coming toward him and said,
"Look, the Lamb of God, who takes away the sin of the world!"
JOHN 1:29

They saw it long before they reached it, the polished white stone almost blinding in the afternoon sun. And the height of it, towering over the streets of close packed houses, the sun glinting off the golden vine that hung down the front wall of the Temple. Yeshua's heart beat faster the closer they came. His parents may have been weary after days of travel over steep, rocky roads, but He was excited at His first visit to the Temple. By age 12 Jewish boys had memorized much of Old Testament Scripture. Now of age, they could take part in Passover.

The streets of Jerusalem were packed with Jews from every country in the known world. The air was filled with the different languages and accents, people who had come far for the yearly service. Going up steep steps, the little family entered the Temple courtyard through one of its nine doorways. As a woman, Yeshua's mother was restricted to the outer court, but Yeshua and Joseph, His father, went into the court of the Israelites with their sacrifice. The bleating of frightened sheep rose over the crowd's murmur. The stench of burnt flesh contrasted with the sweet scent of incense.

In the crowds Yeshua found Himself separated from Joseph. He watched the white-robed priests as with one quick motion they slit the neck of a sacrificial lamb, then placed it on the altar. With the other worshippers He bowed in prayer, clouds of incense swirling above their heads. At night He likely slept in one of the many outer rooms where serious men discussed Talmud from daybreak to sunset, and the rabbis explained Scripture to young boys like Him.

You know the story. How in the confusion of the crowds leaving the city for Galilee, Mary and Joseph did not realize that Jesus had stayed behind. Now He sat at the feet of the learned teachers, questioning them about the prophecies that pointed toward the coming Messiah. Something was happening in His heart. With every hour that passed, with every question that He asked, with every sacrifice that He observed, understanding was dawning in His mind. The Messiah! The Messiah would come to earth not to save—not by military strength, but . . . by the death of a lamb. As the days went by the conviction grew: *I am the Lamb. I am the Lamb.*

And so the child Jesus grew in wisdom. And when His worried parents found Him, He asked with wonder, "Didn't you know I had to be in my Father's house?" (Luke 2:49).

FLUNKING OUT / PART 1

*The Pharisees and Sadducees came to Jesus and tested him
by asking him to show them a sign from heaven.*
MATTHEW 16:1

They were the most successful evangelists in church history. They baptized people by the thousands. They wrote some of the biggest bestsellers in history. They witnessed to kings and queens, traveled the earth, and turned the world upside down for Jesus.

And every one of them flunked his final exams.

Flunked them hard-core, in fact. Straight F's. When the big test came up, they sank like a millstone. When asked, one of them didn't even get the name of his Teacher right.

So why did Jesus have so much faith in them—his bumbling, stumbling disciples?

Imagine the advertisement: Stop fishing for the best Christian education—come to Yeshua's yeshiva and study at the foot of the Master Himself. A three-year program of intense mountaintop classes, fieldwork, and service. You'll get more than an armchair view of ministry; you'll live it. Learn the basics of prayer, parable analysis, eye surgery, scorpion-trampling, spiritual warfare, eschatology, numismatics, and catering. Learn how to preach sermons that will really get your hometown synagogue members rocking. Travel two by two, engaging in practical ministry. Call your financial aid office and learn how you can afford this program . . . for only the cost of all your worldly goods.

And what experiences the disciples had! They learned how to engage in spiritual warfare, how to forgive seventy times seven. They saw blind people receive sight, lepers made whole, the dead raised. They saw demons piggyback off a cliff. They heard Jesus' "don't worry, be happy" message (Matthew 6:25-34), learned the proper place to store their treasures, and found out that true blessing comes from pure hearts, making peace, and even persecutions.

Yet before they encountered the cross, it was all just rhetoric. Their characters, by and large, were still the same. And when things started to look bad, they bailed.

Matthew 16 tells about the Jewish religious leaders asking for a sign. Nothing new here, except Matthew mentions this request right after the feeding of the 4,000. Pretty impressive feat, I'd think, feeding several thousand people out of seven loaves and fishes. But not impressive enough to make the Pharisees believe . . . and not enough to instill true faith and understanding in the disciples, either. Because miracles don't make faith—they only confirm it. *Continued.*

Mission

FLUNKING OUT / PART 2

"A wicked and adulterous generation looks for a miraculous sign,
but none will be given it except the sign of Jonah." Jesus then left them and went away.
MATTHEW 16:4

Jesus told people that, aside from all the miracles they were explaining away, the only sign they'd see of His Messiahship was the "sign of Jonah"—three days in the darkness, then back out again. The disciples wondered, *What kind of sign is that?*

As the cross loomed closer, Jesus repeatedly prepared His disciples for what was coming. Again He says such things as "I'm going to Jerusalem, where the religious leaders will have Me tortured and killed—but don't worry, I'll come back to life."

Peter, one of Jesus' most famous disciples—mostly because he was apparently never at a loss for words—was particularly moved by Jesus' proclamations. He took Jesus aside and began to rebuke Him, saying, "Never, Lord! This must never happen!"

Way to go, Peter! Way to score points with the Messiah! Peter's sure to be first in the kingdom for this one . . . Right?

Not so fast.

Picture the slo-mo here. Jesus turned to Peter and said, "Get behind me, Satan! You are a stumbling block to me; you do not have in mind the things of God, but the things of men" (Matthew 16:23).

Ooooh. Sorry, Peter. Your thinking is human, not divine. But then Jesus spoke the real brain-bender: "If anyone would come after me, he must deny himself and take up his cross and follow me. For whoever wants to save his life will lose it, but whoever loses his life for me will find it."

To work for Jesus, you've got to be willing to put your life on the line, and the cause of Christ, the cross of Christ, ahead of everything else. Ahead of money, ahead of power, ahead of reputation and fame and self-advancement. You must live life by this paradox: that they who want to save their lives will lose them, and that those who lose their life for Jesus' sake will find it.

Church history is full of people who put other things ahead of the cause and cross of Christ. People who put profit first, the status quo, their own position in power. Who embraced the letter of the law, but ignored the spirit of it. Who spoke smooth, eloquent words, but had no love. *Continued.*

FLUNKING OUT / PART 3

He chose the lowly things of this world and the despised things . . .
so that no one may boast before him.
1 CORINTHIANS 1:28, 29

With all that Jesus had to say about death and dying, and all that the religious authorities were doing to make Jesus "go down," the disciples were starting to get paranoid. John 10 tells us about a trip Jesus took to the Temple to celebrate Hanukah. You might think people would let Jesus and company enjoy the holidays in peace. You'd be wrong. Pretty soon a crowd was trying to stone Him because He wouldn't give them the sign they were looking for, and Jesus escaped Judea. So when Jesus announced He was returning to Jerusalem to resurrect Lazarus, Thomas "Think Positive" Didymus spoke for the rest of the disciples when he said, "C'mon, guys. Let's go die with him too."

Fast-forward to the Last Supper. Jesus told His disciples about how much He'd been looking forward to this Passover. He introduced a new covenant, and shocked them with the new revelation that someone was about to betray Him to His death.

And what did they chat about right afterward? That would be the immortal question: *Which of the disciples was the greatest?* Wrong question, Jesus told them. He said that's how the kings of the Gentiles are, lording over people. There was only one Lord, Jesus wanted them to know, and that Lord wasn't any of them. "It's not going to be that way with you," He said. "Let the senior among you become like the junior; let the leader act the part of the servant" (Luke 22:26, Message).

But that night in the upper room, they still didn't get it. Before they understood anything, they'd turn tail and run, each man for himself. They couldn't yet see how Jesus desired them to think and live. They hadn't yet caught the central philosophy that would set the tone for everything they would ever do for Jesus.

In order for them to truly understand what it means to "deny yourself" and "take up the cross," Jesus demonstrated it in the Crucifixion. "Who would you rather be: the one who eats the dinner or the one who serves the dinner? You'd rather eat and be served, right? But I've taken my place among you as the one who serves" (verse 27, Message).

The disciples had three years of presumptions about God's kingdom, and Jesus turned them down in one weekend. When it all sunk in, the disciples were forever changed. They'd never be the same, and neither would the world.

Adventism

THE PALE HORSE

I looked, and there before me was a pale horse! Its rider was named Death,
and Hades was following close behind him. They were given power over a fourth
of the earth to kill by sword, famine and plague, and by the wild beasts of the earth.
REVELATION 6:8

If things looked bad when Jesus opened the second and third seals, the fourth seal takes it to the extreme. We find ourselves in the era of history when the church justified the use of violence, though it contradicted everything Jesus had taught, to force its way through political power. The church forgot the principles of grace and peace that had made it so successful against persecution, and once it tasted power, it became oppressive itself, and its open-mindedness turned into fundamentalism.

Jacques Doukhan writes, "Its conquest of the world had started with the triumph of peace. The scene had opened on a white horse, whose rider, Yeshua the Messiah, bore an empty bow. From the second horse, however, the momentum turned into violence. Whereas the Messiah had fought for the church, the church now considered it its duty to wage war for the Messiah. The religious wars and Crusades testify to a shift in the church's mentality. Action from below replaces revelation from above. The church assumed the prerogative to speak and act on God's behalf. Intolerance always stems from this type of usurping attitude, when God's witness comes to identify himself or herself with God; when success obliterates the revelation from above; when an imperialistic mentality replaces an evangelical concern; when statistics and the number of baptisms prevail over the genuineness of conversion. . . . When humanity replaces God, anything goes. The reason is simple. The need for security always opts for the visible and concrete versus a humble trust in the incomprehensible and invisible God. The success of worldly achievements then leads only to pride and intolerance.

"Violence and oppression are the natural consequences when we usurp God's role. From the Crusades to the concentration camps, each time people have hoisted themselves to God's level to fight in the name of the cross, . . . millions of victims have suffered, and their shouts to the heavens for justice still ring in our ears" (*Secrets of Revelation*, pp. 63, 64).

Jesus always rejected the use of human force and compulsion. When His followers try to force goodness, the opposite inevitably occurs.

ESTHER, WE HARDLY KNEW YE

Who knows but you were chosen to be queen for such a time as this.
ESTHER 4:14, CLEAR WORD

Ah, Esther, everybody's favorite girly Bible character. The charming orphan who trades her humdrum name (Hadassah just sounds all dusty and marbled) for the ravishing new "Esther," and risks her fame to save her people. So sweet, yet so bold. So demure, yet so enticing. What's not to love?

But then comes the day you actually start to think about it and wonder, *Maybe Esther isn't the best role model after all.* After a violent king ditches his first wife because she won't do a jig for his drunken friends, little Hadassah dives in to the competition for Persia's Next Top Concubine. That new pagan name Esther may mean "star," but by not telling anybody about her religion she wasn't exactly letting her light shine. Hide it under a bushel? The bigger the basket the better, thanks. And with apologies to the kids' Bible story books I used to read, Esther won that beauty contest on a little more than good looks and cooking skills, and it wasn't her views on world peace.

Suddenly Esther looks like a story with something to offend everybody, whether ardent feminists or Bible-thumping sexists. Except that, well, Esther is right there in the Bible, and as King Xerxes discovered, there's more to Esther than meets the eye.

Xerxes' advisors feared that if word got out about his wife Vashti's impudence, women all over "will rebel against the king's officials, and there will be no end of contempt and wrath!" (Esther 1:18, NRSV). But if the king bans Vashti, they promise, "all women will give honor to their husbands" (verse 20, NRSV).

Thing is, by the time the story's over, every husband in the tale has followed his wife's advice—Xerxes to his benefit and honor, and the bitter, brooding Haman to his own destruction. The book of Esther comically and subversively upends the notion that men should rule the roost with unquestioned authority. Its star woman not only saves her people from genocide, but saves her husband from his own ego. And thanks to the chauvinistic advisors' counterproductive advice, no one was more honored in the ancient Iranian kingdom of Persia than the Jewish queen.

The same as every Bible character—and every Christian, too—Esther was hardly a paragon of spiritual perfection. But when the moment counted, she trusted God and took a stand.

Science

PICNIC, PARTY, ANYTIME ROLL-UPS

The cheerful heart has a continual feast.
PROVERBS 15:15

These are so much fun to make and to eat that I'm surprised they're not illegal. They've been the only nonsandwich sandwich at church picnics. They're ridiculously easy to put together, and the options are endless. The only thing you must remember is that *less is more*. If you fill them too full, they get messy.

You'll notice that I haven't listed the amount needed for the ingredients. You're smart enough to estimate. If you're cooking for a crowd, you'll use two or three packages of tortillas. If it's just you and a couple friends, one package will do. If you love carrots, grate two. If you don't, just use one. You get the idea! OK, let's get started.

Ingredients:
>   flour tortillas (plain, or use any of the flavored ones, such as
>   tomato, spinach, and basil)
>   cream cheese, softened
>   hummus
>   grated carrots
>   black olives, chopped
>   green onions, finely diced
>   leaf lettuce (green or the red and green variety)

Here's how you put these together:
>   Spread a thin layer of cream cheese *or* hummus over the tortilla
>   almost to the edge.
>   With grated carrots, make a single narrow stripe from one edge of
>   tortilla to the other.
>   Parallel to the carrots but two inches below it, make a stripe of
>   black olives.
>   Below black olive stripe, make a stripe of diced onions.
>   Place leaf lettuce parallel to the vegetable stripes.
>   Taking an edge parallel to the stripes, tightly roll to opposite side.

Cut in one-inch sections. To serve, place on a plate or tray and garnish with leaf lettuce or parsley. An olive on a toothpick stuck in half the roll-ups makes a nice presentation.

Variations: Tofu salad and green olives; a wide strip of vegetarian sandwich meat; sweetened cream cheese, very well-drained crushed pineapple, and finely chopped pecans or walnuts. Go wild. If it sounds good to you, try it. You may create a lifelong masterpiece.

PW

THE VALLEY OF THE SHADOW

I will never leave you nor forsake you.
JOSHUA 1:5

Paulette stood on the square coffee table in the middle of the living room, a sheet twisted around her neck, her head tilted to one side. With one hand she tried to swing the long end of the sheet over an imaginary beam. Her face contorted as she stretched desperately to her tiptoes. She was a good actor, and those of us perched on the couches laughed a little nervously at the charade. "Don't do it," Krista pleaded from her spot on the floor. "You can do this only once."

It was a beautiful fall day at the lakeshore retreat, and the college deans were leading their new staff of resident advisors through a week of orientation. The afternoon's session was about "suicidal intent" and how to ensure the safety of the girls in our halls. Watching Paulette, we tried to imagine confronting the situation in real life.

Several years later I took a class on death and dying. We viewed documentaries, met the bereaved, and spoke with hospice caregivers. Even the terminally ill who were considering suicide as a way out of excruciating disease were afraid of leaving too soon. What would I miss? What if I could wait a little longer?

Fortunately, there are many resources available to help beat back the bewildering darkness of depression. Counseling can relieve the overwhelming sense of worthlessness and guilt, while medicines address the biological causes of mental illness. Still, some Christians suggest that true believers shouldn't experience despair. They imply that being right with God somehow inoculates you against emotional pain and spiritual dullness.

If only. Throughout the Psalms, shepherd-turned-king David, the man after God's own heart, expresses his own frequent anxieties and agony of spirit. He cries, "How long, O Lord? Will you forget me forever? How long will you hide your face from me? How long must I wrestle with my thoughts and every day have sorrow in my heart?" (Psalm 13:1, 2). Yet he also wrote Psalm 23, words that have brought comfort to countless people struggling with fear and desperation: "Even when I walk through the dark valley of death, I will not be afraid, for you are close beside me" (verse 4, NLT).

You are not alone. Hold on.

CR

(If you or someone you know is considering suicide, please call the National Suicide Prevention Hotline at 1-800-SUICIDE [784-2433], or visit www.hopeline.com.)

TAKING GRATITUDE FOR GRANTED

When you have eaten and are satisfied,
praise the Lord your God for the good land he has given you.
DEUTERONOMY 8:10

Sunshine. Puppies. Lilies. Breathing. Making lists of things we're thankful for can be fun, but well, can't it get a little trite? "I'm just thankful to be alive." Well, that kind of goes without saying, doesn't it? As the old saying goes: "I'm thankful for another birthday. It sure beats the alternative."

So maybe we should step back—and recognize that what we should be most thankful for, we're probably not even aware of. Indeed, thankfulness itself, that "attitude of gratitude" pop psychologists like to promote, is essential for happiness and health.

What simple things do you take for granted?

_____

_____

What in your life have you come to be thankful for that at first just seemed like a huge problem?

_____

_____

What unexpected things has God done in your life?

_____

_____

Was it easier to be thankful when you were younger? If so, why?

_____

_____

What are you most unthankful for?

_____

_____

How could God transform that situation—or transform you to better deal with it?

_____

_____

WHAT BIG TEETH YOU HAVE

For I am afraid that when I come I may not find you as I want you to be,
and you may not find me as you want me to be. I fear that there may be quarreling,
jealousy, outbursts of anger, factions, slander, gossip, arrogance and disorder.
2 CORINTHIANS 12:20

Sometimes I've gone to church and felt as if I've entered the Start Wars cantina. There are "doctrinal dragons," legalists of the highest order, folks so established in a hyperrigid form of Christianity that I wondered how they even qualified. I meet wild-tentacled antagonists looking for a biblical fight, or I sit alongside a family bent on controlling the church activities with a dictator's fervor. The place is truly alien.

The truth of it is that whenever you have a large group of people, you'll find conflict. Take any church fellowship, and you're bound to have a token backbiter, gossiper, or doctrinal dragon. Now if for some reason you don't have one, either you have a blessedly small congregation or you have excellent denial skills. But before you let these people wreck your Sabbath, realize that there is a reason for all things—even people's attitudes.

Conflict resolution is a social and psychological process in trying to get through a conflict, even when the "conflict" is frowning in front of you in the potluck line. When you have to deal with a difficult person, do what Little Red Riding Hood did. I've often wondered if she was either terribly naive or a practiced negotiator.

What big ears you have. Listen. Often people who are deemed difficult are prematurely labeled, and you don't label people, right? Right. So get to know the person, make an effort and see if there is a reason (if any) they have the title they have been given. You're not the only person who hurts, and many times people wear hurt as anger and antagonism. The cure is a listening ear.

What big eyes you have. Try to see where this person is coming from or see where they are going. Once you see what and how someone else sees things, you begin to understand. Observe the person. Prayerfully watch your wolf in his or her natural environment. If she's acting nervous, is that why's she acts so tersely? If he looks dejected, could that explain why he's so judgmental?

What big teeth you have. Call someone on his or her junk. Sometimes a person doesn't even realize that they are making a stink. Take on the yoke of Christ and humbly bring your concern to the person. You may be surprised to find that the wolf is a fragile human, and that praying for an ax-wielding woodsman is not necessary after all.

THE SHOTGUN

*Do not take revenge, my friends, but leave room for God's wrath, for it is written:
"It is mine to avenge; I will repay," says the Lord.*
ROMANS 12:19

The car was going 50 miles per hour when suddenly it coughed
and lost power. My grandfather, James, pressed down on the gas. It
revved up for an instant, then died again. Checking for traffic on the
busy two-lane highway, he steered to the shoulder and let the car
stop. Now what? He turned the key. The car growled, then nothing.
The night was dark, the road narrow, and James was anything but a
mechanic. At last, remembering that his gas gauge had been acting
up, he figured he was out of gas, so he began the walk to a gas station
a couple miles up the road.

It was a little frightening, walking in the darkness, cars whizzing by
just a few feet to his left. Then he saw that a car had stopped on the
shoulder just ahead. A man stuck his head out of the window and
called, "You having car trouble? Let me give you a lift."

A moment later James slipped into the front seat, right next to a
shotgun. "Better not touch the gun," the driver told him. "It's loaded.
Just put it in the back seat."

"What are you doing with a loaded gun in the car?" James asked.

"I'm on my way to kill a man," the driver said, adding that he'd
gone home to get his gun and was heading to his enemy's home. "No
one gets away with saying what he said!"

"No, man, you don't want to do that," James objected. "That's a
terrible thing, to take someone's life. Think about what it will do to his
family. Think what it will do to *your* family. Do you have a wife?
Children?" Yes, he did—good wife, good kids. But he didn't care. By
now they were at the gas station. The man filled his own gas can and
put it in the trunk. James' mind raced as they covered the short distance back to his car. "Listen, man, think it over before you do it," he
implored. "Your life is worth more than that. Don't throw your life
away because you're angry. Think of your kids. They don't deserve
having their dad in prison for life."

Without a word the man made the turn necessary to pull up behind
the stranded car. Then he got out and put the gas in himself, refusing
the money James offered. But opening his car door the man said,
"Well, I guess you're right. I reckon I'll head home." And he made a U-
turn on the highway, going back the direction he'd originally come.

James drove on to the gas station to fill up his tank. To his surprise, it held just a few gallons. Whatever the problem, the car had
definitely not been out of gas.

"HOW LONG?"

Then I heard a voice from heaven say, "Write: Blessed are the dead
who die in the Lord from now on." "Yes," says the Spirit,
"they will rest from their labor, for their deeds will follow them."
REVELATION 14:13

When the Lamb opens the fifth seal, John sees victims of religious persecution, "slain because of the word of God" (Revelation 6:9), under a heavenly altar crying, "How long, Sovereign Lord, holy and true, until you judge the inhabitants of the earth and avenge our blood?" (verse 10).

Seals 2 to 4 depicted oppressors, and now seal 5 depicts the oppressed and their cry for justice. Their question echoes the question "How long?" in Daniel 8, to which the reply came, "It will take 2,300 evenings and mornings; then the sanctuary will be reconsecrated" (Daniel 8:14). That prophecy predicted the 2,300 years between Daniel's day and the beginning of the judgment at the end of time. In Revelation the answer is "a little longer" (6:11). The fifth seal echoes language given to the church of Philadelphia, telling us that the prophecy has now reached the era just before the time of the end.

And what of their question? Their haunting "How long?" begs us to remember that the gospel is not just about warm and fuzzy salvation, but about deliverance from oppression. It's about justice in the face of persecution, restoring what God's enemies have stolen.

Like millions throughout history, the martyrs of Revelation 6 beg God to reveal Himself, to stand up and rescue them. It's a cry that everyone who has suffered for following God, for doing the right thing, can instantly empathize with. In so many times and in so many ways, God has seemed invisible and silent while His children suffer. Revelation 6 assures us that, like Abel's blood on the ground after his brother murdered him (Genesis 4:10), God knows our suffering and will not leave it unanswered and unsolved forever.

Though their faithfulness brought them a martyr's death, God hasn't forgotten them. God tells them to rest a while longer—the sleep of death, as we see in Revelation 14:13, today's verse. But that isn't the end of their story. We'll meet these martyrs again in Revelation 20:4, resurrected and judging for God in heaven.

Bible

CATACLYSMS AND SILENCE

I watched as he opened the sixth seal. There was a great earthquake.
The sun turned black like sackcloth made of goat hair, the whole moon turned blood red,
and the stars in the sky fell to earth, as late figs drop from a fig tree
when shaken by a strong wind. The sky receded like a scroll, rolling up,
and every mountain and island was removed from its place.
REVELATION 6:12-14

The moment the Lamb breaks the scroll's sixth seal the earth and heavens break loose. Our world shakes. The sun turns black and the moon blood red. Stars fall, the sky pulls back like a scroll, and every mountain and island is thrown off base.

It is the earth-shattering impact of the Second Coming.

Just as Jesus did in Matthew 24, Revelation 6 borrows language from the Old Testament's Day of the Lord (see Joel 2 and Isaiah 13) to describe His stunning return. The words "as" and "like" imply that these are not symbolic descriptions: these events will be real.

As their world falls apart, the unsaved recoil in horror. Seeking protection from God's glory, they cry "Who can stand?" (Revelation 6:17). Their words echo the Old Testament prophet Malachi's query, "But who can endure the day of his coming? Who can stand when he appears? For he will be like a refiner's fire or a launderer's soap" (Malachi 3:2). God's unshielded glory will destroy the wicked, but it will purify the saved.

The next scene is of God sealing His people, "a great multitude that no one could count, from every nation, tribe, people and language" (Revelation 7:9). His people acknowledge Him as Creator, and the seal certifies that they are His. They have endured everything the world can throw at them, and through faith they've triumphed. An angel declares that the end-time strife won't begin until God's people are locked in. They are protected from such events as the seven last plagues.

When the seventh seal opens, John reports that heaven is silent for a half hour. It is a calm after the storm.

Revelation's seven seals are followed by seven trumpets, which symbolically depict pivotal events in Christian history, from the destruction of Jerusalem to today's conflict between secularism and fundamentalism.

YOU TINY SPECK, YOU

Can you bind the beautiful Pleiades? Can you loose the cords of Orion?
JOB 38:31

When you look up into the night sky and meditate on what God told Abraham, take in deeply that vast array of stars. See the night sky without the pollution of the city lights; escape to the countryside, or just turn off your inside and outside lights and look up. Notice how all those tiny dots are not really dots at all. They're all suns. And all these massive, million-mile-wide suns are just pinpoints to us. And they're millions of light-years away.

A light-year is the distance that light travels in a year. A light-year is approximately 5,879,000,000,000 miles.

The closest thing out there is Proxima Centauri. It is a star that appears to have the same mass and characteristics of our sun, and it's only 4.22 light-years away. If we could somehow break the laws of mass and energy, we might be able to get there in a little less than 5 years. That's a big "if." But in reality, it's currently impossible to get there. Just getting a photo produces a fuzzy dot that makes NASA fanboys geek out.

So here you are, sitting in the loneliest occupied planet in the universe, and you think your prayer is going to make it to God? To keep things in perspective, your voice at its loudest can only carry a few hundred feet before you go hoarse.

Why did God do that? Why did He stick all those stars out of our reach? Is the God of creation so witty that He would just splatter the vacuum with orbs and leave us horribly inaccessible to Him? Why leave us alone like that? Why did He stick us on an island of sorts, leaving us divinely ditched?

Perhaps it's because space and time mean nothing to God. And maybe it's because He wants us to realize how small we are and how valuable we are to Him. Some suppose that we are stuck out here by ourselves as a result of earth's being the headquarters for Satan and that the space is a protecting field for the other sinless planets. But it could also be seen as yet another lesson from our Maker to remind us just how much we need Him. Remember that this is the Creator of the stars and the very cosmos you are floating around in. So before you start to feel tiny and alone in this galaxy, keep in mind that the One who built this place knows exactly where you are.

Here's a Web site that will thrill and chill:
http://antwrp.gsfc.nasa.gov/apod/archivepix.html.

BP

CAUGHT IN THE ACT

If any one of you is without sin, let him be the first to throw a stone at her.
JOHN 8:7

Nothing epitomizes Jesus like the story of the woman caught in adultery. A dramatic showdown between traditional law and true love, vengeance and grace. A story of sexism, hypocrisy, and divine brilliance; of fanaticism and forgiveness. And it includes one doozie of a plot twist.

Scholars have long questioned the story of the woman caught in adultery in John 8, because the earliest copies of the book don't include it. When it does show up, it's not always in the same place in the book. Sometimes it shows up at the end of John, sometimes just a few verses sooner, and sometimes even in the book of Luke.

But, as Jon Paulien notes in *The Abundant Life Bible Amplifier: John:* "The story . . . was not a late invention. It was clearly known in the church as early as the second century. . . . Evidently the story is based on an actual event in the life of Jesus that was remembered by many people in a variety of places. Although it was not included in one of the original Gospels, it was recognized as a unique and authentic witness to a special teaching of Jesus. In the hopes of preserving this witness, perhaps, various scribes sought to attach it to one of the canonical Gospels. The setting after [John] 7:52 became the most common, because the story fits in well with chapters 7 and 8, a setting of controversy and debate where Jesus refuses to pass judgment" (pp. 156, 157).

The "scribes and Pharisees" claimed to be sticklers for the law, yet since they brought only the woman and let the man go free, they were ignoring the part that said both deserved punishment (see Deuteronomy 22:22). This fact has made a lot of people suspect that the man she sinned with was probably in on it with her accusers. They were trying to trap Jesus. Would He go against the laws of Rome, which alone claimed authority to enact a death penalty, or would He go against the Law of Moses? Either way, they figured they had Him cornered.

Jesus ignored their ploy and simply wrote in the dust, words that reminded them that they were hardly in a place to talk or to accuse anybody. By the time Jesus asked the woman, "Where are your accusers?" they'd gotten out while the getting was good. They'd be back, of course, but not before one woman learned that the Judge was on Her side.

NEW WAYS TO PRAY

I will meditate on all your works and consider all your mighty deeds.
Your ways, O God, are holy. What god is so great as our God?
You are the God who performs miracles; you display your power among the peoples.
PSALM 77:12-14

Run out of things to say when you pray? Try these ideas to make prayer more meaningful.

A mighty God. Do a Bible study on God's greatness, such as Psalm 77 or Deuteronomy 4:7: "What other nation is so great as to have their gods near them the way the Lord our God is near us whenever we pray to him?" Then meditate on the greatness of God. How do you perceive God's greatness? When you have spent a few minutes focusing on His greatness, choose a way to express it. Draw a picture or write a poem that describes His greatness.

Palms up, palms down. First Peter 5:6, 7 says, "Humble yourselves, therefore, under God's mighty hand, that he may lift you up in due time. Cast all your anxiety on him, because he cares for you."

It's time to give God everything you stress about, and to receive from Him what you need. Seat yourself comfortably where you can talk to God for a while. Begin by placing your hands on your lap, palms down. In this position, name all the things that you need to give God. Your open hands symbolize releasing those cares to God. You might say to God, "I give You my worry about the test that is coming up next week. I give You my relationship and trust You to be involved." Keep naming things that worry you until you can't think of any more.

Now, turn your hands over, palms facing up. Now it's time to name the things you need to receive from God. The Bible is packed with promises of God's willingness to give us what we need to face our challenges. So you might say to God, "I receive from You wisdom to face that exam." Or "I accept Your strength to face the challenge of standing up for what I believe."

Stay in this position until you have named the blessings you need from God at this time. You may want to finish with praising God for His many blessings.

There's no magic formula to prayer. The important thing is to keep in touch—and to remember that nothing is too big or small to talk about with God.

HC

Mission

BORED TO TEARS

And every day, in the Temple and from house to house, they continued to teach and preach this message: "The Messiah you are looking for is Jesus."
ACTS 5:42, MARGIN, NLT

Church can get boring. There, I said it. Yeah, I know, I'm Captain Obvious on this front, but there are times the whole church racket can bore you to tears. According to Richard Ralley, a British psychology lecturer, boredom is an emotion. And just like anger, happiness, and fear, there are reasons a person gets bored. "We get bored," he says, "because we get fed up when we have nothing to do and feel the need to be productive. We feel bad when we're not productive, and that's what boredom is associated with" ("Boredom Could Be Good for Children," *The Guardian*, Apr. 13, 2006).

By Ralley's definition, the reason you're feeling bored at church is that you've got nothing to do. You're warming the pew. You pass the plate and maybe toss a buck to the kids for the children's story. You nod at the appropriate pauses in the sermon and maybe let an occasional "Amen" slip out. And that's about it. The problem is you are doing only half of what you should be doing. Your boredom triggered when deep down you realized that there's more to Jesus than the weekly clubhouse.

Wake up and smell the wheat; we're smack-dab in the middle of the harvest, and you're just sitting there. You are supposed to take the gospel and take it everywhere, to people you know and those you've never met. You are supposed to take that weekly sermon and use it to charge your next week, not start off your potluck session.

Imagine the members of the early church going from house to house. These are people who have been told firsthand the stories of the Jesus. Some are even the original disciples. These folks were far from bored. They empowered themselves with the knowledge of a God who loved them and faced death on their behalf. They went everywhere. They weren't worried about rejection, because the Spirit ignited a passion to share the gospel. You're called to do exactly the same.

Sure, you could blame the boring sermon, the poor ventilation, or even the glare of the windshields on the parked cars shining in your pew. What it really comes down to is that you need to get off your resting position and take what you know and apply it to the next person God assigns you.

BP

STAY COOL

"In your anger do not sin": Do not let the sun go down while you are still angry,
and do not give the devil a foothold.
EPHESIANS 4:26, 27

When your body gets stressed, your adrenal glands release a hormone called cortisol. Cortisol is a great hormone in a flight-or-fight situation. Your body kicks your blood pressure into gear, you get a temporary boost in immunity, and your pain threshold even increases slightly. Then there's the downside: too much cortisol causes hypertension, muscle loss, and bone degradation. And to make matters worse: since you are in a "danger mode," rather than properly digesting its food your body starts to store body fat.

Meanwhile, it can wreck your sleep. Ephesians tells us not to sleep on a bad mood, to settle our stress before we go to bed. God knew of the cortisol levels and the stress hormones in our body, and the negative effects they can have on a good night's sleep. As for that foothold of the devil, it's actually a cranky you in the morning.

Let's say you ignore that little piece of advice, and you go to bed grumpy. You'll toss and turn, maybe have a couple of nightmares. And when you wake up, you're ready to seize the day—still chock-full of cortisol. You'll fumble grumpily through the hours, snarling the whole way. You probably won't be thinking too clearly, either. That day goes poorly, and you sleep just as badly as the previous night. Repeat this habit routinely, and you'll start a path toward hypertension and even heart disease. There's something to be said about how feeling badly leads people to doing badly.

Even back in Ephesus times were stressful, and the whole day was just as tense as our high-stress culture. Persecution does that, you know. Which comes back to the reason it's so important to relax. On one level, relaxation sounds ridiculous. "What, me relax? I'm way too busy." But relaxing, true relaxing, is actually the only real cure to stress. Real relaxing is not just lying on a couch watching TV—that's vegetating. Prayer, journaling, and even exercise are along the lines of cortisol-busting relaxation. Hey, you could even curl up with your daily devotional before you go to bed.

Check yourself tonight. Are you going to bed with stressful bits of the day stuck in your head? If so, take time to pray and reflect on those things. And instead of letting those stresses create fat cells and a cranky you, give them to God to sort out while you head for bed. He won't lose any sleep over it.

BP

Adventism

THE BEAUTY, THE BABY, AND THE BEAST

Then I passed by and saw you kicking about in your blood,
and as you lay there in your blood I said to you, "Live!"
EZEKIEL 16:6

Throughout the Bible one image pops up again and again: God's people depicted as a woman. In Isaiah 1:21 the prophet laments, "See how the faithful city has become a harlot! She once was full of justice; righteousness used to dwell in her—but now murderers!"

Then there's Ezekiel 16. God compares the city of Jerusalem to an abandoned newborn girl who was left to die in her own blood. God rescues her and ensures that she grow up strong and beautiful. He dresses her in the finest clothes and sandals, and slips bracelets on her arms and a gorgeous necklace around her neck, sparkling rings in her nose and ears, and a crown on her head. But the young woman breaks God's heart, using her beauty and fame to prostitute herself. She even sells her God-given jewelry to pay for her idolatrous lifestyle.

Of course, the Bible's most famous depiction of God's people as a woman is in Revelation. Revelation 12:1 tells of a pregnant "woman clothed with the sun, with the moon under her feet and a crown of twelve stars on her head." A dragon waits to devour her child. The baby boy is rescued at birth and taken to heaven, but the woman flees into the desert for safety.

Yet the next time John the revelator visits the desert to check up on the woman (Revelation 17), he gets the shock of his life: The woman has hopped onto the dragon and made herself comfortable. It's the story of the Christian church through the ages: A meek and persecuted people embracing the violence and coercion that had been trying to destroy them for so long. Dressed in royal purple and the dragon's own scarlet, the once-pure church has become a woman drunk with power—and the blood of Jesus' true followers. As did ancient Israel, it has united itself with worldly powers.

The beast has seven heads and 10 horns, representing seven powers that have oppressed God's people: five past, one present, one future, and an eighth head that is a revival of the seventh. The past are Egypt, Assyria, Babylon, Medo-Persia, and Greece; the present is Rome, and the future one that would die yet come back to life at the end of time is the church-state union of medieval Christianity.

"WHAT SORT OF MAN IS THIS?"

They were amazed, saying, "What sort of man is this,
that even the winds and the sea obey him?"
MATTHEW 8:27, NRSV

Exhausted, Jesus knew that He and His disciples needed to get away from the crowds constantly following Him. They all desperately needed rest. He told the disciples to board a boat and cross over to the western shore of the Sea of Galilee. The lake is, depending upon the season, 685 to 700 feet below sea level, and is surrounded by hills. Masses of dense air can suddenly slide down those slopes—even when the sky is clear—and instantly whip up a violent storm.

As the waves threatened to swamp their small boat, the panic-stricken disciples realized that Jesus had fallen asleep. Waking Him up, they pleaded, "Lord, save us! We are perishing!"

"Why are you afraid, you of little faith?" He asked them. Then, standing, He "rebuked the winds and the sea; and there was a dead calm" (Matthew 8:25, 26, NRSV).

The sudden transformation of the weather naturally amazed the disciples. It would do that to any of us. But their amazement was for still another reason. Mark adds that they were filled with "awe" (Mark 4:41, NRSV) and Luke says that they were afraid (Luke 8:24). All three Gospels have them exclaiming, "What sort of man is this, that even the winds and the sea obey him?" (Matthew 8:27, NRSV).

What astounded the disciples was more than just the calming of the sea. Jesus had done something that only God Himself could do. In the Old Testament, God alone can rebuke the sea (Psalm 104:7). Only He has power over the sea (Job 9:8; 26:12, 13; Psalm 89:9; 107:29; Isaiah 51:9, 10). Craig S. Keener reminds us that "absolute authority over waves and sea in Jewish tradition belonged to God alone" (*The IVP Bible Background Commentary: New Testament*, p. 68). More than that, the Old Testament consistently links the verb form of the word "rebuke" with the most sacred name of God, "Yahweh."

The disciples asked each other what kind of man Jesus was, because He had been doing something they knew only God could do. The Jews considered it blasphemy to claim the prerogatives and power of God. Jesus was either committing blasphemy, or He was truly and fully God. And He again demonstrated that fact when He came ashore and rebuked demons (Mark 4; see also Zechariah 3:2).

GW

Science

CONCENTRIC CIRCLES

The wind blows to the south, and turns to the north;
round and round it goes, ever returning on its course.
ECCLESIASTES 1:6

Here's a stumper for roundtable discussion: if natural occurrence is responsible for how the universe is, what's with all the patterns?

If you've ever seen a model of an atom, you might have noticed that the way electrons orbit protons in an atom is the same as the way planets orbit a sun. The electrons even act similar. When a planet or electron gets closer to the center of their respective cores, they speed up. And while both of these entities have the same patterns, the science behind them differs. Planets have laws of gravity and mass to obey; atoms grapple each other based on their respective forces. And yet you can see the same pattern, one object orbiting another.

The tides of the ocean ebb and flow in a consistent manner, and everything can seemingly be patterned into cycles. As the verse in Ecclesiastes states, even the winds have their respective circuits to follow. There are established cycles for birth and the food chain—a time to live and a time to die, if you will.

There is a cohesive design to everything in our reality. Perhaps that's because our reality was created by a cohesive Creator.

The ability to discern patterns is one of the defining traits of our human brain. In fact, our brains are so adept at finding patterns that we'll manufacture, so to speak, meaning out of totally abstract things. Up to this point, the skeptical type might say that all these similarities, tides and life, atoms and systems, are just coincidental. Just as clouds have no tangible meaning in the world, your brain will turn that cumulus cloud above you into a bunny hiding in a popcorn ball.

But perhaps the reason your brain does that in the first place is that God is trying to tell you something. One of the main ways that God gets in touch with you is through nature. And nature does not stop at camping and developing ivy rashes. Nature spans the entire waking world around you, from the molecular composition of the book in your hand to the comets whizzing past Saturn. It's very possible that these amazingly persistent patterns are nothing more than the autographs of a God who wants you to know that He runs an orderly show.

BP

WATER OF LIFE / PART 1

So he came to a town in Samaria called Sychar. . . .
Jacob's well was there, and Jesus, tired as he was from the journey, sat down by the well.
JOHN 4:5, 6

The relentless sun scorched her face as she strode through town. Puffs of dust swirled around her feet. She looked neither right nor left, not that she would have seen anyone in the hottest part of the day. Long ago she'd stopped trying to join the laughing, gossiping women that drew water from Jacob's well mornings and evenings. This woman had few friends, but it was partly her own fault. When you get a bad reputation, you tend to draw away from people. You protect yourself from further hurt, and years ago she'd had enough hurt to last a lifetime. The Bible doesn't say much about the personal life of the Samaritan woman of John 4 except that she had been married five times.

Who can guess the excitement (or the fear) with which she entered her first marriage still in her lower teens? And because a man could divorce his wife for such a trivial thing as burning the soup, it's possible that that was her first failure. Perhaps her father arranged another marriage for her, but that one didn't work out either. It's likely that at least once she fled physical violence. Perhaps one of her husbands died. As the years passed, hard work, disappointment—failure, even— took a hard toll on her looks. And long before, what self-esteem she'd had as a young woman dissolved in self-hated and despair. After investing hope into five previous marriages, she'd given up and simply moved in with the latest man who was willing to give her shelter in exchange for meals and herself.

She couldn't have been pleased to see a man, a stranger, sitting on the stone ledge that surrounded Jacob's well. She'd looked forward to a long drink of the clear, cold water, and now she'd have to wait until he left. Even worse, as she grew closer she saw that he was a Jew. If the mere shadow of a Samaritan fell across a Jew, he did special washings to cleanse himself from the impurity. Well, she wasn't going to wait for anyone. She'd draw her water and be on her way.

Staying on the opposite side of the well, she bent to lower the leather bucket into the well. In that moment she had the shock of her life.

"Would you give me a drink?" the man asked. *Continued.*

PW

life

WATER OF LIFE / PART 2

Everyone who drinks this water will be thirsty again,
but whoever drinks the water I give him will never thirst.
Indeed, the water I give him will become in him
a spring of water welling up to eternal life.
JOHN 4:13, 14

The man had spoken to her. This Jewish man had spoken to her! She would have been less surprised if he'd gotten up, walked around, and slapped her face. At his words she dared to look toward him. Under his typically dark beard he had a pleasant sun-brown face. She replayed his words in her mind, testing them for hidden meaning, but there was none. No sarcasm. No contempt.

Still, her words came out harsh. "How is it that you, a Jew, ask me, a Samaritan woman, for a drink? Jews don't have anything to do with Samaritans."

He ignored her question. "Listen," he said, "if you knew who I was, you would ask me for water, and I'd give you living water."

What craziness. She called his bluff, a bit of laughter daring to creep in. "Sir, you don't even have anything to draw up the water with, and the well is deep. Are you saying you're greater than our father Jacob, who gave us this well and drank from it himself?"

He didn't back down an inch. At this he looked her right in the eyes and said firmly, "Everyone who drinks from this well gets thirsty again, but whoever drinks of the water that I give will never thirst. In fact, it will be a well of living water to them."

"Living water" was what they called an ever-flowing spring, and that sounded wonderful to her. No more lugging heavy, dripping buckets of water back to her house. No more coming to the well in the hottest part of the day to avoid backbiting women. And somehow, despite herself, she actually believed him.

"Do it, then," she cried, suddenly forgetting who she was, her station in life, and that she was talking to a Jew. "Do it. It would be wonderful never to be thirsty again."

It's curious how quickly she turned from skepticism to trust, from an ingrained fear and hatred of Jews to easy conversation with this stranger. Now see how quickly the man cut through her lifetime of baggage and went in, so to speak, for the kill. "Go get your husband and bring him here," he said. *Continued.*

PW

WATER OF LIFE / PART 3

Then Jesus declared, "I who speak to you am he."
JOHN 4:26

When she first saw him, a Jewish man resting by their well, she was annoyed and almost afraid. Jewish men viewed Samaritan women with disgust. But instead the man made the outrageous claim that he could give her water that would flow forever, then did a 180 and told her to go get her husband.

She frowned. "I don't have a husband," she replied.

The man nodded his head. "You tell the truth when you say that you don't have a husband," he said gently, "for you have had five husbands. And you're not married to the man you're living with right now."

This probing of her inmost soul was almost too much. The best defense is a good offense, so she turned on Him. "Sir," she said, "I can tell that *you* are a prophet." All Jewish men liked to argue, so she changed the subject, eager to turn the attention away from herself. Then she showed off her knowledge of her heritage, saying that Samaritans worship on a nearby mountain but that Jews say the only place to worship is in Jerusalem.

Instead of telling her that Samaritans were wrong, he said that the day would come—and it wasn't far off—that true worshippers would worship God in both spirit and truth. It was a strange thing to say, but stranger still was that he spoke to this woman of spiritual things. The Jews had a saying that to teach a woman religion was as bad as teaching them to be immoral. Something was odd about this situation. Very odd. Then with a chill of insight and a pounding heart, she said, "I know that Messiah is coming, and when He comes He will explain everything to us."

Looking into her soul, the man saw hunger and longing. Hunger for acceptance, for forgiveness, for love, and longing for truth. "I who speak to you am He," he said.

In that moment the woman felt overwhelmed with the certainty that this stranger was truly the Messiah. Somehow she knew that He had looked into her heart. He knew everything she had ever done, every promise she had ever broken, every hurt she had endured, yet He loved and forgave her. She knew that He was the promised Savior. *Continued.*

PW

WATER OF LIFE / PART 4

The woman went back to the town and said to the people, "Come, see a man who told me everything I ever did. Could this be the Christ?"
JOHN 4:28, 29

This stranger had seen into the Samaritan woman's soul, and yet He loved and forgave her. But something else is even more interesting. Bible writers recorded many different encounters and conversations that Jesus had with people, but it is only to the woman of Samaria that He clearly stated that He was the promised Messiah. He honored her, an outcast among outcasts, with this knowledge.

Two things happened just then. Christ's disciples returned from town where they'd gone to buy food. John says that they were surprised to find Him talking to a woman. Jewish leaders didn't talk to women in public. And just about then the woman dropped her water jar on the ground and took off running. She wasn't running away from Christ's disciples; she was running toward town.

Suddenly, she wasn't afraid anymore. She was no longer ashamed. She had no more need to duck her head or avert her eyes from the decent people. She was forgiven. She was free, and freedom lent wings to her feet. She hurried up to the first group of people she saw and cried, "Come to the well. Come meet a man who knows everything I ever did. He knows me inside out, and we just met. Could He be the Messiah?" She ran on, knocking on doors, ducking into shops. "Go to the well. There's a man there who knows everything about me. I think He's the Messiah."

People were surprised. No, they were shocked. What had happened to the dull-eyed woman who hurried through town during the hottest part of the day so she wouldn't meet anyone? Quite a little group followed her to the well, pelting her with questions. And when they met the Teacher, they understood. They talked with Him until evening, then begged Him to stay overnight. He stayed in Sychar two more days, teaching, healing, and making friends.

As for the woman, her life was changed forever. No longer did she hide from her past. She was free. Isaiah 61 describes the Messiah's mission. He came to bind up the brokenhearted, to give freedom to the captives, to release those who are in darkness, to comfort those that mourn, and to impart gladness and praise (verses 1-3). That's exactly what He did for her.

PW

LOVE AND WARNINGS

Then I saw another angel flying in midair.
REVELATION 14:6

Somewhere in the back of your head you've maybe heard of the three angels' messages of Revelation 14. What they had to say, and what it actually means, is probably a little more fuzzy.

I've never quite had a handle on those three angels. I knew they were flying and shouting, and I've seen them in a lot of logos, but their significance? I couldn't have told you if my life depended on it.

So here goes. End-time angel one: proclaims the eternal gospel to everybody in the world, and declares, "Fear God and give him glory, because the hour of his judgment has come. Worship him who made the heavens, the earth, the sea and the springs of water" (verse 7).

Glory. Mission. Judgment. Creation. The first angel foretells the end-time spread of the gospel. But what does it mean to "fear" God? Psalm 33:18, 19 tells us it's all about love: "But the eyes of the Lord are on those who fear him, on those whose hope is in his unfailing love, to deliver them from death and keep them alive in famine."

And what's this about judgment? God's end-time judgment comes in two parts—before the Second Coming, and after. The first angel proclaims God's "pre-Advent" judgment. One thing people don't usually notice in the first angel's message, though, is that it quotes the Sabbath commandment. Revelation 13 tells us that the end-time spiritual crisis will be about worship. The first angel indicates that it will center on the one commandment that, like the tree of knowledge of good and evil in Eden, seems arbitrary: the Sabbath.

The next angel declares, "Fallen! Fallen is Babylon the Great, which made all the nations drink the maddening wine of her adulteries" (verse 8). Aha! So this is why people find Revelation so bizarre. But here's the reality. Babylon is the end-time religious and political forces united against God's people, and represents any system that suggests people can somehow save themselves. But Revelation promises it won't last. The third angel declares that anyone who "worships the beast and his image" (verse 9), which substitutes human-made rules for God's law, will share in the beast's punishment. It's a warning to everyone that in the end, you're either in or you're out.

Bible

THE GOSPEL OF JOHN

In the beginning was the Word, and the Word was with God,
and the Word was God. He was with God in the beginning.
JOHN 1:1, 2

"He Touched Me." It's the name of a popular old hymn, and I've seen some dramatic renditions of people portraying Bible characters who were healed through Jesus' touch. But as nice and, um, touching as those Bible stories are, Jesus hasn't been around lately. Why can't there be a gospel for the rest of us?

There is. It's the book of John.

Scholars believe that John was one of the last books of the Bible to be written. Its target audience: people who were too young to have known Jesus personally—or even to know the people who had. Among its many clever quirks, unique stories, and stylings, I find one fact particularly intriguing. When Jesus heals people in Matthew, Mark, or Luke, He touches them or they touch Him. In the book of John, all it takes is a word.

The man lying at the Pool of Bethsaida? He didn't even know Jesus was coming, but when Jesus said, "Get up and walk," that was that. The royal official's son? The father took Jesus at His word that his son would be healed, and sure enough, he was—the very hour Jesus had declared it from afar. And Lazarus? While Elisha stretched himself over the Shunammite woman's son to resurrect him, Jesus just called out from a good distance away. "Lazarus, come out!" was all it took, and Lazarus stumbled out of his tomb.

But what, you wonder, about the blind guy whose eyes Jesus smeared mud on? Surely that involved some touching, right? Yes—and no. You see, the actual healing didn't happen until the man got at least 1,000 yards away from Jesus, all the way over to the Pool of Siloam. Only then did the blind man finally see.

So what's John trying to say? Simply this: Jesus' word is as powerful to transform your life as His touch. It doesn't matter that Jesus has gone to heaven. In fact, things are almost better that way, because now God is using us. Jesus is the vine, and we're the branches (John 15:5). And even if you never met Jesus personally, you're still connected as much as those who knew Him when He was on earth were.

John is the only book to tell about "doubting" Thomas. The story gives a total shout-out to every one of us who, unlike Thomas, didn't get to examine the evidence up close, yet still believed: "Because you have seen me, you have believed; blessed are those who have not seen and yet have believed" (John 20:29).

I'M DREAMING OF A WHITE CHRISTMAS CHILI

Dill is not threshed with a threshing sledge, nor is a cart wheel rolled over cummin; but dill is beaten out with a stick, and cummin with a rod.
ISAIAH 28:27, NRSV

This is called chili but is more of a stew. It was a tradition in our family to eat this close to Christmas, during those weeks you are enjoying the decorations and family home from college. My mom is a whiz in the kitchen and adapted this recipe from an old one she found in *Southern Living* magazine. This one is a little more veggie-friendly.

Ingredients
3-16-oz cans great northern beans, drained and rinsed
5 cups water
1 large onion, chopped
1/3 cup chopped celery
3-4 1/2-oz cans chopped green chili
1 tsp. McKay's Chicken Seasoning
1 tsp. ground cumin
2 bay leaves
1 tsp. chopped garlic
1 tbsp. chopped fresh cilantro
1 can of Fri-Chik, drained, and diced, if desired

Directions
1. Rinse and drain one can of beans and mash in bowl with a fork until smooth. (May also puree in food processor.)
2. Combine mashed beans and the rest of ingredients in a large saucepan. Simmer over medium heat for 1 hour.

You can serve this with tortilla chips, topped with shredded cheese, salsa, and sour cream, or you could serve it over long-grain rice. Either way, I think you'll love it.

LH

spirit

TUCKER WEBB

Then the King will say . . . , "I needed clothes and you clothed me". . . .
"Whatever you did for one of the least of these brothers of mine, you did for me."
MATTHEW 25:34-40

The December night had descended on the small farm just outside Mesquite, Texas, when Uncle Charlie, his son, Bud, and my grandfather, James, got into the car and headed down the dirt roads to town. James, motherless, lived with his dad's sister and family. His dad's work took him from place to place, and he thought it best that his son have a real home.

Uncle Charlie parked near the train station. "It'll be a while before the train gets in," he said. "We might as well get out and take a walk." Holiday lights shone in a couple stores on the one business street, and that made the cold night special. No kid in town expected many gifts—a ball or bat, a small doll, a new shirt—but it was still exciting. And James's dad was coming, bringing Christmas with him. His cardboard suitcase would be filled with gifts he'd wrapped himself and tied with curly ribbon. While he was there all would be right with the world.

Suddenly shouts broke the silence: "No, boys! Help! Leave a poor man alone!"

"Let's see what's going on," Uncle Charlie said, hurrying Bud and James down the sidewalk. A gang of young men had picked up Tucker Webb and were carrying him into the dry goods store. His knees permanently bent, Mr. Webb's walk was a strange jerky hobble. The boys gasped as the guys lifted the man up and sat him on the checkout counter.

"Just look at this man's jacket," one of the group said. He shouted to the store clerk, "Find this man a new one."

"Look at his shoes," another called. "And that shirt!"

"Don't do this to me," Tucker cried. "I can't pay." But back and forth the clerk went, bringing a warm jacket, a shirt, shoes, socks, and even long underwear. Tucker protested the whole time.

"Well, boys," the clerk said at last, "this comes to a pretty penny." So the guys pulled out bills and pocket change until they had exactly enough.

"Now, Tucker," their leader said gravely, "you've gotta make us a speech." So he did. Using the many flowery words in his well-read vocabulary, he thanked the men for the gifts.

"Uncle Charlie," James said, "those guys surely surprised Tucker Webb."

Uncle Charlie laughed. "He likes to put up a holler, all right," he said, "but you should have heard him last year."

KILLING THE GOOSE / PART 1

My kingdom is not of this world.

JOHN 18:36

For more than 200 years a strict wall of separation between church and state has protected religion in America from the government, and the people from a religion corrupted by power. America has always guaranteed the right to practice religion in whatever way people do or don't wish, and letting people do as they want has actually encouraged faith.

In 1776 America was a surprisingly secular place. It took true freedom of religion, and freedom from religion being forced on them, before people warmed up to going to church again. With the massive religious revival of the early 1800s known as the Second Great Awakening, people returned to religion in droves, and new denominations popped up everywhere.

It wasn't long after the Revolution, though, that conservative Christians began to chafe against their strictly secular government. Surely, they believed, their great nation should in some official way acknowledge their great God. One thing that particularly irked them was the government's 1810 mandate of Sunday mail delivery. How could the government desecrate Sunday—the Lord's day!—by delivering mail on it? Never mind the "peculiar institution" of slavery, this went against God's law! Of course, what really got their goat was that people were gathering at the post office (a popular spot in early small-town America) when they should have been at church.

Christians leaders thundered and railed against what they believed was a sacrilege, until finally in 1828 the Senate Committee on the Post Office and Post Roads took up the matter. Chaired by devout Baptist Richard Mentor Johnson, a senator from Kentucky, who would go on to serve as vice president under Martin van Buren (1837-1841), the committee examined the issue closely.

On January 19, 1829, Johnson reported to Congress on the issue. Opening his report, he acknowledged that a weekly day of rest was a beloved principle of many people's lives. "It should, however, be kept in mind that the proper object of government is to protect all persons in the enjoyment of their religious as well as civil rights, and not to determine for any whether they shall esteem one day above another, or esteem all days alike holy." *Continued.*

Mission

KILLING THE GOOSE / PART 2

Jesus, knowing that they intended to come and make him king by force, withdrew again to a mountain by himself.

JOHN 6:15

"We are aware," Senator Johnson continued, "that a variety of sentiment exists among the good citizens of this nation on the subject of the Sabbath day; and our government is designed for the protection of one as much as for another." The Jews, "who in this country are as free as Christians, and entitled to the same protection from the laws," keep Saturday as their Sabbath, and, Johnson noted, some Christians do the same, while others believe that Sunday has been substituted.

Thus which day people chose to observe, if any, was none of the government's business. "The committee would hope," Johnson said, "that no portion of the citizens of our country would willingly introduce a system of religious coercion in our civil institutions, [for] the example of other nations should admonish us to watch carefully against its earliest indication.

"With these different religious views, the committee are of opinion that Congress cannot interfere. It is not the legitimate province of the legislature to determine what religion is true or what false. Our government is a civil, and not a religious, institution. Our Constitution recognizes in every person the right to choose his own religion, and to enjoy it freely without molestation. Whatever may be the religious sentiments of citizens, and however variant, they are alike entitled to protection from the government, so long as they do not invade the rights of others."

Since Sunday mail service did not interfere with anyone's conscience, Johnson continued, and businesses needed steady communication for the health of the economy (and no one had yet invented the telegraph or the Internet), it would continue. But Johnson didn't leave it at that. He declared that if the government should ever pass a law enforcing a strictly religious idea, "it will be impossible to define its bounds. . . . To prevent a similar train of evils in this country, the Constitution has wisely withheld from our government the power of defining the divine law."

Yet Johnson warned of a lurking danger. *Continued.*

KILLING THE GOOSE / PART 3

I will put my law in their minds and write it on their hearts.
JEREMIAH 31:33

The danger, Senator Johnson explained, was in "extensive religious combinations"—people coming together across denominational lines to enforce their religious views through political power. "All religious despotism," he said, "commences by combination and influence, and when that influence begins to operate upon the political institutions of a country, the civil power soon bends under it, and the catastrophe of other nations furnishes an awful warning of the consequence."

Strong words indeed, and words that are as true today as they ever were, as conservative people of various denominations come together to try to force people to live by the selected beliefs their groups happen to hold in common.

Johnson gave a warning and a suggestion. "Let the national legislature once perform an act which involves the decision of a religious controversy, and it will have passed its legitimate bounds. The precedent will then be established, and the foundation laid, for that usurpation of the divine prerogative in this country which has been the desolating scourge to the fairest portions of the Old World. Our Constitution recognizes no other power than that of persuasion for enforcing religious observances."

If Christians want to "recommend their religion," Johnson said, they should do so by helping those around them. For, he said, "their moral influence will then do infinitely more to advance the true interests of religion, than any measure which they may call on Congress to enact."

"The conclusion," he said, "is inevitable that the line cannot be too strongly drawn between church and state. . . . It was with a kiss that Judas betrayed his divine Master; and we should all be admonished— no matter what our faith may be—that the rights of conscience cannot be so successfully assailed as under the pretext of holiness. . . . Every religious sect, however meek in its origin, commenced the work of persecution as soon as it acquired political power."

Though nationwide Sunday mail service ended in 1912, too little has changed. Christians still think that political power can make up for their inability to change hearts. And some of those who yell "Jesus!" the loudest are the first to betray what He stands for. *Continued.*

Adventism

KILLING THE GOOSE / PART 4

You have heard that it was said, "Eye for eye, and tooth for tooth." But I tell you . . .
MATTHEW 5:38, 39

Attempts by Christians to enshrine Christian tenets in American law and civic life continue today. From state-sponsored prayer in public schools to displays of the Ten Commandments on government property, to coercion only yet envisioned, some Christians believe that human laws can succeed where the Holy Spirit has failed.

Which makes you wonder why Jesus never thought of the idea. When people tried to force their religious beliefs on Him, specifically that He should be their king on earth, He ran and hid. I imagine He has the same reaction to right-wing Christian politics today.

Such attempts at shoving Christianity in people's faces—without context, without love—fly in the face of everything Christianity stands for. And in America, where the golden goose of church-state separation has laid the golden egg of widespread religiosity, enshrining Christianity into American life would kill that golden goose.

The most extreme proponents are known as Dominionists, or Reconstructionists, for their belief that Christians should hold political dominion over the world. Reconstructionists believe that Christians should reestablish Old Testament law over society. Never mind how much Jesus upended the Law of Moses, getting back to its roots of love and compassion; they believe that God would have them punish and execute everyone from Sabbathbreakers to homosexuals. While I suspect that, despite Leviticus 11, most of them still enjoy a good ham, they relish the idea of letting loose on those they believe break God's law. At that point their religion is only fundamentalism calling itself Christianity.

Jesus told a remarkable parable that utterly shatters such concepts. "The kingdom of heaven," He began, "is like a man who sowed good seed in his field" (Matthew 13:24). But an enemy came in and sprinkled weeds among the wheat. Time passed, and the wheat grew—but so did the weeds. The farmer's servants asked if he wanted them to rip out the weeds. "No," the man said, "because you might accidentally pull up some of my good wheat while you're at it. I'm going to let them both grow until it's time for harvest, and only then will I burn the weeds and keep the good wheat."

Force and violence can seem like the way to go, but they bring only destruction.

RETURN ENGAGEMENT / PART 1

After Jesus was born in Bethlehem in Judea, during the time of King Herod,
Magi from the east came to Jerusalem and asked, "Where is the one who has been born
king of the Jews? We saw his star in the east and have come to worship him."
When King Herod heard this he was disturbed, and all Jerusalem with him.
When he had called together all the people's chief priests and teachers of the law,
he asked them where the Christ was to be born.

MATTHEW 2:1-4

The gloomy shadows of the tiny antechamber did little to hide the ravages of the king's continuing physical deterioration, and it especially did nothing to mask his fury, which seemed to intensify constantly with the progress of his disease. The acrid stench of his rage weighted the air.

His military officer paused in the doorway, waiting to be recognized. The king glared at him a moment, then struggled to breathe. The wheeze of his breath hissed in the silence of the room. The soldier bowed.

"Do you remember those foreign mystics that came through here recently?" the king asked, sprawled on a couch patterned after a design from the empire.

The soldier thought a moment. "You mean the ones searching for some divinely appointed leader?"

"Them!" He spat the word. When he tried to seek a more comfortable position on the couch, the king moaned, and his officer feared that the monarch would have another convulsion.

"I've—I've had word," the king gasped, "that they tricked me." He leaned forward, the foul breath of his condition bathing the soldier. But the younger man had disciplined himself to tolerate almost anything.

"Before they left the capital I summoned them secretly and told them to let me know what they discovered when they reached this supposed leader's birthplace." His fist clenched. "But they didn't. Apparently they found whomever they were looking for, then left"—he gasped for air—"without notifying me!"

"Then this prophecy they believed in might be true?" the military officer asked politely. *Continued.*

GW

RETURN ENGAGEMENT / PART 2

Then Herod called the Magi secretly and found out from them the exact time
the star had appeared. He sent them to Bethlehem and said,
"Go and make a careful search for the child.
As soon as you find him, report to me, so that I too may go and worship him." . . .
When they saw the star, they were overjoyed.
On coming to the house, they saw the child with his mother Mary,
and they bowed down and worshiped him.

MATTHEW 2:7-11

"Does it matter?" the king snapped. "Any kind is dangerous. It invites impostors to crawl out from under every rock. If we let this one go on, it's an open invitation to anyone with a grain of ambition."

I'm sure you would know, the soldier thought to himself as the king broke into a fit of coughing. Many strange tales of bloody and bizarre events circulated in the fear-ridden corridors of the palace. But he said nothing. Long ago he had learned how to survive in this insane court.

"You know, it's ironic, in a way," the king finally managed to say.

"How so, my lord?"

The king slumped backward against a cushion and stared into the gloom hovering above the ceiling. Shadows now hid all of his face except for one watery eye. His voice took on the sibilant faintness of old men wandering through their memories.

"It was just beyond that little village the astrologers went to that I fought the single most crucial battle of my entire life." He paused. Had it really been almost four decades? The soldier waited patiently.
"Those were times that make even today seem simple and peaceful," the old king said slowly, as memory took the place of rage. "Even you would admit that if you had lived through them.

"The old Hasmonaean dynasty was in its death throes. The land was a seething pot of forming and dissolving plots and alliances." Despite all that had happened in those intervening years, the old king could still feel the terror of that time. Long-repressed memories crept whimpering from the dungeons of his mind.

In those days he had struggled to gain control of the government, adroitly shifting his allegiance to each new strong man in the emerging empire and using its vast military and political strength to bolster his position. *Continued.*

GW

RETURN ENGAGEMENT / PART 3

When they had gone, an angel of the Lord appeared to Joseph in a dream.
"Get up," he said, "take the child and his mother and escape to Egypt.
Stay there until I tell you, for Herod is going to search for the child to kill him."
So he got up, took the child and his mother during the night and left for Egypt.
MATTHEW 2:13, 14

But another power, the Parthians, from beyond the empire's eastern outposts, had been watching for any opportunity to intervene in the affairs of territory under the domination of the empire. Then Antigonus, the pretender to the throne of the old Hasmonaean dynasty, provided them their chance. If the Parthians would secure for him the throne, he promised them 1,000 talents of money and 500 women of good family.

The Parthian forces immediately swept away any resistance. The invaders occupied the capital and trapped the king (who then held only a lesser post) in the palace area. The Parthian commander assigned 10 officers and 200 cavalrymen to keep him under surveillance. His career and plans appeared hopelessly lost.

Then—unbelievably—the king escaped. One dark night he slipped down into the Tyropoeon Valley and out through the Dung Gate. He and his family and followers straggled through the night, heading south across the wilderness of barren hills and narrow, bone-dry valleys. As he rode along, depression smothered him. Although he was still alive, something seemed to be dying inside him as they fled into the desert.

A crash shattered the night, and a horse neighed in pain and terror. One of the heavily laden wagons had overturned. "Your mother's wagon, sire!" a servant ran to tell him. He swayed in his saddle. It was too much. He couldn't take it anymore. With lifeless hands he fumbled for his sword. He had fought too long and risked too much only to have it come to this.

The metal of the sword was cold from the night chill. Everything was lost. His numb mind could think of only one way out, and he prepared to plunge his weapon down into his heart. Realizing what he intended to do, his attendants forcibly seized him. "You can't leave us leaderless now, after all we've gone through with you," one of them exclaimed. *Continued.*

GW

RETURN ENGAGEMENT / PART 4

When Herod realized that he had been outwitted by the Magi,
he was furious, and he gave orders to kill all the boys in Bethlehem
and its vicinity who were two years old and under,
in accordance with the time he had learned from the Magi.
Matthew 2:16.

Physically restraining him, his men managed to talk him out of his suicide. When he had calmed down, he called for some water to revive his mother. Giving her what care he could, he resumed their desperate trek south.

Dawn slowly outlined the pathetic column of refugees. Most of them were exhausted women and children or court hangers-on, totally useless as a military force. If they were caught now it meant his certain death and the enslavement of his family. Dogs barked as they passed a village, its children beginning to stir from their sleep.

Later a guard shouted and pointed back in the direction they had come. Dust on the horizon. The Parthians and fellow countrymen who opposed them had discovered his escape. His despondency gone, the would-be king rallied what troops he had. They were outnumbered, but he could flee no further.

Each man knew what the battle meant. If they lost, the best they could hope for was slavery. And to their leader it would mean death. One way or another, it would be the turning point of his career. Everything rested on its outcome.

"And I routed them!" the king now hissed at his officer. "There— there near that miserable village where that new pretender is supposed to have been born." He slipped into a fit of coughing and wheezing. Suddenly he grew restless and pushed himself to his feet.

Stumbling to a window, the king stared across the crowded houses to the hills beyond. "I fought off one enemy there and secured my kingdom there." A gasp for breath. "And I'll do it again." Slamming his fist down on the sill of the window, he exploded, "I'm in charge now; I'm ruler here!"

Herod slowly turned to his military officer. "You know what to do." The soldier bowed and departed. A few hours later the mothers of Bethlehem wailed over the bodies of their children.

GW

JUDAS

After saying this Jesus was troubled in spirit, and declared,
"Very truly, I tell you, one of you will betray me."
JOHN 13:21, NRSV.

The disciples' last meal with Jesus had come to a close, and He had the sad task to tell them that one of them would betray Him. Most readers assume that He exposed Judas and his intent before the rest of the disciples. After all, when Peter asks Him whom it would be, Jesus replies, "It is the one to whom I give this piece of bread when I have dipped it in the dish" (John 13:26, NRSV). Then Jesus immediately hands it to Judas and declares, "Do quickly what you are going to do" (verse 27, NRSV). Clearly Jesus indicated who His betrayer would be. Or did He?

For Jesus to hand someone a bit of bread, the person would have to be eating close to Him. Jesus and the disciples were not sitting at a table as depicted in the famous Leonardo da Vinci painting of the Last Supper. People in New Testament times reclined during banquets and formal meals. To reach Judas, Jesus would have had to be next to him. And that was a position of special honor in New Testament society. Furthermore, to give someone bread dipped in sauce at a meal was an expression of honor and friendship.

D. J. Williams comments that "we should take this portrayal of Jesus' action, then, as a sign of His friendship with Judas despite His knowledge of Judas' intentions. It was His last appeal to Judas to change his course. His words 'What you are going to do, do quickly' . . . were in effect a demand on Judas to make up his mind either to respond to Jesus' friendship or to betray him" (*Dictionary of Jesus and the Gospels* [Downers Grove, Ill.: InterVarsity Press, 1992], p. 408).

When Judas made his final decision to betray Jesus to the religious authorities, the other disciples still had no idea of what was going on between the two men. Because Judas was the group's treasurer, they assumed that Jesus was either directing him to buy supplies for Passover or to donate funds to the poor (verses 28, 29).

Jesus still loved Judas despite what he had decided to do, and He kept showing that love. Even now He was giving him every opportunity to change his mind. When Judas brought the Temple police to capture Jesus in Gethsemane, Jesus still called him "friend" (Matthew 26:50). Jesus' love never gives up on any of us.

GW

ARMAGEDDON / PART 1

Then they gathered the kings together to the place that in Hebrew is called Armageddon.
REVELATION 16:16

A few things people might happen to know about Armageddon:
There was a 1998 action movie with that name, about blowing up an asteroid "the size of Texas." It's inspired a lot of video games. It's from the Bible. And it just sounds mysterious and deadly.

What few people know, though, is what it actually means. For starters, the actual word is "Har-mageddon." "Har" means mountain, so the word actually means "mountain of Megiddo." Megiddo was the site of several ancient battles--where Barak and the great judge Deborah defeated Sisera; where Jehu defeated Ahaziah; and where Josiah, the last righteous king of Judah, was killed by Pharaoh Necho. Only problem? Megiddo's on a plain--not a mountain. So what on earth is it talking about?

Commentator Jacques Doukhan suggests the following achingly beautiful prophecy may help us interpret and understand: "And I will pour out on the house of David and the inhabitants of Jerusalem a spirit of grace and supplication. They will look on me, the one they have pierced, and they will mourn for him as one mourns for an only child, and grieve bitterly for him as one grieves for a firstborn son. On that day the weeping in Jerusalem will be great, like the weeping of Hadad Rimmon in the plain of Megiddo" (Zechariah 12:10, 11).

A stunning picture of grieving and loss. What's going on here? It's a picture of what might have been if the first-century nation of Israel had accepted Jesus as the Messiah, and how deep their grief at His sacrifice would have been. (John 19:37 notes that Jesus' piercing on the cross partially fulfilled this prophecy.) Matthew 24:30 says that at the Second Coming, "all the nations of the earth will mourn." Zechariah also alludes to the national mourning for King Josiah's death on the plain of Megiddo.

And who is this Hadad Rimmon? Hadad was a Canaanite god who, according to his people's myth, wept at the death of his only son—similar to the Egyptians when the angel of death struck down their firstborn. Thus Armageddon, mentioned right before the end of the seven last plagues, points back to the final plague of Exodus—a time of celebration for God's followers, but a time of mourning for all who reject Him. *Continued.*

ARMAGEDDON / PART 2

Then I saw three evil spirits that looked like frogs;
they came out of the mouth of the dragon,
out of the mouth of the beast and out of the mouth of the false prophet.
They are spirits of demons performing miraculous signs,
and they go out to the kings of the whole world,
to gather them for the battle on the great day of God Almighty.
REVELATION 16:13, 14

There appears to be yet another intense shade of meaning to the mysterious word "Armageddon." Many scholars believe that the "mountain of Megiddo" that Armageddon refers to is Mount Carmel, which overlooks Megiddo. And what's Mount Carmel famous for? The ultimate spiritual showdown, between Elijah and the prophets of Baal. When Elijah challenged Baal's prophets to make fire come down from heaven, Baal stayed home, but God scorched Elijah's altar clean.

In Revelation 16 Armageddon is mentioned right after the world's final deception, when "spirits of demons" deceive anybody they can. Verse 13 describes these demonic spirits as looking like frogs—a reference to the frog plague of Egypt.

When Moses and Aaron tried to convince Pharaoh to let their people go, they tried to convince him by turning their walking sticks into snakes—but Pharaoh's sorcerers did the same thing. Then they turned water into blood—but Pharaoh's occultic tricksters repeated the trick. Then Moses and Aaron brought a plague of frogs, and the sorcerers replicated it as well—but it was the last time they'd succeed. Thus when Revelation 16 talks about unclean spirits like frogs performing miraculous signs, it's talking about earth's last great deception.

And this time the deception is greater than ever. Unlike the time Elijah stared down the false prophets, this time the false prophets are able to bring fire down from heaven as well. Describing the lamblike beast, Revelation 13:13 says, "And he performed great and miraculous signs, even causing fire to come down from heaven to earth in full view of men."

Thus Armageddon is humanity's last battle—however, it's a battle not between people, but between humanity and God; a battle not on a single spot of land, but in the heart of every person around the world. And true faith in God and knowledge of His truths will be necessary to avoid deception.

Bible

CHRISTMAS

His mother Mary was pledged to be married to Joseph, but before they came together,
she was found to be with child through the Holy Spirit.
MATTHEW 1:18

The Christmas story is a pretty cool one. You've got prophets who want to see the Messiah before they die, Mesopotamian mystics following a star, a murderous king, and the whole world being taxed (OK, maybe not that part). The funny thing, though, is that the Gospel writers hardly touch on it. They almost seem more interested in telling who begat whom—information that doesn't exactly flesh out the story—than in providing important details, such as, say, what Mary's parents or friends thought of her pregnancy or the Magi's actual names. Mark and John don't even bring it up. Their Jesus just strides onto the scene already a thirtysomething rabbi.

Fortunately Matthew and Luke provide plenty for Christmas pageants to embellish on, but one gets the distinct impression that the Gospel writers were more interested in what Jesus had to say and do than events that just happened around Him. Still, I can't help but wonder what that last moment in heaven was like when Jesus said, "I'll see you in 33 years."

How would you react if you discovered you were a parent of the Messiah?

_____

_____

What questions do you have about why Jesus chose to solve the problem of sin the way He did?

_____

_____

Why might Jesus have come to earth as a baby instead of showing up in an adult form?

_____

_____

What is your favorite thing about the Christmas story?

_____

_____

SPIRITUALISM

These are demonic spirits, performing signs.
REVELATION 16:14, NRSV

"Death—don't worry about it. It isn't permanent."

I noticed the bright -purple bumper sticker with its cursive script as I was leaving a shopping center. It expressed the desperate hope of most human beings throughout the centuries. Documents from the very beginning of recorded history depict humanity's search for assurance that human existence somehow continues after death. The ancients thought they could contact the dead and ask for their help. The Egyptians put letters in family tombs, requesting that their dead loved ones intercede for them with the gods. One letter, for example, pleads that a daughter-in-law will have a child.

In 1848 the Fox sisters, the daughters of a farmer living in Hydesville, New York, became convinced that the mysterious raps they heard came from a murdered man who had been buried in their cellar. Their lectures about their experience led to a great interest in spiritualism that quickly spread throughout the United States and then to Great Britain, South Africa, New Zealand, and the rest of the English-speaking world.

The massive casualties of the American Civil War further intensified the interest in spiritualism. People wanted assurance that their fathers, sons, and male relatives were not lost forever, but had "passed on" to a better world. Within a few years after the war spiritualists numbered in the millions in the United States. Spiritualism had another spike in interest after the horrific slaughter of World War I.

The belief intrigued even the upper classes and intellectuals. Thomas Henry Huxley, the ardent supporter of Charles Darwin and the theory of evolution, was one of the few major scientific figures of the time in Britain who did not dabble in spiritualism. He did not believe in any form of the supernatural. Other scientists were willing to accept evolution as long as it allowed for human beings to have an immortal soul.

Spiritualism will take new and perhaps even more subtle forms in the last days as people continue to seek assurance of life after death. That bumper sticker does have some truth in it. Death is not permanent, and we don't need to worry about it—as long as we place our trust in God and the resurrection He promises, and not in some inherent immortality of our own.

GW

spirit

THE HAMMER AND HANUKKAH
PART 1

At that time the festival of the Dedication took place in Jerusalem.
JOHN 10:22, NRSV

The Old Testament ends with the Jews and Palestine under the control of the Persians. But in 334 B.C. Alexander the Great launched an attack on the declining Persian Empire. In 331 B.C. he marched across Palestine on his way to conquer Egypt. After his death Alexander's most powerful generals divided his empire among themselves. Palestine at first came under the control of the Ptolemies, the Greek rulers of Egypt. The Jews lived peacefully under the Ptolemies until the Seleucid Empire, based in Syria, defeated Egypt and took over Palestine.

Alexander had decided that the best way to control his highly diverse territories was to encourage a common language and culture in them. Many Jews, especially those of the higher classes, were attracted to Greek culture. Other Jews muttered about that but didn't do much about it. Then one Seleucid king, Antiochus IV, decided that he needed to strengthen his empire by making it more culturally uniform. He feared the growing power of the new Roman Empire. When Antiochus robbed the Jerusalem Temple treasury, abolished Jewish law, and established a new order of worship (the cult of the "lord of heaven"), other Jews began to resist.

Realizing that Judaism would always be a potential threat to the way the Syrian kings wanted to control their empire, the Seleucids decided to destroy the faith of the people of Palestine and replace it with one based on Greek religion. They outlawed the Jerusalem Temple sacrifices and offerings and substituted altars to pagan gods. They did everything they could think of to dishonor the Sabbath. If a mother had a boy circumcised, the Seleucid authorities would put her to death and hang the dead child around her neck. Many people fled the towns and villages and hid in the countryside. Others gave their lives in martyrdom to remain loyal to God and their religion.

The book 2 Maccabees (written in the years between the Old and New Testaments) tells how the Syrians arrested seven brothers and their mother and tried with whips and thongs to force them into eating pork. When they announced that they were ready to die rather than "transgress the laws of our ancestors" (2 Maccabees 7:2), the Syrian king flew into a rage and determined to make mother and sons reject their faith. *Continued.*

GW

THE HAMMER AND HANUKKAH,
PART 2

Others were tortured and refused to be released,
so that they might gain a better resurrection.
HEBREWS 11:35

No matter how harsh the Syrian king made the torture, it did not break the will of the seven brothers. They clung to their faith in God and the divine promise that they would meet again in the resurrection. After the seven brothers died, the king had their mother put to death. (Hebrews 11:35 may have this story in mind.)

The religious persecution spread through the land. When Syrian troops came to the village of Modein and ordered its inhabitants to sacrifice and eat a pig, Mattathias, a local priest, and his sons Judas, Jonathan, and Simon fled into the wilderness and started a guerrilla war.

The Syrian authorities thought they could quickly stamp out the rebellion. Confidently one Syrian general after another set out to wipe out Judas's little ragtag army, only to find themselves defeated in an amazing ambush or a surprise raid. When the people of Palestine saw that Judas could defeat even the mighty Syrian forces, they joined him and his brothers in the first war for religious freedom. Military strategists still admire the tactics Judas employed against his vastly larger enemy. Finally the Syrians sought a truce with the Maccabeans. (Maccabees apparently meant "hammer," referring to the way Judas repeatedly struck the Syrian armies.) But the brothers wanted complete independence as well as religious freedom. Eventually they conquered additional territories and established an independent Jewish nation that lasted until Roman domination in 63 B.C.

The Feast of Dedication, or Hanukkah, commemorated the rededication of the Jerusalem Temple. The Seleucids had desecrated it by building an altar to Zeus and sacrificing pigs on it. Tradition says that the Jews had only a one-day supply of sacred oil for the Temple lamps, but the lamps burned for eight days until they could make more oil. Thus another name for Hanukkah is the Festival of Lights.

If the Maccabeans had not resisted the Seleucid Empire, the Syrians could have destroyed the Jewish people, their religion, and its temple in their attempt to make the entire empire Greek in culture and religion. Perhaps it might have made it more difficult for Jesus, the true light of the world, to come as Messiah to the Jewish people and to be able to teach in the Jerusalem Temple. The Maccabees helped preserve God's people during a dangerous time.

GW

THE END OF SIN

They marched across the breadth of the earth and surrounded the camp of God's people,
the city he loves. But fire came down from heaven and devoured them.
And the devil, who deceived them, was thrown into the lake of burning sulfur,
where the beast and the false prophet had been thrown.
REVELATION 20:9, 10

One of my favorite authors is a novelist and essayist named Frederick Buechner. His writings explore Christian faith with a freshness and vitality I find in few other writers. But there's one area I have to disagree with him. Buechner is a universalist, and believes that because God is love He will save and transform everyone in the end.

Depending on the mood you're in, it might sound like a nice idea. Surely God could transform even the vilest criminal if He wanted to? Just tweak them a little bit, flip their switch from "bad" to "good"? The problem is, they wouldn't be themselves anymore. The person saved might look, sound, and walk like the original, but it is our choices that make us human, and thus our choices that make us who we are. And God chooses to honor our free choices. And if our choices mean that heaven would be an unhappy place for us, God won't force us to live there—or turn us into something plastic to jam us in.

Sin is toxic. The devil and his minions live only because, in the original irony, God's power sustains them. I think that if it were not for God's sustaining power and choice to let sin manifest itself until the universe understood it, sin would destroyed Satan the moment he first coveted. The same goes for every one of us. We live only because God wants to give us a sacred chance to get to know Him, to grow through working for Him, and to accept His free gift of eternal life.

Revelation 20 describes the wicked, having been resurrected 1,000 years after the Second Coming, now perishing in a lake of fire. I don't know just how literal that fire is, but its effects will be real. Sin and all who cling to it will be gone forever, leaving only memories. It will be the hardest thing God will ever do. Even harder, perhaps, than letting Jesus die for a weekend, but a necessary act. Once everyone who's ever lived has gained a clear picture of what their life on earth meant, God will withdraw His life-giving power from the unsaved, and they'll cease to exist.

I don't know what I'll feel watching that moment. But I know I'll be grateful for a new beginning.

RESURRECTUS

I will ransom them from the power of the grave; I will redeem them from death.
HOSEA 13:14, NIV

My mother's friend Lynn just died. A cancer survivor, her sudden passing comes as a great shock to everyone; her absence compounds the deep ache of previous losses. We can't help thinking *This wasn't supposed to happen*.

The first lie ever told slipped reassuringly over the serpent's lips: "You will not surely die" (Genesis 3:4). Curiosity overpowering her better judgment, Eve bit into the fruit. And every creature since has experienced the sting of death.

I think of the ones we personally celebrate, such as Fred and Metta, gone after a lifetime of generosity and faith. Others, such as Wayne and Vic, and Lynn, were interrupted midstride. A few, like Ian and Ashley, are gone just as they were beginning. Yet others, like Kitty and my grandfather, sink beneath the tide of Alzheimer's before they draw their final breaths.

Mary and Martha, their grief fresh after the unexpected death of their brother Lazarus, were confident of his eventual resurrection, but still pained by the senselessness of their bereavement. They confronted Jesus: "Lord, if you had been here, he would not have died!" (see John 11:21, 32).

According to the favorite passage of every child ever required to learn a memory verse, "Jesus wept" (verse 35). The One who came to bring eternal life felt their sadness and shared their longing.

Years later the exiled apostle John had a vision of the future home God is preparing for all believers. "He will wipe every tear from their eyes. There will be no more death or mourning or crying or pain, for the old order of things has passed away" (Revelation 21:4).

The Second Coming may be only a short time away, but it seems very long to those of us who look forward to it and to the promised reunion with loved ones we've laid to rest.

I think that's why I like to visit cemeteries. The peaceful beauty and quiet anticipation stills and soothes my soul.

CR

Adventism

THE NEW EARTH

The city streets will be filled with boys and girls playing there.
ZECHARIAH 8:5

My friend Audrey slips out of her shoes and leaps across my parents' lawn, her skirt swirling around her legs. It's just past sunset, so I adjust my camera's metering as I snap photos. Audrey grew up in a southern California suburb, so my parents' two acres of uninterrupted green is a fresh adventure for her. I end up with some fantastic portraits of Audrey's glee at experiencing a slice of pure freedom.

Two years later my 6-year-old niece holds on tight as I spin and spin and spin my way around the yard. Larissa shrieks with delight as we finally tumble onto the ground, and her giggling 3-year-old brother jumps on. "My turn!" he happily announces. When I've regained my balance enough to stand, I whirl Xander around and around. Xander's face—eyes squinting, mouth open wide—displays pure bliss. I wish I could capture the moment in a jar like a firefly, and hold on to it for eternity.

Eternity. We feel trapped on this planet, trudging through the mud and sludge of daily life. The creative freedom of a brand-new existence—free of stress, free of pain, free of backbiting and politics and poison and everything that maims and divides us—seems as distant as the fireflies that sparkle light-years away in the night sky. Yet someday we'll swim past those stars, doing cannonballs off nebulae and deep-sea diving into black holes, splashing in all the light they say just can't escape its density.

Eternity. It won't be just giraffe rides and hugging hippopotamuses. It will be fresh discoveries, stretching limits, new skills, and enhanced relationships. We'll revel in our favorite hobbies, cherish our friendships, and feel our minds infinitely expand as we swallow whole ideas we could never have jammed in now.

Eternity. It's becoming everything we were ever meant to be. It's life without excuses for boredom or aggravation. And it's life finally without the masks that blur and obscure our view of God.

What will it be like to know God? Will we ever stop being surprised by a new side to Him? How many shades to Him will we find—a cosmic king, an ecstatic inventor, a nurturing mother, a tickling brother, a stunning beauty, a merciful judge, a dancing child?

SELECTED BIBLIOGRAPHY

Interested in learning more about some of what you've read in this book? Here's a very short list of books you might enjoy.

About Ellen White:

Meeting Ellen White, Reading Ellen White, and *Walking With Ellen White,* by George Knight.

Escape From the Flames: How Ellen White Grew From Fear to Joy, and Helped Me Do It Too, by Alden Thompson.

About Christian history:

A Short History of Christianity, by Stephen Tompkins (Wm. B. Eerdmans Publishing Company, 2005).

The Great Controversy, by Ellen G. White.

About the Bible:

Saints and Sinners: Bible Biographies, by Gerald Wheeler.

About Bible prophecy:

What the Bible Says About the End-Time, by Jon Paulien.

Secrets of Daniel and *Secrets of Revelation,* by Jacques Doukhan.

The Revelation of Jesus Christ, by Ranko Stefanovi (Andrews University Press, 2002).

MY TIME WITH GOD

Prayer — *What I want to talk to Him about?*

_____

_____

_____

_____

_____

_____

_____

_____

_____

_____

_____

_____

_____

_____

_____

_____

_____

_____

MY TIME WITH GOD

Reflection — *What is God saying to me?*

_____

_____

_____

_____

_____

_____

_____

_____

_____

_____

_____

_____

_____

_____

_____

_____

_____

_____

_____

_____

MY TIME WITH GOD

Application — *Things I want to accomplish for God.*

_____

_____

_____

_____

_____

_____

_____

_____

_____

_____

_____

_____

_____

_____

_____

_____

_____

THE STIRRING STORY OF A YOUNG MAN

WHO YEARNED TO BELONG

Suspended

Between

Ancient Terrors

and Modern Insanities,

a Young Navajo

Searches for Truth

Spirit Warrior

DAVID GEORGE

Kee Nez, a Navajo boy, finds himself suspended between ancient terrors and the insanities of the White man's world, searching for truth and belonging. His fascinating journey reveals the rich Navajo culture, the spiritual battles with the darkest side of "bad medicine," and his difficulties after encountering Christianity. Paperback, 128 pages. 978-0-8280-1925-0.

AN UNBELIEVABLE STORY
OF GOD'S LEADING

An Unforgettable Story
of Fear, Courage,
and a Run for
Freedom

A Way of Escape

Doru Tarita
with Kara Kerbs

After years of food shortages, sporadic work, disappointment, and a hundred other problems, a desperate family tries to escape Communist Romania. This true story tells of a family who asks for God's protection— then takes a risk that can cost them their lives. Paperback, 139 pages. 978-0-8280-1869-2.